AF560242

MEN WITHOUT HATS

MEN WITHOUT HATS

Dialogue, Discipline and Discontent in the Madras Army, 1806-1807

JAMES W. HOOVER

MANOHAR
2007

First published 2007

ISBN 81-7304-725-1

Published by
Ajay Kumar Jain *for*
Manohar Publishers & Distributors
4753/23 Ansari Road, Daryaganj
New Delhi-110002

Typeset by
Kohli Print
New Delhi-110051

Printed at
Lordson Publishers Pvt. Ltd.
Delhi-110007

Distributed in South Asia by
FOUNDATION BOOKS
4381/4 Ansari Road, Daryaganj
New Delhi 110002
and its branches at Mumbai, Hyderabad, Bangalore, Chennai, Kolkata

Contents

Preface

As an undergraduate at the University of California—Berkeley, I was fascinated by the history of the East India Company, and by the cultural issues surrounding the old sepoy armies. I wrote a thesis on the culture of the Bengal Army and the causes of the Indian Mutiny of 1857. It seems to me that the most compelling reason for studying the sepoy was that they were a relatively large group of ordinary people whose lives were intensively documented by the Company's bureaucracy. I wondered whether or not such record could be used to trace sepoys back to their villages, and learn about the ways in which villages were (and are) connected with the larger world. I was also convinced that a better understanding of sepoys was necessary in order to comprehend fully the inner workings of the British Raj. The recruitment and affective command of Indian soldiers was essential to the survival of the colonial regime—indeed, one might argue, it was essential to the survival of the British Empire in Asia and East Africa.

The work of Eric Stokes and his students had a profound impact on my developing views of rural India under colonial rule, but I was dismayed by the absence of the sepoy. While I concurred that it was necessary to examine 'peasant' insurgency, it seemed equally necessary, to me, to study sepoys as a way to determine why so many Indians chose to be loyal to the British Raj even though that choice did not serve their own interests. Sepoys, after all, often suffered terribly because of their loyalty to the British. The existing literature on the history of the Indian Army did not satisfactorily answer, in my opinion, the vital question of why sepoys rebelled. I began to wonder, also, about the many small-scale mutinies that preceded 1857, primarily military events rather than part of a general revolt.

I decided to turn to south India and conduct a study, similar to that of Seema Alavi (1995), of the Madras Army. Examining the Madras Army meant engaging in an intensive study of south India history, culture, geography. A familiarity with south Indian languages, especially Telugu, was also required. Meanwhile, as I was preparing myself, a small group of scholars emerged who shared my interest in the Company armies. Their work, however, focused almost exclusively on the period 1815-57; they were loathe to study the Company's armies on campaign. Military history as social history was just barely respectable in academic circles in the mid-1980s, but no one was interested in studying the Company's armies as the aggressive tool of British expansion that they quite clearly were. At that time we all wished to avoid being viewed as 'military historians'. Indeed, I would still reject this term as my work is primarily socio-political and cultural. Those of us interested in the early history of the Indian Army began to organize ourselves, with a series of panels at the Annual Conference on South Asia at the University of Wisconsin–Madison, in order to expose our work to the larger field. In 1997 Clive Dewey organized the First Conference on Indian Military History at Cambridge University, which drew some fifty scholars from all over the world—mostly scholars of South Asia, and only a handful of them what one would call 'military historians'. We were people studying India, but concerned about the impact of military institutions.

In 1995-6, I conducted eleven months of archival research on the development of the Madras Army. I went to India planning to study sepoy recruitment, with only a vague idea of what the archives might contain. However, I immediately encountered a problem: recruitment records for the eighteenth century had been destroyed or lost. I had to turn from recruitment, therefore, to other aspects of the Madras Army's development—a choice that led me into the labyrinth of the Madras Military Consultations, over half a million pages of hand-written, mostly un-indexed documents providing a day-by-day account of the Army administration from the 1750s down to the end of the Company Raj. I collected information regarding a variety of subjects: finance, supply matters, transport, fortifications, training, and discipline. I examined court martial records, medical reports, petitions of all sorts, and lengthy consultations regarding military policy. I also travelled to the scenes of the Army's operations, to half-ruined fortresses, the palaces of the 'Southern Poligars', and to Pondicherry to study the French *corps de cipayes.* I was able to visit all the places described in this work, except Nandidurgam and Bellary. Later, during another visit to India, I was able to visit both Nandi Hills and Seringapatam (Srirangapatnam).

The sepoys always seemed to lie somewhere just beyond my line of sight. I could find a few glimpses of their character and lifestyle, but nothing very satisfying—usually just anecdotes filtered through official memoirs and reports. I also became aware that the Military Consultations told only a fraction of the story of the Army. In fact, all of the departments of the Madras Government, in particular the Revenue Department, recorded much valuable information about the army. My initial elation quickly gave way to numbing anxiety. The Company-period papers in the Madras Record Office are a data set of such magnitude that no scholar could explore them all, even superficially, in an entire lifetime. I knew that it would be impossible to synthesize such a mass of information into a complex military and political history at south India during the later eighteenth century without producing a work that was either thousands of pages long or worse, a superficial summary. As my research funds were almost exhausted, I was forced to make the decision that led me to focus on the Vellore Mutiny.

Robert E. Frykenberg had first made his copies of part of the Vellore Papers available to me in 1994, but I had been unable to do much with the materials. After two years of archival research in India and Britain I returned to the Vellore Papers, convinced that they contained valuable information—in fact, the very key to the sepoy culture that I had been seeking. Working with the documents at my disposal, however, was nearly impossible, as they had not been properly identified according to series title and volume. I was only able to begin to organize the documents when I found overlapping sets of materials on microfilm. In this way, I gradually pieced together all of the Vellore Papers—something that had not been done before. What emerged was very exciting—the sepoy telling his own story, explaining his way of life, his personal relationships, and motivations. I realized that the Vellore Mutiny, in fact, was a good prism through which to view the whole Madras Army.

As always happens when conducting research with primary sources, many false leads had to be explored. I had hoped that the secondary sources for the Vellore Mutiny would provide a basic understanding of the Vellore Papers, but they proved to be more misleading than helpful. Indeed, the secondary works contained much information that was either garbled or incorrect. Like so many who have looked at the Vellore Mutiny before me, I brought several assumptions to the project. I assumed that in the transcripts of court martial and court of enquiry proceedings, the depositions of the accused (and some witnesses) were probably a fabric of lies and half-truths. This is easily inferred by the naturally cynical mind of the historian, but it cannot be proven. I also was convinced that the Vellore Mutiny must have been linked to political disturbances caused by the recent conquest of south India by the British—by the annexations of Thanjavur, the Carnatic, and half of Mysore—and by the *rayatwari* settlement and missionary activity. By anything, in fact, except the Army's newly-issued turban (or *topi*, as sepoys called it) which the soldiers said was the cause of their discontent. I devoted months to trying to trace the 'obvious' connection between the Vellore Mutiny and other events, only to conclude that there was no substantive, direct connection.

As I organized the records, however, and came to know them in detail, I realized that I needed to look within the Vellore Papers, and to view these documents as the remnants of a process rather than an event. It became clear that the Vellore Mutiny was primarily a military protest rooted in military culture, albeit one with important social and political consequences. I also came to understand that a lot was missing from the Vellore Papers. Despite their great detail, the documents did not touch more than a small part of everything that must have happened in connection with the Madras Army disturbances of 1806. Thus, great caution was necessary in order to convey the essence of the Vellore Papers. I refrained, ultimately, from trying to find all of the pieces of the puzzle, for it became apparent that the evidence—much of it contested testimony—did not permit the construction of a teleological account. Thus, my work focuses on the investigative and dialogic processes underlying the Vellore Papers—the inquisitorial stance of the Raj, on the one hand, and the position of sepoys on the other, sometimes but not always deferential. Sometimes, in the Vellore Papers, sepoys criticised the Government, railed against each other, mused nostalgically about pre-colonial life, and lamented the depravity of contemporary society. It seemed prudent, to me, at the end of the day, to leave the events surrounding the Vellore Mutiny open-ended, allowing the informants to tell their stories. Indeed, if this work contributes anything to the general study of South Asian history, it is a sense of the early Raj engaged in a dialogue, sometimes chilling, sometimes comical, often at cross-purposes, and occasionally profound, with the voice of 'pre-colonial' India.

JAMES HOOVER

Acknowledgements

The researching and writing of this work, though at times arduous, has not been without its rewards, both academic and personal. No academic work can be done in isolation, and this one could not have been produced without the assistance and encouragement of a number of individuals and institutions. I would like to acknowledge the advice and support offered, over the years, by Professors Robert E. Frykenberg and Andre Wink, under whose supervision I took my M.A. and Ph. D. degrees in South Asian History at the University of Wisconsin-Madison. Professor Frykenberg, my advisor, was particularly helpful in obtaining most of the funding required for the research upon which this work is based. I also must make mention of other scholars at the University of Wisconsin whose assistance contributed to the completion of my project. Michael Chamberlain, James Donnelly, and Johann P. Somerville of the History Department, and Joseph Elder, Muhammad Umar Memon, and Narayan Rao of the South Asian Program in the Department of the Languages and Cultures of Asia.

Among members of the larger academic community, I owe debts of gratitude to so many people it would be impossible to name them all. Those deserving specific mention, however, include Professor Eugene Irshick, my undergraduate advisor at the University of California-Berkeley, George Hart, Ronald Goldman, and Ira Lapidus, who introduced me to South Asian and Islamic History, and who gave me my first insights into India's religious systems and schools of philosophy. Among the so-called military historians of South Asia, I must mention those who share my interest in the Company's sepoy armies, who offered advice and encouragement over the years:

Douglas M. Peers, Clive Dewey, Pradeep Barua, Seema Alavi, Stewart Gordon, Martin A. Wainwright, Channa Wickremesekera, Jean Deloche, Raymond Callahan, and Arnold Kaminsky. Among more general military historians, I must also recognize Jeremy Black and John Lynn. It was also a privilege to interact with Frank Conlon, Richard Eaton, Indira Petersen, Cynthia Talbot, David Ludden, Sita

Raman, and the late Burton Stein. All of these people taught me much through their work, and offered encouragement, especially in the early stages of my project, when everything seemed hopeless. Among scholars in India, who helped me gain access to the archives I acknowledge Professors Atluri Murali and Rattan Hanglu of the Central University at Hyderabad. Professor Murali, in fact, is directly responsible for persuading me, in the end, to trust my feeling that the focus on the Vellore Mutiny was the right way to approach the historiographical questions in this work.

Without the work of the archivist—the guardian and organizer of priceless records—the historian's task is a hopeless one. I must express my gratitude to the directors and staffs of a number of archives and libraries, in particular Dr. P. Krishnamurti and Dr. Kausamakumari, Assistant Directors of the Andhra Pradesh State Archives, who guided me through the process of conducting research in India. Similarly, I must acknowledge Dr. N. Ramaswamy, Director of the Tamil Nadu State Archives—Madras Record Office, whose staff provided me with excellent, courteous service and invaluable advice. I also thank the librarian of Central University at Hyderabad, the Director and staff of the British Museum Manuscript Reading Room, and of the British Library's Oriental and India Office Collections; and the staff of the Microfilms Division of the University of Wisconsin's Memorial Library. Finally, I thank the Interlibrary Loan Departments at University of Minnesota—Minneapolis, the Cleveland Public Library, and Pennsylvania State University.

In India, quite a number of individuals provided me with assistance that made my work not only easier, but in many ways a pleasure. Among them I wish to recognize Dr. Narayana Shenoy and his family, of Hyderabad; C. Deepak, also of Hyderabad; Mr. and Mrs. David of Cochin; François Houllier of the Institute Français in Pondicherry; Anita Bali and her sister, Roshel Mirchandani, of Secunderbad; and Rani Remadevi Tondaiman, of Pudukkottai, who allowed me to stay in her guest-house while touring southern Tamil Nadu. I thank Jennifer Howes, who was also conducting research in south India at that time, for her companionship, and allowing me to tag along during her exploration of the old palaces and forts of Kerala and Tamil Nadu.

Finally, I thank Curt and Shirley Frey, and their daughter, Heidi, my fiancé, for believing, even at the very worst of times, that it could all be done.

Note on Transliteration

In this work, I have made every attempt to transliterate terms from South Asian languages according to the forms currently used in most scholarly works. I have decided, however, not to employ a precise transliteration, using diacritical markers, as this would give a false impression of the very transitional state of Indian languages in the eighteenth and early nineteenth centuries.

There are, of course, some exceptions in the text to the above rules of transliteration. Place names, especially in south India, are always problematic, but I have tried to be judicious in my decisions whether to employ old or new spellings. In some cases, in which older spellings are still used, and are more widely recognized than newer transliterations, I have kept the old form: Madras (Chennai), Mysore (Maisur), Hyderabad (Haidarabad), Trichinopoly (Tiruchirappalli), and so on. However, in some cases the new transliteration has become more common and widely known than the old spelling: Tirunelveli (Tinnevelly), Palaiyamkottai (Palamcottah), Chitradurga (Chittledroog), etc. I have followed more or less the same line of reasoning with respect to Indian loan words in English. I have used an English plural ending for most Indian terms, to avoid confusion, with the exception of the word *mard-i-admi*, for which I have used the more readable Urdu plural, *mard-i-admiyan*.

With respect to Indian personal names, I have tried to match the old, often variable spellings found in the Vellore Papers with modern forms, but this has not been possible in every case. In such cases, I have retained the old spelling to avoid undue confusion, and to aid those who may wish to use my work as a guide to reading the Vellore Papers for themselves. Most old English transliterations of words in Indian languages were phonetic, and are easily recognizable to anyone familiar with South Asian languages and their scripts. However, there was no standard transliteration form in 1806, such as was later adopted by the Madras Government. Consequently, one finds in the records some remarkably twisted and often comical renderings of indigenous terms.

Glossary

Adjutant	An officer, either European or Indian, responsible for translating, explaining, and enforcing military regulations.
Adjutant-general	The member of the Military Board responsible for publishing and interpreting Army regulations.
Akhbar nawis	A correspondent; an intelligence officer. Both Indian princes and the East India Company employed such people at each other's seats of government to obtain political information.
Amildar	In Mysore, Hyderabad, and the pre-annexation Carnatic, the chief revenue collector of a *zilla* or district.
Amir	A nobleman, or important courtier. (Plural *umara*).
Articles of War	General body of laws governing all British armed forces, including the Company's armies.
Arz	Petition.
Ball Cartridge	A paper container, of the same shape and size as a roll of coins, filled with gunpowder, to which a lead ball is attached with a cloth patch and thread. Essentially, it is ammunition for a smooth-bore musket that is ready to be used.
Bania	A grain dealer.
Basti	Servants' quarters.
Bastion	A heavily-built segment of a rampart, usually protruding from the base line of a fort wall.
Begam	A Muslim queen, princess, or aristocratic lady.
Benki nawab	In Mysore, the chief of artillery.
Bhang	Hashish.
Bawarchikhana	A detached cooking shed.

Board of Control	Regulatory body, under the supervision of Parliament, established by the India Act of 1784 as a check on the Court of Directors of the East India Company.
Cantonment	An area used by the Army for barracks and storage. Cantonments in India usually were not fortified, and many contained bazars, villages, temples, and other civilian areas.
Canister Shot	A tin container, filled with musket balls, extensively used before the invention of shrapnel.
Cavalier	As used in this work, a small, triangular bastion extending out from a wall, enabling soldiers to prevent an escalade by firing at the ground immediately under a rampart or bastion.
Chobdar	A mace-bearer; one of the attendants of an Indian ruler.
Choultry	A shelter for pilgrims and travellers, usually supported by an endowment; in south Indian cities, old *choultries* were often used as public offices, police outposts, law courts, and jails.
Choultry Plain	Suburban area of Madras where the Madras Army Headquarters was located.
'Chuckler'	Archaic form of *chakkiliyan*, the Tamil leather-working caste.
'Colleries'	Archaic form of Kallan, a numerous caste in southern Tamil Nadu.
Conductor	A staff sergeant in charge of manual labourers (coolies) and the movement of military stores.
Corps	Flexible term used for any primary tactical unit, either of regimental or battalion strength.
Coup de main	A frontal assault on a fortified position, made without a formal siege.
Court of Directors	Executive governing body of the East India Company, elected by vote-casting members of the Court of Proprietors.
Court of Proprietors	Shareholders of the East India Company, only some of whom had voting privileges.

Crownwork	A low, broad bastion with several projecting cavaliers.
Curtain Wall	A section of rampart lying between two bastions or cavaliers.
'Cutcherry'	A magistrate's offices; a court house.
Dargah	A Sufi hospice and place of religious study.
Deohra	A suburban pleasure garden, especially in Hyderabad.
Dharma	Duties specific to an individual; these include duties to self, to community, and to humanity in general. They are determined by the totality of one's existence, taking into account such variables as age, the period of one's existence, location, social status, etc.
Diwan	Official concerned with the financial and diplomatic affairs of a kingdom; the chief minister under an Indian ruler.
Dragoon	A heavy cavalryman armed with a saber and carabine, or short musket.
Drug	A precipitous rock outcrop, usually crowned with a fort or temple, and sometimes with both.
Faqir	A Sufi *pir* or one of his followers. In the eighteenth and early nineteenth centuries, British observers applied the term to both Muslim and Hindu holy men.
Farash	A mercantile agent
Faujdar	A district military officer in a princely state.
Firelock	The mechanism of a musket; the word was used at the time of the Vellore Mutiny, however, to refer to the entire weapon.
Galloper Gun	Horse-drawn gun attached to cavalry regiments.
'Gentoo'	Archaic term used in the Madras Presidency to refer to Telugu, but also sometimes synonymous with 'Hindu'.
Glacis	Sloping earth embankment in front of the ditch surrounding a fort.

Gopuram	Tower of a Hindu temple, several towers usually sited over temple gateways.
Governor-in-Council	The governing body of the Madras Presidency, consisting of a council presided over by the Governor.
Governor-General	Highest executive officer in British India, 1774-1858.
Grenadier	Elite infantry soldier, chosen for size, strength, and courage, armed with grenades as well as a musket and bayonet, to make assaults on fortified places.
Harkara	Messenger or intelligence agent.
Havildar	Indian non-commissioned officer corresponding to a British Army sergeant.
Havildar-Major	Equivalent of a British Army sergeant-major.
Hindavi Nawis	Writer of indigenous languages, especially Urdu or Hindi.
Horse Guards	Office of the Commander-in-Chief of the British Army, controlling all patronage matters in the King's Army.
Invalid	Indian or European soldier no longer on active duty, but still under military discipline.
Iqbal	Sustained good fortune.
Izzat	Literally 'brilliance', a word used to convey a sense of good reputation and honour.
Jemadar	Indian commissioned officer corresponding to a lieutenant in the British Army.
Kafir	An 'infidel', a term often applied by Muslim sepoys to Europeans.
Kanakapillai	accountant, or bookkeeper.
Khas Mahal	The Sultan's favourite wife, usually the mother of the heir-apparent.
Kot Havildar	Indian staff officer-in-charge of a company's equipment.
Kotwal	Town constable.
Lakh	One hundred thousand.
Lascar	Term used in the Madras Army to denote troops used for manual labour, especially in the Artillery.

Lashkar	Range of huts belonging to a prince's soldiers; any military encampment.
Leadenhall	Offices of the East India Company in London.
Light Infantry	Troops selected for agility, marksmanship, and intelligence; troops trained to move quickly and fight in loose order.
Lines	Quarters for soldiers.
Madrasa	Muslim theological seminary.
Magazine	Ammunition depot.
Mahal	Private apartments of a palace, as distinct from public assembly halls.
Maidan	Open area, or parade ground.
Main Guard	Shelter for troops assigned to guard duty during a particular watch.
Makan	Building; in the Vellore Papers, sepoys use this term to refer to *dargahs.*
'Malabars'	Archaic term for Tamil, often incorrectly used by newly-arrived British officials to refer to the people of Malabar.
Mard-i-admiyan	Gentlemen companions of a prince.
Masjid	Mosque.
Moniyagar	Estate manager, a petty revenue officer.
Muharram	Muslim holiday during which the martyrdom of Hussain and Hassan are commemorated with parades and ceremonies.
'Naigue'	Archaic form of *naik*, equivalent of a corporal in the British Army.
Nallah	Seasonal water course.
'Nautch'	From *nachna*, 'to dance', referring, in south India, to a performance of *bharatanatyam.*
Nawab	Regional warlord serving, theoretically, as a local viceroy of the Mughal Emperor.
Nayaka	Hindu warlord of pre-colonial south India, especially one controlling several subordinate warlords. Similar to a north Indian maharaja.
Nizam	The ruler of Hyderabad, as they were known to the British; referred to themselves by the title *Nawab.*

Other Ranks	Term used in the British Army to refer to all non-commissioned soldiers; often used with distinct class overtones.
'Puckalie'	Water-carrier, corresponding to the north Indian *bhisti*. In the Madras Army, *puckalies* were carried on the regimental strength to provide water to troops.
Pagoda	A south Indian gold coin, of which there were several varities circulating at the time of the Vellore Mutiny. The official coin of the Madras Government was the Star Pagoda. The term was also used to refer to the *gopuram*, or tower, of a temple.
Palaiyakkar	Tamil version of *palegaru*, a local warlord controlling a small domain.
Palaiyam	Tamil version of *pallem*, area supporting a *palaiyakkar*.
Paltan	Body of troops; sepoys derived the word from 'platoon', but used it to refer to an entire battalion.
Paraiyar	General term for 'untouchable' communities.
Peshkar	Chief revenue collector under the Nizam of Hyderabad.
Pettah	Market town, especially one located next to a fort.
Pir	Muslim religious leader.
Platoon	Largest subdivision of an infantry company, consisting of approximately thirty men.
'Poligar'	Archaic term for *palaiyakkar* or *palegaru*.
Presidency	Regional administration under the Government of India. The three presidencies of British India were Bengal, Madras, and Bombay.
Rayat	Arabic term used in south India (especially in Telugu areas, i.e. *grama rayalu*) to refer to a small landholder.
Route March	Routine movement of troops in peace time.
Sangar	Stone redoubt, usually guarding a hillside.
Sarkar	Government.

Sowar	Cavalryman, sometimes transliterated *sawar.*
Subadar	Indian commissioned officer corresponding to a British captain.
Talaiyar	Commander of watchmen, or peons.
Tappal	Postal service.
Thanadar	Commander of a police outpost.
Trace Italienne	System of earthworks and ditches surrounding the stone walls of a fort, drawn in a geometric pattern to guard all possible approaches of an enemy force.
Umara	Plural of *amir.*
Ustad	Tutor or teacher; in the Madras Army sepoys used this term to refer to drill *havildars.*
Zenana	Women's quarters in a palace or large house.

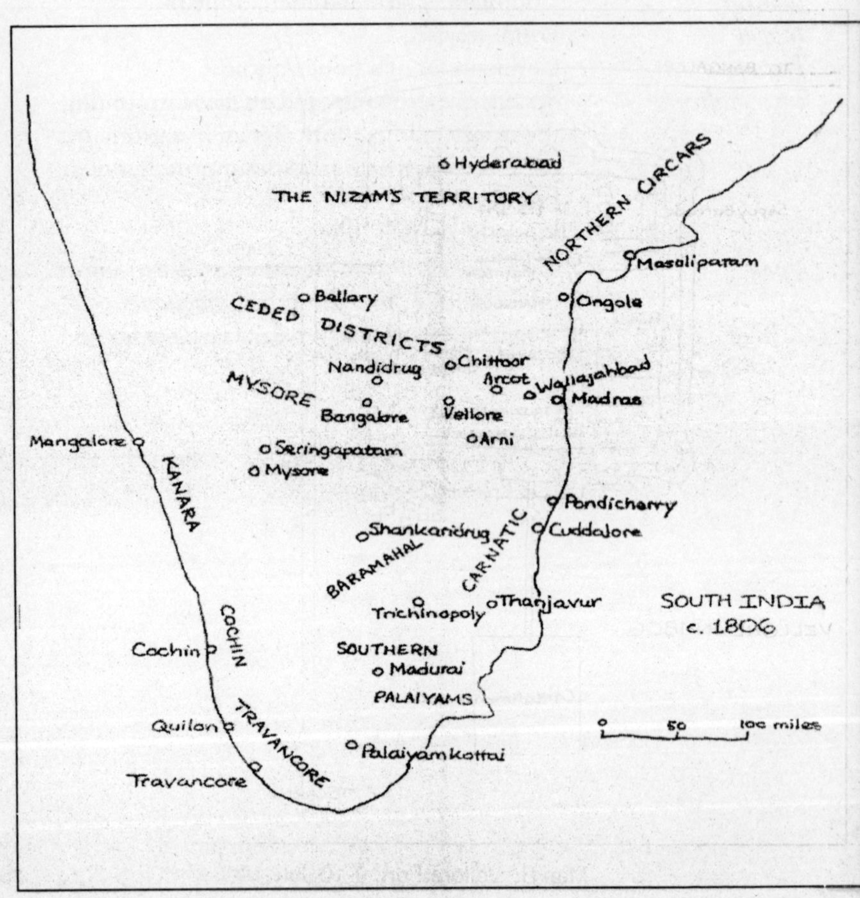

Map A: The Vellore Crisis in South India, 1806-7

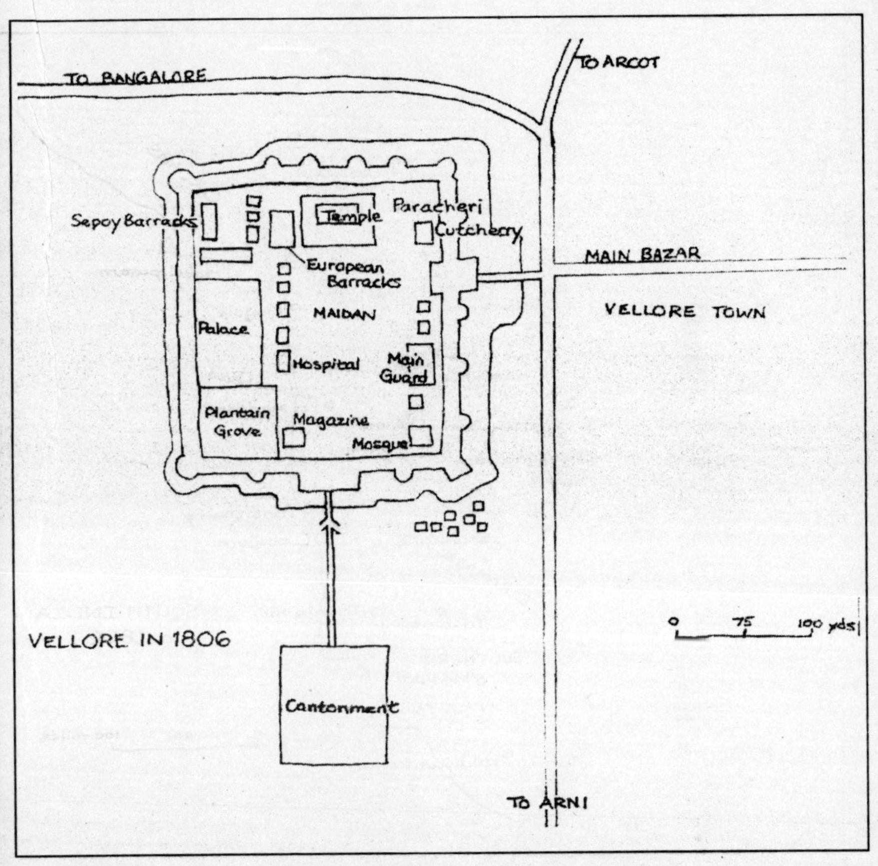

Map B: Vellore Fort, 9-10 July 1806

1806 saw [illegible]
in the East India [illegible]
of 1857, the Vellore Mutiny [illegible]
affected one quarter of the [illegible]
happened. Vellore Mutiny [illegible]
on 10 July 1806 [illegible]
context of [illegible]
historical [illegible]
ideas underlying [illegible]
arz (petition) [illegible]
own view of the [illegible]
Government [illegible]

The Vellore [illegible]
the main [illegible]
Asian historiography [illegible]
episodes of anti-colonial [illegible]
Because the Vellore Mutiny [illegible]
of a new [illegible]
topi, or hat [illegible]
incidents in which [illegible]
against British military [illegible]
shaped cutbans [illegible]
asserting that the [illegible]
forced conversion [illegible]
historiography [illegible]
time reinforcing the official [illegible]
and essentially [illegible]
aldermost [illegible]
similar [illegible]
with the [illegible]
was assigned [illegible]

Introduction

1806 saw the most violent and politically significant sepoy mutiny in the East India Company's armies prior to the great Indian uprising of 1857, the Vellore Mutiny. A year of investigations and disturbances affected one-quarter of the troops of the Madras Army after it happened. 'Vellore Mutiny' refers here to the uprising at Vellore Fort on 10 July 1806; the 'Vellore Crisis' refers to the wider historical context of the event. In this introduction, I briefly outline the historical significance of the Vellore Crisis, and introduce the main ideas underlying my thesis by examining a remarkable document—an *arz* (petition) in which a group of sepoys at Hyderabad offered their own view of the Crisis, as well as a stinging critique of the Madras Government's policies.

The Vellore Crisis lies in a very complex context, and this is perhaps the main reason why the event has been so marginalized in South Asian historiography, despite being one of the most well documented episodes of anti-colonial resistance in the history of British India. Because the Vellore Mutiny followed a protest against the introduction of a new style of turban—thought by many sepoys to resemble a *topi*, or hat—historians, have been quick to ascribe it to a series of incidents in which sepoy 'religious prejudice' gained the upper hand against British military discipline, never quite specifying why a hat-shaped turban could move men to mutiny, although sometimes asserting that the turban was connected with vague fears about forced conversion to Christianity.[1] Military historians follow colonial historiography, denying sepoys political agency while at the same time reinforcing the official view that sepoys were simple 'sons of the soil', essentially loyal, but inclined to be swayed by irrational considerations of personal and caste honour, religion, and custom.[2] In a similar vein, there has been a tendency to connect the Vellore Mutiny with the exiled sons of Tipu Sultan. The mutinous garrison of Vellore was assigned the task of guarding the fallen Sultan's sons and their families; contemporary witnesses and generations of historians have assumed that the sepoys must have been instigated to rebel by the captive Princes.[3] This particular reading of the Vellore Crisis, for which there is only the most scant evidence, renders the episode a mere footnote in the postscript of the Anglo-Mysore Wars. Alternatively, the Vellore Crisis has been seen as an episode in the political career of Lord William Bentinck, the Governor of Madras, and a future Governor-General of India.[4] Since some army officers chose to blame Christian evangelism for the Mutiny—desperate scrabbling at straws—the Vellore Crisis also became a talking point in the ongoing debate about Company policy *vis-à-vis* the access of Protestant missionaries to India.[5] More recently, there have been attempts to connect the Vellore Mutiny with other disturbances, a wave of localized protests, riots, and insurrections that swept across south India during the period 1795-1804.[6] There are significant problems with all of the above points of view, yet one can see, just from this list, that the Crisis lies at the intersection of numerous issues and debates regarding colonial rule in Indian.

The Vellore Mutiny occurred during a formative stage of colonial rule in south Inida. Indeed, a study of the Vellore Crisis offers remarkable insights into the transition from pre-colonial to colonial modes of political thought and action.[7] The thousands of pages of the Vellore Papers illustrate how Company officials struggled to understand and control the military crisis. This is not the confident colonial state encountered by Ranajit Guha in Bengal, however, but an administration flailing between panic, repression, and conciliation in response to possible insurrection. The Vellore Papers underscore the ignorance and limited effectiveness of colonial authorities, even in the management of their own military forces, and they reveal the extent to which important policies were hotly contested in the early stages of colonial rule.[8]

Ranajit Guha has noted that colonial records dealing with resistance, although part of the dominant elite's process of control, are shaped by their subjects, and hence contain at least an echo 'rebel consciousness'.[9] The considerable portion of the Vellore Papers that consist of confessions, testimonies, and letters translated from south Indian languages may be viewed in this light. Indeed, the information contained in these particular documents is more useful than most such records, because the colonial state's informants, with only a few exceptions, were not accustomed to bureaucratic procedures, such as the recording of evidence. In the Vellore Papers, we hear all sorts of ordinary people, from sepoys to village women, speaking their minds—often criticising the Raj, or praising the wisdom of the pre-colonial order. While some of the testimonies recorded by the various courts of enquiry were undoubtedly coached, much of the evidence rings true—which is to say that it has a certain authenticity, even if contested, contradictory, or inconsistent, as memories (especially memories of violent events) often are. Apart from offering an unusually clear view of the insurgent's ideas, the Vellore Papers also provide an unparalleled glimpse of the inner life of sepoy battalions, allowing us to explore the world of the sepoy as never before, and to break free of the tropes used to construct most European accounts of the early colonial Indian Army. Significantly, the Vellore Papers allow us to examine how sepoys encountered the British attempts to Westernize the colonial military system—a reform that presented sepoys with many difficult choices, compelling them to deeply consider their loyalty to the Company, on the one hand, and their sense of communal solidarity on the other.

Perhaps the best way to introduce the themes and ideas of this work is to examine a document that illustrates the points made above—in fact, one of the most important and least well known of the primary documents concerning the Vellore Mutiny. It is an *arz*, or petition, translated from Urdu by J. Munro, Persian Interpreter to the Adjutant-General of the Madras Army. The anonymous authors of the petition described themselves as eleven sepoys—probably native commissioned officers—of the Subsidiary Force stationed at Hyderabad, the scene of several disturbances during the Crisis.[10] Sir John Francis Cradock, Commander-in-Chief of the Madras Army, placed the soldiers' letter before the Governor-in-Council on 7 July 1807. But this time, the Vellore Crisis was ending, and this is one of the reasons why this particular *arz* is so important; it presents an indigenous analysis of the entire Crisis, as well as a cutting critique of British Policy. In fact, the *arz* also demonstrates the high degree of political awareness that was common among native officers of the Madras Army at that time—a consciousness that later historiography sought to suppress.[11] The authenticity of the *arz* had been confirmed by the Military Board's translator, and was not doubted by British authorities.

The opening paragraph of the *arz* positions the document in a tension between discontent and mutiny, on the one hand, and deference and loyalty on the other hand—a classic subaltern stance.

European officers, if they shou'd [*sic*] remain a hundred years in this country, wou'd [*sic*] find it difficult to understand the hearts of the people. The secrets of the natives are to be learned from natives only. It is therefore necessary to treat them with respect. By observing this rule, the gentlemen of the Company's service will obtain considerable advantage.[12]

This statement expresses a number of important concepts underlying the relationship between the sepoys and the Company. The first of these ideas, of course, was that the British could not rule India without indigenous soldiers—a point that the *arz* underscores more than once.[13] The second idea is that effective command, in the Indian context, required the maintenance of a dialogue with indigenous intermediaries—the only way in which the British might know the 'secrets of the natives'. The third idea contained in this passage is less apparent than the others, but no less important: that an implied contract bound sepoys to the Company, one that might be considered broken if Indian soldiers thought they were no longer 'treated with respect'. As we will see, for sepoys respect had many shades of meaning—not just respect for religious beliefs and customs, but also material maintenance. Like most people, sepoys were idealistic to a certain extent; they wanted to serve their employers loyally, but not to feel exploited.

The final chapter of this work discusses the recruitment of the Madras Army, endeavouring to explain who sepoys were, and what sorts of cultural knowledge informed their attitudes about loyalty, service, and mutiny. In the *arz* from the sepoys at Hyderabad, the petitioners claimed to speak for all Indian soldiers, and thus provide their own history of the Army. An important part of sepoy 'memory' of Company expansion was a comparison of the Company's territorial possessions in the mid-eighteenth century with the vast empire that it had acquired by the time of the Vellore Mutiny.

When the English first arrived, and possessed a very small extent of country, their justice and moderation were exemplary. At that time we all said, 'Those strangers have small possessions, but the principles of their governments are excellent. If providence should increase their prosperity and dominion, they will undoubtedly manifest still more justice and wisdom.' The sepoys, under the influence of those impressions, abandoned the service of their own nabobs, and many persons of high family embraced that of the Company.[14]

During the Carnatic Wars (1746-63) tens of thousands of men were drawn into the sepoy battalions of the Madras Army, attracted by the perceived prosperity, justice, and wisdom of its regime. Prosperity and dominion were important elements of what sepoys termed *iqbal*, or sustained good fortune. *Iqbal* was typically thought to arise from a ruler's justice and wisdom—or, to use a Hindu term, his maintenance of *rajdharma*. The concept of *rajdharma* was important throughout pre-colonial Indian history, and well into the colonial era, as an anchor of mass loyalty. The subaltern classes could be loyal to the idea of a justly governed kingdom even while in revolt against a particular raja; thus the political structure itself was never challenged. The Vellore Crisis was much the same; sepoys might oppose the Company's policies, but not the Company itself.[15]

The British were vaguely aware that sepoys were attracted to the apparent invincibility of the 'Company Bahadur', but they did not often perceive the fundamental connection between *iqbal* and *rajdharma*. The linkage of these two ideas was very important, however, for sepoys.

> Since the days when the gentlemen of the Company's service first left their own country and arrived in the Carnatic, all the natives were desirous that their prosperity should increase, and that the humble and poor should receive their protection. Almighty God accordingly exalted the Company to power, and we were all well pleased. From that time to the present moment, the diligence, attention and assiduity with which we have served the Company's government is well known. . . .[16]

The British, in taking their place among the many rulers of India, acquired the obligations that long-accepted tradition and religious texts imposed on *nawabs* and rajas—an obligation to protect the weak, and to honour and provide for loyal servants. In this passage 'the humble and poor' should be read as a double entendre, referring not only to the truly destitute, but also to the subordinate condition of sepoys as loyal servants of the Company. Sepoys expected 'protection', and they expected to receive it in proportion to the success of their employers. In return for this 'protection'—one might also read the sense of this word as 'patronage'—the sepoys offered 'diligence, attention, and assiduity'. British officers, especially those serving with the King's Army in India, repeatedly registered their surprise regarding the appearance and discipline of Indian troops. Captain Innes Munro of His Majestry's 71st Highlanders wrote, in 1780, that

> . . . the Company's officers have acquired just praise by their steady adherence to the duties of their profession, which the excellent order of their sepoys clearly confirms. It is hardly credible, though true, that few troops in Europe cut a better appearance upon the parade; and I have been told by some veterans here that, when led on by European officers, they behave in the field with astonishing conduct and intrepidity.[17]

Note the difference between this passage, however, and that of the sepoy's *arz* that precedes it; contemporary European sources, whether official or unofficial, rarely presented sepoys in such a positive light except as the product of European endeavour. Whenever sepoys behaved well, it was because they were trained by British officers; if they ran away from the enemy, it was because they were 'natives' and 'unsteady'.[18]

The petitioners expressed, in their *arz*, the view that the Company's wars of expansion in south India had been extremely bloody and arduous contests that tested the limits of sepoy loyalty.

> The subadars, jemadars, havildars, naigues and sepoys of the Carnatic have forsaken their wives and children, accompanied the gentlemen of the Company's service to different countries, and sustained all kinds of dangers and hardships on their account. The conduct of the sepoys in this respect is undoubtedly well known. The Company's government first subdued the Carnatic; then the Sultan's dominions; then those of the Mahrattas and Nizam.[19]

Here and several other times in the Vellore Papers, sepoys clearly articulate their feeling that it was they who conquered the Company's empire. They also clearly saw through the system of subsidiary alliances, through which the British exerted indirect control over Mysore, Hyderabad, Travancore, and Cochin. The sepoys keenly felt the price that had been paid for the empire, referring to the 'immense numbers of sepoys' who had been killed in the Company's wars, especially in the wars with Haidar Ali and Tipu Sultan of Mysore.[20]

The petitioners refer, more than once, to the hardship of leaving their families. Hindu or Muslim, sepoys belonged to a family-oriented culture, in which separation from relatives was dreaded. Military service required soldiers to undertake long marches, and sometimes overseas voyages, often for extended periods. Madras Army sepoys were more amenable to these demands than their counterparts in the Bengal Army, but they nevertheless found that the rewards for their hard and loyal service often fell short of their expectations. 'We all enter the Company's service for the purpose of supporting our wives and children with respectability and honour', the petitioners wrote, but added that the dependants of their comrades killed in action were 'destitute and ruined'.[21]

What, then, bound sepoys to the Army? The *arz* was specific about the anchor of sepoy loyalty: '. . . the invalid and pension establishments alone. If they did not exist, all sepoys wou'd abandon the service'.[22] Company troops were always aware that they could earn more, at least in theory, in the service of the Nizam or one of the Maratha *sardars.*

> The common sepoys of the Nizam and Mahrattas are better off than your subadars and jemadars. They eat and drink with their wives and children, and are comfortable and happy. Let the truth or falsehood of this account be determined by the report of any officer who was marched through the Nizam's or Mahratta country. While this is the case, the Company proclaim throughout the country that they display the greatest possible favour and indulgence to their native tropps.[23]

Regular pay and the promise of a pension and a place in one of the invalid units, however, was a strong attraction for those interested in securing a stable income. Nevertheless, the pay of an ordinary sepoy was rather dismal—about as much as could be earned, at Madras, by unskilled coolies. To the ambitious, primarily native officers recruited from the more socio-economically advanced sections of south Indian society, the Company offered very little compared with what might be gained in a princely state. In the first years of the nineteenth century, however, the military labour market in South

Asia was rapidly contracting as each new British conquest led to the demilitarization of another tract of territory. Those who hoped to support themselves by bearing arms found few choices other than Company service. Indeed, the strength of the Madras Army had been maintained, in the years preceding the Vellore Crisis, primarily by absorbing the manpower of indigenous armies. This was, in fact, an important factor in bringing about the Vellore Mutiny; sepoys who had seen service in other armies usually brought with them pre-colonial modes of political thought. Their sense of loyalty was less rigid than that of sepoys who had known only British military discipline, and they were likely to countenance mutiny much more readily, viewing protest as a form of negotiation.

The Madras Army came into being, as a fully-articulated field army, during the Carnatic Wars, through a process of linking local military traditions with British systems of organization, by forming cohesive groups of mercenaries and their leaders into companies and sepoy battalions under European officers.[24] In the early stages there usually were only two British officers attached to a sepoy regiment. This system of command stressed the importance of dialogue between ranks rather than discipline imposed from above. Much of the dialogic exchange that enabled British officers to lead sepoy regiments effectively passed through an Indian officer known as the Native Commandant. This rank, however, was abolished in 1785, as the Army began to acquire more European officers.[25] The need to operate effectively alongside British regulars had forced the Madras Army to adopt a regimental system more like that of the King's Army.[26] These changes in organization had a profound effect on the dialogic interaction that had enabled Indian martial traditions to thrive in a quasi-European military environment.

> On the abolition of the rank of commandant, a [subadar] was appointed native adjutant in every corps. After the expiration of some years, the native adjutancies were exclusively given to jemadars. A jemadar is not fit for the situation of adjutant of a corps of cavalry or infantry. A jemadar's heart is confined, and he cannot extend support and assistance to the sepoys. When subadars were adjutants, the sepoys received assistance and protection from them. At present the native adjutants . . . are all jemadars.[27]

In this passage, we see the sepoy's view of how military reforms eroded the power of Indian commissioned officers. Once the topmost rank among native officers was removed, authority became hydra-headed. For a time, subadars appointed to act as native adjutants enjoyed first-among-equals status, considerable influence, some powers of patronage. Under this system, effective dialogue between British and Indian officers, and between the latter and sepoys, was still possible. It was also possible, although somewhat harder, for sepoys to unite, in the face of grievances, in order to seek redress. By increasing the number of European officers in each sepoy battalion the Cornwallis reforms of 1796 greatly enhanced the significance of the European adjutant, reducing the status and effectiveness of native adjutants.[28] As adjutants, jemadars found themselves awkwardly located in the chain of command, with insufficient political or financial resources to perform their duties to the satisfaction of either superior officers or subordinate soldiers. In practice, native adjutants suppressed even serious grievances, stifling the flow of dialogue between ordinary sepoys and European officers. Subadars, meanwhile, became effectively useless—a body of ageing men (having attained their rank by seniority) whose duties were duplicated, under the Cornwallis reforms, by an influx of young, inexperienced, and poorly-trained British officers.

These changes happened to coincide with one of the most active periods of the Madras Army, in which almost every battalion was permanently in the field, often on active service for months at a time. In cantonments, officers were pressed by the Military Board to implement new systems of discipline in an effort to bring sepoys up to (largely imagined) European standards of discipline. As the petitioners described the situation in their *arz*.

> [The] . . . condition . . . of a horse keeper or seykeelgar [*sic*] is respectable and happy. He earns each month two or three pagodas, and remains in comfort at one place, among his friends, and has but to rub his horse. To scour his musket and clean his arms, to dress in a variety of ways, and to march from country to country, where everything is scarce and dear, are the occupations of all the sepoys. They must also expose their lives in battle; and besides these things, the sepoys experience privations, hardships and distresses that exceed all description.[29]

To make matters worse, the Cornwallis reforms were implemented, at the company level, by junior British officers who did not quite understand the new system of drill and discipline. Indeed, the orders an officer had to give to direct close-order manoeuvres could be confusing to all concerned, as the sepoy's *arz* relates:

At parades and field days, the European officers, in giving the words of command in exercising the men, in leading their companies, and in other things, frequently commit mistakes and then abuse the sepoys, asserting that they have spoiled the performance of the corps. Having in this manner accused the poor sepoys unjustly to the commanding officer, they obtain their punishment by double duty or drill. At those times, the European officers treat the subadars and jemadars, in the presence of the men, with the utmost indignity. What sepoys will respect subadars and jemadars who are used in this manner by their superior officers?[30]

One must not think of the Madras Army as a professional military force in the modern sense of the word; few of its officers received formal military training, despite the development of a cadet corps in the late eighteenth century. Indeed, in that period formal military training was a relatively new concept. In Britain, formal training was thought useful primarily for gunners and engineers, superfluous for prospective infantry officers, and pointless for those entering the cavalry. Young men pursuing careers as army officers of the Company came out to Madras as teenagers, having been appointed, with scant reference to their abilities, by patrons who were members of the Court of Directors.

Our old European officers formerly considered the subadars and jemadars as their equals, and treated them with kindness and respect. Every new European officer who has arrived from Europe within the last ten years manifests no consideration or regard towards a [subadar] or jemadar, and deems them more unworthy than his cook or mooty [*sic*] boy. At those times, our hearts are sick of existence.[31]

These young European joined sepoy battalions as cadets, there to learn soldiering by trial and error. Before 1806, there were no standard regulations systematizing military procedure and discipline, and thus the quality of British officers was extremely variable. Much depended on the character and diligence of individual battalion commanders.[32]

In the Madras Army, on the eve of the Vellore Mutiny, there was a widespread feeling that the Company had failed to honour the unwritten contract that bound sepoys to its service. The Company had failed to 'protect' its loyal adherents, despite a string of conquests. Sepoys keenly felt the disparity between the manner in which they were treated and the growth of the Company's empire.

In . . . [the countries recently conquered by the Madras Army], a number of [*amirs*] entitled to elephants and thousands of palanquins and horses have been displaced by the Company through the assistance of their native troops. Let the Company sat what subadar, jemadar or sepoy they have distinguished by an elephant, by a palanquin, or by conferring on him the means of living with dignity and comfort? Under the Company's government, so far from finding ten or twenty men distinguished by palanquins, we cannot find that number of persons who have been rewarded even with horses.[33]

Indeed, far from honouring its sepoys, the Company was neglecting their welfare. Salaries did not keep up with inflation, and the poverty of the soldiers was made worse by droughts, famines, and periods of acute scarcity, which caused the price of basic provisions to surge, especially in and around the garrison towns where most sepoys and their families lived. During the Second Anglo-Mysore War (1780-4), the Madras Army nearly collapsed. As one British civilian recorded, 'I found [the Army] few in number, and the seapoys [*sic*] so dispirited, from want of proper care and encouragement, as to be daily deserting.'[34] According to the sepoy petitioners at Hyderabad, the government was slow and inept even in paying pensions and death benefits.

If the Company's government had been protectors and supporters of . . . [its soldiers' families], the wives and children of . . . [sepoys killed on campaign] would not have been disgraced. It is an astonishing thing that [subadars], jemadars, havildars, naigues and sepoys shou'd [*sic*] be called during their whole life by the Company's name, and after their death that their wives and children should be reduced to want and compelled to beg. The people of the Carnatic are ashamed of this state of things. . . . At present the result of the Company's service is bread to the sepoys while they live, and dust to their families when they die.[35]

There may be more than a grain of truth in the above statement. The Madras Military Consultations are full of letters complaining about the functioning of the pension establishment and the system for paying sepoy's remittances. In particular, sepoys stationed at Hyderabad, and sepoys' families living in the Northern Circars, lost a considerable percentage of their income due to the need to exchange Star Pagodas for local currency.[36]

Sepoys could not help but notice the steadily increasing distance between themselves and their European officers. The Hyderabad *arz* contrasted the service conditions of British officers with those of sepoys: 'Horses, palanquins, carriages, lofty houses, ample tents, couches, pleasure and enjoyment, gratification and delight: whatever yields joy is the portion of the European officer.' Many indebted junior officers might have quibbled with this statement, for it was almost impossible for a Madras Army officer to live on his pay, given the extraordinary expenses required by his position. Nevertheless, we are here concerned primarily with how sepoys felt—and they were not happy with their lot. 'Rain, wind, cold and heat', the petitioners wrote, 'fatigue and hardship, trouble and pain and the sacrifice of life itself . . . these are all the portion of the sepoy'. Sarcastically, they conclude: 'It is possible that Almighty God may have constituted this the justice of the English.'[37] Sepoys judged British officers by the pre-colonial standards that had prevailed in princely states, expecting them to adopt courtly traditions of gift-giving. Sepoys did not mind their officers living well, but they expected to share in the riches.

Elsewhere the sepoy petitioners provide an even more cutting illustration of the distinction between British officers and themselves—one of many passages carrying the subtle message that, despite religious and racial differences, Europeans and Indians were essentially equal in their needs and desires.

> In comparison with the station and dignity of a sepoy, jemadar or subadar, the prostitute attached to a European officer enjoys considerable pre-eminence. European officers, in compliance with their wishes, procure agreeable and beautiful women, and give them the pay 30 or 40 Star Pagodas. If the native officer received a pay in proportion to their just claims, they also wou'd be able to enjoy the pleasures desired by their hearts. At present, it is difficult for a native to obtain the love of a handsome woman, and we are ashamed to shew [*sic*] even our faces to a fine woman. Everything is dependent on gold. Why shou'd I write more? A hint is sufficient to a wise man.[38]

Some armchair historians of the colonial Indian Army have subtly praised the keeping of mistresses by British officers as part of an effective means of controlling sepoys, inferring that such women were able to teach officers about indigenous culture. Indeed, in later Army slang, the Indian mistresses of British officers were sometimes called 'sleeping dictionaries'. Sepoys, however, do not seem to have held British officers in greater esteem simply because they kept *zenanas.* Nor were such officers always very effective commanders.[39] Indeed, the sepoy petitioners at Hyderabad were no doubt aware of the great scandal that had occurred when Lieutenant James Achilles Kirkpatrick, the former British Resident, married Khair-un-Nissa, niece of Mir Alam, who was to become the Nizam's *diwan* shortly before the Vellore Crisis, in which he played an important role.[40] Some native officers, in fact, may have seen British officers as socio-economic and even sexual competitors. However, the above passage is best read in the context of several others which were included in the *arz*, all of which decry the considerable difference between the salaries enjoyed by British officers, and those given to subadars and jemadars.[41]

Throughout the *arz,* the sepoy petitioners at Hyderabad made it clear that they felt exploited by the Company. The strength with which they articulate their grievances is all the more understandable because this was not the first time sepoys of the subsidiary force had sent a petition of this nature to their officers. In Hyderabad, the Indian troops were concerned about material issues, such as pay, but they also voiced dissatisfaction with less tangible aspects of military service, such as their experience of contempt, ridicule, and racism at the hands of British officers and soldiers. The abolition of the rank of native commandant, for instance, was viewed by the sepoys as an attempt to consolidate all authority in sepoy battalions in the hands of European officers, while saving the Company the cost of the commandants' salaries.[42] Indian officers began to feel slighted as they began to be treated not as commission-holding officers, but as the equivalent of British NCOs.

When a sepoy is centinel [*sic*] and an European officer passes, on seeing the officer, he carries or presents his arms, according to orders. When a European soldier is centinel [*sic*] and a native commissioned officer passes, what is the reason that he does not carry arms to the native officer, but manifests a total disregard to him? How is it proper for the Company to allow European soldiers to shew [*sic*] this disrespect to subadars and jemadars?[43]

The sepoys were acutely aware of the prevailing opinion, among British officers, that Indian officers were not trustworthy or efficient. They complained, for instance, about the practice of assigning British sergeants to command detachments under subadars and jemadars, ranks formerly the equivalent of captain and lieutenant.[44] The petitioners pointed out, in their *arz*, that sepoys often were better acquainted with most military duties than their European officers, yet were blamed for every problem. As a result of such treatment, their 'hearts [were] alienated from the Company's service'.[45]

The petitioners in Hyderabad were particularly concerned about systematic inequalities based on race that diminished the prestige of native officers. They pointed out, for instance, that Indian officers, instead of having their own tents, like European officers of equivalent rank, were forced to share with common soldiers.[46] Similarly, on the very rare occasions when subadars were presented with palanquins, as a special honour, the Company did not provide an allowance sufficient to maintain the requisite number of *palki*-bearers, let alone the *mussalchi*, or torch-bearer, whose services were necessary for night travel. To the petitioners, the reason for this was clear—as was the remedy:

The gentlemen certainly do not consider the natives worthy of being borne in palanquins, for with the greatest reluctance and difficulty they put the Company to the expense of 10 pagodas as an addition to the allowances of the native officer whom they honour with a palanquin. It would be better . . . to [withhold] the bounty altogether than to confer such a lame palanquin. It might have been proper . . . to shew some respect to justice at least in their conduct towards their native troops.[47]

Sepoys had noticed, however, that European officers, as a group, resented the attempts of Indian officers to claim symbolic privileges of high status, especially those symbols valued in both British and Indian military culture.

Among the subadars and jemadars, some few having restricted their expenses in regard to clothes and food, and purchased horses, incur the resentment and envy of European officers whenever they appear mounted on those horses. For the European officers view with contempt the endeavours of black men to ride horses or to appear in any respect on an equal footing with themselves [*sic*]. While European officers entertain those sentiments of jealousy and enmity towards us, how can we come in competition with them?[48]

If the statements contained in the petition from Hyderabad are compared with many others that appear throughout this book, voiced by sepoys stationed all over south India, it becomes apparent that a general dissatisfaction with service conditions prevailed in the Madras Army on the eve of the Vellore Mutiny. The reasons for this dissatisfaction were complex. Sometimes sepoys were upset by problems common to the whole army, but often their grievances were particular to battalions, or even to specific companies. Grievances ranged from complaints about pay and hard duty to issues concerning respectful treatment. Even more significant than particular grievances, however, was the fact that the Army's dialogic system of discipline was replaced by one that prevented a sepoy from pleading his case before the concerned superior. The system of deference and reciprocal 'protection' upon which the subaltern status of the sepoy had rested, was allowed to collapse, in many sepoy battalions, in the ten years between 1796 and 1806. The breakdown of dialogue hastened the collision of interests that led to the Vellore Crisis. It was in this over-heated context of mounting grievances and stifled communication that the infamous 'new' turban and regulations acquired a symbolic power that transfigured their significance. When sepoys rejected the new turban and regulations, they did so because they saw them as symbols of a complex matrix of grievances.

The Vellore Mutiny left the British puzzled. As was noted above, the Council of Fort Saint George was divided in its assessment of the Mutiny. Civilian officials, for the most part, blamed it on the new turban and the new Army regulations, making the arguments that these 'obnoxious' innovations had outraged the 'religious prejudice' of the Indian troops. Military officers, for the most part, blamed the Mutiny on conspiracies hatched by local elites—conspiracies that turned out to be imaginary, once investigated. Unfortunately, the officers' conspiracy theories were pressed so vigorously that they are still given credence today. In this book I repeatedly underscore the fact that even most of the Vellore mutineers questioned by the British after the Mutiny denied or downplayed the involvement of Tipu Sultain's sons and their servants in the uprising. The *arz* from Hyderabad, in fact, demonstrated a remarkably clear understanding of what had happened at Vellore.

When, in consequence of the new turbans, a certain event occurred at Vellore, it is reported that some gentlemen declared that it was occasioned by the sons of Tippoo Sultan. This declaration is false. If at that conjucture all the subadars, jemadars, havildars, naigues and sepoys had been united, Vellore wou'd not have been retaken. The cause of the mutiny proceeded from the folly of a few persons, and from the European officers having ill treated the subadars and jemadars on every occasion.[49]

In the paragraph that follows this, the sepoy petitioners criticise the indiscriminate manner in which British troops slaughtered the Indian soldiers found inside the fort on the morning after the mutiny, pointing out that 'three portions of the native troops were ignorant of the intention to mutiny, and were faithful to their duty'. Their assessment closed with a warning: 'If another insurrection shou'd occur in the army, all the men will be united in the sentiment and action, in consequence of Colonel Gillespie's undistinguishing vengeance.' Although the government applauded Gillespie's bloody suppression of the revolt, the sepoys at Hyderabad found his 'folly . . . incontest-able'.[50] In another passage, the petitioners made the particularly bold statement that bringing additional European troops to India would not save the Raj if the Company succeeded in alienating the people of India ' . . . [T]he natives at this moment are faithful to their duty', they wrote. 'At the time when all the natives shall entertain hostile designs, nothing can be effected [*sic*] by any force. This is known to God, and what He wills shall be accomplished.'[51] The petition thus chides the Government's short-sighted reliance on the sort of brutal suppression carried out by Gillespie at Vellore, and urged the Company to return to the old process of dialogue, compromise, and conciliation.

It is significant that the sepoys in Hyderabad denied the conspiracy theory regarding Tipu Sultan's sons, and singled out the new turban as the cause of the Mutiny. However, one must view the turban both as a cause of mutiny and as a symbol of more widespread discontents. In the Vellore Crisis, sepoys were particularly concerned about the denigration of their status, and for them, social position was bound up with caste traditions and religious affiliation. The *arz*, from Hyderabad is particularly eloquent in its explanation of how sepoys felt about such matters.

Every man, whether a Mussulman or Hindoo, is happy in following his own history and religious usages. But if endeavours shou'd be used to abolish these usages and introduce Christianity in their place, what sepoy will be satisfied? To prohibit the wearing of rings on the hands, of the mark on the forehead, and of ornament on the ears; to forbid the use of music at festivals, to forbid marriage processions from passing after 8 o'clock; and, if women are carried in doolies, to pry at them with idle curiosity and ridicule; if those orders and practices obtain, what sepoy will be pleased with the Company's service? At present, to serve the Company is the same with renouncing one's religion, abandoning his customs, and washing his hands from the most sacred ties that connect him with society.[52]

Given that the East India Company's official religious policy denied Protestant missionaries access to India at the time of the Vellore Mutiny, the sepoys' argument about the introduction of Christianity must not be accorded more than rhetorical value. What is important in this passage is that the grievances listed by the sepoys mostly concern cultural rather than strictly religious matters. The new regulations approved on the eve of the Vellore Mutiny prohibited the use (while on duty) of *vibhuti*, or sacred ash, to make 'caste marks', as the British called them—the sectarian devices worn on the foreheads of many Hindu devotees, especially in the early nineteenth century. The other grievances listed above were specific to Hyderabad, where newly adopted garrison standing orders banned the use of tom-toms, restricted marriage processions, and compelled the residents of the cantonment and surrounding villages to pass through a series of checkpoints and face tedious enquiries and searches. In Hyderabad covered litters, used mainly to carry women of rank, were searched primarily to discourage desertion from sepoy battalions, which was a serious problem at that particular station. We thus see how military regulations, especially those touching tradition and custom, could easily be cast as an affront to religion. This was partly because sepoys did not separate religious and cultural values, and partly because British officials viewed Indians as a people driven primarily by religious ideas, and interpreted Indian customs in that light.

NOTES

1. The classic anti-missionary view of the Vellore Mutiny can be found in James Mill, *History of British India*, V. 1 (London, 1844), pp. 123-44. After 1857 other historians took up Mill's essential argument, but from the missionary point of view, arguing that the Vellore Mutiny occurred because the East India Company paid more attention to Hindu than to Christian 'faith'. See Henry Beveridge, *A Comprehensive History of India*, V. 2 (London, 1862), pp. 811-16; John Clark Marshman, *The History of India, from the Earliest Period to the Close of Lord Dalhousie's Administration*, V. 2 (London, 1867), pp. 208-15; Charles E. Trevelyan, *The Mutiny of Vellore: Its Parallelisms and Its Lessons* (Calcutta, 1857). A revival of the idea that the revolt was primarily religious in nature is found in Susan Bayly, *Saints, Goddesses and Kings: Muslims and Christians in South Indian Society, 1700-1900* (Cambridge, 1989), p. 224. For more comment on Bayly's position, see Chapter 1.
2. J.W. Wilson, *History of the Madras Army*, V. 2 (London, 1887); E.G. Phythian-Adams, *Madras Infantry, 1748-1943* (Madras, 1943); V. Longer, *Red Coats to Olive Green: A History of the Indian Army, 1600-1974* (Bombay, 1974), pp. 49-59; Philip Mason, *A Matter of Honour: An Account of the Indian Army, its Officers and Men* (London, 1974), pp. 236-7.
3. Edward Thornton, *A History of the British Empire in India*, V. 4 (London, 1843), pp. 57, 68-9. A nationalist spin was put on the conspiracy idea in Haripado Chaudhuri, 'The Vellore Mutiny: A Reappraisal', *The Modern Review*, 98, 1955, pp. 125-8; and in Ramesh Chandra Majumdar, *History of the Freedom Movement in India* (Calcutta, 1962), p. 115.
4. Maya Gupta, 'The Vellore Mutiny, July 1806', *Journal of Indian History*, 49, 1971, pp. 91-112; Gupta, *Lord William Bentinck in Madras and the Vellore Mutiny, 1803-1807* (New Delhi, 1986).
5. S.K. Mitra, 'The Vellore Mutiny of 1806 and the Question of Christian Mission to India', *Indian Church History Review*, 8, no. 1, 1974, pp. 75-82.
6. K. Rajayyan, *South Indian Rebellion: The First Indian War of Independence, 1800-1801* (Mysore, 1971); Perumal Chinnian, *The Vellore Mutiny: The First Uprising against the British* (Madras, 1982); P. Chinnian, *The First Struggle for Freedom in South India in 1806: Sporadic Events after the Vellore Mutiny* (Erode, 1983).
7. Major studies of the pre-colonial political systems of south India and the Deccan which have shaped my study include Kate Brittlebank, *Tipu Sultan's Search for Legitimacy: Islam and Kingship in a Hindu Domain*

(Delhi, 1997); Velcheru Narayana Rao, David Shulman, and Sanjay Subrahmanyam, *Symbols of Substance: Court and State in Nayaka Period Tamilnadu* (Delhi, 1992); Nicholas Dirks, *The Hollow Crown: The Ethnohistory of an Indian Kingdom* (Cambridge, 1987); André Wink, *Land and Sovereignty in India: Agrarian Society and Politics under the Eighteenth-Century Maratha Swarajya* (Cambridge, 1986); David Ludden, *Peasant History in South India* (Princeton, 1985).

8. Work that has influenced my interpretation of the early British Raj in south India includes Pamela G. Price, *Kingship and Political Practice in Colonial India* (Cambridge, 1996); Eugene F. Irschick, *Dialogue and History: Constructing South India, 1795-1895* (Berkeley, 1994); Burton Stein, *Thomas Munro: the Origins of the Colonial State and His Vision of Empire* (Delhi, 1989).
9. Ranajit Guha, *Elementary Aspects of Peasant Insurgency in Colonial India* (Durham, 1999), p. 15.
10. Use of the term 'native' here and elsewhere in this work merely reflects the usage of the Madras Army during the period under study. The term was used, at that time, to distinguish Indian troops from British forces, with no pejorative or racist connotations. Indeed, a striking feature of the Vellore Papers is the absence of discourse concerning race, for the racial attitudes that later informed so much of British policy in India had not yet formed or hardened into an established world-view. Terms such as 'black men' and 'black officer' appear a few times in the records, but always as a translation of the testimony of indigenous people referring to themselves. It would seem that race was an implicit but not overtly articulated factor shaping both British and Indian interpretations of the Vellore Mutiny. An interesting and revealing discussion of Indian racial attitudes in the period may be found in Michael H. Fisher, *The First Indian Author in English: Dean Mahomed (1759-1851) in India, Ireland, and England* (Delhi, 1996), pp. 220-1. For a more in-depth examination of the concept of race in this context see Channa Wickremesekera, '*Best Black Troops in the World*': *British Perceptions and the Making of the Sepoy, 1746-1805* (New Delhi, 2002).
11. Until recently, much of our knowledge of the life of the sepoy was based on Lieutenant-Colonel Norgate's very clever reworking of the memoirs of Sita Ram Pande, a veteran of the pre-Mutiny Bengal Army. See: Sita Ram Pande, *From Sepoy to Subedar, Being the Life and Adventures of Subedar Sita Ram, a Native Officer of the Bengal Army, Written and Related by Himself*, Lieutenant-Colonel Norgate, tr., James Lunt, ed. (London, 1970). Recently, however, Michael H. Fisher has

offered us a more reliable view of the Indian officer's world. See Michael H.H. Fisher, *Travels of Dean Mahomet: An Eighteenth-century Journey through India* (Berkeley, 1997) and *First Indian Author in English: Dean Mahomet (1759-1851) in India, Ireland, and England* (Oxford, 1996).

12. USL, 'Grievances of Native Soldiers', *Wellington Papers,* WP1/184/8, ff. 1v-1r.
13. In 1806, the strength of the Madras Army was 7,200 European soldiers and 48,000 sepoys and Indian cavalry under 1,500 European officers. These regular forces were supported, throughout the Presidency, by locally-recruited quasi-military formations of various kinds.
14. USL, 'Grievances of Native Soldiers', *Wellington Papers,* WP1/184/8, ff. 12r-13v.
15. Gautam Bhadra, 'The Mentality of Subalternity: *Kantanama* or *Rajdharma*', *Subaltern Studies VI,* ed. Ranajit Guha (1989), pp. 54-91.
16. USL, 'Grievances of Native Soldiers', *Wellington Papers,* WP1/184/8, ff. 2v-3r.
17. Captain Innes Munro to 'My Dear Friend', March 1780, published in Arthur H. Haley, ed., *The Munro Letters* (Liverpool, 1992), p. 26.
18. The training of sepoys, in fact, was undertaken not by British officers, but by Indian officers and British NCOs.
19. USL, 'Grievances of Native Soldiers', *Wellington Papers,* WP1/184/8, ff. 8r-8v.
20. Ibid., f. 10v.
21. Ibid., f. 10v.
22. Ibid., f. 22r.
23. Ibid., ff. 9r-9v.
24. Henry H. Dodwell, *Sepoy Recruitment in the Old Madras Army* (Calcutta, 1922).
25. Excellent discussions of these issues are found in Samuel C. Hill's 'The Old Sepoy Officer', *English Historical Review,* 28, 1913, pp. 260-91, 496-514 and *Yusuf Khan: The Rebel Commandant* (London, 1914).
26. Wilson, V. 3, pp. 151-68.
27. USL, 'Grievances of Native Soldiers', *Wellington Papers,* WP1/184/8, ff. 4v-5v.
28. Cornwallis to Dundas, 7 November 1794, *Cornwallis Correspondence,* V. 2, p. 574; also see Callahan, pp. 122-6.
29. USL, 'Grievances of Native Soldiers', *Wellington Papers,* WP1/184/8, ff. 19r-20r. A 'Seykeelgar' (*saikalgar,* in Hindi, and *chikilidarudu,* in Telugu) was a knife-grinder and sword-sharpener. Since such people used leather straps in their work, they usually were of low caste.
30. USL, 'Grievances of Native Soldiers', *Wellington Papers,* WP1/184/8, ff. 22v-23r.

31. Ibid., ff. 15r-15v. 'Mooty body' may be a reference to the *mutasaddi* or accountant. Most British commanders entrusted battalion accounts and business to a *mutasaddi,* and these individiuals often abused their positions in ways that inflicted economic hardship on sepoys.
32. In 1775, the Madras Army began to assign newly-arrived cadets to sepoy battalions, in which they were supposed to receive four months of rudimentary military training before receiving their commissions. As this system proved ineffective in practice, the cadets were collected in small groups at the major cantonments, to undergo instruction together. A cadet company was not formed, however, until 1800, but this institution soon developed into a full-fledged academy, where students learned not only military science, but also south Indian languages. *See* Dodwell, *Nabobs of Madras,* pp. 45-7.
33. USL, 'Grievances of Native Soldiers', *Wellington Papers,* WP1/184/8, ff. 8v-9r.
34. Lord Liverpool to Lieutenant-General Sir Eyre Coote, February 1781, *Liverpool Papers,* BL/Add. MSS., no. 38405, f. 128.
35. USL, 'Grievances of Native Soldiers', *Wellington Papers,* WP1/184/8, ff. 10v-11v.
36. TNSA. William Gordon, Paymaster at Masulipatam, to GC/FSG, 28 January 1802, *MMC,* V. 293-A, pp. 1288-1302. Encloses several documents pertaining to remittances and exchange rates.
37. USL, 'Grievances of Native Soldiers', *Wellington Papers,* WP1/184/8, ff. 17v-18r.
38. Ibid., 17r-17v.
39. For example, see George Elers, *Memoirs of George Elers, Captain in the 12th Regiment of Foot, 1777-1842,* Lord Monson and George L. Gower, eds. (New York, 1903).
40. The Madras Government investigated Kirkpatrick's relationship with Khair-un-Nissa, fearing that the young woman had been the victim of what would now be termed 'date rape'. The so-called Clive Enquiry exonerated Kirkpatrick, but his relationship with Khair-un-Nissa ultimately led to his dismissal by the Supreme Government.
41. USL, 'Grievances of Native Soldiers', *Wellington Papers,* WP1/184/8, ff. 16r-17r. Also see ff. 3v-4r.

    If we should pass our whole lives in the Company's service we may, perhaps, with infinite difficulty and exertion, acquire the rank of subadar. After attainment of that rank, further advancement is impracticable. . . . According to the constitution of the Company's service, three portions of the life of a man must elapse in passing through the ranks of sepoy, naigue, havildar and jemadar: and attaining the situation of subadar afterwards, at the end of 18 years, if a man should happen not to be dead, but to have survived, will receive the pay of 20 pagodas. . . . The gentlemen must imagine that great benefits are derived to the Company's interest from this system.

42. Ibid., ff 4r-4v.
43. Ibid., ff. 7r-7v.
44. Ibid., f. 7v.
45. Ibid., ff. 23v-24v.
46. Ibid., ff. 7v-8r.
47. Ibid., ff. 9v-10v.
48. Ibid., f. 14v.
49. Ibid., ff. 5v-6r.
50. Ibid., ff. 6r-7r.
51. Ibid., ff. 15v-16r.
52. Ibid., ff. 24v-25r.

1
The Mutiny at Vellore—Memory, Ideology, and History

In my book I examine discipline, loyalty, and mutiny in the East India Company's sepoy military system, focusing on these issues through the lens of the Vellore Mutiny, one of the last acts of violent resistance to British authority in south India.[1] The Vellore Mutiny of 10 July 1806 is of interest in its own right, yet the details and context of the event point suggest a broader and more profound significance. The Indian soldiers who took part in the rising were guarding the exiled and imprisoned families of Haidar Ali and Tipu Sultan, the former rulers of Mysore, and their rising has been linked, in much of the historiography of the Mutiny, to the supposed political aspirations of these recently displaced elites.[2] Related incidents, following the Vellore Mutiny, were reported from every part of the Madras Presidency, raising doubts about both the loyalty of the Army and the stability of alliances between the Company and Indian rulers such as the Nizam of Hyderabad. Were these events evidence of a widespread anti-British movement orchestrated by a conspiracy of displaced and disgruntled élites? One thing is certain: the British were panicked by the rising of their troops at Vellore. In the summer of 1806, the colonial administration in south India was only a few years old. No one yet knew whether the structure of the Raj was fragile or strong, and British officials had no precedent on which to fall back. In the absence of known procedures for facing a combined civil and military insurrection the Madras Government developed a template for handling such emergencies in the future, even though the Vellore Mutiny itself stopped far short of becoming a popular revolt.

Quite understandably, the British expected the worst from regions newly-conquered or annexed, and they assumed that the Company

Raj might be swept away if, as the Vellore Mutiny implied, the goodwill and self-interested loyalty of its Indian servants were lost. Yet the Company Raj did not fall as a result of the Vellore Mutiny and its aftermath, which I call the Vellore Crisis. The mutiny was crushed before the fighting could spread beyond the fort, and subsequent disturbances and incidents, none of which resulted in serious, open mutiny, were investigated with great care by both military and civilian officials. The various local agents of the colonial state acted to restore calm and order, sometimes in indirect and subtle ways, sometimes by intrusive and violent means, and sometimes in a panic, jumping to false conclusions and heaping blunders over insult and ignorance. While the Vellore Crisis exposed some of the weaknesses of the colonial state, it also revealed some of the strengths of the Raj. Most of all, however, the Vellore Crisis marked a transition from negotiated and essentially dialogic transactions to the bureaucratic governance that characterized the consolidation of British rule in India. In any event, the investigation of the Vellore Mutiny and its aftermath led to one of those drawn-out, intricate controversies, laced with political faction fights, blunders, and scandals, that shaped British policy toward India in the early years.

This work offers a new interpretation of the military crisis that swept through the Company's sepoy battalions in south India in 1806-7. Drawing upon the Vellore Papers and a variety of contemporary and secondary sources, this study explores the mutiny and the sepoys' growing discontent with deteriorating conditions of military service during the late eighteenth and early nineteenth centuries. My central thesis is that the military reforms of 1796-1806 undermined a dialogic relationship between Indian soldiers and British officers, a relationship that had been the basis of discipline in the old Madras Army. The drive for Europeanization unleashed by these reforms destroyed, in many battalions, an unwritten but psychologically powerful contractual relationship upon which the Indian soldier's loyalty to the Company was founded. The sense of betrayal which arose with this change accelerated the breakdown of the Army's dialogic disciplinary process. The new regulations drafted in 1806 stressed 'strict discipline' rather than dialogue, but they reflected a trend already prominent in the Army by the early 1790s. Finding no way in which to express and resolve discontents, many sepoys became estranged both from their Indian and European officers. In the months preceding the Vellore Mutiny, the negative changes came to be associated with a new, hat-like turban ordered to be adopted by regiments of 'native' infantry in the Madras Army.

This study also examines contemporary allegations that the sons of Tipu Sultan, courtiers close to the Nizam of Hyderabad, and certain groups of non-*tariqa faqirs* played an important role in fomenting sepoy discontent on the eve of the Vellore Mutiny. In contrast to recent works which make much of alleged connections between displaced indigenous interests and the Company's disgruntled troops, this paper rejects the argument that the Vellore Crisis reflected a powerful convergence of anti-British forces. Focusing on the mutineers' own stories, I assert, instead, that the Vellore Mutiny was a multi-dimensional but primarily military protest against a new article of clothing that, in the complexity of cross-cultural exchange, had come to symbolize the discontents of the Company's sepoys.

THE BACKGROUND AND CONTEXT OF THE VELLORE MUTINY

After Tipu Sultan died during the storming of Seringapatam his sons became political prisoners. On 18 June, forty-four days after surrendering to the British, the princes were escorted, under a strong guard, from the old city palace of Seringapatam to the seventeenth-century fort of Vellore, at the foot of the Eastern Ghats.[3] Vellore was both an administrative centre and a major cantonment. Indeed, the town was a recruiting location for the Madras Army, having been a magnet for soldiers even in pre-colonial times. After the arrival of the exiles from Mysore, with their retinues—altogether some three thousand people—Vellore also became a court city once again. Around 1700 it was a seat of Muslim power in the Carnatic, attracting a large number of soldiers, courtiers, and *sufis.* The character of both the town and many of the surrounding villages was decidedly Muslim; Vellore was an Urdu-speaking pocket in a predominately Tamil and Telugu-speaking area. Nevertheless, the old Muslim community did not develop close ties with the new-comers. During the Second Anglo-Mysore War, Haidar Ali had besieged British-held Vellore, but to his dismay local Muslims had aided the Company garrison with men and supplies. Haidar Ali's forces had retaliated against the people of Vellore by brutally torturing all civilians who fell into their hands—cutting off ears and noses. A prominent local *sufi*, in fact, had been killed at Haidar Ali's own command, although local legend claimed that he repeatedly rose from the dead, after numerous executions.

Confined to the interior of Vellore fort, where they were spied upon by a British Paymaster of Stipends and a network of *harkaras*, Tipu Sultan's sons nevertheless lived luxuriously, supported by allowances more generous than those they had received from their father. Indeed, the British did not discourage the princes from surrounding themselves with large retinues, especially *mard-i-admiyan*, or gentlemen attendants.[4] These individuals absorbed most of the princes' stipends, thus preventing the prisoners from amassing the sums necessary for grand political intrigue. The princes were not, however, incapable of financing petty intrigues, a few of which will be discussed in the next chapter. The interior life of the unusual political prison at Vellore, however, was not widely known. The only European officer with direct access to the princes was their Paymaster, Colonel Thomas Marriott, a talented officer born and raised in India and fluent in Urdu and Persian.[5] If a vague connection had not been drawn between the mutineers and the adherents of the Mysore princes, it is likely that the rising at Vellore would be as little-known today as any other minor sepoy mutiny. The presence of Tipu Sultan's sons, however, and the possibility of their involvement in the mutiny, aroused the dire fears of British officials, and this in turn brought a shroud of controversy and obfuscation down upon the facts and testimonies collected during the investigation of the revolt and its aftermath.

The Vellore Mutiny was all the more alarming to British officials because it occurred shortly after the conquest of south India and the establishment of the colonial administration of the Madras Presidency. Before the Fourth Anglo-Mysore War, the Company's directly-held territories had consisted of the Northern Circars, Guntur District, Madras city, the Chingleput District surrounding Madras, Baramahal, and a few other coastal enclaves. By 1801 the British also had acquired Kanara, the Ceded Districts, Thanjavur, and all of the Carnatic districts which formerly had belonged to the Nawab of Arcot. Scarcely five years had elapsed in which to consolidate the Company's hold on these far-flung and diverse territories before the shock of the Vellore Mutiny was felt. Neither the army nor the civil service had faced a major internal threat, as yet, and no one knew how well they would stand the pressures of a serious crisis. In fact, there were few *palegaru* left in 1806 who possessed either the will or the resources to fight the Company. After the defeat and public hanging of Kottabomma Nayaka, the Raja of Panjalamkurichi, only minor rebellions had occurred in Dindigul and the Chittoor *pallems*. Small detachments had put down these risings easily—so easily that the reports to the Madras Government announcing their occurrence also described their prompt suppression.[6] South India was almost completely demilitarized in 1806, but the collapse of resistance and the acceptance of the Company Raj had come so swiftly after 1801 that even the British themselves were unaware of how complete their victory had been.

The internal politics of the colonial establishment contributed much to the seriousness with which the Board of Control and the Court of Directors of the East India Company regarded the Vellore affair. The governorship of Lord William Bentinck (1803-7) had become mired in controversy regarding fiscal and military policies, the powers and jurisdiction of the Crown court in Madras; the institution of a *rayatwari* settlement throughout the Presidency, and charges of improper patronage in the appointment of a new Third Member of the Council of Fort St. George. Indeed, at the centre of all of these conflicts—at the centre of the Vellore story itself—was the Council. Bentinck, Governor and President of the Council, was the son of the Duke of Portland, who himself was Home Minister, having served first William Pitt, then Henry Addington. Born to one of the greatest fortunes in the British Empire, Bentinck was a young, liberal intellectual who agonized over questions touching 'good government'.[7] Liberalism was an inheritance from Bentinck's father, a leader among the progressive Whigs, who briefly had served as Prime Minister in the immediate aftermath of the American Revolution, and who became Prime Minister again only a few months after word of the Vellore Mutiny reached London.[8]

William Petrie, a Company servant of long standing and the Second Member of the Council of Fort St. George, served as a counterweight to the idealism of Bentinck. Petrie was wary of the expansionist policies that had led to the overthrow of Tipu Sultan and the subsequent Second Anglo-Maratha War. In every respect, he was an experienced and shrewd judge of the Indian scene.[9] While Bentinck was inclined to take his cues from the expansionist Governor-General, the Marquess of Wellesley, Petrie consistently urged him to be mindful of the conservative Court of Directors. At the outbreak of the War of the First Coalition, Governor-General Cornwallis, before his departure from India, had outlined a policy of retrenchment and limited engagement in India's internal politics. The Court of Directors had seconded these policies, but Wellesley had pursued a string of conquests and interventions, presenting each to his outraged superiors as a *fait accompli.* As soon as the Maratha Wars were successfully concluded, Wellesley was ordered home—if not in disgrace, at least to his own and the Court of Directors' considerable annoyance. Bentinck, to some extent, was blinded by his admiration for Wellesley, and like Wellesley he overestimated the tolerance of the Court of Directors.[10]

At the beginning of the Vellore Crisis, the Third of Council was James Strange, son-in-law of Henry Dundas, who headed the East India Board of Control. Strange was appointed to the Council of Fort St. George by Bentinck, in violation of the long established order of precedence governing the promotion of the Company's covenanted servants.[11] In the middle of the Vellore Crisis, Strange was removed from the Council by an order of the Court of Directors and replaced by Thomas Oakes, who, like Petrie, was another veteran Company servant. At the height of the Vellore Crisis, when it seemed that Bentinck might lose control of the Council, Oakes buried any resentment he may have harboured against the Governor for being passed over in favour of Strange. Indeed, Oakes' support for Bentinck's proposals contributed much to the timely resolution of the crisis. The appointment of Strange, however, had raised the Directors' ire against Bentinck even before news of the Vellore Mutiny reached them; it did not take much, after that, to persuade them to recall Bentinck from Madras.[12]

The Fourth Member of Council was the Commander-in-Chief of the Madras Army, Lieutenant-General Sir John Francis Cradock—the scapegoat blamed for setting in motion the series of actions that led to the uprising. Like his more successful friend, Sir Arthur Wellesley, Cradock had been born into the elite. His father had been the Anglican Archbishop of Dublin who on his death left his family in genteel poverty. John Cradock, at the age of fourteen, was compelled by adversity to seek a future in the Army, and his father's political connections stood him in good stead. Rather quickly, Cradock was able to obtain an appointment to the Lord-Lieutenant's staff at Dublin Castle, thus assuring that he would be noticed by the powerful and influential soldiers who commanded the Army of Ireland in the late eighteenth century. Under Sir Ralph Abercrombie and Cornwallis, Cradock acquired expertise in military administration and a powerful belief in the importance of strict military discipline and efficiency— what in those days was called the 'internal economy' of an army. Cradock has been described as a 'martinet', but such a description does not do justice to the range of his personality. Although inclined to express himself bluntly, Cradock's feelings were quite complex. Politically, for instance, he believed in the authoritarian ethos of the Anglo-Irish aristocracy, violently opposing nationalist sentiments as a member of the Irish Parliament. However, unlike his fellow staff subaltern at Dublin Castle, the future Duke of Wellington, Cradock did not demand of himself the strict adherence to discipline and orders that he insisted upon in others. He took part in the dueling mania of the period, for instance, in violation of military regulations. Cradock also pursued both honours and allowances with an enthusiasm that struck his superiors—even in an age when such behaviour was expected of a young military officer—as opportunistic, if not indecent. Nevertheless, Cradock was successful in his personal quest; he moved quickly up the ranks and married into a wealthy and well-connected old Anglo-Irish family.[13]

In an era of gifted soldiers, Cradock was a mediocre leader of men. He was personally brave—twice wounded in action, once in the Irish Revolt and again during an expedition to the West Indies—but could not handle large bodies of troops under fire.[14] Cradock was not an inspiration to his men, and his ineptitude did not pass unnoticed. Sir John Moore, who served with him in Egypt, wrote in blistering terms of his poor generalship and reliance on patronage.[15] After the signing of the Peace of Amiens, fearing exile to the half-pay list, Cradock eagerly accepted command of the Madras Army, under the impression—as he later claimed—that he eventually would be made Commander-in-Chief of the Bengal Army on the death, recall, or retirement of Lord Lake, and consequently Commander-in-Chief, India. The hot and steaming climate of Madras, however, did not agree with Cradock, and although he commenced an ambitious reform of the Madras Army's disciplinary system, he quibbled about his pay and privileges, complaining that he had not realized how expensive it would be to maintain a Commander-in-Chief's household in India. The resumption of war in Europe further aggravated Cradock, and he begged the Court of Directors to transfer him back to Britain—pleas that fell on deaf ears.[16] Compared with other members of the Council of Fort St. George, all polished and scholarly men, immersed in Enlightenment theories of 'civil society' and 'the rule of law', Cradock was a blunt, passionate, and rather short-sighted soldier, intellectually out of his depth.

By his own admission, Cradock was ignorant of south Indian languages and culture, but this impediment scarcely distinguished him from most other officers who had served as Commander-in-Chief of the Madras Army. High-ranking British officers were forbidden by Company anti-corruption regulations from associating freely with Indian civilians. Arthur Wellesley, who sailed home to England from Madras in 1805, just as Cradock was arriving, had taken an interest in the command of Indian troops, and could speak with them in Hindustani, but he was very much the exception to the rule. Cradock, as chief of the Military Board of the Madras Presidency, deferred to the experience of his staff officers regarding the management of sepoy battalions—in particular to the Adjutant-General, Lieutenant-Colonel Patrick Agnew, and to Agnew's assistant, Major Frederick Pierce. These two officers, in turn, saw Cradock's arrival as an opportunity to advance their own interest in the drafting of a new system of military regulations for the Madras Army.

The absence of a single, coherent system of discipline for the Madras Army was a serious impediment to the standardization and improvement of the sepoy battalions. Each regiment followed its own procedures and regulations, which were supplemented by General Orders handed down, as necessary, by the Military Board and the Governor-in-Council. A similar problem had hindered the reform of the British Army until the publication of Dundas' regulations.[17] Cradock himself had helped Abercrombie enforce the new reforms in the Army of Ireland, an experience that had confirmed his belief in the importance of standardized military regulations. Cradock immediately approved Agnew's plan to draw up and publish, in the form of a small book, available to every European officer of the Madras forces, a single system of regulations based on those established for the British Army nine years earlier. Cornwallis had contemplated such a standardization at the time of his own reforms in 1796, but because most of the sepoy battalions were on active service almost continually until the summer of 1805, the project had been indefinitely abandoned. Cradock thus hoped to complete what Cornwallis had begun.[18]

Major Pierce's 150-page draft of the new regulations was completed by November 1805, and at that time was reviewed, point-by-point, by the Military Board. During this process, Cradock drew the Board's attention to a new regulation requiring sepoys to appear on duty without jewellery or 'caste marks'—the application of *vibhūtī*, or sacred ash, to the forehead to designate affiliation with either the Śaiva or Śri Vaiṣṇava sects of Hinduism. Sepoys also were required to trim their beards and moustaches in a particular manner. Cradock, to his credit, asked his staff if any of the above changes might annoy the Indian troops under his command, but both Agnew and Pierce insisted that the new regulations merely reflected existing practice in 'well-disciplined' battalions. Reassured that the regulations would not be received by sepoys as an affront, Cradock allowed their inclusion in the final draft sent to the Governor-in-Council for approval. Due to heated debates in the Council regarding the Presidency's finances and the *rayatwari* settlement, the new Army regulations were set aside and not approved until March 1806. Lord Bentinck later admitted that the busy Council did not read the new regulations, but merely accepted them under the assumption that they contained nothing likely to alarm the Company's Indian troops. The Council then returned its attention to the problem of the revenue settlement until the outbreak of the Vellore Mutiny interrupted normal government business.[19]

Cradock sought to reform the sepoy's appearance as well as his discipline. Indeed, he viewed the two projects as complimentary. Attempts had been made to 'improve' sepoy uniforms since the Army first adopted more or less standard red coats in 1754. European observers often identified, as the most distinctive feature of the

Company's sepoy military system, the use of clothing that blended the military fashions of both India and Europe. The British had taken the concept of dressing Indian soldiers in quasi-European uniforms much further than the French and their other European rivals. The clothing of troops in the Madras Army was a 'privilege' of battalion commanders. In fact, the allowances of officers detached to command sepoy corps initially had been paid out of the savings derived from 'clothing stoppages' deducted from soldiers' pay. From 1754 to 1802, despite dozens of changes in the style and cut of sepoy uniforms, the method of procurement remained the same. Each battalion provided its own clothing, purchasing broadcloth from the Company and contracting the tailoring and decoration of the uniforms with local craftsmen. The system was simple, but in practice it was very inefficient.

From the moment of the formation in 1748 of the Madras Army until the conclusion of the Third Anglo-Maratha War in 1805, sepoy battalions were constantly on active service, putting down local revolts or fighting the Mysoreans. When not on the march, sepoys often were scattered in small detachments, on escort, guard, or recruiting duty. British officers found it almost impossible, under such conditions, to keep the clothing of their battalions 'complete'. Following a lengthy debate about these problems, the Military Board decided to form a central depot for military clothing in 1802, but the Second Anglo-Maratha War broke out. Cradock's decision to introduce a new turban as part of the sepoy's uniform was not an innovation, but rather part of a process begun long before his arrival at Madras. Indeed, Cradock could not have anticipated that the new turban would arouse such strong feelings among the Army's Indian troops. Sepoys selected to model the new turban for the Military Board said that the headgear was an excellent improvement, as it did not fall off as easily as the old turban. Only a very unusual sepoy, however, would have the nerve to say anything else in the presence of his Commander-in-Chief and an Adjutant-General whose ill-treatment of those who brooked his authority was notorious.[20]

The Military Clothing Department produced a sample turban for each battalion and sent them to the depots of the various regiments in March 1806. In keeping with standard military practice, the 'pattern men' of each company were to make turbans resembling the depot sample, and their fellow soldiers then would follow their lead in fashioning their own headgear. The first cantonments to which the new turbans were sent were those within a hundred miles of Madras—Wallajahbad, Ranipet, Vellore, and several other lesser posts such as Arni and Chittoor.

The new turban was not actually 'new'. Indeed, in making it, sepoys used the wire frames and broadcloth of their old turbans, merely altering the shape of the frame and adding the decorations stipulated by the General Order accompanying the depot samples. Among the decorations was a leather cockade; at Vellore, the cockades were produced by untouchable *chakkiliyan* craftsmen who worked for one of the Anglo-Indian military contractors attached to the garrison. Ironically, however, it was not the leather cockades that caught the attention of sepoys at Vellore, but rather the new shape of the turban. The tailor, who first opened the box of pattern turbans sent to the Vellore arsenal immediately said that they looked like 'Portuguese' drummers' *topis*, or hats. A fellow sepoy, standing with him, urged the *darzi* sepoy never to repeat what he had just said. The company tailor, however, retorted that it would be quite obvious to all who saw the new turban that it was not a turban at all, but a hat—and not just any hat, but a European *topi*, such as was worn by European soldiers and the musicians of sepoy battalions.[21]

Not long after sepoys of the 2/4th Native Infantry first noticed that the new turban resembled a drummer's *topi*, the men of the battalion began to grow apprehensive. It was suggested by some sepoys, and by servants of the Mysore princes, that the new turban must be part of an arcane British plot to undermine the social status of both Hindu and Muslim sepoys. The Indian troops were told that if people saw them wearing the new turban, no one would want to intermarry with them. Some soldiers apparently were told by their own wives that they would refuse to cook or sleep with them if they wore the foreigners' hat. Such gossip and threats played on powerful fears embedded in the socialization of soldiers recruited from the middling castes of the south Indian peasantry. Nevertheless, soldiers in any part of the world are set apart from the larger society surrounding them, and there were many sepoys who scoffed at all the banter about the new turban.[22]

British officers first became aware of the impending crisis when the grenadier company of the 2/4th Native Infantry was ordered to be the first unit in the entire Army to make up the new turban. The grenadiers made a rather chaotic but spontaneous protest, and their irate commander, Lieutenant-Colonel John Darley, accused them of mutinous behaviour. Hoping to force the issue, Darley personally asked each grenadier whether or not he would wear the new turban: a number of sepoys, both Muslim and Hindu, remained steadfast in their refusal, saying that to wear the new turban would violate the customs of their castes and lead to their ostracism. Darley arrested the disobedient grenadiers, and panic spread through the garrison. The sepoys of the 1/1st Native Infantry did not protest themselves, but they seem to have encouraged the rest of the 2/4th to support the stand taken by their grenadier company. At evening parade, therefore, a large number of sepoys of the 2/4th turned out without their bayonet scabbard belts—a violation of the battalion regulations, but also a subtle message that indicated their unwillingness to move beyond mere protest to violent resistance. In the face of what seemed, on the surface, to be a united opposition, Darley flew into a rage, yelling at his men; then he lost his nerve and turned to the garrison commander for help. Colonel Fancourt, who commanded the Vellore cantonment, handled the affair according to the unwritten rules of the old Madras Army, in which 'mutiny' was understood as a form of negotiation. Fancourt pretended not to know what was happening, hoping that the protest could be suppressed without the need for a formal report; he tried to convey to Darley, as subtly as possible, that a soldiers' protest was only a mutiny if one called it a mutiny, and that to do so was unwise if one hoped to retain the trust and loyalty of Indian soldiers. Fancourt thus relied on dialogue rather than discipline to restore order to the 2/4th Native Infantry. Native officers, taking their cue from the garrison commander, rapidly restored order in the 'mutinous' companies while their British officers looked on helplessly. Darley considered himself to be disgraced and begged to be relieved of command.[23]

On the parade ground, facing angry and resolute men, Fancourt followed the old rules, but when he returned to his quarters, he seems to have reconsidered the event in more abstract terms. Ultimately, he had to admit that there had been a mutiny—at least according to the technical language of the Articles of War, which classified every refusal to obey orders, no matter how trivial, as a mutiny. Fancourt decided to proceed with a formal investigation of the 'disturbance'. This, too, often was part of the old system of discipline, for a demonstration of the inexorable operation of British military law tended to terrify disgruntled soldiers and shake out the 'ringleaders' from among the mass of men who merely had been misled in a moment of weakness. Ironically, however, when a court of enquiry was convened at Vellore, Darley sought to blame the 'mutiny' on the very Native officers who had restored the battalion's discipline. Unfortunately for Darley, this was not part of the script for the proceedings of a traditional Madras Army court of enquiry. The court perceived the inconsistencies in Darley's allegations, and decided not to take any drastic measures.[24] Two hapless sepoys were selected as 'examples' to stand court martial in Madras, and Darley escaped with a stern reprimand. It was hoped that this sacrifice would uphold both the chain of command and military authority, and protect the *izzat*, or honour of the 2/4th Native Infantry.[25]

The incident at Vellore was followed by a very minor disturbance among the grenadiers of the 2/14th Native Infantry stationed at Wallajahbad, which was commanded by the designer of the new turban, Lieutenant-Colonel Bose.[26] These 'mutinies' alarmed Cradock, who had gone to Nandidurgam, in the Mysore hills, to escape the summer heat. Warned by British officers sympathetic to Indian sensibilities that sepoys' concerns about the new turban should not be taken lightly, Cradock wrote to the Governor-in-Council for direction.[27] Bentinck, however, did not believe the matter warranted intervention by the highest executive body of the Government, and he urged Cradock to uphold his own authority by punishing all sepoys guilty of disobedience of General Orders. Bentinck argued that it was unwise to reward protestors, as British rule in India was founded not on consent, but on compulsion. He also suggested that the controversy surrounding the new turban might be abated if the Government did not imbue it with more significance than it warranted. Bentinck apparently did not see how his advice, strictly implemented, might bring about exactly the opposite of the results that he intended.[28]

As a precautionary measure, the 2/4th Native Infantry had been moved from Vellore and replaced by the 2/23rd, one of the Army's youngest battalions. No further problems were reported from Vellore, and the men of the 1/1st and the 2/23rd made up copies of the new turban without complaint. British officers and others at Vellore were warned, however, that a mutiny was to take place, but they disregarded these reports on one pretext or another. Then, at two o'clock in the morning on 10 July 1806, the sepoys of the Vellore garrison armed themselves and attacked their British officers and the European troops stationed in the fort. Over one hundred officers and British soldiers, including Colonel Fancourt, were killed, and many others were wounded, but the mutineers failed to gain undisputed control of the fort—a failure that proved fatal. At dawn, British dragoons and Indian cavalry arrived from Ranipet; the gates of the fort were blown open, and the cavalry charged in, slaughtering hundreds of sepoys. In the chaos that attended the terrifying recapture of the fort, hundreds of other sepoys managed to escape, but most of them were arrested and brought back to Vellore during the weeks that followed. In the crowded Main Guard, the captured fugitives joined those sepoys who had been fortunate enough to be taken prisoner in the mop-up of the mutiny. Together, in dread and confusion, they waited behind bars for more than a year while the Madras Government tried to decide their fate. While they waited, further disturbances rippled through the Army, but none resulted in the sort of violence which had been displayed by the insurgents at Vellore.

SOURCES, HISTORIOGRAPHY, AND METHODOLOGY

Our primary sources are voluminous. Almost all of these are the court martial records of the Madras Army, and official consultations and reports generated by the Company Raj and British authorities in London. Indigenous voices are present in these records, but they are filtered through the pens of European officials. No trace remains, apparently, of the original court of enquiry and court martial records made in south Indian languages by local scribes.[29] If these were retained after the Vellore Crisis, they doubtless were destroyed when the Madras Record Office's military holdings were culled under Field Marshall Roberts in the early 1880s.[30] Occasionally, one finds transliterations of Urdu, Tamil, and Telugu words and phrases used by those who testified before the various courts and commissions of enquiry, and that is all.

The Vellore Mutiny raised a great storm of controversy, one that was to be reflected by its historiography. Indeed, the meaning of the uprising has been studied more than the mutiny itself, especially by historians concerned primarily about the impact (or lack thereof) of Christian missions on south Indian society.[31] The tendency to consider the events of the Vellore Crisis as irrelevant to understanding the meaning of the Vellore Mutiny constitutes a significant historiographical problem. In this study, I will leave these ancillary discussions aside, concentrating instead on the military and cultural contexts of the Vellore affair, and on the Madras Government's resolution of the crisis. However, I must demonstrate how my methodology and findings differ from those of others who have written about the Vellore Mutiny.

Serious study of the Vellore Mutiny—as distinct from the partisan polemics of the post-Mutiny 'Pamphlet War' of 1807-10—began with John Malcolm's *Sketch of the Political History of India*. This important work was published first in 1811, on the eve of the crucial debate in Parliament regarding the extension and amendment of the East India Company's royal charter. Among its other accomplishments, Malcolm's work transformed the oral traditions of the Madras Army into a formal text, laying the foundation of an idealized image of the relationship between British officers and Indian sepoys—an image that persists to this day, having been nurtured and carefully maintained over the years to meet changing political needs. Significantly, Malcolm's general discussion of sepoy identity hinged upon his analysis of the causes of the Vellore Mutiny. Sepoy loyalty, from that point on, would always be discussed in a context of military crisis and mutiny, in a perpetual tension between discipline and discontent. Malcolm argued that the deterioration of the Madras Army stemmed from the Cornwallis reforms of 1796, in particular the increase in the number of European officers attached to sepoy battalions. These officers, mostly very young and unfamiliar with Indian customs and sensibilities, quickly appropriated the privileges and responsibilities which formerly had belonged to Indian commissioned and non-commissioned officers. Most British officers, however, were unable or unwilling to develop the cultural sensitivity and language proficiency necessary to command Indian troops effectively. They also distanced themselves from Indian officers, who were viewed as redundant, inefficient vestiges of the era of military adventuring. Malcolm himself had favoured Cornwallis' reforms as a young officer, hoping for promotion, but within three years, his attitude was entirely transformed. He wrote, in a cautionary epistle to the Madras Government, that 'the system on which [the Army] is at present arranged is of that cold, confined, and depressive nature that it cannot . . . fail, if not radically amended, of some day bringing a misfortune on the state'.[32]

Although a cautionary tale, based on personal impressions rather than archival materials, Malcolm's assessment of the Vellore Mutiny contained significant insights. Malcolm's fluency in Hindustani and his lively interest in south Indian culture, enabled him to mingle with sepoys and other indigenous people on terms of unusual familiarity. As a young officer attached to a sepoy battalion, he had gained, in the early days of his service, a clear understanding of unedited Indian attitudes toward the Company Raj. As a marginalized, middle-class Scotsman, compelled to succeed through merit as a scholar rather than political patronage, Malcolm's own views on British India and Company policy could be quite critical. He empathized with Indian complaints about the Raj even if he did not support them himself, hearing in them the echo of his parents' generation's grudging acceptance of English domination in Scotland.

The essential points of Malcolm's argument were used by James Mill in the first edition of his *History of British India*, which appeared in 1819. Hoping to curry the favour of the Court of Directors, however, Mill cast Cradock and Bentinck as the 'villains' of the Vellore story. Furthermore, Mill reintroduced the idea that sepoy discontent originated in an irrational fear of Christian missionary activities. 'There can be no reason to seek any other origin of the mutiny', Mill wrote, 'than the dread of religious change inspired by the military orders.' Sepoys—unable to understand the Company's rather inexact separation of politics and religion—had been unable to distinguish between European military officers and missionaries, although they assumed the latter must have some great influence over the former. In Indian kingdoms, after all, *purohits* and *qazis* sometimes played an important role in secular affairs. On the other hand, however, rajas and *nawabs* rarely allowed themselves to be guided by priests or *ulema* in their pursuit of *artha*. Nevertheless, Europeans often embraced the simple, expedient fiction that all Indians were blinded by religion in their secular pursuits, for it helped them construct order amid the apparent chaos of contemporary Indian politics.[33] Mill, consciously or unconsciously, merely adopted a stereotype that had been held so long that it was assumed to be an accurate reading of the collective Indian mind. Indeed, Mill's argument was merely a refinement of an earlier argument made by Cradock himself in his attempt to defend himself before the Court of Directors at the time of his recall.[34]

In the 1860s, John William Kaye produced another analysis of the Vellore Mutiny based on Malcolm's insights. As an evangelical Christian, however, Kaye did not share the anti-missionary sentiments of James Mill.[35] Writing in the immediate wake of the Indian Mutiny of 1857, Kaye's attention was drawn to issues of race and caste, about which Malcolm had said very little. The introduction of a lengthy discussion of racism and caste-consciousness into the study of sepoy mutinies was a significant step, one that was to have a lasting influence on the writing of Indian military history. Although inclined to view the sepoy as an irrational simpleton, Kaye nevertheless perceived the importance of threats to sepoy identity within the context of both British India's military culture and indigenous systems of belief and social status.[36] Kaye's views continue to resonate, having been adopted over a century later by two influential writers at both ends of the ideological spectrum, the evangelical ex-I.C.S officer turned amateur historian, Philip Mason, and the don of the subaltern school, Ranajit Guha.[37] Robert E. Frykenberg's study of the Vellore Mutiny draws many of the same conclusions as those of Malcolm and Kaye, albeit in more modern language. Frykenberg does not, however, acknowledge the influence of either author.[38]

Although dismissed by Company officials, contemporary allegations that an extensive and potentially powerful anti-British conspiracy lay behind the Vellore Mutiny have proved remarkably persistent. The idea that the Raj was beleaguered by secret foes was particularly appealing to nationalist historians seeking to uncover evidence of pre-colonial popular resistance to British rule, thus supplying the twentieth-century Freedom Struggle with a grassroots heritage. K. Rajayyan and Perumal Chinnian, in particular, present a nationalist interpretation of the Vellore Mutiny—one tinged with the regional chauvinism of the modern Tamil movement. While

Rajayyan has brought to light many little-known but important documents concerning south Indian resistance to Company expansion in the late eighteenth and early nineteenth centuries, both his work and that of Chinnian suffer from significant methodological problems,[39] in particular their attempt to link all of their evidence into a grand pattern of conspiracy, and to use archival sources in an indiscriminate manner. Even so Rajayyan's idea of a popular anti-British conspiracy has influenced the work of more widely-read scholars such as Susan Bayly. In her *Saints, Goddesses and Kings*, Bayly enters into an extended but poorly-informed discussion of the Vellore Mutiny, which she characterizes as a 'dramatic but short-lived "Islamic" warrior's insurgency'. Bayly describes the Vellore affair as a full-scale rebellion, a dress-rehearsal of the Great Mutiny of 1857. Her many mistakes, however, stem from her reliance on Rajayyan and Chinnian rather than on the primary sources. Indeed, if Bayly had made use of the Vellore Papers, she would have found important primary sources for her study of south India's non-*tariqa sufis*, in particular their connection with the region's Islamic military culture.[40]

The most serious modern studies of the Vellore Mutiny are those of Ainslie T. Embree, Maya Gupta, and Pakkianathan Samuelraj. Embree deals with the Vellore Crisis in the context of Charles Grant's defence of Company policy and the recall of Bentinck. He concludes, on the basis of a short but well-focused examination of part of the Vellore Papers, that Madras Army sepoys actually feared an attempt to destroy their religious, cultural, and socio-economic status. Embree asserts that, because south Indian society was 'traditional' there was 'little distinction . . . between custom and religion'. In this context, something as mundane to Western eyes as a mere change in military costume was construed, by Hindu and Muslim sepoys, as the imposition of alien cultural values and religious identities.[41] Maya Gupta echoes Embree's conclusions in both her study of the Vellore Mutiny and her longer work on Lord Bentinck's governorship of Madras. Gupta exonerates Cradock, Bentinck, and the Christian missionaries, but she accepts the idea that some sort of limited anti-British movement lay behind the Vellore uprising. Unwilling to identify the agents of such a movement, however, Gupta raises more questions than she answers.[42] Meanwhile, apparently unaware of Gupta's concurrent work in India and England, Pakkianathan Samuelraj produced a comprehensive doctoral thesis on the Vellore

Mutiny in Canada in 1972. This work remains unpublished, and therefore it has not been used in previous studies of the Vellore Crisis. Samuelraj examines most of the important primary sources regarding the Mutiny, but unfortunately his interpretation lacks the scholarly rigour necessary to build a convincing argument. Samuelraj falls into the trap of attempting to reconstruct a coherent, teleological account of the Mutiny, and in so doing, overlooks the essentially contradictory and contested nature of the Vellore Papers. The most significant weakness of his work, however, is a failure to view the Vellore Mutiny in its wider political and military context. Ultimately, Samuelraj does not tie the details of his narrative into a convincing analysis, and thus he does not synthesize fully-developed, satisfactory conclusions. He sees the Vellore Mutiny as merely the axiomatic reaction of indigenous people to the imposition of foreign rule—a finding that is unenlightening and of somewhat dubious value.[43]

Channa Wickremesekera, in a recently-published study of how the British constructed the identity of sepoys in the eighteenth century, touched on the Vellore Mutiny in a more general discussion of early sepoy mutinies.[44] Wickremesekera's few words on the meaning of the Vellore rising deserve close attention, due to his wide reading on the old sepoy armies and his familiarity with the relevant India Office records. Wickremesekera notes that although a strong mercenary spirit moved the sepoy armies, by the 1790s the mutiny of Indian troops increasingly stemmed from religious causes. While recognizing that the Vellore Mutiny 'had religious overtones' Wickremesekera nevertheless points to some of the lesser disturbances in the Madras Army at that time, noting that these petty affairs also suggest that 'deep-seated grievances relating to intolerable service conditions like low pay and excessive drill' also contributed to sepoy unrest.[45] To a certain extent, these arguments are valid, and are supported by my own research. However, an examination of Wickremesekera's sources reveals methodological problems. In assessing the causes of the Vellore Mutiny, he cites Wilson's *History of the Madras Army*, but although this source is unparalleled in its treatment of the organization and operations of the army, it does not provide an in-depth analysis of the political or cultural factors that shape military history. Wilson's opinions regarding the causes of the Vellore Mutiny, in fact, merely reflect the popular understanding of the late nineteenth century, which held the captive princes guilty of organizing a conspiracy.[46] In speaking of the other Madras Army disturbances of 1806, Wickremesekera's work rests on firmer foundations, as he cites evidence from original documents concerning alleged acts of insurbordination at Wandiwash, but once again, his methodology bears close scrutiny.[47] The Madras government's investigation of the incidents at Wandiwash was inconclusive, much of the collected evidence being second-hand, or uncorroborated. Furthermore, although the sepoys at Wandiwash doubtless spoke their minds about the grievances that most concerned them, British authorities held that their annoyance was quite understandable, as they had been sent off after morning parade to their barracks to clean equipment, without their customary meal break.[48] Piecemeal use of the Vellore Papers poses problems because the evidence is so voluminous, complex, and contested. For this very reason one should not be quick to link the Vellore Mutiny and the other, related disturbances into a coherent pattern. As my own study demonstrates, service conditions—and sepoy attitudes about them—varied greatly from one battalion and cantonment to another, while sepoy discontent usually was embedded in local socio-economic and political concerns.

My own work rests on the understanding that the Vellore Papers consist mainly of contested testimony and the correspondence of various parties within the colonial bureaucracy with an interest in the outcome of the post-Mutiny enquiries and trials. As very few unequivocal facts were established regarding the causes of the Vellore Mutiny, it is impossible to develop the sort of teleological presentation that forms the basis of Samuelraj's study. A blow-by-blow account of the rising can only be reconstructed if much contradictory (but equally valid) evidence is selectively disregarded. It is necessary to accept the limitations inherent in the Vellore Papers, to understand that our knowledge of what happened at Vellore and other cantonments will always reflect only a fraction of the truth. Ultimately, with respect to the very idea of truth, the historian also must acknowledge the interplay of occurrence and perspective. In the Vellore Papers, for instance, we find that two sepoys, standing side by side, saw the very same events, yet remembered and interpreted them in different ways.[49] In this work, I argue that the Vellore Crisis was multi-dimensional, meaning different things to different participants. Such is the nature of historical events; being past, they are merely constructions fashioned out of myriad perceptions of former realities.

NOTES

1. By 'sepoy military system' I refer to the Indian units of the Company's three armies. The three Presidencies of British India—Bengal, Madras, and Bombay—each had their own armies, with general staffs and supporting services. Although European troops, both Crown and Company, were stationed in each Presidency, the core of each army was its sepoy battalions, two of which composed a regular Indian infantry regiment. The word 'sepoy' was an Anglicization of the Persian *sipahi*, which by 1800 had come to designate a musketeer. The word, however, had developed a range of meanings over time. For more details, see Henry Yule, et al., *Hobson-Jobson: A Glossary of Colloquial Anglo-Indian Words and Phrases, and of Kindred Terms, Etymological, Historical, Geographical and Discursive*, William Crooke, ed. (Calcutta, [1886] 1994), pp. 809-11. The term sepoy was replaced, around the time of the Second World War, by the term currently used to refer to Indian soldiers, *jawan*, which has no colonial associations, and simply means 'young man'.
2. Haidar Ali Khan, a mercenary in the Raja of Mysore's army, overthrew his employer in a military coup in 1759, establishing a new, Islamic regime in the southern Deccan. Haidar Ali's programme of expansion brought him into conflict with the British, resulting in a series of hard-fought wars. Tipu Sultan inherited his father's position in 1782, proclaiming himself Sultan of Mysore and doing away with the fiction of being a mere general, ruling the kingdom for the deposed Wodeyar Raja. Tipu's reign (1782-99) was highly controversial, and historians today have found both the Sultan and his kingdom difficult to explain. A bold and vigorous commander, Tipu Sultan posed a significant threat to the Company's position in south India, and consequently, the British availed themselves of every opportunity to weaken Mysore and surround it with allied states. Finally, in 1799, a disastrous war was forced on Tipu, culminating in the siege and storming of his capital. Following Tipu's death in the final assault on Seringapatam, his extended family and their retainers—more than three thousand people—were moved to the fort of Vellore, in the Tamil country, where they remained at the time of the mutiny.
3. The royal family of Mysore, during Tipu's reign, inhabited a rambling old palace inside the city of Mysore. The Daurya Daulat Bagh 'palace' outside Seringapatam was too small to accommodate the Sultan's family, while the newly-built Lal Bagh was allowed to stand empty. As the Lal Bagh had been used by Cornwallis as his headquarters in 1792, Tipu Sultan considered it defiled.

4. BL/OIOC (British Library/Oriental and India Office Collection), Harcourt to GC/FSG, 9 August 1806, 'Abstract of Males of the Blood of Hyder Ally', *HMS* (*Home Miscellaneous Series*), V. 508, pp. 93-8. Also see TNSA (Tamil Nadu State Archives), Abstract of the Princes, their Relations, Domesticks, Women, and Children Residing in the Fort of Vellore, April 1806, *MSS* (*Madras Secret Sundries*), V. 2-A, p. 1079. According to the census cited last above, there were 1,344 court ladies, attendants, children, and female servants living in the *zenanas*, most of them in the households of Haidar Ali and Tipu Sultan. By contrast, there were only 248 male domestic servants and *mard-i-admiyan*. Several hundred other people, both Mysore royal family members and servants, lived in Vellore town, visiting the prisoners in the fort as required. Although the total number of prisoners was large, the fact that so many were women and young children meant that the British garrison's security problems were minimal. Smuggling, in fact, posed more of a problem for the British than attempts to escape.
5. Marriott had been one of the officers assigned to move the Mysorean royal family from Seringapatam to Vellore in 1799.
6. For example, see George Parrish to Bentinck, 25 June, 6 July, and 20 August 1804, UN (University of Nottingham), Portland MS, PwJb/34, ff. 17-22; TNSA, Collector to MBOR (Madras Board of Revenue), 2-3 and 12 July 1804, *Coimbatore District Records*, V. 597, pp. 100-9; Major James Leith's Memorandum on the Chittoor Poligars, 14 November 1804, Portland MS., PwJb/26, ff. 21-3, 32-5, 40-1, 43.
7. These observations are based on my own study of Lord Bentinck's Madras Papers, part of the Duke of Portland's Manuscript Collection. These papers fill 87 reels of microfilm, and include both confidential and public correspondence, as well as some private material. The best published studies of Bentinck's governorship are Demitrius C. Boulger, *Lord William Bentinck. Rulers of India Series* (Oxford, 1897) and Maya Gupta, *Lord William Bentinck in Madras and the Vellore Mutiny, 1803-1807* (New Delhi, 1986). The account of Bentinck's career found in John Rosselli's *Lord William Bentinck: The Making of a Liberal Imperialist, 1774-1839* (London, 1974) is poorly researched and slavishly skewed to advance the author's ideological agenda. For more about Bentinck's family background, see John Colville, *Strange Inheritance* (Salisbury, 1983) and Amanda Foreman, *Georgiana, Duchess of Devonshire* (London, 1998).
8. Lord Bentinck did not ask for his father's help during the Vellore Crisis, even after he became aware of the extent to which the Court of Directors was disillusioned with his efforts. At the same time, the Duke of Portland

offered no defence or even excuse for his son's handling of the Vellore affair.

9. K.N. Venkatasubbha Sastri, 'Petrie Papers', *Indian Historical Records Commission,* V. 18, pp. 288-96.
10. With Wellesley's recall, Cornwallis returned to India to take charge of Company affairs, but died shortly after his arrival in Bengal. At the time of the Vellore Mutiny, the acting Governor-General was George Barlow, the Second of Council of the Bengal Presidency.
11. Love, V. 3, pp. 138, 162, 348-9; Bentinck to Charles Grant (confidential), 21 March 1807, UN, Portland MS., PwJb/155, f. 157.
12. When Bentinck was recalled from Madras in 1807, Petrie briefly took over as acting Governor until George Barlow arrived from Bengal as the new chief of the Madras Presidency. Petrie then was rewarded for his service by being appointed Governor of the Straits Settlements in the East Indies.
13. The only full account of Cradock's life is a fairly long and detailed article in Sir Leslie Stephen and Sir Sidney Lee, *Dictionary of National Biography,* V. 4, pp. 936-7. For more information about the Cradock family, see Ibid., pp. 1359-60. Anecdotal information regarding Cradock's staff appointment at Dublin Castle may be found in G.R. Gleig, *Life of Arthur, Duke of Wellington* (London, 1889), p. 8.
14. John W. Fortescue, *History of the British Army,* V. 4, Part 1 (London, 1906), pp. 352, 357; Musgrave, pp. 812-13.
15. Carola Oman, *Sir John Moore* (London, 1953), p. 295; for more on Cradock's misadventures in Egypt, see Fortescue, *History of the British Army,* V. 4, Part 2, p. 855.
16. Sir John Francis Cradock, 'Sketch of the Situation of Sir John Cradock', *HMS,* V. 510, pp. 897-928.
17. Henry Dundas, at the time, was both Secretary at War and chief of the East India Board of Control.
18. TNSA, Cradock's Minute, 12 March 1805, *MMP* (*Madras Military Proceedings*), Range 255, V. 48, pp. 1246-8; BL/OIOC, Pierce to Cradock, 26 July 1806, *HMS,* V. 507, pp. 463-5.
19. BL/OIOC, Code of Regulations (1806), Section 11, Para. 10; BL/OIOC, Cradock's Minute, 2 October 1806, *HMS,* V. 510, pp. 274-5; Petrie's Minute, 29 July 1806, Ibid., V. 507, pp. 508-15.
20. BL/OIOC, Agnew to Cradock, 18 July 1806, *HMS,* V. 507, pp. 345-50; Pierce to Cradock, 26 July 1806, Ibid., pp. 450-61.
21. UN, Kot Havildar Shaikh Imam's Defence, Portland MS, PwJb/57, pp. 103-4.
22. UN, Court of Enquiry Proceedings, 17-24 May 1806, Portland MS., PwJb/57, pp. 17-18.

23. Ibid.
24. Ibid.
25. UN, Deputy Judge Advocate General Watson to Cradock, 12 June 1806, Ibid., p. 119.
26. UN, Bose to Harcourt, 10 June 1806, Ibid., pp. 167-71.
27. UN, Cradock to Agnew, 16 June 1806, Ibid., p. 172; Cradock to GC/FSG (Governor-in-Council at Fort St. George), 29 June 1806, Ibid., pp. 175-8.
28. UN, GC/FSG to Cradock, 4 July 1806, Ibid., pp. 179-81; Bentinck to Cradock (private), 4 July 1806, Ibid., pp. 192-3.
29. For a reference to these original transcripts, see Lieutenant-Colonel Ross Lang to GC/FSG, 10 July 1807, Portland MS., PwJb/60, ff. 1806-7.
30. J.W. Wilson, *History of the Madras Army*, V. 1 (London, 1887), Introduction.
31. The best account of this aspect of the Vellore Mutiny is Jörg Fisch, 'A Pamphlet War on Christian Missions in India, 1807-1809', *Journal of Asian History*, 19.1, 1985, pp. 22-70. Also see S.K. Mitra, 'The Vellore Mutiny of 1806 and the Question of Christian Mission to India', *Indian Church History Review*, 8, no. 1, 1974, pp. 75-82.
32. John Malcolm to Josiah Webbe, CSG (Chief Secretary to Government), 3 October 1799, quoted in John William Kaye, *Life and Correspondence of Major-General Sir John Malcolm* (London, 1841), pp. 95-6.
33. Gyanendra Pandey, *The Construction of Communalism in Colonial North India* (Delhi, 1992), pp. 23-65.
34. James Mill, *History of British India*, V. 1 (London, 1844), pp. 123-44.
35. Nihar Nandan Singh, *British Historiography on British Rule in India: The Life and Writings of Sir John William Kaye, 1814-1876* (Patna, 1986).
36. John William Kaye, *A History of the Sepoy War in India, 1857-58* (London, 1896), pp. 204-25.
37. Philip Mason, *A Matter of Honour: An Account of the Indian Army, its Officers and Men* (London, 1974), pp. 236-7; Ranajit Guha, *Elementary Aspects of Peasant Insurgency in Colonial India* (Delhi, 1983), pp. 267-8.
38. Robert E. Frykenberg, 'New Light on the Vellore Mutiny', *East India Company Studies: Papers Presented to Sir Cyril Phillips* (Hong Kong, 1986), pp. 207-31.
39. K. Rajayyan, *South Indian Rebellion: The First War of Independence, 1800-1801* (Mysore, 1971); Perumal Chinnian, *The Vellore Mutiny: The First Uprising against the British* (Madras, 1982); P. Chinnian, *The First Struggle for Freedom in South India in 1806: Sporadic Events after the Vellore Mutiny* (Erode, 1983).

40. Susan Bayly, *Saints, Goddesses and Kings: Muslims and Christians in South Indian Society, 1700-1900* (Cambridge, 1989), pp. 224-6, P. Chinnian, *The Vellore Mutiny* (Madras, 1982), p. 24.
41. Ainslie T. Embree, *Charles Grant and British Rule in India* (New York, 1962), p. 238.
42. Maya Gupta, 'The Vellore Mutiny, July 1806', *Journal of Indian History*, XLIX, 1971, pp. 91-112. Also see Gupta (1986), pp. 211-15.
43. Pakkianathan Samuelraj, *The Mutiny at Vellore and Related Agitations, 1806-1807* (University of Saskatchewan Ph.D. Thesis [unpublished], 1972).
44. Wickremesekera, pp. 161-4.
45. Ibid., p. 163.
46. Ibid., pp. 163-4, op. cit., J.H. Wilson, *History of the Madras Army*, V. 3 (Madras, 1886), pp. 188-200. Wickremesekera also draws evidence from Maya Gupta, *Lord William Bentinck in Madras and the Vellore Mutiny, 1803-1807* (Delhi, 1986), pp. 219-34.
47. Ibid., p. 163, op. cit., BL/OIOC, Adjutant-General's Report to GC/FSG, 27 July 1806, *HMS*, V. 507, pp. 483-5; BL/OIOC, Evidence of Mrs. Revier, 28 July 1806, *HMS*, V. 507, pp. 494-5. Note: The full text of these documents clearly reveal Mrs. Revier's biases, as well as the fact that her information was obtained from her 'servant maid', an Indian Christian named Catherine, who 'overheard' the remarks while walking past the sepoy barracks.
48. BL/OIOC, Petrie's Minute, 29 July 1806, *HMS*, V. 507, pp. 515-16. In this instance, even Cradock admitted that the local authorities had misrepresented the complaints of their men. See Cradock's Report on Wallajahbad, Ibid., pp. 587-8.
49. For an illustration of this problem, and the basis for my methodology, see TNSA, Sepoy Grenadier Ramru's Testimony, *MSS*, V. 2-A, pp. 972-7. Sepoy Ramru and Sepoy Ramjani were detailed to guard the doors of the princes' quarters on the night of the Vellore Mutiny. Just a few minutes before the rising began, they discussed their recruitment, the new changes in military uniform, and their diverging opinions regarding loyalty and mutiny; they were engaged in a rather heated argument when the first shots of the rising interrupted them. Ramru's testimony is particularly vivid, yet quite candid and believable.

2
'Our Negative Friendship'

Colonel Thomas Marriott, the Paymaster of Stipends for political prisoners at Vellore, never harboured illusions about the feelings of Tipu Sultan's eldest sons. He first met them, shortly after the fall of Seringapatam, while serving as one of the officers of the escort that conducted the four elder—and presumably most dangerous —princes into captivity. Shortly before the Mutiny, in April 1806, Marriott penned a detailed, private report about the princes to Lord Bentinck, remarking on the changes that had come over them during nearly seven years of exile and surveillance. Marriott warned the Governor that Tipu Sultan's sons were far from reconciled to their situation; they merely had learned how to conceal their real views.

> It is most material to suppose, and certainly most advisable to believe (in order to guard against the consequences) that the Princes themselves must ever look upon the English as their enemies, and the destroyers of royalty in their family. The very splendid and liberal establishment allowed them, not to mention the kindest attentions and treatment they receive from us, may be supposed to make them feel thankful and grateful, but these can never possibly be expected to extirpate and expunge their original and deep-rooted ideas of our enmity, or at least our negative friendship toward their family. It will always, therefore, be advisable to expect the worst from their intentions; and too many precautions cannot be taken relative to the security of their persons. Experience will, in time, I hope, prove to them the superior happiness they now, in reality, enjoy, to the ideal probability of what they might have found under contrary and opposite circumstances. Contentment and happiness, however . . . cannot be dictated to the breast of any one, and must, therefore, be left to time and the voluntary operations of their own feelings to impart.[1]

During the march from Seringapatam to Vellore, Marriott recalled, the princes had been 'generally distinguished by modesty, an un-assumption [*sic*] of pomp, and a readiness to accommodate themselves to everything that was proposed'. One month later, after their arrival at Vellore, there had been 'a most astonishing change in their behaviour and conduct, which . . . was now arrogant and nearly insulting'. During the absence of Lieutenant-Colonel Gabriel Doveton, the first Paymaster of Stipends, Marriott had taken charge of the prisoners, and it seems that they tested his authority over them. They refused to stand when he entered their rooms, and they argued against his every suggestion. Each prince insisted on 'having the state pomp and ceremony of his household conducted on as near a plan as possible to that established by [Tipu Sultan] for the . . . administration of a large kingdom'. Indeed, Tipu Sultan never had allowed his sons the luxury they enjoyed as prisoners of the British. As much a self-made man as Haidar Ali, Tipu Sultan seems to have noticed the princes' capacity for arrogance and extravagance, which he had curbed by limiting their allowances and setting them to arduous tasks. In exile, the four eldest princes now had large incomes, but none of the vigorous activity and scope for exercising power to which they had become accustomed. Unable to alter their fate, at least for the time being, they resisted through displays of insolence. Two of the eldest princes had lived, as young teenagers, at Madras as hostages of the Company, held under the terms of the treaty that had ended the Third Anglo-Mysore War. It seems that familiarity with foreigners bred in them a contempt; having been played as pawns by their father and the Company, they were, quite understandably, furious—both with their own families and with the British.[2]

Never before, in their conquest of India, had the British locked an entire royal lineage into a fortress prison. The British would become quite adept at this exercise of internal exile, and they learned much from the mistakes made at Vellore. The handful of domestic servants who followed the eldest princes from Mysore were joined shortly by 'creatures equally ready to appeal the folly, as the wisdom, of every sentence uttered by their idol'. Collectively known as the *mard-i-admiyan*, or gentlemen companions, these individuals ensconced themselves in Vellore before Lieutenant-Colonel Doveton implemented the Governor-in-Council's suggestions for a well-regulated system of security. In 1799, no policies or procedures existed to guide Doveton's organization of a palace-prison, and the *mard-i-*

admiyan had sprung into being in much the same way that British officers acquired retinues of Indian servants at that time, the entertainment of one creating the cause for the hiring of another. Each prince thus had placed himself at the head of a miniature court, even to the extent of assuming the title 'Sultan'—a ridiculous affectation with which Marriott was far from pleased. Nevertheless, Marriott noted that the princes were attached to their *mard-i-admiyan*, and that their expulsion would be construed as 'a great hardship, even harshness'.

In any event, the interests of most of the *mard-i-admiyan* were pecuniary rather than political. A number of the companions acted as agents of the *pettah* merchants, securing contracts for the provisioning of the various *mahals*, while others among them supplied the princes with horses or women. Marriott had his hands full trying to curb the excesses of the worst of the *mard-i-admiyan*, yet he tolerated them as a group because he could set them against each other, or even persuade them (forcefully, if necessary) to act as a check on their masters' behaviour. The companions served the Company's interests most directly by absorbing the princes' stipends, preventing them from amassing fortunes with which to stir up revolt or plot an escape. Only Prince Abdul Khaliq managed to build up any considerable sum, mainly by hoarding his payments, and thus Marriott viewed him, rather than his brothers, as his most dangerous charge.[3]

The two eldest princes, Fatteh Haidar and Abdul Khaliq, were bitter enemies—a pattern typical of the royal lineages of Islamic India. In the south Asian Muslim tradition, there was no recognized order of succession, and thus opposing factions within a regime pinned their hopes to the aspirations of younger princes, pitting them against the heir-apparent. Few elder princes succeeded peacefully to their father's thrones, the death of a sultan being followed, if not preceded, by a fratricidal slaughter among his sons. The Persian chronicles that recorded these transactions summed up this grim political reality with the maxim *takt-ya-takta*—'a throne or a bier'.[4] When the British stormed Seringapatam, Tipu Sultan's death immediately raised the possibility of civil war. Fatteh Haidar, with the survivors of the Mysorean army, was encamped on the north bank of the Kaveri, quite capable of fleeing to continue resistance to the British and make his own bid for power. Abdul Khaliq, who had remained in the capital, was among those who had surrendered, he led his father's funeral procession through the shattered streets of Seringapatam under the eyes of thousands of its inhabitants. Aware of these developments, Fatteh Haidar's officers urged the eldest prince to follow his father's last orders to retreat to Chitradurga, from which the fight against the British could be carried on from a network of formidable hill forts in northern Mysore.[5] However, Tipu Sultan's Brahmin *diwan*, Purnaiya, advised Fatteh Haidar to leave the army and throw himself on the mercy of the British, who then might be inclined to recognize him as Tipu's successor. It did not take long for Fatteh Haidar to suspect that Abdul Khaliq's surrender had been a ploy to gain British support for his own bid for power. Indeed, Purnaiya may have planted the seed of this idea in Fatteh Haidar's mind. Throwing caution to the wind, the eldest prince abandoned his troops and gave himself up to the British.[6]

Purnaiya, ably scrambling to save his own position, offered Fatteh Haidar to the British as 'another Umdat-ul-Umara', but his diplomacy was poorly timed. By then, the victorious allies already had agreed to oppose any attempt to revive the legacy of Haidar Ali and Tipu Sultan. The British, in fact, had signed a secret treaty pledging to restore the fallen Udaiyar Dynasty. Once aware of this, Purnaiya wasted no time transferring his allegiance, and that of his own extensive entourage, to the restored Hindu king—who was, at that time, a child raja. For Fatteh Haidar, 'hopes of even a limited authority were suddenly changed into the gloomy ideas of a prison', Marriott wrote, 'for amongst Eastern governments it seldom happens that there is any medium between those extremes, a throne and a dungeon.'[7] Vellore fort, in its new function as a pen for royal exiles, had been designed to be just such a medium—a claustrophobic, gilded purgatory haunted by memories of lost greatness.

MARRIOTT'S VIEW OF THE PRINCES

Defeated and ashamed, Fatteh Haidar was deeply depressed after his arrival at Vellore. Most British officers who met him at the time were irked by his gloomy disposition, short temper, and striking resemblance to his father. In 1799, most people had viewed Tipu Sultan as a tyrant, his death a cause for celebration—an utterly self-interested usurper whose fruitless wars had cut swathes of desolation and misery across a region already blighted by misrule, revolt, drought, and famine. At the time of the Vellore Mutiny, and for many years afterward, the oral traditions of the Madras Army elaborated hair-raising tales about the horrors experienced by British officers and sepoys in Tipu Sultan's dungeons. Hundreds of sepoys who did not agree to join his army were said to have been sewn into sacks and thrown from the soaring cliffs of Nandidurgam and other hill forts—an atrocity for which no evidence ever was produced. However, no story seemed too terrible or spectacular to be believed if it was attributed to Tipu. Indeed, Tipu Sultan's memory was resolutely beaten into that requisite straw man of Enlightenment apologia for empire, the Oriental despot—the 'Tiger of Mysore'. In the immediate aftermath of the Anglo-Mysore Wars, British officers transferred their hatred of Tipu Sultan to his entire family.

In time, however, as British officers came to know Fatteh Haidar, they thought him, at worst, annoying. By the time Marriott became Paymaster of Stipends, the eldest prince had become 'unreserved and more pleasant in conversation, more polished and affable in manners. . . .' Yet, he also had acquired a voracious appetite for political news, especially intelligence regarding the progress of the wars between Britain and France. During the summer of 1803, as acting Paymaster, Marriott had uncovered a spy ring organized by Fatteh Haidar to relay reports from Madras and Pondicherry, the latter place having been reoccupied by the French during the short-lived Peace of Amiens. Outwardly, Fatteh Haidar professed his attachment to the Company, yet Marriott was certain that, in his heart, he hoped the French would defeat Britain and demand his restoration as Tipu Sultan's 'heir'. Indeed, he was deeply upset to learn that the French, in negotiating the Peace of Amiens, made no mention of Mysore at all.[8]

Fatteh Haider could not have known that Napoleon had decided to pursue his interests in India indirectly, through French mercenaries serving in the Maratha armies, or through the squadrons of privateers that plundered the Company's ships from one end of the Indian Ocean to the other. Such bargain-basement, proxy warfare tied down more British ships and regiments than the grand, expensive, and often doomed military expeditions with which the French had challenged the British in India during the eighteenth century. Napoleon longed to restore French trade with Asia, but militarily he saw India only as a distraction for the British, who he hoped would fly to its defence, and thus draw forces away from the European theatre of war.[9] Ironically, Fatteh Haidar may have gained an exaggerated sense of French interest in his affairs from the British themselves, many of whom still feared a direct attack on India. Such fears did not subside until the very eve of the Vellore Mutiny, when the Madras Government received official word of Nelson's annihilation of the Franco-Spanish fleet at Trafalgar in October 1805.

Abdul Khaliq's story was quite different from that of Fatteh Haidar. In 1792, he and his younger brother, Muiz-ud-Din, had been selected to accompany the British to Madras as hostages, securing Tipu Sultan's compliance with the treaty that ended the Third Anglo-Mysore War. For three years, Abdul Khaliq had lived apart from his family, among their enemies. Company officials, it seems, had hoped to make a positive impression on their young hostages by exposing them to as much European culture as possible. The princes' education had even included theatrical performances, in which they observed members of the Council of Fort St. George performing in costumes and make-up. They seemed to endure their captivity with patience and grace. After the return of his sons from Madras, however, Tipu Sultan was dismayed, for their pent-up anger and frustration surfaced at once. Viewing their insolence as the result of an association with the British, Tipu Sultan soon made arrangements with his French agents to have his sons sent to Paris for their education. Paris was one place, he reasoned, where a prince might acquire a European education without also acquiring an attachment to the cultural values and political ideas of the British. This project, however, was doomed—by the outbreak of Tipu's final war with the Company.

When Marriott wrote his first report on the princes, on 23 July 1799, he informed Governor-General Wellesley that Abdul Khaliq was 'good natured and obliging', although scarcely regal in his behaviour or thinking. Indeed, Marriott was struck by the prince's indifference to court pomp and the company of women—the characteristic distractions of the 'Oriental despot' of European imagination. Abdul Khaliq spent much of his time with a Brahmin accountant, reviewing his finances. 'If experience has given me reason to alter my opinion', Marriott reported in April 1806, 'it is only on this one point, that I mistook for good nature what . . . was only a cloak to cover the deformity of the most malicious and rancorous heart.' The Paymaster was convinced that Abdul Khaliq's earlier affability had been a mere ploy to secure the Company's favour and perhaps a larger stipend. Frustrated in these hopes, Abdul Khaliq seems to have pursued his goals by more devious and desperate means. He planted evidence implicating Fatteh Haidar in a correspondence with Dundiya Waugh, whose guerrillas, at that time, were still fighting the British in northern Mysore. One of his own servants, however, later confessed that the intercepted letters were the work of Abdul Khaliq, who had stamped them with a seal stolen from Fatteh Haidar's rooms. Later, evidence was uncovered indicating that Abdul Khaliq had tried to contact the French during their reoccupation of Pondicherry in 1803. What he hoped to gain from communication with the French, however, is not known.[10]

As far as Marriott was concerned, the 'real' heir of Tipu Sultan was Muhyi-ud-Din. The mother of this prince, Ruqaya Banu Begum, one of Tipu's first wives had died of illness during the siege of Seringapatam in 1792. Marriott, however, had noted that Newal Begum was Muhyi-ud-Din's mother, a rare but interesting mistake, as it suggests the limits of British knowledge regarding Tipu Sultan's family. Toward the end of his reign, Tipu Sultan had married Muhyi-ud-Din to Fasl-ul-Nissa, the daughter of his *mir bakhshi*, who was also a distant relative. When the young prince arrived at Vellore, his wife was still a child, but rather than associating with concubines, as some of his younger brothers did, Muhyi-ud-Din took up a life of study. He was particularly fond of history, both ancient and modern, with a taste for biographies. Marriott had never found any cause to be displeased with the third prince, for to the Paymaster he was both a model prisoner and an excellent human being. Marriott's assessment of Muhyi-ud-Din, in fact, tells us almost as much about the Paymaster's own well-concealed attitudes regarding Indians as about the manifest goodness of his charge.

He is the only native of India, with one exception, and that is the present Rajah of [Coorg], in whom I have met with every appearance of being really satisfied with the dispensations of providence, and of being really contented with his condition. I may carry the similitude further by saying that they are the only two natives in whom I could never see the least attempt at duplicity, prevarication, or deceit.[11]

The youngest of the four eldest princes, Muiz-ud-Din, was quite unlike Muhyi-ud-Din. Even in 1799, Marriott had found his character to be complex, ever-shifting. He could be 'fur[ious] and sometimes passionate, but as easily calmed as enflamed . . . good-natured, lively, affable, and generous; extremely anxious for communication with the English . . . .' Muiz-ud-Din was particularly fond of his stable of horses, and he went out frequently to watch his *syces* feed, water, and comb them. Occasionally, he exercised the horses in an adjoining paddock. Marriott often found Muiz-ud-Din sitting with illuminated manuscripts, looking at pictures of horses. The Paymaster attributed his 'very high spirit' to his mother being from Delhi, noting that he had the 'characteristic features of the northern Mussulman. . . .' The prince's interest in equestrian matters also contributed to Marriott's sense that Muiz-ud-Din was a Mughal at heart. Indeed, as a cavalry officer, the Paymaster bonded with Muiz-ud-Din, although their connection was mostly that of amused father-figure and precocious son.[12]

Yet, there were those who considered Muiz-ud-Din to be cruel, and their views were not without foundation. Many observers, for instance, noticed that the prince treated his horses brutally despite his deep emotional attachment to them. Marriott, however, thought him merely 'careless', not inclined to reflect on consequences before acting. The Paymaster recalled that once, a horse had given Muiz-ud-Din trouble, and the prince had ordered it to be thrown down and gelded on the spot—unconcerned that the beast would surely die as a result of the ordeal, entailing 'the loss of a thousand or fifteen hundred rupees which he had paid for the horse but two days before'. This side of Muiz-ud-Din disturbed Marriott, but more often than not the Paymaster found his predicaments amusing rather than alarming.

His views are all venal. In short, he is a true Moor man. Believing in fatality, he will live today and let the morrow take thought for itself. He is always deep in debt, and always endeavouring to borrow. In society, he puts on a mild and warming countenance, and you would think him the most modest and least debauched of mankind. This is not, I believe, done with the intention of deceiving you, but rather to give pleasure, and induce you to visit him the oftener, for five minutes after, he will ask permission to bring a dancing girl, or anything else. He talks on all subjects, and [shows], by the naïvté of his questions on politics, that he has not made them his study. . . . Whatever is his hobby horse, he will soon ride to death; even [from] his horses, women, & musicians, he sometimes [re]tires to reading, chess, and catching of birds. He lately sold off all his horses on a matrimonial scheme, but soon purchased, or rather coaxed, them back again from his brother [Muhyi-ud-Din].[13]

Three of Tipu Sultan's sons had been adolescents at the time of their father's death. Muhammad Yassun Sahib, the eldest of these princes, was born in 1785 after Tipu Sultan's union with the daughter of the Mufti of Arcot, one of the many women his soldiers captured during their occupation of the Wallajah-i capital during the Second Anglo-Mysore War. Following the death of his own wife, with whom Yassun Sahib seems to have been deeply in love, the young prince sought peace in religion, devoting himself to a sedentary life of prayer and theological study. Marriott noted that he was 'extremely corpulent for his age', but 'tractable' and willing to do 'whatever [was] pointed out to him'. The next in age, Muhammad Subhan, was the son of one of Tipu Sultan's concubines. 'Lively and quick, without much passion or anger in his disposition', Marriott had found him willing to comply with most suggestions.

The youngest of the adolescent princes, however, was the most troublesome, both for his family and for Marriott. When Muhammad Shukr-ullah first arrived at Vellore, the Paymaster recalled, he 'promised to be the best disposed, as he was the handsomest', of Tipu's sons. His mother, a 'Delhi lady', was believed to be the source of Shukr-ullah's 'high and haughty spirit'. Nevertheless, Marriott did not rule out the possibility that Doveton had made a mistake in giving the young prince full control over his stipend before he was fifteen years old. Perhaps dazzled by his unrestricted access to so much wealth, Shukr-ullah had rebelled against his mother, threatening to kill her on at least one occasion. His disposition had 'changed into a passionate and unbridled badness of temper', Marriott recorded, adding that Shukr-ullah's irritability was compounded by a physical illness brought on by his addiction to opium 'prepared and mixed with sweetmeat'.[14]

THE YOUNGER PRINCES AND THEIR FAMILIES

The five youngest sons of Tipu Sultan, all under the age of thirteen at the time of the Vellore Mutiny, still lived in the womens' quarters of the palace complex, their stipends carefully managed by the Paymaster. Besides these children, a few of Tipu's close male relatives also had been confined at Vellore, including his deranged brother, Karim Sahib, and his nephew Haidar Hussain Khan. The latter had made his way to Scindia's court after the fall of Seringapatam, and in 1803 the Maratha *sardars* considered sending him to Mysore to renew the lost cause of Dundiya Waugh. After the British victory at Assaye, however, Major-General Arthur Wellesley demanded Haidar Hussain Khan's surrender as a preliminary step to the negotiation of peace, and thus he finally fell into the hands of his uncle's enemies.

Karim Sahib, meanwhile, was among those members of Tipu Sultan's family whom the British thought harmless and allowed to stay in Seringapatam. Yet, as had happened even during Tipu's reign, opponents of the régime and would-be adventurers employed the name of the Sultan's brother in an attempt to recruit support for their cause. Oblivious to these machinations, Karim Sahib had been viewed by Tipu Sultan as the harmless, sole inhabitant of his own unique universe. His occasional, mysterious disappearances always had been forgiven. The British, although inclined to continue this lenient policy at first, soon decided that Karim Sahib's mere presence at Seringapatam offered too much hope to Udaiyars' enemies. Once, in a daze, the Sultan's brother had wandered away, vanishing for an extended period; as soon as he turned up again, the British decided to pack him off to Vellore, where his family could care for him. He would be far less likely to 'wander' out of Vellore fort than out of poorly-guarded Seringapatam.

It is now necessary to turn to the women. The women of the *zenanas* were an important part of everything that happened at Vellore. Indeed, their lives formed the very structure that shaped the internal dynamic of the strange political prison. Most of those sent to Vellore by the British were women and children, and together with their servants, they far outnumbered the princes and their adult male attendants. In picturing the Vellore *mahals* at the time of the rising, we must imagine a palace complex inhabited primarily by children under the age of twelve—a sprawling nursery closely-guarded by a full brigade of troops.[15]

Immediately after the fall of Seringapatam, the British officers in charge of Tipu Sultan's enormous family were baffled by the complex relationships that bound its members together. The large number of 'first rank' concubines in the Sultan's personal *mahal* was particularly perplexing. Some of them were aristocratic ladies, but others were simple village women—all swept up in the course of Tipu Sultan's wars and state-building efforts over the course of many years. Furthermore, the relationships between the women of Tipu's *mahal* and those of Haidar Ali's *zenana* often seemed at odds with the almost census-like registers with which the British sought to keep track of the members of the fallen and captive dynasty. A few of Haidar Ali's women had come to Mysore from Delhi, but having arrived after his death, they had been inherited, along with the kingdom, by his son. One of the Paymaster's tasks was to study the members of the extended family and determine the ranks, privileges, and interests of each. Seeking the favour of their captors, the women of the various *zenanas* frequently petitioned both Marriott and the government, requesting special enquiries to adjust disputed claims.

Petitions also were sent to the government by people outside Vellore, claiming that some of the women in the *mahals* were captives taken in Tipu's wars, and should be returned to their families. Whenever such requests reached Madras, the government routinely forwarded them to the Paymaster for investigation. The most alarming of these cases arose immediately after the Mysore prisoners were marched to Vellore. Arthur Wellesley had written to Gabriel Doveton on 24 December 1799, relaying the subject of a recent meeting with the Abbé Dubois, an itinerant Roman Catholic missionary well-known across south India.[16] The padre had come to British military headquarters representing a number of men in Malabar and Kanara whose wives allegedly had been forced into Tipu Sultan's harem—presumably at the time of the wholesale exile of many Indian Christians from those areas to Seringapatam. The Abbé claimed that no less than two hundred 'Christian' women had been 'taken . . . in the most tyrannical manner, accompanied by acts of cruelty', and now, ironically, had been marched into a second exile at Vellore alongside the very people who had deprived them of their liberty.

Wellesley, in his cover letter, denied the priest's accusations, informing Doveton that 'the Company having taken . . . [Tipu Sultan's] family under protection, it is not proper that anything should be done which can disgrace it in the eyes of the Indian world, or which can in the most remote degree cast a shade upon the dead or violate the feelings of those who are alive.' Wellesley was not entirely a slave of policy, however, for he added that Doveton should discuss the matter with the princes, urging them to allow any women held against their will to return to their families. At the end of his note—and rather uncharacteristically—Wellesley changed his mind, concluding that preserving the dignity of Tipu Sultan's lineage was 'not of a very urgent nature'.[17]

The complexity of Tipu Sultan's family, for our purpose—which is to understand the prisoners' connection with the Vellore Mutiny—need only be traced back as far as the Sultan's own marriages. Haidar Ali had hoped that Tipu Sultan would marry the daughter of Imam Sahib Bakhshi, a Navayat relative of the so-called 'Pondicherry Nawab'. The women of the *zenana*, however, had favoured Ruqayya Banu, daughter of Lala Miyan and sister of Burhan-ud-Din. Haidar Ali's wishes were opposed even by his own principal wife, who wielded considerable influence over his domestic decisions.[18] Haidar Ali's difference of opinion with his women was not resolved until 1774, when Tipu married both of his parents' choices in a convenient, double wedding ceremony.[19] After Ruqayya Banu died during the siege of Seringapatam in 1792, Tipu Sultan married Khadija Zaman Begum, daughter of Sayyid Sahib. In 1797, shortly after giving birth to a son, who did not live long, she also died. At the time of his own death, Tipu was thought by most people to have only one wife, the daughter of Imam Sahib Bakhshi, commonly known by her title of Padshah Begum.[20]

However, Marriott identified another principal wife of Tipu Sultan: Buranti Begum, the daughter of a Delhi nobleman connected with the family of the Subahdar of Kashmir.[21] Roshani Begum, the mother of Fatteh Haidar, was ranked as a concubine by the British, although her son insisted that she had been promoted to the rank of *khas mahal* before Tipu's death.[22] Many women in the *zenanas* rejected Fatteh Haidar's claim, however, a rejection apparently attributed to class feeling. Roshani Begum, formerly Pum Kum, was originally a dancer from Adoni, who, together with her sister, had been captured by Tipu's army during the First Anglo-Mysore War. Somehow the young woman had made the most of her situation, rapidly gaining Haidar Ali's favour. Fatteh Haidar had been born in 1771 or 1772, and was seven years older than Abdul Khaliq; since Roshani Begum's son had come of age by the time of the Third Anglo-Mysore War, it is not surprising that Tipu Sultan came to rely on him, grooming him to be his successor. Indeed, the fact that Fatteh Haidar was not offered to Cornwallis as a hostage indicated, to most of Tipu's courtiers, that he now was the Sultan's heir apparent. The matter was never fully settled, but it could not be denied that the status of Fatteh Haidar's mother had risen with his own.

Tipu Sultan had expanded the influence of Mysore through matrimonial alliances as well as military conquest. Fatteh Haidar had been married to Zinat-ul-Nissa, great granddaughter of Chanda Sahib through the female line.[23] Through his wife, the eldest of the princes at Vellore thus was attached to many of the principal Muslim families of the Carnatic, including the jagirdars of Kaveripakkam and Palaur.[24] Abdul Khaliq and Muiz-ud-Din also had been married into the Navayat aristocracy of the Carnatic.[25] In addition, Abdul Khaliq had been married, when still a child, to the Bibi of Cannanore in order to help build an alliance with the Mappillas of Malabar.[26] The only exception to this pattern was Muhyi-ud-Din, who had been married into Tipu's own family.[27] The younger princes remained single in 1806, but the Madras Government was not opposed to their marrying into 'respectable'—and politically safe—Muslim families of the Carnatic or Mysore. Indeed, Marriott already had begun to make the financial arrangements necessary for the construction of new palaces in Vellore fort—one to house each of the younger princes and their households as soon as they could be married.

Six of Tipu Sultan's eight daughters were in Vellore on the night of the Mutiny, some living in the fort with their brothers, others in the *pettah* with their husbands.[28] Umir-ul-Nissa, the eldest of Tipu's daughters at Vellore, had married Raiza Hussain Khan, son of the *qiladar* of Bangalore, in a government-sanctioned ceremony in February 1805; she and her husband lived in a house in the *pettah*. Fatima Begum, the next daughter, had married Muhammad Ibrahim, son of the *benki nawab*, or (former) commander of the Mysorean artillery, in March 1805.[29] Also married that year were Bude-ul-Nissa and Umdah Begum. The former had been married in June to Sayyid Hussain, while the latter had married Haidar Hussain, Tipu's nephew and son of the Nawab of Sannur. Both women were living in the fort at the time of the Mutiny, waiting for their own houses in the *pettah* to be finished. Nur-ul-Nissa's marriage celebration commenced on 3 July 1806, but was interrupted—to put it mildly—by the Mutiny on the night of 9-10 July.[30] The youngest daughter, Kulima Begum, was to have been married immediately after Nur-ul-Nissa's ceremonies were finished. Nur-ul-Nissa's marriage to Nizam-ud-Din was not to be solemnized or consummated until several years after the beginning of the ceremonies in 1806. Unfortunately for the young couple, some of the groom's attendants emerged as prominent suspects in the investigation that followed the Mutiny, and this made Nizam-ud-Din, in the eyes of the British, a potential traitor.

SECURITY ARRANGEMENTS AT VELLORE

When the victorious allies first decided to exile the princes of Mysore to Vellore, Governor-General Wellesley himself made it clear to Lieutenant-Colonel Doveton that their confinement was to be as dignified as possible.[31] Under the general policy adopted at that time, the princes were granted every freedom consistent with their own protection and the Company's interests, but they were not to leave the fort without an armed escort.[32] Unlike the French prisoners of war interned at the Presidency, who could travel freely within the town limits of Madras, Tipu Sultan's sons were not trusted to adhere to the conditions of their parole. On the other hand, the princes enjoyed more material comforts than their French counterparts—the most important being their place of residence. Umdat-ul-Umara, the Nawab of the Carnatic, had sympathized with the plight of fallen and displaced Muslim royalty (a class into which his own descendants fell less than two years later), and thus he offered the exiles the unlimited use of the palaces at Vellore. These palaces were part of the Wallajah ruler's private estate, although the fort itself belonged to the Company.[33]

Putting Wellesley's 'liberal policies' into practice, however, was not an easy task, requiring—at the bare minimum—the garrison commander's full cooperation with the Paymaster of Stipends. And such harmony rarely existed at Vellore. The Paymaster himself had to be an officer incapable of corruption, yet clever and subtle enough to perceive the most closely-guarded secrets of an Indian court. Furthermore, the Paymaster had to be something of a detective and a spy-master, alive to all of the possibilities for trouble offered by a sprawling garrison town frequented by transient strangers. He also had to be sensitive to the broad range of cultural practices and religious beliefs that were to be accommodated within the security system that assured the peace not only of the fort, but also of the adjoining *pettah* of Vellore. Perhaps the Paymaster's most important qualification, however, was his ability to befriend the princes and simultaneously spy on them, which required a certain innate sense of paternal justification. He had to reconcile the prisoners to their fate while at the same time reassuring the government that his charges were both safe and harmless. Also, the Paymaster had to be fluent in either Urdu or Persian, the two languages of the captive court, a requirement that reduced the pool of officers who could serve as the princes' keepers to a handful. A civilian—a mere accountant—was unlikely to possess the range of skills and experience necessary to serve as Paymaster of Stipends.[34]

The garrison commander, meanwhile, had to keep the Vellore brigade under strict military discipline. Failure to maintain absolute adherence to orders could destroy all the Paymaster's security arrangements. The troops had to be alert and thorough at all times while on duty in order to prevent unauthorized communication between the prisoners and the outside world. At the same time, however, the soldiers had to be kept at arm's length—further, whenever possible—from the princes in order to avoid offending their dignity. Indeed, government insistence on 'hands-off' security was the main idea that shaped Vellore's complex system of surveillance—a system British in its original conception, but altogether Indian in the dynamics of its daily operation. The delicate protocols of guarding a political prison in which the prisoners nevertheless were to enjoy an exhalted (if hollow) status, could not be lost on the garrison commander without making the Paymaster's job extremely difficult.[35]

The broad outline of the Vellore security system was worked out in the first few months of 1800 by Doveton, in consultation with the Marquess of Wellesley and the Madras Government.[36] No attempt was made, however, to force people in Vellore to conform to a detailed plan. Rather, the details of the security system were allowed to arise gradually, taking shape in response to actual problems and changing conditions. Indeed, the four eldest princes had helped Doveton frame an initial set of procedures that would allow their families to live as comfortably as possible under the circumstances.[37] Furthermore, the demographics of the palace-prison changed considerably between 1800 and 1802, as the younger princes and the women and children of the *mahals* moved from Seringapatam to Vellore. In the summer of 1802, due to the presence of large numbers of élite Muslim women, all British soldiers were removed from those guard duties in which they were likely to come into contact with the prisoners.[38]

However, even the deployment of sepoy sentries was restricted by the demands of *purdah*. The original Vellore palace, built by the shrewd and paranoid Murtaza Ali Khan, was designed to shield its chief occupants from view, but at the same time numerous secret passages within and under the building enabled the *qiladar* to observe his guests, occasionally engaging in kidnappings and stealthy murders. The old palace was built around an inner courtyard, its doors and windows facing inward, and to the four sides of this structure the British added new wings, one for each of the eldest princes, plus separate areas for the *mahals* of Haidar Ali and Tipu Sultan. Each section of the palace, like the original, was built around a central courtyard, duplicating the basic plan of most south Indian palaces. The outer walls of the complex were, for the most part, blank faces of brick, the few windows being small, and set so high that anyone attempting to crawl out of them would very likely kill or injure themselves if they fell—an occurrence that was not unknown. A second wall surrounded the palace complex and separated it from the rest of the fort. One set of sepoy guards was placed at the main gate leading into this outer compound from the fort *maidan*, while a smaller detail occupied sentry boxes inside the central courtyard of the old palace—two soldiers at the gates of each of the *mahals*. Far from being a panopticon, the palace-prison was a warren, hiding its occupants from the gaze of their captors. Yet, Marriott observed, in a report penned shortly before the Mutiny, that *purdah* worked for rather than against the Company's plans. The presence of the princes' families gave the government far more power over the men than might have been attained by filling the palace with sepoys. The princes would never abandon their families—at least not in the hands of the British, who, unlike other Indian powers, did not barter hostages. Nor could the princes, encumbered by so many women and children, hope to lead an escape *en masse*.[39]

At the core of Doveton's security system was an establishment of *harkaras*, or intelligence agents, and *hindavi nawis*, or Hindustani scribes. The former roamed freely through every part of the *pettah* and the fort, being barred only from the *zenanas* within the *mahals*. The *harkaras* kept the Paymaster informed of every curious detail of life in both the town and the palace-prison. Generally, each *harkara* worked independently, sometimes being unaware of the identity of the other spies. Because of these multiple sources of information, the Paymaster could prevent his spies from fabricating stories by comparing their reports, or prevent corrupt *harkaras* from colluding with the princes. Those *harkaras* who knew their business, of course, probably also knew who the other spies were, but their reports and testimonies indicate that although the princes had identified some of the Paymaster's informants, none had ever been suborned. In any event, the *harkaras* were just one part of a multi-faceted surveillance system. Several of the princes' domestic servants also acted as spies, as did the tutors. Under Marriott, up to 130 *pagodas* a month in bonuses had been distributed to the intelligence staff for accurate, corroborated information about the inner life of the *mahals*.[40]

The Hindavi writers, meanwhile, kept a daily, detailed record of the movements of everyone associated with the prisoners. One group of writers was posted in the *pettah*, another at the main gate of the fort, and a third at the gate leading into the palace complex. With the *harkaras'* assistance, the writers recorded the names of all non-military personnel entering or leaving the fort. Each of the princes' servants and followers held a ticket, signed by the Paymaster, allowing them to pass freely through the gates until ten o'clock at night—at which time all of the gates were closed until the morning. These tickets, however, gave their holders access only to the apartments of one of the princes; one of the tasks of the sepoy commander of the interior guard was to make sure that all visitors went only to those areas of the palace to which they had been granted access. Muslim visitors to the fort always endured closer scrutiny by the scribes than others—a precaution stipulated, rather bluntly, in the Garrison Standing Orders. Thus the Paymaster, through his minions, was able—to some extent—to control the movement of the princes' followers and servants within the palace compound.[41]

Controlling the movement of the prisoners' attendants within the *pettah*, on the other hand, was a nearly impossible task. Approximately 1,800 registered servants lived in Vellore town, as well as some 1,200 unregistered individuals identified by the authorities as relatives of the Mysorean princes or their *mard-i-admiyan*.[42] With the help of his *harkaras* and a detail of *talaiyars*, the Paymaster confiscated weapons at the town gates, intercepted letters, and tried to keep track of suspicious characters. More than half of the population of the *pettah* consisted of recent migrants from Mysore and the Madurai country—people who could be placed in the 'suspicious characters' category by one measure or another.[43] All intelligence collected by the Paymaster—no matter how trivial—was relayed to the Governor-in-Council, via the Political and Secret Department, in reports issued every ten days. Often the reports were routine, empty assurances that all was well, but there had been certain weeks when they had run into several pages of detail regarding some impropriety, scandal, or strange occurrence. Vellore was a large, straggling town, with ruined walls and numerous gates, a policing nightmare. We can be sure that the Paymaster was only ever aware of a fraction of what was happening.[44]

Clearly, the weak link in the Paymaster's security system was the military detail posted at the sentry boxes inside the palace. Doveton had insisted that no European other than the Paymaster be allowed to enter the palace unless invited in by the princes and approved by the Paymaster. This rule originally was intended to isolate the princes from contact with French agents and unwanted intruders, but in practice it merely prevented British officers from directly inspecting the sentries outside the doors to the various *mahals*. Indeed, in this respect, the security system was at odds with the Army's most important regulations, which required all guard posts to be checked by a European officer. Failure to perform such a check was a serious offence, one rarely sent to trial, but technically punishable by death.[45] The sepoy sentries in the palace were part of a small naique's detail, detached from the troops assigned to the Main Guard, which also supplied the sentries for the main palace gate. The composition of the Main Guard detachment was determined by duty rosters maintained by the battalion Havildar-Writers, while the native officer commanding the detachment selected the men who would form the palace guard detail during a given watch.[46] What this meant was that no European officer had ever selected the men who actually guarded the princes—a seemingly trivial but quite important oversight on the part of Doveton and his successors, Dallas and Marriott.

Most of the naique's guard stayed in a small shelter near the gate to the palace compound.[47] At regular intervals, eight sepoys were taken into the palace to relieve the sentries at the doors to each *mahal*. Doveton's amendments to the Garrison Standing Orders forbade any conversation between the sepoys and any of the princes or their servants. Nevertheless, whenever the princes appeared, the soldiers were to present arms and pay them 'every military compliment'.[48] Whenever one prince visited another, or went to the stables, the naique commanding the guard formed a detail to escort him directly to his pre-stated destination. Even when the princes visited the small mosque located inside the fort, across the *maidan* from the palace, they were shadowed by the naique and his guards, who followed at a 'respectful' distance. Even though the sentries' muskets were never loaded, none of the princes ever attempted to escape.[49] Shortly after the princes' arrival at Vellore, a troop of HM 19th Dragoons was posted to the fort to escort them should they choose to go horseback riding in the surrounding countryside. This freedom to leave the fort for brief periods was seen by the British as a gesture of good will, but the princes clearly disliked being followed by dozens of dragoons while being gawked at by the local population. After the novelty of these field trips wore off, they stopped asking for permission to leave the fort, and the dragoons were withdrawn to their main cantonment at Arcot. Marriott read these changes as a gradual acceptance of their lot, the breaking of their spirit that the British had hoped to achieve, and on the eve of the Mutiny, he happily reported that 'were the gates of the fort thrown open to their individual flight, there is not one of . . . [the princes] who would avail himself of the opportunity. . . .'[50]

In the day-to-day administration of the palace-prison, the Paymaster was much more concerned about keeping unauthorized persons and contraband out of the *mahals* than about keeping the prisoners from escaping. In 1800, Doveton recognized that the use of *palanquins* by women of rank coming in from the *pettah* to visit their relatives seriously compromised his security measures. Consequently, all 'covered *doolies*' were ordered to be stopped and searched in the presence of the European officer commanding the Main Guard. Marriott himself tried to discourage the use of *palanquins* by palace visitors, but he could not suppress them altogether. In this matter, he was up against the nearly impenetrable wall of *mamul*, or custom, surrounding the institution of *purdah*, and the princes well knew that in any matter touching their women, the British tended to stop dead in their tracks for fear of outraging Muslim opinion in a predominantly Muslim town. Muhammad Shukr-ullah, for one, had made use of *palanquins* and other devices to smuggle opium into the palace, a traffic that both Doveton and Dallas chose to ignore. Marriott, however, took pains to stop the opium smuggling operation, hoping thereby to break the prince's addiction.[51]

Most of the elder princes were interested mainly in smuggling women into the palace. Fatteh Haidar, for instance, managed to import the daughter of a *pirzada* from Arcot, to whom he was secretly married in his *zenana* before the Paymaster could discover the transaction. Fatteh Haidar was not the only denizen of the palace-prison who soon learned that it was easier to obtain forgiveness than permission from the British. At the time, the Paymaster even went so far as to allow Fatteh Haidar to employ the woman's brother as part of his entourage, and to provide a stipend for her father, an old servant of the former Nawab of Arcot. However, Marriott considered some of the *mard-i-admiyan* to be nothing more than pimps, who earned their living by bringing women to the princes under all sorts of false pretences.

> In this traffic, the most diabolical practices were put into execution, and sometimes with the connivance of . . . [the princes]. I have found that promises of marriage, and of large sums of money, were most frequently made use of, under the Prince's seal, to induce parents to part with their daughters, and when once secured, the authority of the paper denied, and the assertion made that the seal was forged, or put to the paper by stealth. . . .[42]

Few of the parents of these unfortunate women ever complained to the British authorities, but Marriott understood their reluctance to come forward. The *mard-i-admiyan*, in seeking out women, preyed on poor widows, who, in their desperation, were willing to gamble the lives of their children on the mere promise of security in the princes' trains. Marriott feared that even his own servants were being bribed by the *mard-i-admiyan* to steer petitioners away from him. Others, he felt, despaired of justice, no doubt assuming the British authorities to be ignorant of their language. In any event, the customs of *purdah* effectively prevented widows from presenting themselves before a European official even in what was often a matter of life or death.

Marriott stressed, in his reports to Bentinck, that whoever held the post of Paymaster had to be fluent in local languages. Every report, whether written or verbal, had to be checked personally by the British officer-in-charge of the princes. Marriott himself made a conspicuous habit of riding around the fort and town in the evening, just as darkness was falling. He noted that many people came to him during these rides, slipping in and out of the shadows to seek redress for some grievance that could not be openly expressed, or to convey intelligence in the hope of a petty reward. Many of his investigations, Marriott confessed, began with such clandestine, nocturnal meetings. Most of his detective work merely led him in circles, or uncovered some trivial affair, yet the process of constant probing into the princes' activities allowed him to build a store of crucial knowledge about the details of daily life in the palace-prison.

In discussing the smuggling of women into the fort, Marriott never mentioned the important fact that any means of conveyance capable of sneaking people into the fort presumably could as well be used to sneak people or contraband out into the world. When the princes first arrived at Vellore, they were not allowed to send any money outside the fort unless purchasing goods or provisions in the *pettah*. At the time, this measure was intended to prevent the prisoners from contacting or funding insurgents fighting the British in Mysore and the Carnatic. Even in the Chittoor Pallems, scarcely a day's march from Vellore, Company troops had been involved in extensive and rather protracted operations against rebel *palegaru* as late as 1804. However, after the suppression of the Chittoor 'disturbances', no one remained in south India who was in a position to help the princes escape—except, of course, the numerous local elites who had made their peace with the British, and who had never wished Tipu Sultan's family anything but ill. In any event, although the princes found a way to smuggle money out of the fort, their motivations had nothing to do with raising revolt or plotting their escape.

Abdul Khaliq, for one, pared down his establishment to a small personal staff in order to save most of his stipend of fifty thousand rupees a year—a sum that he then sought to enlarge by loaning it at interest. To this end, the prince ordered a special *hackery* to be built, with a false bottom in which large amounts of cash could be secured.[53] Twice a day, this *hackery* was sent out of the fort 'under pretense of exercizing the bullocks'. Abdul Khaliq's chief client was the *moniyagar* of zilla Arcot, one of the Nawab's officials, who required a substantial loan to cover the cost of his revenue farm. Abdul Khaliq, however, had second thoughts about sending the *moniyagar's* loan, perhaps fearing discovery (more likely, suspecting that the official must have realized he was in a position to withhold repayment and deny any knowledge of the loan).[54]

Abdul Khaliq eventually turned to a more certain means of raising money. He sent his servants on secret missions—not to plot with rebels in the hills, but to purchase 'every valuable article', especially gold, silver, and jewels. These luxuries were sold or loaned to his brothers, but this thriving business also had its dangers, especially whenever Muiz-ud-Din was involved. As Marriott observed,

> [Muiz-ud-Din] takes great delight in vexing Abdul Khalick on account of his stinginess. The latter made up a pillow chair, and [Muiz-ud-Din], at his next visit, made a bargain with him, promising to give him so many thousand plantains for it. Abdul Khalick, after some days, sent to demand the plantains, but [Muiz-ud-Din] returned for answer that he had just ordered the trees to be planted, and when the fruit was ripe, it should be sent him.[55]

Before the Vellore Mutiny, British suspicions about the princes were focused on the secretive, irritable, and constantly busy Abdul Khaliq. His attempt to subvert Fatteh Haidar after the fall of Seringapatam was widely known, while his eagerness to hoard money caused the Paymaster to ponder his possible motivations. By 1806, Abdul Khaliq's personal fortune had increased to some two and a half lakhs of rupees—an amount sufficient to raise several thousand armed men.

Marriott claimed to be able to mention 'hundreds of instances' of Abdul Khaliq's duplicity and avarice.

The Paymaster also had to admit that Abdul Khaliq was a sadist, who sometimes tortured servants in his private quarters. One woman, suspected of concealing some of the prince's jewels, had her hands bound with oil-soaked cloth by Abdul Khaliq's servants. When the bonds were set on fire, however, she managed to escape by throwing herself over the parapet of the roof-top terrace where her torture was being conducted—a method of flight that might have proved fatal, except that her fall was broken on a stack of coir-fibre matting in the adjoining courtyard, where she was rescued by the women of one of the other *mahals*. Marriott also mentioned, in his pre-Mutiny report to Bentinck, 'complaints of certain boys that this descendant of Sodom had refused to pay them the sums offered as the price of satisfying his unnatural and brutal lusts.' Yet, there were those who were even less fortunate than these victims. Two women were tortured by having brands applied to their 'thighs'. Somehow, the women managed to escape into Fatteh Haidar's *mahal*, and from there out of the fort, where they took refuge in the house of a sepoy pensioner. Abdul Khaliq refused to countenance their flight. First, he offered them promises of money and better treatment if they returned, but upon their adamant refusal, the prince decided to demonstrate that although he was a prisoner, he could destroy those who crossed him just as easily as any reigning prince.

> . . . At last, sending for an Afghaun attendant, he gave him the powder of a poisonous root, which he ordered to be mixed with sugar and administered to them. This servant, as far from acting on any malice of his own, did not even know where the women lived, and was obliged to take another person to shew them to him. He succeeded, however, in getting one to take the dose (under pretense of reconciliation, when it is customary for Mussulmans to eat sugar) of which she died in great agonies after a few hours. The other, refusing to partake of the sugar, escaped with her life. . . .

An enquiry was held at Vellore following this last incident, resulting in the framing of murder charges against Abdul Khaliq—charges that were referred, automatically, to the Governor-General. Wellesley, in due course, directed that the case be tried before the local civil magistrate. The matter was still pending at the time of the Vellore Mutiny.[56]

NOTES

1. TNSA, Marriott's Report on the Family of Tipu Sultan, April 1806, *MSS*, V. 2-A, ff. 1038-9.
2. Ibid., pp. 1046-52.
3. Ibid.
4. Strictly speaking, 'throne' should be rendered '*masnad* platform', as thrones (in the Western sense) did not exist in India.
5. Tipu Sultan's orders were not without merit, and they demonstrate his remarkable grasp of both history and strategy. He was well aware that supply problems had turned the British back from Seringapatam before, and that the arrival of the monsoons would cut the allied armies off from their supplies unless they retreated. In 1799, the Company's forces had nearly run out of provisions before capturing Seringapatam, and it is very unlikely that they could have marched in pursuit of Fatteh Haidar.
6. Tipu Sultan's partisans later castigated Purnaiya for offering such advice to Fatteh Haidar, and to this day many people in south India despise him as a 'traitor' in much the same way that Americans continue to scourge the name of Benedict Arnold.
7. TNSA, *Marriott's Report on the Family of Tipu Sultan*, April 1806, *MSS*, V. 2-A, pp. 1052-5.
8. TNSA, *Marriott's Report on the Family of Tipu Sultan*, 1 August 1806, *MSS*, V. 2-A, pp. 957-60.
9. Siba P. Sen, *The French in India*, 1763-1816 (Calcutta, 1958).
10. TNSA, *Marriott's Report on the Family of Tipu Sultan*, April 1806, *MSS*, V. 2-A.
11. Ibid.
12. Ibid.
13. Ibid.
14. Ibid., pp. 957-60.
15. BL/OIOC, Harcourt to GC, 9 August 1806, 'Abstract of Males of the Blood of Hyder Ally', *HMS*, V. 508, pp. 93-8.
16. Dubois was well known in Madras, but not yet generally famous. His classic description of south Indian Hinduism, *Hindu Manners and Customs*, was submitted to the Company for publication at the time of the Vellore Mutiny. Major Mark Wilks, the Resident at Mysore, was proofreading Dubois' manuscript when he was called upon to deal with the 'mutinies' at Nandidurgam and Bangalore. Dubois' work, although not entirely genuine, nevertheless represents a Jesuit view of south Indian customs during the period 1750-1806, and one must allow

that it offers a glimpse, frequently prejudiced but also quite perceptive, of the cultural context of the Vellore Crisis.

17. Wellesley to Doveton, 24 December 1799, quoted in Rajakaryaprasakta Rao Bahadur, *Modern Mysore: From the Beginning to 1868* (Bangalore, 1938), pp. 362-3.
18. Hasan, p. 190. Lala Miyan was Tipu's father-in-law. Burhan-ud-Din, meanwhile, was an important Mysorean commander. Later, he was killed leading a cavalry charge against the British at Satyamangalam.
19. Kirmani, p. 155.
20. TNSA, Wellesley to Mornington, 19 August 1799, recorded in consultation of 4 September 1799, *MMC*, V. 257-B, p. 5868; BL/OIOC, Marriott to Josiah Webbe, 2 July 1800, *HMS*, V. 461, p. 172.
21. Ibid., p. 173.
22. TNSA, Doveton to Wilks, 30 November 1799, recorded in consultation of 19 December 1799, *MMC*, V. 261-A, p. 7513.
23. Chanda Sahib had married into the line of *nawabs* that had preceded the Wallajahs, and in the early 1750s he had attempted, with French aid, to wrest control of the Carnatic from Muhammad Ali and his English protectors. He himself was killed by the Raja of Thanjavur, leaving a line of poor but prestigious Navayat descendants in the French enclave of Pondicherry. Thus the English referred to the eldest member of the family as the 'Pondicherry Nawab'. The people of the Carnatic also used this term—but usually in a pejorative sense, implying that the independent authority of the Navayats had been squandered through helpless dependency on foreigners.
24. TNSA, *Marriott's Report on the Family of Tipu Sultan*, April 1806, *MSS*, V. 2-A, pp. 159-61.
25. Ibid., pp. 1068, 1077-8.
26. Logan, *Malabar*, V. 1, part 2, pp. 453-6.
27. TNSA, *Marriott's Report on the Family of Tipu Sultan*, April 1806, *MSS*, V. 2-A, p. 1071.
28. The two eldest daughters were the absent ones. Bibi Begum, married to a close relative of the Sultan, had been allowed to remain at Chandal, near Seringapatam, supported by a small Company pension. The second eldest daughter, Asmut-ul-Nissa, had been invited to visit Vellore by her mother before the Mutiny, but she did not arrive until 22 July 1806. See TNSA, *Marriott's Report on the Family of Tipu Sultan*, April 1806, *MSS*, V. 2-A, pp. 159-61.
29. The 'Binkey Nabob' of the British records was Muhammad Raiza, former commandant of Tipu Sultan's artillery.
30. Nur-ul-Nissa's husband-to-be, Nizam-ud-Din, was son of the late Sayyid Mukhdun of Bailur, a town near Nagamangalam in Mysore. She was a

full sister of Muhyi-ud-Din, and he was a descendant of the Sayyids of Gulbarga, whose family was closely tied many times over with that of Tipu Sultan.

31. TNSA, Extract of a Letter from the Marquess of Wellesley to Lieutenant-Colonel Gabriel Doveton, 5 July 1799, *MSS*, V. 5, pp. 2271-5.
32. TNSA, Josiah Webbe to Doveton, 11 September 1799, *MSS*, V. 5, pp. 2275-83.
33. Sydney C. Grier, 'The Mutiny at Vellore in 1806', *Bengal, Past and Present* (October-December, 1924), pp. 166-7. As private family property, the Vellore palaces remained the property of the Nawabs of Arcot even after the annexation of the Carnatic in 1801.
34. TNSA, Mark Wilks (then Military Secretary to Government) to Doveton, 11 February 1800, *MSS*, V. 5, pp. 2283-9.
35. TNSA, Doveton to Wilks, 20 March 1800, *MSS*, V. 5, pp. 2290-2300.
36. During the period 1799-1800, Lord Mornington resided at Madras to monitor the Army's operations in Mysore. While at Fort Saint George, he acted both as Governor-General and Governor-in-Council, effectively displacing the local authorities.
37. Montgomery Martin, ed., *Despatches, Minutes, and Correspondence of the Marquess Wellesley* (London, 1837), V. 2, pp. 80-1.
38. BL/OIOC, Marriott's Report, *HMS*, V. 508, pp. 252-3. When the princes first arrived at Vellore, many of their followers inhabited tents until new wings could be built on to the existing palace for their accommodation. Guard duties, at that time, were assigned to HM 33rd Foot, the soldiers being screened from the princes' women by a 'temporary tent wall'. After receiving several complaints from the princes, however, the British decided to compromise with the prisoners by deploying sepoys, who they assumed would be better behaved.
39. TNSA, *Marriott's Report on the Family of Tipu Sultan*, April 1806, *MSS*, V. 2-A, pp. 1039-40.
40. TNSA, Marriott to Major-General Pater, 4 October 1806, *MSS*, V. 5, p. 2329.
41. TNSA, Garrison Standing Orders issued by Lieutenant-Colonel Doveton, *MSS*, V. 2-A, pp. 1030-3.
42. BL/OIOC, Marriott's Deposition, *HMS*, V. 508, p. 238. Only a few of these unregistered inhabitants were permitted to enter the fort.
43. TNSA, Marriott's Testimony, *MSS*, V. 2-A, pp. 931-4. There were police outposts at four of the town gates, the other gates of the city supposedly remaining closed at all times. The policy against carrying weapons was enforced so strictly that even the Paymaster's *talaiyars* and the Collector's peons were forbidden to carry arms in the *pettah* unless escorting prisoners or treasure.

44. BL/OIOC, Doveton to Wilks, 10 April 1800, *HMS*, V. 459, pp. 152-4.
45. This particular standing order was incorporated in the Madras Army's first regulations, which were issued by Major Stringer Lawrence in 1749, and which were adapted almost word-for-word from the Articles of War governing the British Army. The purpose of this order was to make sure that sentry-duty was taken seriously at all times, and that no unreliable men were ever posted to guard key installations.
46. TNSA, Marriott's Testimony, 1 August 1806, *MSS*, V. 2-A, pp. 946-51. A small party of British soldiers also formed part of the Main Guard detail, detaching men, in rotation, to guard the garrison magazine, the gates to the British barracks yard, and the main fort gate.
47. 'Naigue', derived from *nayaka*, is the origin of the modern rank of *naik* (corporal). The old Anglo-Indian spelling captures the Telugu and Tamil pronunciation of the word.
48. Ibid.
49. Muzzle-loading muskets of the sort used by the Madras Army in 1806 could not be kept loaded for long, as the powder charge spilled whenever the gun was moved. The testimony of the sentries after the Vellore Mutiny uniformly indicates that none of the soldiers had their weapons loaded and ready for use when the uprising began. In any event, no sepoy was allowed to load his weapon, much less fire it, without direct orders from his naique or some other superior officer.
50. TNSA, *Marriott's Report on the Family of Tipu Sultan*, April 1806, *MSS*, V. 2-A, pp. 1039-40.
51. TNSA, *Marriott's Report on the Younger Princes*, 1 August 1806, *MSS*, V. 2-A, pp. 957-60.
52. TNSA, *Marriott's Report on the Family of Tipu Sultan*, April 1806, *MSS*, V. 2-A, pp. 1048-9.
53. *Hackery*, an Anglio-Indian term of possible Portuguese origin, referred to a light, two-wheeled bullock cart used, in south India and Sri Lanka, for personal transport.
54. TNSA, *Marriott's Report on the Family of Tipu Sultan*, April 1806, *MSS*. V. 2-A, p. 1068.
55. Ibid., p. 1076. Indeed, a large grove of plantain trees eventually grew up inside the fort, along one side of the palace.
56. TNSA, *Marriott's Report on the Family of Tipu Sultan*, April 1806, *MSS*, V. 2-A, pp. 1065-7.

3
The Vellore Mutiny

The Vellore rising was planned in advance, but its timing and execution gave it the appearance of a spontaneous, mass movement. The mutineers succeeded in taking the British by surprise, but gained very little from their initial advantage. In fact, the rebels were not really prepared to begin their insurrection, and had been forced into premature action. Consequently, most sepoys in the fort were just as surprised and confused as their British officers by the bloodshed that ensued. Only a handful of native officers—the leaders of a conspiracy to take the fort—were fully informed about the plot and its goals, but even they were forced to improvise at the last minute. The general bewilderment of the surviving participants thus established the tone of the post-Mutiny investigations, making it very difficult for the British to discern the causes of the rising.

THE PLOT

There had been warnings of impending trouble at Vellore. Even before the grenadiers of the 2/4th Native Infantry protested against the new turban, Colonel Marriott and Lieutenant-Colonel Forbes had been aware of rising agitation among the sepoys of the 1/1st Native Infantry. A Muslim teacher, engaged by the sepoys of the battalion to teach their children to recite the Koran, made a cryptic remark about the new turban, and was whipped out of the town after being reported to the authorities.[1] Although material evidence, this matter was nevertheless withheld during the proceedings of the court of enquiry that investigated the disturbances in the 2/4th Native Infantry, in which Marriott and Forbes were the chief investigating officers. In the aftermath of the Mutiny, of course, British officials learned that the adherents of the princes had been acting as agent provocateurs since at least early May, when Sepoy Alagiri had been told, by one of the *mard-i-admiyan*, that

> . . . the Feringhees have conquered the country. Now when they shall have made you Christians by putting on those hats, they will put a stop to all our religious ceremonies both Musselman and Hindoos. You must all eat together. Nobody will give you wives or even water out of . . . [their] hands. . . . Do not wear that hat. If you do, we shall become Feringhees. If you sepoys consent to wear that hat, what will become of us? The whole country will be ruined; bazaar people, ryots, and all of us will be obliged to wear it.[2]

Jamal-ud-Din, foster-brother of Prince Muiz-ud-Din, seems to have been the most committed anti-British activist among the *mard-i-admiyan*, but the testimony of the insurgents later indicated that, although he encouraged mutinous behaviour, he did not instigate it himself. After being told by Sepoy Imam Khan that the men of the 1/1st Native Infantry would rather die than wear the new turban, Jamal-ud-Din opened his house in the *pettah* to all soldiers who sought a private refuge in which to discuss their grievances.[3] These casual meetings allowed sepoys to air their complaints, but they came to nothing until early June, when the 2/1st Native Infantry halted at Vellore during a route march from Seringapatam to Wallajahbad. Because both battalions of the 1st Regiment were at the same station—a rare circumstance—their Indian officers met at Amin Pir's tomb to discuss the anger and fear aroused by the appearance of the new turban. One of those present, Sheikh Qasim, later confessed that the native officers of the 2/1st told those of the 1/1st that it was their responsibility to take the lead, should mutiny become necessary, as they were the senior battalion not only of the regiment, but of the Madras Army. If the men of the 1/1st were prepared to lay their lives on the line, those of the 2/1st were ready to stand by them. However, the officers of the junior battalion also warned that the men of the 1/1st would be held responsible if they stood mute and idle in the face of what had come to be seen, in many quarters, as a 'threat' to all sepoys and their families. Immediately after this meeting, a complex conspiracy began to form, and thus the informal sepoy *panchayat* was a catalyst for much of what followed.[4]

The original conspirators at Vellore were soldiers of the 1/1st Native Infantry, but when the officers of the 2/23rd were invited to join the plot, one of them, Subadar Sheikh Adam, quickly became the acknowledged leader.[5] The number of sepoys brought into the would-be mutineers' confidence increased rapidly, but their understanding of and commitment to the plot varied. Outside the small, core clique of conspirators, few sepoys had detailed knowledge of the projected plan and goal of the mutiny, and to help maintain the requisite secrecy, all those informed of the plot were compelled to swear an oath to strict silence, and to kill all Europeans when signaled to act. Some men, an inner circle of co-conspirators, about whom more will be said in due course, also swore to establish a new sultanate under prince Muiz-ud-Din.[6]

Indeed, the would-be mutineers at first took such pains to protect their plans that even Muiz-ud-Din was unaware of them until 23 June, when Jamal-ud-Din informed him that the sepoys were plotting to capture the fort, after which they would call upon Muiz-ud-Din and Muhyi-ud-Din to 'come out and join' them. Interpreting this report as an attempt to trick him, however, Muiz-ud-Din requested that the sepoy leaders decide who they wished to be their new sultan. He refused to associate himself with their designs unless this matter was addressed to his satisfaction.[7] Meanwhile, Jamal-ud-Din encouraged the plotters by making wild promises on behalf of his master—including an agreement to raise the sepoys' monthly pay from Rs. 7-0-0 to Rs. 17-8-0.[8] In reading Jamal-ud-Din's testimony, one is struck by the conspirators' lack of concern about the life-or-death problem of seizing the fort. Indeed, they apparently were so star-struck by post-Mutiny possibilities that their immediate difficulties were recklessly set aside or explained away.[9]

By mid-June, the veil of secrecy around the plot had begun to fray, but the conspirators were saved—for the time being—by their British officers, who dismissed warnings of impending mutiny as idle gossip. For instance, at midnight on 16 June, Sepoy Mustafa Beg went to Colonel Forbes' house in the *pettah* to warn him about the plot. Several native officers were sitting with Forbes at the time, however, and they immediately intervened. Mustafa Beg, the Colonel was told, had the worst reputation in the battalion; only a drunkard or a lunatic would so malign the *izzat* of the most distinguished *paltan* of the Madras Army. Despite his pleas, Mustafa Beg was arrested on the spot, bound in irons, and confined in a shed within the walls of the fort.[10] Another warning—much more public—was given by Rustam Ali Shah, a *faqir* from Cuddapah, who walked through the Vellore bazaars, shouting, 'One sepoy has joined with many . . . yet in seven days, all the [*kafirs*] will be killed. . . . Rivers of blood will flow; heaps of dead will be carried away. . . . [A Muslim] flag will be hoisted.' Few British officers at Vellore knew enough Urdu or Telugu to interpret Rustam Ali Shah's warning. The fact that he was a *faqir* led most people who heard him to dismiss his cries as a mystical prophecy—or perhaps as insanity. The *faqir's* warning, however, was the clearest premonition of what was in store for the people of Vellore.[11]

A European woman offered yet a third warning, but her words, too, were dismissed. Colonel Marriott later recalled that a woman who claimed to be the widow of an Irish soldier had tried to warn Colonel Fancourt about 'what she had heard'. Her first name has been lost, but she was known in Vellore, where she had lived for twenty-two years, as Mrs. Burke. Shortly before the Mutiny, she was living in the *paracheri*, or Paraiyar's quarter, of the *pettah* under the protection of an invalid magazine vendor named Kalla. The records imply that Mrs. Burke had become Kalla's common law wife, and was looked upon as such by the people of the neighbourhood and the soldiers of the garrison. After a quarrel, Kalla turned Mrs. Burke out of his house, and as headman of the *paracheri*, he threatened to expel her from the *basti* as well. James Frost, the seventeen-year-old Anglo-Indian son of Garrison Staff Sergeant Frost, subsequently took Mrs. Burke into his home and attempted to make peace between her and Kalla.[12] Mrs. Burke, however, was uninterested in reconciliation, she told Lieutenant-Colonel Fancourt that he had uttered treason about the impending overthrow of the Company Raj.[13] The irate woman apparently did not realize that, in the eyes of the European community at Vellore, her word carried less weight than that of Kalla, who was a community leader and a veteran of the Company's service despite his outcaste status. Furthermore, Mrs. Burke was known to accost the Garrison Staff Sergeants on a regular basis, demanding prize money allegedly owed to her former husband. Fancourt dismissed Mrs. Burke's accusations, assuming them to be incapable of proof, and probably mere slander.[14]

Why were the European officers at Vellore so incredulous in the face of these reports? Upon closer examination, it is misleading to conclude that the British at Vellore were incompetent—although their fate was sealed, in part, by their ignorance of local languages. Apart from a few officers above the rank of captain, and those who served as battalion adjutants, few British officers of the Madras Army commanded local languages sufficiently to follow even bazar *gup*. Furthermore, those Indian servants who could speak English—the *dubashes*, or interpreters, employed by almost all officers—were selective about the information they conveyed to their masters' ears. Thus it was that yet another warning about the Mutiny was quashed by a *dubash*, who thought it too unimportant to convey to his patron, Colonel Forbes, until after the Mutiny. None of this, however, explains Marriott's silence, for he not only knew Indian languages, but was responsible for monitoring the activities and conversations of suspicious strangers such as Rustam Ali Shah, who—although a *faqir*—had taken up residence in the sepoy lines. The truth may be that Marriott knew less about the internal life of Vellore than his reports suggested—or at least less than he imagined. The image of the obtuse Englishman, oblivious to his Indian surroundings and blinded by the force of bureaucratic procedures, is a standard component of modern images of the Raj—a trope which too many historians have used, in defiance of a mass of contrary evidence. Rather than dismissing the British at Vellore as fools, it seems wise to consider the warnings that they received in the context of the historical moment. The authorities at Vellore had to weigh a few scattered, cryptic warnings against what seemed to be overwhelming evidence that all was as it should be—thousands of disciplined soldiers calmly going about their duties, the ordinary, quiet bustle of a prosperous market town, and the Mysore royal family preparing for wedding celebrations.[15] Furthermore, both the 1/1st and the 2/23rd had received orders to make up the new turban, and they had done so cheerfully. Indeed, the men had been so eager to expedite the process that they had procured, on their own initiative, the materials needed to make most of the turban ornaments. Their officers reasonably assumed that the sepoys of the two battalions did not share the disaffection that had undermined the discipline of the 2/4th Native Infantry.

The conspiring native officers at Vellore successfully intercepted, discredited, and silenced Mustafa Beg, but the incident had been a very close call for them. Time was running out, and it must have seemed to the plotters that, sooner or later, a trusted Indian officer or sepoy would convince an alert British officer that the mutiny was more than a rumour. Ironically, the British themselves took steps that would incite the Vellore garrison to mutiny before the conspiracy could be betrayed. On the afternoon of 9 July, the men of the 2/23rd Native Infantry were told that they would parade for firing practice the next morning—a routine exercise that Madras battalions performed once or twice a month. To avoid delaying the morning parade and firing drill, the sepoys were allowed to draw six rounds of ball cartridge and take their firelocks to the barracks inside the fort, which were much closer to the firing range than the infantry lines.[16] These orders plunged the conspirators into heated debate, since it offered them what might be the best of all possible conditions for taking the fort. Most of the men of the 1/1st were scheduled to be on guard duty that night. Normally, the numbers of British and Indian troops inside the fort were equal at any given time, but on this particular night, the armed sepoys would outnumber the Europeans by almost three to one. By coincidence, the wedding of one of the Mysore princesses was being celebrated that evening, and many of the guests were expected to remain in the *mahals* after the gates closed at ten o'clock, thus providing the conspirators with an even larger pool of potential supporters. The pressure of the moment was too much for Jamadar Sheikh Hussain, however. He became intoxicated and swaggered through the barracks, shouting the details of the plot to all who might be listening. His fellow conspirators, alarmed by this, hastily reached a decision: they would commence the uprising at two o'clock in the morning, giving themselves just enough time to organize their followers to take advantage of a favourable situation. The mutineers agreed to strike just as the guard was being changed, for at that hour, the sound of men moving through the fort would arouse no suspicion.[17] Jamal-ud-Din informed Muiz-ud-Din of the change in plans, but although the prince was excited, he was even more alarmed by the news.[18]

Captain J. J. Miller, the Officer of the Day on 9 July, also made a decision that strengthened the conspirators' hand considerably. Miller informed the senior Indian officer of the Main Guard, Subadar Sayyid Hussain, that he was 'indisposed', and thus unable to inspect the guard posts. Miller must have known that it was strictly against military regulations for anyone other than a European officer to inspect sentries, but his order was unquestioned by his men. Sayyid Hussain agreed to inspect the guards, but later decided that he, too, was 'indisposed'. The Subadar ordered Jamadar Sheikh Qasim to see to the changing of the guards, apparently unaware that the Jamadar was part of the conspiracy. Indeed, few native officers of the rank of Subadar had been brought into the plot, as they were considered, with good reason, too attached to their British superiors, or at least to their considerable pay and benefits. Shortly before two o'clock, Sheikh Qasim set out on his rounds, accompanied by a small escort and a drummer carrying a lantern. After passing through the *mahals*, where he checked and changed the sentries, the Jamadar dismissed his escort, and, when they had passed out of sight, slipped away through the shadows to the sepoy barracks to give the signal for the rising to begin. Thinking on his toes, he had managed to place trusted fellow conspirators at most of the key guard posts inside the fort.[19]

VELLORE FORT AND THE PLAN OF ATTACK

The layout of Vellore fort and its environs holds the key to the course of the Mutiny and the tactical reasons for the mutineers' failure. The town and fort of Vellore are located at the western edge of a rock outcrop, or *durgam*, that rises some five hundred feet above the surrounding plain. Three old *sangars*, or stone redoubts, may be seen at different points on the rocky slope of the *durgam*, and if held by an enemy armed with European artillery, were close enough to command the ramparts and interior of the fort. Vellore fort itself, first built before the introduction of gunpowder weapons, is sited on level ground, to the north-west of the town. Anticipating a direct assault and escalade rather than a European-style siege, with its bombardments and regular approaches, the original architects of the fort dug a broad moat around the position, which later became famous for its legendary, man-eating crocodiles.[20] Such a fort was unusual in the generally dry landscape of the Carnatic, and, unlike the moats of other such forts—Thanjavur, for instance—that at Vellore never ran dry, being fed by the waters of a large tank.[21]

The *pettah*, or town of Vellore, meanwhile, consisted of several straggling bazars and clusters of houses ringed by a ruined stone wall. The town stood on slightly rising ground, between the *durgam* and the fort, and was separated from the east wall of the fort by the Arni Road. An early nineteenth-century description of Vellore gives a good impression of its appearance at the time of the Mutiny. The *pettah* was

> . . . close under the hills, and joined by connecting battlements with the old castellated works on the triple peaks above. It is a large and populous town, with an exceedingly busy bazar, containing many good houses, interspersed with a large proportion of Mussulman tombs, thickly-wooded with coconut trees, but without any public buildings of note, the white-washed mosque of [Chanda Sahib] being the most remarkable edifice.[22]

Only on the south side of the fort, near the sally port, did the *pettah's* houses encroach upon the glacis, possible because, until 1801, the town had been under the jurisdiction of the Nawab of Arcot. A new and half-finished line of British officers' bungalows, as well as part of the sepoy lines, stood approximately one-half mile further south of the fort, astride the main road to Arni. When not on duty in the fort, the sepoys of the garrison lived with their families either here or in the outlying neighbourhoods of the *pettah*.[23]

Because the fort was surrounded by a moat, the only practicable points of entry (or exit) were two bridges. One of these was a narrow foot-bridge extending from the sally port cut into the crownwork of the southern rampart. The other was a draw-bridge connecting the main gate with a fortified causeway that led to the town. With three loopholed outer gates, the zig-zagging causeway was designed to foil a *coup de main* by slowing the pace of an attacking party and funneling it into a point-blank cross-fire. Robert Orme, visiting the fort in 1756 to negotiate with its then *qiladar*, Safdar Ali Khan, at that time declared it to be 'impregnable'.[24] Experienced British military engineers, however, noticed that the fort was fatally exposed to artillery fire from the *durgam*. After Vellore fort passed into British hands, it became a major military base, and steps were taken to upgrade its defences by raising a *trace itallienne* of earthworks to shield the medieval stone walls. During the Second Anglo-Mysore War, however, when Vellore was besieged by Haidar Ali's forces, Colonel Ross Lang, the commander, defended the *sangars* on the *durgam* at all costs, for both Haidar Ali and Tipu Sultan instantly realized that the easiest way to reduce the fort was to take its exposed outworks.

The walls of Vellore fort enclose a roughly rectangular space of approximately one-quarter square mile. Constructed of blocks of blue granite, without mortar, the ramparts rise only fourteen feet above the water of the moat. Oxidized with age and exposure to the monsoons, the granite blocks have become rust-coloured due to their high iron content. The British, upon taking over the fort from Safdar Ali, filled the space between its exterior and interior walls with rammed earth to form a firing platform for infantry and artillery, to which ramps were added to aid the movement of men and equipment. Military engineers added cavaliers to the four angles of the fort to provide covering fire along the curtain walls, while the curtains themselves were strengthened further, at irregular intervals, by rounded bastions that probably were built by the Marathas during their occupation of Vellore. The British also added the southern crownwork as a main redoubt, covering the sepoy lines and the only point from which a besieging army could open trenches against the fort.

The interior of the fort was divided into four more or less distinct quarters that enclosed a central *maidan*, or parade ground, some one hundred and fifty yards across from east to west. The north-east quarter, where the causeway entered the main gate from the town, contained the post office, the magistrate's office (*cutcherry*), a row of shops, and an abandoned temple. This 'pagoda', formerly dedicated to Siva in the form of Jalakanteswara, had been used, by turns, as a prison, arsenal, and warehouse. At the time of the Mutiny, the temple contained the garrison stores, including several artillery pieces and the equipment, powder, and ammunition required to serve them. The north-west quarter of the fort contained a European barracks, capable of accommodating eight hundred men, British officers' bungalows built around a central garden, and ranges of sepoy barracks enclosing an open square large enough to permit an entire battalion to assemble for roll call. The south-west quarter, lying next to the sepoy barracks, was dominated by the palace complex described in the previous chapter. The palace was separated from the *maidan* by the garrison hospital, and by several houses occupied by British officers and the garrison Staff Sergeants and their families. West of the palace, filling a relatively large space between its walls and those of the fort, was a grove of plantain trees, either owned or rented by the princes, closely planted around the entrance to a subterranean, 'bomb-proofed' magazine containing thousands of rounds of ball-cartridge ammunition and a store of gunpowder. The south-east quarter of the fort, on the other side of the *maidan* from the palace and hospital, contained a small *masjid*, storage godowns, the Main Guard, and several old, two-storey houses where most of the senior officers of the garrison lived. Nineteenth-century photographs of the fort offer some idea of the general atmosphere, which resembled a thriving town rather than a military installation. Most of the spaces between the main buildings were crowded with small bazars and servants' *bastis*, penetrated only by narrow alleys scarcely wide enough for two people to pass. Most other spaces within the fort not being used as thoroughfares or parade grounds also were planted with trees and gardens, as they would be in any south Indian village, providing both fruit and shade.[25]

The conspirators' plan to seize the fort hinged on their ability to overpower and wipe out the men of HM 69th Foot, while simultaneously preventing European officers from reaching the Sepoy Barracks and the Main Guard after the fighting began. Their daring scheme called for a simultaneous assault on the European Barracks and all of the guard posts where there were British soldiers or officers, including the post that covered the Pagoda and the Magazine. Other parties of mutineers were to attack the junior officers in their quarters, thus preventing them from making contact with those sepoys who might be either loyal or wavering in their views. A cadre of dedicated volunteers, meanwhile, apparently agreed to place themselves in positions to assassinate Marriott, Fancourt, and Lieutenant-Colonel McKerras, who commanded the 2/23rd Native Infantry. When all of these objectives had been attained—ideally within an hour or so—the conspirators then planned to call upon the princes to emerge from their captivity and take charge of any further operations.

In planning their coup, however, the would-be mutineers made a number of fatal mistakes. First, they made far too many assumptions about their ability to overpower their British counterparts, and made no attempt to plan for contingencies. What, for instance, would happen if the attack on the barracks failed? The conspirators had no alternate plan at all for meeting a counter-attack by HM 69th, assuming that the redcoats would not act if their officers could not reach the barracks to take command. Second, although they had discussed holding the fort, the would-be insurgents do not seem to have appreciated that Vellore, for all its apparent strength, was a trap. They gave no thought to organizing their men to take over and hold the ramparts, nor did they make arrangements to bring the hundreds of sepoys outside the fort inside the walls. The European officers who lived in the *pettah* had been forgotten entirely even though they were, potentially, more of a threat to the conspirators than the officers inside the fort. There was nothing to stop these officers from rallying the sepoys still staying in the lines, nor did anything prevent the British from occupying the *sangars* on the *durgam*. These mistakes were so transparent that even the princes realized that the mutiny was doomed to end in blood and tears. Only Muiz-ud-Din went so far as to consult with the chief conspirators during the Mutiny—a brief interview that apparently convinced him not to entangle himself further in such a hopeless cause.

THE ATTEMPT TO TAKE THE FORT

The Mutiny began shortly after two o'clock in the morning. At the Sepoy Barracks, the men of the 1/1st Native Infantry were awakened by Sheikh Qasim and his confederates. A few minutes later, sepoys of the 2/23rd also were aroused from their sleep. Many of the sepoys hurriedly dressed and equipped themselves for action, but others demanded to know the meaning of this nocturnal tumult. Subadar Sayyid Nabbi of the 2/23rd even ordered his grenadiers to return to their beds, and threatened to arrest Sheikh Qasim if he dared to return.[26] Sepoy Arnachalam, meanwhile, informed a mob of would-be mutineers that he would not open the battalion stores and magazine to them without orders from the commander or adjutant. He was shoved aside. Breaking open doors and locks, the sepoys armed themselves as quickly as possible. In the barrack square, they assembled under Sheikh Adam, who formed them into divisions and explained that they were about to take over the fort, following which they would receive a reward of five pagodas. In the confusion, someone thought to rush to the battalion gaol to liberate Mustafa Beg, who was confined there in irons. The grateful sepoy did not tarry, for otherwise he probably would have been the first casualty of the uprising.[27]

Only fifteen minutes after rising from their cots, parties of sepoys marched to attack the Main Guard, the European Barracks, and the officers' lines. At the front gate of the European Barracks, a platoon of mutineers drew up opposite the sentry boxes, the British soldiers standing guard there thinking nothing of their presence until, suddenly, the sepoys halted, turned to face them, and fired a volley. Most of the British sentries were killed or wounded by this fusillade, while those who survived fled into the Barracks, dragging their wounded with them, and shouting the alarm.[28] The noise of the volley awakened the men of HM 69th Foot, but before they could respond, the mutineers pushed through the compound gates, reloaded, and fired a second volley into the verandahs and open windows of the Barracks. Sergeant Cosgrave, one of the survivors of the first volley, reached the Barracks only to discover that it was a trap rather than a refuge. The insurgents, firing through the windows, pinned the survivors behind hastily-constructed barricades of overturned cots and trunks, while dozens of soldiers lay dead or dying in debris-strewn, smoke-filled rooms lit only by the repeated flash of the sepoys' muskets. For the moment, there was little that Cosgrave could do to restore order, for the soldiers' weapons were locked in racks mounted on the walls, and these could not be reached through the terrible cross-fire that had been unleashed from every angle. In any event, Cosgrave himself soon was hit by a ball and severely wounded.[29]

Across the *maidan*, the British soldiers at the Main Guard began to stir, alarmed by the sound of firing in front of the European Barracks. In an instant, a second party of mutineers rushed out of the darkness to attack them, but even as they tried to defend themselves, they were cut down by the sepoys who shared their guard posts. Only one of the soldiers survived, by falling down and feigning death. The lone British sentry at the 'bomb-proofed' Magazine, meanwhile, put up a fight in the darkness of the plantain grove, holding his assailants at bay for a few minutes as he reloaded and fired. As soon as he expended the last of his ammunition, however, he was rushed, overpowered, and killed. The mutineers at once carried away all of the ball-cartridge in the bunker, leaving only a few barrels of loose gunpowder.[30]

The European officers living in the fort awakened to the sound of musketry and shouting. In the darkness, from their doors and windows, they could make little sense of the situation, but some officers managed to keep their heads, assuming the worst. Lieutenant John Ewing disarmed the sentries outside his bungalow before they themselves realized what was happening.[31] Most of the officers, however, immediately sought security in numbers, collecting in three small groups, each determined to fight its way to safety.[32] Escape from the mutineers, however, was nearly impossible, for the obstacles intended to keep attackers out of the fort now served to trap the British inside the walls. Only a few Europeans were prepared to expose themselves to both the cross-fire from the mutineers and the voracious crocodiles in the moat.

Several officers were cut down during the first hour of the uprising. Colonel Fancourt, ignoring the advice of several sepoy sentries, ran toward the Main Guard, but was shot, en route, by Havildar Abdul Qadir—one of the conspirators who had volunteered to assassinate the key officers of the garrison.[33] Not long afterward, the same havildar also killed Lieutenants O'Reilly and Popham, who had escaped from the Main Guard.[34] Lieutenant-Colonel James McKerras, running up the steps of the *tappal* (post) office, was told by Sepoy Sheikh Dumas, the sentry there, that the sound of firing meant 'nothing at all'. Then, having caught McKerras off guard, Sheikh Dumas shot him and finished him off with a bayonet thrust.[35] Other officers managed to live for two or three hours, hidden or hunted, before being cornered or ambushed and killed. Many, such as Lieutenant Smart, fell prey to their trust of Indian soldiers; Smart opened a window to hail a passing sepoy of his company, who answered him with a shot through the head. In the morning, Smart's companions, Captain Miller and Lieutenant Tichbourne, were found dead at the bottom of a bathing pool.[36] Captain David Willison, meanwhile, was dragged from his house near the wicket of the Main Gate. Thirty sepoys shoved him about and 'abused him for wearing a cap and making them wear topees'. The mutineers then shot Willison and kicked his corpse, 'asking if he considered them a parcel of chucklers to make them wear hats'.[37] Lieutenant John Ely, shot and wounded near the Sepoy Barracks, managed to stagger home only to witness the killing of his infant daughter before he himself was hauled back to the Barracks by his cross-belts and stabbed to death in the guard room.[38] Sergeant Frost was shot and killed in his house near the Main Guard, but the sepoys who fired at him were restrained from killing the Englishman's Indian wife by a signal from one of the princes' servants.[39] Another sergeant's wife, Charlotte Watters, watched the mutineers kill her husband, but she, too, was rescued by a palace servant.[40] Only a few officers who lived in the fort were able to escape from the mutineers. Lieutenant Coombs, the unpopular adjutant of the 2/23rd, narrowly escaped a volley that ripped through the front of his bungalow. He ran from his back verandah to Marriott's house, leaving his own home to be set ablaze by the insurgents.[41]

The testimonies of the European, 'Anglo-Indian', and Indian women trapped in the fort that night are particularly important to an accurate reading of the course of the uprising. Unlike most of the officers and soldiers who survived the Mutiny, these women were not constrained by military conventions in the presentation of their accounts. Furthermore, women were the only Europeans who interacted with the mutineers during the revolt and lived to tell about it. Their descriptions of the Mutiny are both vivid and credible, indicating that neither the insurgents nor the British military were organized or disciplined. Rather, they describe the struggle for the fort as a bloody and chaotic affair, an extremely violent riot rather than a pitched battle.

At the house of Samuel Gill, Conductor of Garrison Stores, several sepoys banged on the door, demanding the keys to the arsenal at the old temple. Mrs. David Potter, who was staying with Gill, went to the door to answer them, and was told to run away when Gill appeared behind her, accompanied by a civilian named William Mann, who was Deputy Commissary of Stores. The sepoys immediately fired, hitting Gill. As Mrs. Potter fled away, with her children, Mann pushed her aside in his own flight. A second volley almost hit Mrs. Potter, but was deflected by a pillar. One of her children, however, was shot through the knee, and had to be carried to safety.

The wife of Surgeon William Pritchard, in a letter to a friend, described how the rebels burst into the compound, shouting, '*Din,*

din vallekarrah!' Her cowardly husband, she added, immediately abandoned her and her children to their fate, scrambling up to the roof top.

[He] had not left me a minute when 15 or 20 sepoys rushed upstairs, some with burning brands and all with fixed bayonets. On entering the room I was in, they fired two or three shots, and pointed their bayonets at [me] while my poor women and dear children were clinging to me, the former entreating them to have mercy on me and the latter screaming with terror. Finding there was not an officer or European man in the house, they turned their attention from murder to plunder. Everything in the upper rooms was presently demolished. My cot, drawer, glasses etc., broke to pieces. My cloths and every article of value packed up, ransacking every box and place for money and repeatedly coming to me to ask where it was deposited. During this perilous time, I was sitting on a window. . . . When the ferocious monster [*sic*] had loaded themselves [*sic*] with spoil, they left the house. . . .[42]

Havildar Mallaiyandar and Sepoy Ballagaru later found Mrs. Pritchard crouched in a *bawarchikhana* with her children and hurried them to the Sepoy Barracks, where they were given blankets and hidden away from the mutineers.[43]

Amelia Fancourt, meanwhile, had been hiding in her bedroom, where her husband had sent her before rushing out to the Main Guard. Emerging under the cover of darkness, she made her way down the hall toward the back verandah, where she was startled by the sudden appearance of 'a figure'.

It was so dark I . . . was dreadfully frightened expecting to be murdered. . . . I had however the courage to ask who was there? The answer I received was, 'Madam, I am an officer.' I then said, 'But who are you?' To which the gentleman replied, 'I am an officer of the Main Guard.' I enquired what was the matter. He said it was a mutiny, that every European had already been murdered on guard but himself, and that we should all be murdered. I made no reply but walked away to the room where my babes and female servants were. The officer went out of the opposite door of the hall where we had spoken together and never got downstairs alive, for he was butcher'd most cruelly in Col. Fancourt's dressing room. . . .[44]

The officer in the above account was either Lieutenant O'Reilly or Lieutenant Popham, and Amelia Fancourt's description suggests that he may have been suffering from psychological shock. Amelia Fancourt herself, like most of the other women in the fort, remained calm. Eventually, a sepoy discovered her, leading her away to a chicken coop, where he hid her away with her children. All through the night, the sepoy discreetly watched over her, leaving only once to find some bread for her to eat.

THE FIGHT FOR THE FORT

It was daybreak when the British troops in the fort finally began to fight back. A party of European officers, dislodged from their hiding place by the mutineers, made a dash for the European Barracks and managed to scramble through its windows. The scene that they discovered within was not encouraging. The insurgents had brought up two six-pounders, and with the help of a few artillery lascars (and perhaps some of the princes' followers), they had begun to fire round shot into the already devastated Barracks. Some of the British troops, however, had been able to reach their own weapons, and had begun to return the mutineers' fire. A shot had killed one of the few rebels who seemed to know how to work the guns, but the other six-pounder continued to fire from a position in front of Lieutenant Coombs' burning bungalow. Lieutenant Mitchell, the first officer to reach the Barracks, already had taken stock of the situation, which he rapidly explained to the officers who had just joined him. Two hundred British soldiers remained who were capable of bearing arms, and they all had at least five rounds of ball cartridge in their boxes. If these survivors could withdraw from the Barracks, somehow, they might be able to make a useful sortie against the mutineers.

Captain MacLachlan, the highest-ranking officer present, assumed command. He seems to have realized that the only hope of British survival was somehow to reach the ramparts and move around the fort, along the top of the wall, capturing the Main Gate. If they were able to do that, the next logical move would be to push the sortie toward the Magazine and try to capture the fort's supply of small arms ammunition. Ordering the survivors in the Barracks to leave the dead and wounded, MacLachlan had the soldiers fix bayonets and led them through the back windows and into the adjoining *paracheri.* The mutineers had not anticipated this sudden movement, and consequently the British troops climbed up to the north wall of the fort without too much difficulty. Once outside the Barracks, and with officers to take command, the soldiers' sense of discipline returned, and they swiftly charged along the ramparts, taking several cavaliers and bastions from a handful of ill-prepared rebel defenders. Mutineers fired at the redcoats from the *gopurams* of the Jalakanteshwara temple, but although MacLachlan was hit and wounded, the men of HM 69th Foot pushed on, eventually capturing the section of wall above the Main Gate. This objective attained, Captain Barrow ordered Lieutenant Mitchell to lead a sortie down the stairs near Captain Willison's house, hoping thereby to open the Main Gate. However, Mitchell and his men were met on the stairs by a burst of musketry that seemed to come from the direction of the palace.[45] They retired to the top of the wall, Mitchell severely wounded with a ball through his arm.[46]

At this point in their sortie, the morale of the British troops began to waver, and several of them dropped down from the top of the wall above the Main Gate to the causeway below, running away into the still quiet city. Those who remained, however, stood fast under Captain Barrow; they regrouped and charged along the wall to take the south-east cavalier. The mutineers, ready for this attack, raked the top of the wall, firing from the roof-tops of the palace complex; Barrow, shot through both legs, fell, and command of the British troops passed to Surgeon John Jones of the 1/1st Native Infantry. The only other European officer still standing was Assistant-Surgeon John Dean of the 2/23rd Native Infantry, and thus it was that two medical officers completed the mission to capture the Magazine.[47] Finding the Magazine all but empty, Jones immediately ordered his men to fall back on the Main Gate, pausing only to cut down a flag—later to become a rather important scrap of evidence—that someone had run up a staff on the southern crownwork.[48]

Thus far the Mutiny had been confined to the fort.[49] Most British officers living in the *pettah* passed the night awestruck and idle, apparently unable to comprehend what was happening behind the walls of the fort. Two officers staying in the Cantonment near the Native Infantry lines managed to enter the fort from the south, but were warned by sepoy sentries there that they would be killed if they proceeded further.[50] Sepoys outside the fort, whether in the *pettah* or the lines, were torn. Some three hundred of them, including the highest-ranking native commissioned officers, loyally fell in under their European officers. Others entered or tried to enter the fort to join the mutineers, some of those sick in hospital even crawling from their cots to lend what aid they could to the insurrection.[51]

Lieutenant-Colonel Forbes was the only senior officer not inside the fort when the Mutiny began. As soon as he realized what was happening, he contacted and organized the officers living in the *pettah*. Collecting the British soldiers who had fled from the Main Gate, he sent them, with a few loyal sepoys, to occupy the commanding hill fort of Sazarao.[52] Major J.K. Coates, who commanded the wing of HM 69th Foot trapped inside the fort, mounted his horse and galloped to Ranipet to warn the cavalry brigade there.[53] Around six o'clock in the morning, Coates arrived at the extensive cavalry exercise grounds near Arcot, where he found Colonel Robert Rollo Gillespie preparing to dismiss HM 19th Dragoons and the 7th Native Cavalry from morning drill. Hearing Coates' report, however, Gillespie immediately ordered a squadron of the 19th Dragoons (his own regiment) to march to Vellore with part of the 7th Native Cavalry. Lieutenant-Colonel Joseph Kennedy was ordered to bring the rest of the cavalry, with their regimental galloper guns, as soon as possible. Only a small party remained to cover the cantonment.[54] Huddlestone, left in command at Ranipet, reported these orders to Colonel Harcourt at Wallajahbad within three hours. Harcourt at once ordered out all those at his disposal who could be spared, which included most of the 2/4th, 2/14th, and 1/23rd Native Infantry battalions. Marching toward Vellore, Harcourt paused only to send a dispatch to the Adjutant-General, forwarding his own short report with that of Huddlestone. The express rider who carried these reports arrived at Choultry Plain, the headquarters of the Madras Army, later that very afternoon.[55]

Within a few hours of sunrise on 10 July, the British had mobilized a brigade-sized contingent to put down the Vellore Mutiny. Gillespie reached the fort, with the vanguard of this force, shortly before eight o'clock in the morning. Marching swiftly along the esplanade in front of the *pettah*, the main body of the cavalry—a mixed force of dragoons and *sowars*—formed up facing the causeway leading to the Main Gate. The rest of the troopers continued down the Arni Road, swinging out across the open country to the south of the fort. Sepoys already were slipping across the footbridge, trying to reach the Native Infantry Lines. Some of the dragoons chased after them, while the others plunged into the lines, shooting and cutting down every sepoy they encountered. Meanwhile, Gillespie, with the main body, examined the approach to the Main Gate. The mutineers had left the drawbridge down, but the causeway was swept by the desultory fire of a party of insurgents gathered in the cavalier to the left of the Main Gate. Gillespie rather cautiously chose to wait for Kennedy to bring up the guns before attacking the position.[56] When the rest of the cavalry and the guns appeared, Captain John Blakiston of the Engineers directed one of the crews to load with round shot and push their gun across the drawbridge and along the causeway, under fire, right up to the Main Gate. The first discharge smashed the bolt, and 'the gate flew open'. The gunners immediately wheeled their cannon out of the way, but Gillespie was not yet ready to commit his dragoons.[57]

In order to ascertain the situation within the fort, and the resistance that his force would encounter, Gillespie himself climbed up to the top of the wall to join the survivors of HM 69th, who had been pinned down there since shortly after dawn. Accompanied by Sergeant Brady, Gillespie observed the mutineers' 'positions' from the top of the Main Gate, from the corner of the Paymaster's House, and from the north-east cavalier.[58] There were no uninjured King's officers left on the wall, and thus Gillespie reorganized the infantry himself, leading them down the steps beside Captain Willison's house. With bayonets fixed, the redcoats charged and drove away a party of mutineers trying to form up in front of the now gaping Main Gate, and at almost the same instant, the dragoons charged across the causeway a few horsemen at a time. Gillespie was knocked down and trampled, but managed to crawl to safety.[59]

Few of the mutineers resisted the attack. Most of the sepoys, still scattered around the fort, were drinking, looting, or simply milling about. The dragoons fanned out in small groups, putting every person in sight to the sword. Several mutineers fled into the European Barracks, pursued right into the building by dismounted dragoons, who swiftly overpowered them. Other mutineers collected on the flat sections of the Palace roof, firing at the dragoons as they crossed the *maidan*. As the slaughter proceeded, however, the rebels abandoned these positions and scattered in flight. Another party of insurgents fell back into the old temple, but the dragoons pushed in after them, cutting them down and picking them off with carbine shots, offering no quarter. Most of the sepoys caught on the open *maidan* moved at once toward the narrow footbridge leading out of the fort from the sally port, but as they emerged on the other side of the moat, they found their path blocked by more dragoons and *sowars*. In the confusion, hundreds of sepoys—together with the princes' servants and hapless civilians—ran in all directions through the *pettah* and the cantonment. Dragoons spurred after these crowds of refugees with drawn sabres, leaving a tell-tale swathe of bodies across the countryside.[60] One of those who survived the chase later recalled indiscriminate slaughter—civilians and sepoys shot or cut up without discrimination, the former including even servants, concubines, and dancing girls from the palace.[61]

When the cavalry discovered the bodies of Lieutenant Jolly and forty British soldiers who had been dragged from the fort hospital and killed, they rushed to the gates of the Palace, intent on revenge. There, however, they were stopped by Colonel Marriott, who refused to allow the troopers to harm the princes—an act which surely saved the lives of Tipu Sultan's sons, and probably those of many others inside the palace.[62] Later, Marriott allowed the *mahals* to be searched properly, but only under his supervision. One hundred fugitive sepoys were found in various corners of the palace during the search. They were marched away by the dragoons, pushed up against the wall near the Sepoy Barracks, and mowed down by salvoes of canister shot.[63] Only seventy-five sepoys found in the fort were allowed to surrender and live, but in this battered remnant were many of the chief conspirators.[64]

The fighting over, casualties were counted and the damage assessed. The interior of the fort presented a scene comparable with the aftermath of a pitched field battle. Hundreds of bodies were strewn across the *maidan*, both inside and outside the various buildings. It took the soldiers and coolies who cleaned up the human debris three days to separate all of the European dead from the sepoys and others who had been killed. Corpses were piled onto carts and pushed out of the fort, to a nearby burial ground, where the mutineers' bodies were flung upon a huge pile of burning wood, their bones and ashes later to be interred in a large pit. Fifteen British officers had been killed and three wounded. Eighty-three British 'other ranks' had been killed and ninety-four had been wounded, fifteen of the latter mortally. One European child had been killed, another wounded. Finally, one of Marriott's *harkaras* had been found wounded in Muiz-ud-Din's quarters.[65] How many mutineers were killed or wounded? An exact count of the Indian bodies scattered around the fort was not made at the time, and the available sources defy attempts to establish a reliable estimate of their number. In July the weather is quite sweltering. Given the extreme heat, the piles of corpses, and the looming danger of disease, the British ordered the dead to be disposed of as quickly as possible. Questions were raised immediately, of course, about the number of mutineers who might have escaped from the fort, and thus the British officers at Vellore had every reason to count the fallen. In their haste to remove the dead, however, the authorities merely offered an estimated number of sepoy casualties to the government, revising the number more than once over the course of the year. Chinnian estimates, in his study of the Vellore Mutiny, that 3,000 sepoys, palace servants, and 'townspeople' were killed in the fort, but his figure is a guess based on very suspect reasoning and wildly inaccurate claims made at the time of the Mutiny.[66] Rajayyan, following Furnell and the records, offers a more conservative figure of 350 mutineers killed.[67] However, based on an examination of estimates given in the various post-Mutiny reports, and on the muster rolls of the 1/1st and 2/23rd Native Infantry battalions, it seems likely that at least 600 or 700 sepoys were killed in or around the fort, most of them falling during the first twenty minutes after the dragoons entered the fort.[68] Apart from the human casualties, there also had been an extensive destruction of property. Nearly two lakh *pagodas* worth of cash and goods were reported stolen, and several buildings were damaged or completely destroyed.[69] Some of the damage done to the fort and temple, in fact, remains visible to this day, such as the sabre-marks on the Nayaka-period statues carved on the pillars of the *kalyana mantapam*, made by Gillespie's dragoons as they plied their weapons inside the old shrine.

The *prima facie* evidence all around him convinced Colonel Gillespie that the captive princes must have been the authors of the mutiny, but he had no idea what to do about them, given Marriott's insistence that they not be harmed or even questioned. Gillespie wanted to send them all to Madras, without delay, but was forced to content himself with doubling the guard.[70] Meanwhile, the irate dragoon officer ordered his second-in-command, Lieutenant-Colonel Kennedy, to organize and preside over a Military Court of Enquiry, which was to 'trace the whole business to its origin'.[71] This body opened its proceedings immediately, commencing even before all the bodies had been removed from the fort. By 12 July, Gillespie had heard enough of the survivors' horror stories to confirm his initial suspicions. He wrote to Harcourt, who had stopped with his troops at Arcot: 'It appears in such strong colours, as almost to amount to positive proof . . . that the whole was carried on at the instigation of [Muiz-ud-Din] . . . for the express purpose of enabling him to . . . escape to Mysore, where . . . he expected to be joined by a numerous train of followers.'[72] Harcourt himself arrived at Vellore with his troops on 13 July and assumed temporary command of the garrison. In his own report to Lord Bentinck, Harcourt repeated Gillespie's remarks and added a prediction that the Military Court of Enquiry would establish the guilt of Tipu Sultan's sons.[73]

NOTES

1. BL/OIOC, Sheikh Ahmad's Testimony, *HMS,* V. 507, pp. 383-4. The documents do not indicate directly whether or not this man was a *faqir,* but I suspect that he was merely an ordinary school master of the sort often employed by sepoys to educate their sons.
2. BL/OIOC, Sepoy Allegarry's Testimony, *HMS,* V. 507, pp. 278-80.
3. TNSA, Jamal-ud-Din's Testimony, *MSP,* V. 25, pp. 4267-8; TNSA, Sheikh Ramjuny's Testimony, *MSP,* V. 25, pp. 4257-8.
4. TNSA, Sheikh Qasim's Confession, *MSP,* V. 20, pp. 1225-45.
5. TNSA, Report of Forbes and Coombs, 15 July 1806, *MSP,* V. 25, p. 4225. The newly-recruited 2/23rd N.I. was sent to Vellore from Tiruchchirappalli to replace the 2/4th N.I., which, after its 'mutiny', had been transferred to Fort Saint George.
6. BL/OIOC, Sheikh Nattar's Deposition, *HMS,* V. 508, pp. 204-5; TNSA, Sheikh Qasim's Confession, *MSP,* V. 20, pp. 1225-45; TNSA, Jamal-ud-Din's Deposition, *MSP,* V. 25, pp. 4279-81.

7. TNSA, Jamal-ud-Din's Deposition, *MSP*, V. 25, pp. 4272, 4284.
8. TNSA, Sheikh Qasim's Confession, *MSP*, V. 20, pp. 1225-45; TNSA, Jamal-ud-Din's Deposition, *MSP*, V. 25, pp. 4272-3.
9. TNSA, Jamal-ud-Din's Deposition, *MSP*, V. 25, pp. 4277-9. Apparently, many of the would-be mutineers assumed that all of the Indian troops in the area would support them, which would have included the wing of the 1/1st guarding the collectorate at Chittoor, the 2/1st at Wallajahbad, and the cavalry stationed at Ranipet and Konnatur. However, the conspirators made no effort even to inform these troops of their intentions.
10. TNSA, Forbes' Deposition, *MSP*, V. 25, pp. 4245-51; BL/OIOC, Forbes' Deposition, *HMS*, V. 508, pp. 123-35; BL/OIOC, Sepoy Mustafa Beg's Deposition, *HMS*, V. 508, pp. 182-5.
11. TNSA, Rustam Ali Shah's Deposition, *MSP*, V. 25, pp. 4311-18.
12. Despite his age, James Frost already was a successful local businessman. Indeed, his leather-working shop had obtained the contract to produce the leather cockades for the sepoys' new turbans. As most of his workers were Paraiyars, Frost apparently had an interest in the internal affairs of the *paracheri* where they lived and worked.
13. TNSA, Mrs. Burke's Deposition, *MSS*, V. 2-A, pp. 964-5; James Frost's Deposition, *MSS*, V. 2-A, pp. 966-7.
14. TNSA, Mrs. Burke's Deposition, *MSS*, V. 2-A, pp. 964-5; BL/OIOC, Marriott's Deposition, *HMS*, V. 508, p. 207. According to Marriott, Mrs. Burke was notorious for slandering people. The matter of her claim to prize money, however, has never been investigated. As garrison commander, Fancourt should have forwarded Mrs. Burke's information to the Military Board in Choultry Plain, where it could be compared with the prize list in question, but I have not been able to find any record of such a correspondence. Marriott emphasized Mrs. Burke's 'bad character', but it is not clear whether he referred to her general disposition or to her liason with Kalla.
15. UN, Marriott to Bentinck, 17 July 1806, Portland MS, PwJb/, pp. 354-7.
16. TNSA, Forbes' and Coombs' Report, 15 July 1806, *MSP*, V. 25, pp. 4229-31.
17. TNSA, Sheikh Qasim's Confession, *MSP*, V. 20, pp. 1225-45.
18. TNSA, Jamal-ud-Din's Deposition, *MSP*, V. 25, pp. 4287-8.
19. BL/OIOC, Jamadar Rangappah's Deposition, *HMS*, V. 507, pp. 303-5; BL/OIOC, Subadar Sayyid Hussain's Deposition, *HMS*, V. 508, pp. 212-13.
20. According to local folklore, there were ten thousand crocodiles in the moat—a rather large number for such a small one. Travellers' accounts

of the seventeenth century mention the crocodiles, and they remained a menace, particularly to local children, until hunted to extinction by British officers in the first part of the nineteenth century. However, there were still crocodiles in the moat in 1806, which explains why no one, either British or Indian, thought of trying to swim across it, either to enter the fort or escape, during the Mutiny.

21. The Suryagunta Tank, located near the Vellore railway station, still provides water to the fort moat.
22. Walter Hamilton, *The East India Gazeteer*, V. 2 (London, n.d.), p. 695.
23. Arthur F. Cox, *A Manual of the North Arcot District in the Presidency of Madras* (Madras, 1881), pp. 187–8; W.H. Bayley, ed., *A Gazeteer of Southern India* (Madras, 1855), pp. 275–7.
24. Robert Orme, *Military Transactions of the British Nation in Indostan*, 4th edn. (Madras, 1861), V. 1, pp. 418-20.
25. Cox, pp. 191-3. For the precise locations of the various structures, see Map B.
26. Only a few hours later, the unfortunate Subadar, trying to leave the fort by swimming across the moat, was attacked and killed by one of the infamous crocodiles.
27. BL/OIOC, Mustafa Beg's Deposition, *HMS*, V. 508, pp. 184-6. Mustafa Beg escaped from the fort and went into hiding until 28 July. When he returned to Vellore, he was, at first, confined with the other survivors of the Mutiny, but later exonerated and held up by the government as an example of loyalty and discipline. The Company gave him a cash award of Rs. 7,000, a subadar's pension for life, a gold medal, and a badge of honour. Notification of these rewards was published in a special General Order, for the text of which see BL/OIOC, General Order of Government concerning Mustafa Beg, *HMS*, V. 508, pp. 70-2.
28. TNSA, *MMP*, Range 255, V. 75, pp. 6169-72. The guard in front of the European Barracks that night consisted of Sergeant Cosgrave, two corporals, and twelve privates.
29. TNSA, Sergeant Cosgrave's Deposition, *MMP*, Range 255, V. 75, pp. 6169-72.
30. TNSA, Corporal Piercy's Deposition, *MMP*, Range 255, V. 75, pp. 6169-72.
31. Lieutenant Ewing kept the battalion records of the 1/1st Native Infantry in his bungalow, hence the presence of a guard detail.
32. TNSA, Surgeon John Jones' Report, *MMP*, Range 255, V. 74, pp. 5383-96; BL/OIOC, Assistant Surgeon John Dean's Report, *HMS*, V. 508, pp. 156-8, 258-9.
33. Fancourt did not die immediately. Two sepoys dragged him to cover and hid him through most of the evening, bringing him water to drink

until he succumbed to his wounds about two hours later. See BL/OIOC, *HMS*, V. 508, pp. 222-3.

34. TNSA, *MMP*, Range 255, V. 80, pp. 8887-93.
35. BL/OIOC, James Frost's Deposition, *HMS*, V. 508, pp. 186-8.
36. BL/OIOC, Ramji's Deposition, *HMS*, V. 507, pp. 329-32. Ramji was Lieutenant Smart's servant.
37. BL/OIOC, Lakshmi Bee's Deposition, *HMS*, V. 507, p. 354; BL/OIOC, Marriott's Deposition, *HMS*, V. 508, p. 151. 'Chucklers' (*chakkiliyan*) are leather-workers, a south Indian 'untouchable' caste similar to the *chamars* of north India.
38. BL/OIOC, *HMS*, V. 508, pp. 210-11.
39. TNSA, Mrs. Frost's Deposition, *MSS*, V. 2-A, p. 968.
40. TNSA, Charlotte Watter's Deposition, *MSS*, V. 2-A, pp. 967-8. She was the wife of Garrison Staff Sergeant James Watters, and she had lived at Vellore for seven years. Like Mrs. Frost, she recognized the palace servant who saved her life, having seen him in the fort many times before.
41. BL/OIOC, Marriott's Deposition, *HMS*, V. 508, pp. 155-7.
42. Samuelraj, pp. 105-6, op cit., UE, *MSS* 913.
43. TNSA, *MMP*, Range 255, V. 80, pp. 8774-7.
44. Samuelraj, pp. 105-6, op. cit., BLO, *MSS*, Eng. Misc., b. 30, f. 32.
45. The angle of fire, however, suggests that these shots were fired either from the European Barracks, or from the row of bungalows in front of the Sepoy Barracks.
46. TNSA, Surgeon John Dean's Deposition, *MSS*, V. 2-A, pp. 940-5.
47. Ibid.
48. TNSA, *MMP*, Range 255, V. 74, pp. 5587-96.
49. TNSA, Surgeon John Dean's Deposition, *MSS*, V. 2-A, pp. 940-5. According to Dean, as his party advanced toward the Magazine, they were fired at by sepoys concealed in 'the small houses on the glacis'. This is the only reference in the Vellore proceedings to fire entering the fort from outside the walls.
50. BL/OIOC, Captain Marrett's Deposition, *HMS*, V. 507, pp. 358-9. Marrett (1/1st Native Infantry) and Bissel (HM 69th Foot) did not explain how they managed to enter the fort, although it seems likely that they slipped across the unguarded footbridge. They advanced as far as the north-west angle of the palace, where Naik Venkataram stopped them. After this, they withdrew along the walls as far as the Main Guard, where they hid until the recapture of the fort in the morning. That they could move so far, undetected, indicates that the mutineers gave no thought whatsoever to manning the ramparts.

51. BL/OIOC, Forbes and Coombs to Harcourt, 1 September 1806, *HMS*, V. 509, pp. 129-42.
52. BL/OIOC, Gillespie to GC, 11 July 1806, *HMS*, V. 507, pp. 172-3.
53. TNSA, *MMP*, Range 255, V. 78, pp. 6167-74.
54. BL/OIOC, Gillespie to GC, 10 July 1806, 11:00 a.m., *HMS*, V. 507, pp. 157-61.
55. BL/OIOC, Huddlestone to Harcourt, 10 July 1806, 9:00 a.m., *HMS*, V. 507, p. 155; BL/OIOC, Harcourt to Agnew, 10 July 1806, Ibid., p. 154. These reports were addressed to Agnew because Cradock was then on leave to Nandidurgam and Bangalore.
56. BL/OIOC, Gillespie to GC, 10 July 1806, *HMS*, V. 507, pp. 157-61.
57. John Blakiston, *Twelve Years' Military Adventure in Three Quarters of the Globe . . . between the Years 1802 and 1814* (London, 1829), pp. 290-5.
58. TNSA, *MSP*, V. 22, p. 2851.
59. BL/OIOC, Gillespie to GC, 11 July 1806, *HMS*, V. 507, pp. 168-74.
60. For an example of the experiences of those pursued that morning, see BL/OIOC, Naik Akkelundum's Deposition before the Magistrate of Salem, 11 August 1806, *HMS*, V. 508, pp. 538-40. Thirteen other sepoys arrested with the deponent in Salem District all gave similar accounts. See ibid., pp. 536-53.
61. BL/OIOC, MacDowall to Cradock, 17 July 1806, *HMS*, V. 507, pp. 360-2. This report encloses a translation of a Persian letter from Hasan Ali Khezari of Arcot to Bahar Sahib, of Seringapatam.
62. TNSA, *MSP*, V. 22, pp. 2852-3; BL/OIOC, MacDowall to Cradock, 17 July 1806, *HMS*, V. 507, pp. 360-2.
63. Blakiston, p. 295.
64. BL/OIOC, Gillespie to GC, 11 July 1806, *HMS*, V. 507, pp. 168-75.
65. BL/OIOC, Forbes' and Coombs' Report, 6 September 1806, *HMS*, V. 509, pp. 129-42.
66. Chinnian, p. 84.
67. Rajayyan, p. 291, op. cit., S.S. Furnell, *The Mutiny of Vellore*, pp. 7-9.
68. As will be demonstrated in the following chapters, it is, in fact, doubtful exactly how many of the sepoys in the fort really were 'mutineers'. Many loyal sepoys stayed in the fort, unable or unwilling to leave their posts; in the morning, they were massacred along with the others, or were forced to run for their lives and surrender later.
69. TNSA, *MMP*, Range 255, V. 75, pp. 5988-98.
70. Gillespie had become friends with Colonel and Mrs. Fancourt, and before the Mutiny had often made the short journey from Ranipet Cantonment to visit them. Arriving at Vellore to find his friend dead certainly must have primed the rather hot-headed Gillespie for revenge.

71. BL/OIOC, Gillespie to GC, 11 July 1806, *HMS*, V. 507, pp. 168-74.
72. BL/OIOC, Gillespie to Harcourt, 12 July 1806, *HMS*, V. 507, pp. 187-90. All of Gillespie's correspondence with Harcourt, of course, was forwarded to the Military Board, and then to the Governor-in-Council without delay.
73. BL/OIOC, Harcourt to Bentinck, 13 July 1806, *HMS*, V. 507, pp. 201-7.

4
Evidence and Contested Testimony

The Governor-in-Council in Madras received several reports from Vellore within twenty-four hours of the insurrection, and the matter was considered in secret proceedings even before the hundreds of dead strewn about the ravaged fort could be collected and burned.[1] Colonel Rollo Gillespie immediately had assembled a court of enquiry to investigate the causes of the Vellore rising. However, as a close friend of Colonel Fancourt, who had been killed by the mutineers, Gillespie was probably not entirely rational in his decision-making during the crucial days following the mutiny. The only witnesses available to his court of enquiry at that time were psychologically shocked women and children—British, Indian, and Anglo-Indian—whose husbands were either dead or missing, or who themselves had survived only by chance. Almost all of these witnesses had seen their homes burned and looted. Their testimony, some of which was recounted in the previous chapter, was often harrowing, painting a picture of strangely deliberate bloodshed amid an atmosphere of general chaos.[2]

In Vellore *pettah*, many people were on edge in the aftermath of the uprising. Lieutenant-Colonel Harcourt, who soon arrived from Wallajahbad with reinforcements, assumed command of the garrison and imposed martial law. The Mysore migrants crowding the Muslim *mohalla* were particularly angry, and Lieutenant Ewing, the unpopular adjutant of the 1/1st Native Infantry, was confronted there by a furious mob. Spat upon, the hapless lieutenant was chased from the bazar amid cries of, '*farangi bahinchut*!'[3] Such incidents merely confirmed Gillespie in his unfounded opinion that the mutineers had been pawns in the hands of Tipu Sultan's sons, and he declared in his reports to the government that he would quickly find proof with which to condemn the princes.

FRAMING A CONSPIRACY

Cradock rushed from Nandidurgam to Vellore and within three hours of his arrival was convinced by Gillespie of the princes' guilt. The Commander-in-Chief issued proclamation ordering 'every person to aid in the discovery of the [horrid] plot'.[4] In Madras, however, the civilian authorities were less inclined to jump to conclusions.[5] William Petrie, in particular, was conscious of the political implications of the rising, reminding his fellow members of Council that the Directors in London would expect a full, detailed account of both the mutiny and the steps taken to quell the crisis that had caused it.[6] The Council noted that Gillespie had not sought its sanction before assembling his court of enquiry, and it was made clear to him that although his court could continue to collect testimony and evidence, it was only a military commission. A joint military-civilian committee of enquiry, appointed and authorized by the Governor-in-Council, was to be sent to Vellore, as soon as possible, to take charge of the proceedings.[7] Bentinck ordered Cradock to return to Madras at once and join the rest of the Council in secret consultation.

For the time being, Cradock was reminded of his subordinate position in the Madras Government, but he must have realized, when he was ordered to rescind the command regarding the new turban, that he was likely to be blamed for the mutiny. Cradock suffered a moment of doubt, reflecting that perhaps the sepoys had been motivated by a genuine religious grievance. Writing to Agnew on 15 July, he confessed to feeling 'the most likely inquietude . . . that infringement of the right and prejudices of the Natives, dear to them as life, should originate with me'.[8] Gillespie's court of enquiry, however, issued a report the same day outlining what amounted to a charge of treason against the princes. The court laid the blame for the mutiny at their feet and described a conspiracy hatched by 'Moormen of the *pettah*' and a cadre of disgruntled native officers, ringleaders of which had hoped to establish a new Mysorean sultanate. The rebels had advanced their cause by taking advantage of the 'temporary dissatisfaction . . . of the sepoys [due to] . . . the introduction of the new turban. . . .' The officers of the court concluded that the Vellore mutiny was not a spontaneous rebellion, but a well-planned, long-awaited coup attempt, the ultimate goal of which was the overthrow of British power in south India.[9]

As soon as Cradock arrived at Fort St. George, a battle of wills ensued between the Commander-in-Chief and Lord Bentinck—a battle that could result only in the Governor's triumph, but which strained the already uneasy relationship between the two men. When asked to rescind the order regarding the new turban, Cradock's response was to make the revocation 'conditional'. Battalion commanders were ordered to revert to or maintain the old pattern of turban 'unless the native officers and men should desire to wear that which it was intended to adopt'.[10] At the same time, Cradock criticised the Mixed Commission, arguing that its members were not qualified to investigate the Vellore Mutiny, and suggesting that Bentinck and Petrie should preside over the proceedings—a proposal that flew in the face of the normal procedures of government.[11] Finally, without seeking the Council's advice, Cradock ordered the court martial of the prisoners at Vellore on 18 July. Bentinck stayed this command, and furthermore compelled the Commander-in-Chief to rescind the 'obnoxious' order introducing the new turban.[12] A General Order of Government also was drafted, announcing that the Vellore Mutiny was an isolated incident concerning only the 'two battalions composing the unhappy garrison'. The rest of the Army, the Order assured, continued to display that 'spirit of zeal, fidelity, and attachment which the Native troops have so frequently displayed in the service of the British Government'.[13]

The proceedings of the Vellore enquiries, meanwhile, were coloured by the political priorities of the Madras Government, and also shaped by a stream of orders sent to Fort St. George by the Supreme Government in Bengal. The focus of the enquiries also changed as news of other military disturbances reached Vellore, along with rumours alleging the existence of a widespread conspiracy against British rule. Cradock and most other King's officers in the Madras Presidency shared the prevailing notion that revolt was a symptom of the hidden workings of an élite cabal. Both Cradock and Bentinck had served in the army of occupation in Ireland, where periodic risings against the Crown were attributed by the British to Jacobin conspiracies hatched by élite radicals, and it was Bentinck's father who had drafted the draconian laws prohibiting public meetings and suspending *habeas corpus* during the early years of the Napoleonic Wars, when the British aristocracy feared an insurrection led by radical fifth columnists of the French Revolution. Viewing society as a network of interests rather than a mass influenced by broad historical forces, contemporary Britons, especially aristocrats, did not consider 'popular' movements possible. Ordinary people—'common folk' or peasants—were unlikely to swerve from their habits of deference to authority unless duped into lawless courses by interested provocateurs. Such thinking had much to do with the Madras Council's rather abrupt decision to view the Vellore rising as a conspiracy, and to see the captive princes—as the élites on the scene—as obvious suspects. In seeking a Mysorean connection with the Vellore Mutiny, however, British officers opened Pandora's notorious box, releasing fears that had been suppressed since the fall of Tipu Sultan, fears about all of those who had been displaced by the sudden ascendancy of the Company Raj. The vision of British officials became clouded with the spectre of conspirators, and everywhere they looked, colonial officials saw Indian élites with very good reason to hate them and plot their downfall.

The politics of conspiracy-hunting began to play out immediately. Cradock and Petrie took the first step by questioning Colonel Thomas Marriott's performance as Paymaster of Stipends. Surely, they suggested, the rising could have been thwarted if Marriott had been attentive to his duties?[14] Even the princes' friends and relatives argued that Marriott's *harkaras* were corrupt, and that his predecessor had provided the captives with better security.[15] Fortunately for Marriott, neither Bentinck nor James Strange concurred with this view. Marriot himself vigorously defended his pre-mutiny security arrangements as well as his actions during the mutiny. As the officer responsible for the princes he had supervised the interrogation of twenty-two of the princes' servants who had been charged with aiding the mutineers. On the basis of this questioning Marriott had concluded that the princes themselves were innocent, and he insisted that it was the turban—not some political conspiracy—that was the cause of the mutiny.[16] When questioned about the rising themselves, the princes merely scoffed, regarding the very suggestion of their guilt as an insult.[17]

EVIDENCE AND CONTESTED TESTIMONY

The testimony against Tipu Sultan's sons and their servants must be examined carefully, especially since so many authorities have assumed and asserted so much about their connection with the insurrection.

Essentially, there were two categories of testimony heard by the Vellore enquiries: one regarding activities alleged to have occurred *before* the mutiny, another concerning activities alleged to have occurred *during* the mutiny. Four common elements stand out when the first category of evidence is analysed. Several sepoys reported being teased by palace servants about the forthcoming alteration of their dress. Later, after the patterns for the new turbans arrived, sepoys discussed them with two 'emissaries' from the princes. According to many witnesses, these discussions led to several meetings and numerous oath-taking ceremonies in which sepoys were sworn not to inform British officers of their activities. Finally, it was generally agreed that for a period of two weeks before the mutiny, there was talk in Vellore about an immanent rising that would restore the fallen sons of Tipu Sultan, and it was specifically stated that the flag of Mysore would be raised over the fort. The second category of testimony revolved around five major problems. The most important question concerning the mutiny itself was whether or not the princes directly interacted with the mutineers. Directly associated with this question were three inter-related matters. Did Muiz-ud-Din give the sepoys the flag of Mysore that British soldiers had found raised over the southern crownwork? Did Sayyid Hussain, the son of one of Tipu Sultan's commanders, try to take charge of the mutineers, and, if so, did he act on his own, or at the request of Muiz-ud-Din? Two other questions, somewhat less important, also were raised. What role did the palace servants play in the rising? Finally, why was Muiz-ud-Din's horse found saddled, apparently ready to spirit the prince away to the nearby Mysore hills?

The Mixed Commission considered the second category of testimony first. After hearing the depositions of several European and Anglo-Indian survivors of the mutiny, the court listened to the stories of several loyal sepoys. These sepoys corroborated most of the preceding testimony, adding important details of their own. Sepoy Maniyappah of the 1/1st Native Infantry, for instance, said he had heard the mutineers calling out to the princes in front of the palace, following which 'someone' came to a window and made a signal.[18] Sepoy Ramdu of the same battalion recalled that when the Mysore flag was raised, Sepoy Muhammad Jafar had turned to him, saying that Tipu's standard was the cause for which they fought, and that there were not fighting against the new turban.[19] Meanwhile, Sepoy Ramaswami, one of the palace sentries, claimed he had heard Muiz-ud-Din order an attack on the *sangars* on the hillside above Vellore town.[20] Havildar Qazi Khan, speaking under promise of pardon, seconded Ramaswami's testimony, and added that Muiz-ud-Din had ordered Sayyid Hussain to take command of the fort and lead the attack on the outlying redoubts. Havildar Yusuf Khan, captured south of the Kaveri, and questioned at Trichinopoly, reported that the princes had sent the mutineers food and water during the rising.[21]

The Mixed Commission sifted through such testimony day after day in the steadily-rising heat of a Carnatic summer, their work slowed by the need to translate the depositions of Indian witnesses into English. It was apparent, by the beginning of August, that few hard facts were likely to emerge, leaving the Commission to make the best of fragmentary and contradictory testimony. There was scarcely a scrap of information before the Commission that was not contested by one party or another, while some suspects questioned by the British officials simply refused to divulge anything about the mutiny—apparently aware that silence regarding the entire affair was their best defence. The identity of the *mard-i-admiyan* who had consulted with the mutineers remained unknown for some time, but eventually one of the prisoners broke the oath of secrecy and named Jamal-ud-Din as the sepoys' main connection to the princes, and to Muiz-ud-Din in particular. The Commission strongly suspected that Muiz-ud-Din and his servants had known about the plans for mutiny, and had kept them from Marriott. Almost all of the testimony presented the mutiny as a premeditated action, but as one witness gave way to another, the Commission became increasingly confused about the cause of the rising, noting that it was 'not easy to calculate upon the motives which may have actuated a large body of men, composed of different castes, religions, and countries, and acting for a period of time sufficient to admit of new feelings and interest calculated to divert the original impression to a different object'. This left open the possibility that Muiz-ud-Din and his servants had co-opted the mutineers for their own benefit even if they had not been concerned with the original causes of the revolt, or even with the initial plot to capture the fort.[22]

Marriott's insistence upon the innocence of the princes was

supported by a number of witnesses, including sepoy sentries, Company *harkaras* who had been inside the palace during the mutiny, and the eunuchs of the princes' *zenanas.*[23] These observers explained that a crowd of mutineers had entered the *mahals*, uninvited, but had received no cooperation from the princes.[24] Several captured mutineers, however, contradicted these statements, depicting Muiz-ud-Din, in particular, as a willing participant in the rising. Indeed, these witnesses offered specific examples of instructions given to them by the prince during their battle for control of the fort.[25] Most of those who spoke for or against the princes, however, delivered carefully constructed depositions. Indeed, there is enough similarity among many of the depositions to suggest that several of the witnesses brought before the Commission may have been coached, perhaps by Marriott himself. He, as chief interrogator of the prisoners, certainly had both the motive and the opportunity for such tampering. Since many of the prisoners were initially confined together, however, it is not unreasonable to imagine that the conspirators also may have influenced what was said to the Commission. The words of Sepoy Shaikh Imam of the 1/1st Native Infantry, however, have the ring of truth about them. His description of the mutiny was not a scripted series of actions, but rather an impressionistic account of a fundamentally chaotic event. He vividly portrayed both the frustration of the mutineers, who could not convince the princes to take action, and the confusion of Muiz-ud-Din, who vacillated at the very doors of his *mahal*, unsure whether to go out and join the rebels, or to close the gates against them. In Shaikh Imam's account, the mutineers were driven by excitement and fear rather than by any particular plan; Muiz-ud-Din himself remained silent, although his body language displayed deeply torn feelings.[26]

The Mysore flag taken by HM 69th Foot as a trophy of the fight for the fort was the only scrap of material evidence connecting the princes with the mutiny. Everything about the flag, however, was immersed in mystery and contradictory testimony.[27] The Mixed Commission was shown the flag, which was believed to have been sold along with other war loot taken after the fall of Seringapatam, eventually finding its way into the hands of the princes via a Vellore merchant named Naoroji Parsi. The Commission remarked that the flag was 'an old one, bearing the late Sultan's insignia, a sun in the centre, with green tiger [*sic*] stripes on a red field'. Naoroji, however, denied ever having sold the princes a flag, or even the material with which to make a flag.[28]

The Commission's enquiries regarding Sayyid Hussain also ended in consternation. The son of a former Madras sepoy who had become one of Tipu Sultan's most beloved commanders, Sayyid Hussain proved a difficult suspect. He flatly denied every charge brought against him, and even framed his denials so as to suggest that Marriott and the other British commanders had been remiss in their duties! Unable to prove anything against Sayyid Hussain, the Commission dropped all charges against him.[29] Other palace servants of lower rank were accused of taking part in the rising, but while their confessions corroborated the charges, the Commission found no evidence that they acted with their masters' blessing.[30] Even the saddling of Muiz-ud-Din's horse appeared to be a mere coincidence. The prince's terrified *syce* had saddled the horse at the request of two sepoys, who had threatened to beat him if he did not do as they said.[31] When cross-examined, one mutineer, Qasim Ali, confessed that although he had 'seen' the princes and their servants take part in the uprising, he did not himself know what they looked like.[32]

When all available testimony is examined closely, it becomes clear that the handful of servants who joined the mutineers did so only after the sepoys' initial attacks on the British garrison. Not until three o'clock in the morning did Muiz-ud-Din's rebel followers leave the palace or enter the fort from the *pettah*. Two hours later, after the surviving British troops broke out of their besieged barracks and captured the Main Gate, these same individuals fled into the palace. There is no pattern to their individual movements, in fact, that cannot be explained by the physical ebb and flow of the battle for the fort. Ultimately, Jamal-ud-Din was persuaded only be the threat of condemnation to confess that he had negotiated with the mutineers on behalf of his master, Muiz-ud-Din.

As a result of Jamal-ud-Din's confession, the Mixed Commission eventually reassembled in Madras to investigate Marriott's conduct, but Bentinck made sure that the meeting was a mere formality. The palace servants arrested after the mutiny had been turned over to civil magistrates for trial, compelling the officers at Vellore to treat the prosecution of the sepoy prisoners as a court martial, in which only crimes of a strictly military nature could be discussed.[33] Thomas Oakes, who had succeeded James Strange, further pointed out that a proper investigation of the princes could not be carried out, as they were being transferred to a new place of exile in Bengal. Marriott himself did not testify before the reconvened Commission, as he was busy overseeing the arduous task of moving the princes. Instead, the Paymaster submitted a lengthy report regarding the security procedures of the Vellore garrison.[34] In his report for April 1806, which Marriott forwarded to the Commission, he had made it clear that although the princes were not exactly well behaved in captivity, they had not contemplated escape.[35] Marriott now took the opportunity to remind the Commission that none of the princes had been seen even to leave the palace during the eight hour period when the fort, for all practical purposes, was controlled by the mutineers; this fact vindicated his belief that the princes would do nothing that might endanger or dishonour their families.[36] Indeed, the Paymaster's report swayed Petrie's opinion, leading him to view the Vellore Mutiny as an event which must have had multiple causes.[37] Finding himself isolated, Cradock also was forced to adjust his opinions. The Commander-in-Chief was keenly aware, as were Agnew and Pierce, that with Marriott's exoneration and the departure of the princes for Bengal, the Mixed Commission's attention would return to the new turban, and to the policies of the Military Board. Cradock's subordinates had no intention of sharing responsibility for the Vellore Mutiny with their superior officer.

UNRAVELLING CONSPIRACY

As the enquiry progressed, it became apparent to the officers who interrogated the sepoy prisoners that the mutiny had originated as the project of a very small group of Indian soldiers and palace servants. Both evidence and testimony repeatedly pointed to the activities of certain key individuals. Under strongly-worded threats from the court of enquiry, suspected sepoys had quickly crumbled, divulging information about the conspiracy and those who had participated in it. Following these leads, the court isolated the ringleaders of the rising among hundreds of prisoners, producing a distinct, unusual group of sepoy mutineers. Very few sepoys at Vellore had been willing participants in the uprising. Some had taken advantage of the situation to run amok and loot their officers' bungalows, but most had only done their best to survive a nightmarish ordeal. The conspirators, far from finding themselves at the head of willing followers, had been compelled to force compliance through dire threats and physical violence.

During the mutiny, most of the Indian troops at Vellore had wandered around the fort, wondering what was happening, and what they should do next. Sepoy Ramru had fretted in his sentry box, pleading to anyone who would listen that he would be held accountable by his officers for the six rounds of ammunition in his pouch, and thus could not use them.[38] An old subadar had paced before the palace, demanding to know how the mutineers could have killed Colonel Fancourt, a married man with children.[39] Amid such surreal scenes—and the cross-fire of bloody skirmishes—a very small group of individuals had been dashing from one part of the fort to another, trying to organize the sepoys and take charge of the situation. From the first, they had compelled obedience through force. The Commission learned that sepoys had been kept silent prior to the mutiny by their non-commissioned officers, who threatened to retaliate against anyone who revealed the plot. A select group of *jamadars, havildars,* and naigues of the 1/1st and 2/23rd had taken steps to ensure that neither higher-ranking Indian officers nor British personnel would come to know of the conspiracy.[40] A band of tough enforcers among this clique of mutineers had taken drastic steps to persuade other sepoys to join them. Sepoy Venkatchellam, for instance, had been shot in the head and left for dead for refusing to help the insurgents remove powder from the magazine.[41] Other sepoys had followed, out of fear, but had escaped from the fort at the first opportunity.[42] The mutineers had overpowered not only their European officers, but also those Indian officers and soldiers who tried to stop them.[43]

Who composed this inner clique of mutineers? British officers at Vellore soon realized that they would gain access to the real causes of the mutiny if they could answer this question. Sepoy Grenadier Shaikh Nattar was the first conspirator to confess details of a deeply-laid plot, drawn out by a promise of pardon.[44] Much of what Nattar said was corroborated by Jamal-ud-Din, and further information was offered by Jamadar Shaikh Qasim, who voluntarily confessed even though he knew that cooperation would not alter the sentence of death already passed upon him.[45] The Commission thus came to learn about the conspiracy already described in detail in the previous chapter.

The mutineers' easy familiarity with the palace servants was explained, eventually, by the discovery that most of the inner clique of insurgents had served Tipu Sultan before 1799. Indeed, few of these men could be described as 'typical' sepoys. Sepoy Grenadier Muhammad Jafar, for instance, was the son of one of Muhammad Ali Wallajah's servants, who had been carried off to Mysore as a military slave in 1781. Serving in Tipu Sultan's artillery, Muhammad Jafar had attained the rank of *jamadar* by the time of the fall of Seringapatam. After the fall of the city, unemployed and penniless, he had been forced to join the Madras Army as a common sepoy in December 1801. Education and connections, however, assured Muhammad Jafar an unusual degree of influence in his corps. Captain John Coombs, adjutant of the 1/1st Native Infantry, reported that Muhammad Jafar tutored several young Muslim soldiers in the battalion, teaching Islamic theology and Arabic. Such soldiers—Muslim, literate, and former soldiers of Tipu Sultan—spent much of their free time in the company of the princes' *mard-i-admiyan*. As mentioned before, the small *dargah* attached to the tomb of Amin Pir, standing immediately outside the Main Gate of the fort, had served as a convenient meeting place for the conspirators, and was the one place in Vellore where Marriott's *harkaras* could not spy on them. One of those who frequented the *dargah* was Sepoy Jafar Beg, who had been one of Tipu Sultan's bodyguards. After the fall of Mysore, he had fought with Dundiya Waugh, and later had made his way to Hyderabad, where he joined a recruiting party of the 1/1st Native Infantry in September 1801.[46]

Desperate for men to serve in their depleted battalions, Madras Army officers usually did not ask questions about a sepoy recruit's origins, caste, or political leanings. Many British officers, in fact, did not believe sepoys capable of political behaviour. However, there were thousands of Tipu Sultan's former soldiers serving in the Madras Army by the summer of 1806—in addition to thousands of former *palegaru* peons and the discharged veterans of the French *corps de cipayes.* Most of those who were prominent participants in the Vellore Mutiny had been students or friends of Muhammad Jafar and Jafar Beg, and no less than six of them had fought for Tipu Sultan. Generally young men, they served in the elite companies of their corps—the light company or the grenadier company—companies to which men were assigned on the basis of merit rather than seniority. Sepoy Rahman Sahib, for instance, was noted as 'perfect at his drill', and an 'excellent soldier'.[47] He had served as a British officer's personal servant for several years before becoming a sepoy recruit. Sepoy Grenadier Shaikh Nattar had grown up as a European officer's orderly, yet before the mutiny he had volunteered to kill his battalion's commanding officer.[48] It is possible that such men may have had personal motivations to join the plot, for officers' servants were often treated with great cruelty, and General Orders forbidding physical assaults upon Indian servants by British officers were frequently repeated. Most British officers who had been cut down during the revolt were killed by members of this same small group of men who were veterans of Tipu Sultan's elite *paltans*; furthermore, these conspirators had marked certain unpopular officers for assassination well before the mutiny began.

Only one of the leaders of the mutiny was not a Muslim. Almost all the sepoys who risked their lives to save British soldiers and officers' wives during the mutiny were Hindus. This communal distinction, however, must be treated with caution, for the only sepoy who came forward prior to the mutiny to warn the British was Mustafa Beg, a Muslim.[49] Nevertheless, Lieutenant-Colonel Forbes and Adjutant Coombs, in their report on the causes of the mutiny, made much of the prominence of Muslims among the mutineers.[50] Blaming the revolt on a handful of disgruntled Muslims served three purposes. The idea of Muslim resentment of the recently-established Company Raj was understandable, and did not suggest long-term problems regarding the morale of the Madras Army or the policies of the civil administration. The Company, after all, had overthrown or subverted every Muslim court in South Asia with the sole exception of the minor emirates of Sind. Furthermore, viewing the Vellore Mutiny as a Muslim conspiracy supported Cradock's argument that the interests of the Mysore family had undermined the loyalty of the garrison. Finally, Muslim leadership of the rising 'proved' that Cradock's orders had not been the cause of the mutiny. Only Hindus, it was argued, could possibly object to the new turban on religious grounds, while Muslims were not likely to risk their lives to uphold 'Gentoo prejudice'. Forbes and Coombs concluded that the mutineers' motivations had been political—namely the hope of forming a new Muslim regime in south India under one of the princes of Mysore.[51]

The Mixed Commission noted, in their report of 9 August 1806, that it was only natural for Tipu Sultan's sons to take an interest, however slight, in activities that might have resulted in their liberation. The Vellore enquiries, however, did not reveal evidence sufficient to demonstrate that any of the princes, including Muiz-ud-Din, took an active part in the insurrection. The quixotic Muiz-ud-Din probably sympathized with the conspirators, but his refusal to join them openly indicates that he not unreasonably expected them to fail. Providing the rebel sepoys with food and water—even with a flag, if indeed he did so—constituted a very low level of commitment to the mutiny. What the rebels desired most—his open recognition and personal leadership—he wisely held back. Although viewed as something of a fool by Marriott, the young prince demonstrated considerable talent for survival on the night of the mutiny. Keeping his thoughts to himself under very trying circumstances, he probably saved his family. As for the palace servants captured under arms after the mutiny, it seems best to regard them as independent actors who hoped to achieve personal goals by throwing their master to the fore of a rebellion that he himself did not support. The British nevertheless decided to move the princes from Vellore to Calcutta. Safely exiled in Bengal, Tipu Sultan's sons would be too far away from Mysore to pose any sort of threat to the Raj or its allies.[52]

The goals of the Vellore insurgents had been at best vague. No practical preparations had been made by the mutineers to hold the fort in the event of their success. Indeed, some of the mutineers had taken up arms convinced that they would be killed.[53] Witnesses reported arguments about the reason for the mutiny among the insurgents themselves. For Muhammad Jafar and Jamal-ud-Din, of course, the rising had been a bid to restore the lost glory of Mysore. Sepoy Shaikh Ahmad, however, insisted that the mutiny was a response to the new turban. He pointed out that the men of the garrison had been threatened with ostracism by their caste elders if they wore the new *topi*, and that hundreds of men had been upset by such warnings. The men had agreed to 'go along' with the designs of Muhammad Jafar and his friends, but for them the liberation of the princes was a secondary goal.[54] A palace eunuch, meanwhile, recalled being told by a sepoy that 'the reason for the fight was . . . their being ordered to wear new turbans, which made them look like Christians'. The soldier added that they were fighting for their religion, and were responsible for their own actions—apparently meaning that the princes had nothing to do with the mutiny. Although fundamentally loyal to their officers, the sepoy explained, no soldier could obey the order to accept the new turban and retain his self-respect.[55] The majority of the sepoys at Vellore, however, did not support the mutineers. Yet, they had been powerless to halt the rising, for it had taken them—as it had taken the British—completely by surprise. Sepoy Grenadier Thandava Murti must have represented many of the hapless sepoys at Vellore on that fateful night. He had thought only of how the uprising reflected on his own character, dashing the achievements of a lifetime of military service. Overcome by these thoughts, he had crumbled to the floor of his sentry box, crying and shouting that he simply wanted to be a good sepoy and do his duty. When the dragoons burst into the fort, however, he had realized that he was indistinguishable from the real mutineers, and deserted his post in order to save his life.[56]

RUMOURS AND FALSE ALARMS

The General Order of Government that had been published in late July, informing the Army that the Vellore Mutiny was an isolated disturbance, must have sounded odd to many sepoys who heard summaries of the proclamation read at the head of their companies.[57] Far from reassuring the European officers, the General Order may have led some of them to view every sepoy, but especially the Muslim soldiers who composed such a substantial part of most battalions of the Madras Army, as a potential mutineer. Some British officers openly took precautions against mutiny. Captain James Welsh of the 1/3rd Native Infantry, an experienced officer, who ought to have been more discerning, interpreted the 'suspicious' behaviour of two Maravar sentries at Palaiyamkottai as the beginning of a mutiny.[58]

Recalling that a sepoy had told him that Maravars were a 'treacherous race', Welsh asked for and obtained permission to disarm and turn out of the service 161 Maravar sepoys of his battalion as a 'political as well as military measure'.[59] Welsh's actions were approved by the Governor-in-Council, but this merely reflected a sudden change in attitude occasioned by reports of unrest and suspicious activities at Wallajahbad and Hyderabad in late July.[60]

A few days after Welsh's panic at Palaiyamkottai on 22 July, the Madras Government's faith in its Army was shaken still further by reports of unrest at Wallajahbad Cantonment. After Lieutenant-Colonel Harcourt's departure for Vellore, command of the garrison passed to Lieutenant-Colonel Ross Lang. There were three sepoy units stationed at Wallajahbad: the 2/1st, 2/14th, and 1/23rd Native Infantry. Two of these units were sister battalions to those which had mutinied at Vellore.[61] Following morning parade on 25 July, Lieutenant Richard Crew, Adjutant of the 1/23rd, ordered the battalion to their barracks to clean their equipment—apparently forgetting that the men had not yet eaten breakfast. By noon, however, Crew realized his mistake and ordered the sepoys to be released from their barracks. By this time, however, the sepoys had grown angry, and milled through the lines in a 'tumultuous' manner. Some of the soldiers allegedly said that it would be better to kill such officers as Crew, even if it resulted in one's death, rather than serve as slaves for a paltry seven rupees a month.[62] When word of this was brought to the attention of Lieutenant-Colonel Lang, he quietly asked the battalion commanders to employ 'confidential persons' to spy on the troops—a measure that merely generated more alarming stories.[63]

Lang allowed himself to be misled by the information that he received from his 'confidential persons'. Every rumour of the cantonment bazar, every serving woman's report, was deemed worthy of attention and relayed to Choultry Plain by express *tappal*.[64] By 26 July, Lang was convinced that the Wallajahbad garrison was about to mutiny, and acting on his fears, he sent to Arcot for European troops, and ordered the 1/23rd to fall in, under arms, and march ten miles toward Poonamallee.[65] A wing of HM 19th Dragoons arrived at Wallajahbad on the morning of 28 July only to find the station perfectly quiet. Nevertheless, Gillespie assumed that the 1/23rd had intended to mutiny, and consequently marched the battalion back to its lines, where it was paraded before the assembled garrison and disarmed.[66] The non-commissioned officers of the battalion were arrested and confined, the sepoys placed under guard. Meanwhile, a court of enquiry sat to discuss the evidence against the men of the 1/23rd Native Infantry.[67]

Lieutenant-Colonel Lang's official summary of the Wallajahbad court of enquiry proceedings bore almost no relation to the circumstantial evidence and rumours divulged by the various witnesses. Lang merely confirmed Cradock's interpretation of the Vellore Mutiny. Some European officers sought to explain the behaviour of the 1/23rd on the basis of the battalion's composition, pointing out that the unit consisted of '[Kallans] and Southern [*palaiyakkars*] of noted enmity'. Close scrutiny of the muster rolls later revealed, however, that less than 10 per cent of the men of the battalion hailed from Tirunelveli, the seat of the 'Southern Poligars'.[68] William Petrie, examining the reports from Wallajahbad, urged the Council to proceed cautiously, pointing out that the sepoys of the 1/23rd had been neglected by their adjutant, who ought to have sent them to prepare their breakfast, and that Lang may have overreacted in the face of understandable grumbling.[69] Cradock, however, felt that the insubordination of the sepoys at Wallajahbad justified resuming the court martial proceedings against the Vellore mutineers, and he was now able to convince the Governor-in-Council to support him.[70] Thus within scarcely a week of publishing a General Order that defined the Vellore mutiny as an 'isolated incident', the Madras Government took steps that indicated a new assessment of the situation. The Vellore mutiny was now seen as a manifest symptom of an army-wide crisis. Letters were dispatched to Bengal, asking the Supreme Government to postpone the Secretary at War's order transferring HM 19th Dragoons and HM 94th Foot from south India to Europe.[71]

When Cradock went to Wallajahbad to investigate the incident there, however, he soon found that the whole affair had been misrepresented. After reviewing the court of enquiry proceedings, and conducting his own interviews, the Commander-in-Chief concluded that Lang and his subordinates had acted too hastily on the basis of spurious remarks made by uninformed residents of the cantonment bazar. Indian officers of the 1/23rd Native Infantry insisted that their men had been angry only because they had been hungry, and they offered to prove their loyalty to the Company by volunteering for overseas service.[72] In his report to Bentinck, Cradock nevertheless supported the idea that serious disaffection existed in the Wallajahbad garrison. Ignoring evidence to the contrary, he told the Governor that 'there may be some evil disposition among individuals', adding that the officers must have had good reason to suspect their sepoys of disloyalty, or else they would not have sent to Arcot for British troops.[73] At about this time, Cradock's suspicions seemed to be confirmed again by the arrival of news that a 'mutiny' had been narrowly averted at Hyderabad.

NOTES

1. BL/OIOC, GC (Governor-in-Council) to Thomas Brown, Acting Secretary to the GGC, 11 July 1806, *HMS*, V. 507, pp. 163-4; BL/OIOC, Bentinck to Colonel Harcourt, 11 July 1806, ibid., pp. 161-3.
2. For examples, see TNSA, Mrs. Potter's Testimony, *MSS*, V. 2-A, pp. 913-16; Charlotte Watter's Testimony, ibid., pp. 267-8.
3. BL/OIOC, Lt. Ewing's Testimony, 19 July 1806, V. 507, pp. 309-10.
4. UN, Marriott to Bentinck, 15 July 1806, Portland MS, PwJb/25, pp. 367-72; BL/OIOC, Proclamation by his Excellency, the Commander-in-Chief, 14 July 1806, *HMS*, V. 507, pp. 225-8.
5. BL/OIOC, Bentinck's Note in Secret Consultation, 12 July 1806, *HMS*, V. 507, p. 180; BL/OIOC, GC to Brown, 13 July 1806, ibid., pp. 190-1.
6. BL/OIOC, Petrie's Minute, 21 August 1806, *HMS*, V. 508, pp. 509-13.
7. BL/OIOC, GC to Major-General James Pater, et al., 12 July 1806, *HMS*, V. 507, pp. 181-2. This Mixed Commission commenced its proceedings on 21 July, concluding them on 9 August. The members of the Commission were: Major-General James Pater, Lieutenant-Colonel G. Dodsworth of HM 34th Foot, Senior Judge Nathaniel Webb, 2nd Judge of Circuit J.H.D. Ogilvie, and Major W. Dowse, a staff officer of the Military Department. James Leith, the Judge Advocate General, served as Secretary of the Commission, and was responsible for translating indigenous language testimony into English.
8. BL/OIOC, Cradock to Agnew, 15 July 1806, *HMS*, V. 507, pp. 233-6.
9. BL/OIOC, Harcourt and Gillespie to GC, 15 July 1806, *HMS*, V. 507, pp. 243-6. Encloses the report of the military court of enquiry.

10. BL/OIOC, Agnew to Commanding Officers, 17 July 1806, *HMS*, V. 507, pp. 371-2.
11. BL/OIOC, Cradock to GC, 15 July 1806, *HMS*, V. 507, pp. 239-43.
12. BL/OIOC, Cradock to GC, 18 July 1806, *HMS*, V. 507, pp. 322-3; BL/OIOC, GC to Cradock, 14 July 1806, *HMS*, V. 507, pp. 193-6. Signed, 'Bentinck, for Council'. This was one of the rare instances in which Bentinck issued an order without awaiting consultation with the Council. Bentinck claimed that he knew nothing about the new regulations regarding 'caste marks' and jewellery until this time.
13. BL/OIOC, GOG, 24 July 1806, *HMS*, V. 507, pp. 389-93.
14. BL/OIOC, Report of the Mixed Commission, 9 August 1806, *HMS*, V. 508, pp. 103-21; BL/OIOC, Petrie's Minute, 21 August 1806, *HMS*, V. 508, pp. 509-13.
15. TNSA, Mirza Chandmand Ali's Deposition, *MSS*, V. 2-A, pp. 951-3; BL/OIOC, Mirza Chandmand Ali's Testimony, 21 July 1806, *HMS*, V. 508, pp. 137-9.
16. BL/OIOC, Marriott's Testimony, 25 July 1806, *HMS*, V. 508, pp. 148-66.
17. TNSA, Proceedings of the Mixed Commission, 6 August 1806, *MSS*, V. 2-A, p. 987.
18. BL/OIOC, Sepoy Maniyappah's Deposition, *HMS*, V. 507, pp. 209-11.
19. Portland MS, PwJb/59, Second Report of Forbes and Coombs, Appendix 4, p. 4477. Sepoy Ramdu's recollection is significant, as Muhammad Jafar later was identified as one of the leaders of the mutiny.
20. BLK/OIOC, Sepoy Ramaswamy's Deposition, *HMS*, V. 508, pp. 190-2; also see *HMS*, V. 507, pp. 332-6.
21. TNSA, Confession of Havildar Yusuf Khan, *MSS*, V. 5, pp. 1183-9.
22. BL/OIOC, Report of the Mixed Commission, 9 August 1806, *HMS*, V. 508, pp. 103-21.
23. An interesting note on the eunuchs who served the princes' families may be found in John Shortt, 'The Kojahs of Southern India', *Journal of the Anthropological Institute of Great Britain and Ireland*, 2, 1873, pp. 402-7.
24. TNSA, Muhammad Martaba's Testimony, 5 August 1806, *MSS*, V. 2-A, pp. 978-86; Sepoy Murti's Testimony, ibid., pp. 921-4; Harkara Gurrappah's Testimony, ibid., pp. 905-8.
25. BL/OIOC, Sepoy Shaikh Ahmad's Testimony, *HMS*, V. 507, pp. 272-5; TNSA, Sepoy Ramjunny's Testimony, *MSS*, V. 2-A, pp. 1000-1; TNSA, Havildar Yusuf Khan's Confession, *MSP* (*Madras Secret Proceedings*), V. 5, pp. 1173-82.

26. TNSA, Sepoy Shaikh Imam's Testimony, *MSS*, V. 2-A, pp. 998-1000.
27. TNSA, Sepoy Grenadier Shaikh Nattar, *MSS*, V. 2-A, pp. 909-12; Sepoy Shaikh Imam's Deposition, ibid., pp. 998-1000; Sepoy Grenadier Ramru's Testimony, ibid., pp. 972-7; Ibrahim Syce's Testimony regarding the activities of Qadr Khan, muezzin to Muiz-ud-Din, ibid., pp. 924-5; Barber Puchan's Deposition, *MSP*, V. 5, pp. 1190-5.
28. BL/OIOC, Comments of the Mixed Commission and Naoroji Parsi's Testimony, *HMS*, V. 508, pp. 112-13.
29. TNSA, Sayyid Hussain's Testimony, *MSS*, V. 2-A, pp. 953-5. Sayyid Hussain was the son of Sayyid Ghafur, a former Madras Army sepoy, who had gone over to Tipu Sultan's service, and had risen to command the Mysorean artillery. Upon receiving news of Sayyid Ghafur's death, Tipu Sultan had rushed to the ramparts of his besieged capital, where he shortly met his own violent end at the hands of British troops.
30. BL/OIOC, Sepoy Bawa Singh's Testimony, *HMS*, V. 508, pp. 146, 193; BL/OIOC, Muhammad Hasif's Deposition, *HMS*, V. 507, pp. 283-6; BL/OIOC, Chumeen Khorah's Testimony, *HMS*, V. 507, pp. 282-3; Sepoy Allagurry's Testimony, ibid., pp. 276-81; TNSA, Qasim Ali's Testimony, *MSS*, V. 2-A, pp. 903-4; Qutb Shah's Testimony, ibid., pp. 987-8.
31. TNSA, Ibrahim Syce's Testimony, *MSS*, V. 2-A, pp. 924-5.
32. TNSA, Qasim Ali's Testimony, *MSS*, V. 2-A, p. 905.
33. BL/OIOC, Bentinck's Minute, 23 September 1806, *HMS*, V. 509, p. 377; BL/OIOC, Buchan to Special Commission, 26 September 1806, ibid., pp. 379-80.
34. Most of the documentation for chapter two is drawn from this report.
35. TNSA, Marriott's Report on the Family of Tipu Sultan, April 1806, *MSS*, V. 2-A, pp. 957-1067.
36. TNSA, Marriott's Testimony, 1 August 1806, *MSS*, V. 2-A, pp. 960-1.
37. BL/OIOC, Petrie's Minute, undated, *HMS*, V. 509, pp. 185-92. This minute was read in secret consultation on 12 September 1806.
38. TNSA, Sepoy Grenadier Ramru's Testimony, *MSS*, V. 2-A, pp. 972-7.
39. BL/OIOC, Havildar Taqir Muhammad's Testimony, *HMS*, V. 507, pp. 269-71.
40. TNSA, Havildar Yusuf Khan's Confession, *MSP*, V. 5, pp. 1183-9.
41. UN, Sepoy Venkatchellam's Testimony, Portland MS, PwJb/59, Appendix no. 29, pp. 4564-5.
42. BL/OIOC, Sepoy Ramaswamy's Testimony, *HMS*, V. 507, pp. 332-6.
43. BL/OIOC, Havildar Vendameli's Testimony, *HMS*, V. 507, pp. 356-8.
44. TNSA, Sepoy Ramjani's Testimony, *MSS*, V. 2-A, pp. 1000-1; Sepoy Shaikh Nattar's Testimony, ibid., pp. 1001-3.
45. UN, Jamal-ud-Din's Confession, Portland MS, PwJb/59, Appendix no.

12, pp. 4507-9; BL/OIOC, Jamadar Shaikh Qasim's Confession, *HMS*, V. 508, pp. 7-17.
46. UN, Second Report of Forbes and Coombs, Portland MS, PwJb/59, p. 4423.
47. Ibid., p. 4492.
48. Ibid., pp. 4493-6.
49. UN, Rustam Ali Shah's Deposition, Portland MS, PwJb/59, Appendix no. 2, pp. 4473-4; Longer Examination of Rustam Ali Shah, ibid., Appendix no. 28, pp. 4557-64.
50. UN, Second Report of Forbes and Coombs, Portland MS, PwJb/59, pp. 4403-22.
51. Ibid., pp. 4403-30.
52. Although a large part of the princes' extended families eventually joined them in Bengal, many of the women remained at Vellore, where they were joined, over the years, by other exiled royal families. Vellore fort remained a special place of captivity for toppled south Indian royalty until the late 19th century, when it began to be transformed into a political prison for arrested nationalists. After 1947, Vellore remained a maximum security prison, although part of the old palace became a police academy. Today, the fort houses a number of Tamil Tigers, and most of the area beyond the *maidan* is 'off limits' to the public.
53. BL/OIOC, Jamadar Shaikh Qasim's Confession, *HMS*, V. 508, pp. 7-17.
54. TNSA, Sepoy Shaikh Ahmad's Testimony, *MSS*, V. 2-A, pp. 919-21.
55. TNSA, Muhammad Martaba's Testimony, *MSS*, V. 2-A, pp. 978-86.
56. TNSA, Sepoy Grenadier Thandava Murti's Testimony, *MSS*, V. 2-A, pp. 925-6.
57. One of the duties of a battalion adjutant was to prepare a summary of General Orders, to be read before each company, as well as full-text translations in Persian, Urdu, Tamil, and Telugu, which were posted at battalion headquarters.
58. Welsh thought he had seen one of the sentries loading his musket and fixing his bayonet while on guard duty.
59. BL/OIOC, Dyce to Buchan, 23 July 1806, *HMS*, V. 507, pp. 600-1; Dyce to Assistant Adjutant-General at Trichinopoly, 23 July 1806, ibid., pp. 601-4; District Orders, 23 July 1806, ibid., p. 605; Welsh to Dyce, 23 July 1806, ibid., pp. 606-7; Welsh to Dyce, 23 July 1806, ibid., pp. 609-13. The order was approved by Lieutenant-Colonel Alexander Dyce, commanding officer of Tirunelveli District. Most of the Maravar sepoys dismissed from the service were new recruits.
60. BL/OIOC, Buchan to Dyce, 1 August 1806, *HMS*, V. 508, p. 2.
61. TNSA, *MMP*, Range 255, V. 73, pp. 4708-9. The 2/1st was commanded

by Major Joseph Hazelwood, the 2/14th by Major Paul Bose, and the 1/23rd by Lieutenant-Colonel Bowness.

62. BL/OIOC, Testimony of Catherine, 'servant maid to Mrs. Revere', and of Mrs. Revere, 'who speaks the Malabar language very fluently', 28 July 1806, *HMS*, V. 507, pp. 494-5. The circumstantial nature of this evidence has been discussed already in chapter one.
63. BL/OIOC, Bose to Lang, 25 July 1806, *HMS*, V. 507, pp. 587-8. These spies were employed in addition to the 'confidential men' already scattered among the troops. 'Confidential men' were trusted soldiers who provided officers with secret reports regarding the morale of the battalion. These individuals, representing every rank from sepoy to subadar, also formed the battalion *panchayat*, which handled minor disciplinary matters.
64. BL/OIOC, Lang to Cradock, 25 July 1806, *HMS*, V. 507, pp. 421-33.
65. BL/OIOC, Lang to Cradock, 26 July 1806, *HMS*, V. 507, pp. 433-6.
66. BL/OIOC, Gillespie to Cradock, 28 July 1806, *HMS*, V. 507, pp. 487-91.
67. BL/OIOC, TNSA, *MSP*, V. 19, pp. 1100-4, 1110-19; ibid., V. 20, pp. 1275-94.
68. BL/OIOC, Cradock's Interviews at Wallajahbad and Related Documents, *HMS*, V. 507, pp. 591-3. Of the 853 sepoys of the 1/23rd Native Infantry, 64 came from Tirunelveli, 671 from the Carnatic and Thanjavur, 72 from Guntur and the Northern Circars, 21 from Madurai and Dindigul, and the rest from outside the Presidency.
69. BL/OIOC, Petrie's Minute, 29 July 1806, *HMS*, V. 507, pp. 515-16.
70. BL/OIOC, Cradock's Minutes, 27 and 29 July 1806, *HMS*, V. 507, pp. 431, 481. The latter includes Gillespie's report to Cradock regarding the 1/23rd Native Infantry. Also see ibid., p. 441.
71. BL/OIOC, GC to GGC, 29 July 1806, *HMS*, V. 507, pp. 475-9.
72. BL/OIOC, Cradock's Report on Wallajahbad, *HMS*, V. 507, pp. 587-8.
73. BL/OIOC, Cradock to GC, 31 July 1806, *HMS*, V. 507, pp. 553-60.

5

Mysterious Disturbances in Hyderabad

Four hundred miles north of Vellore lay Hyderabad, capital of the Nizam's dominions and headquarters of a large Company subsidiary force in which a mysterious 'disturbance' occurred on 11 July 1806. The immediate significance of this disturbance was that it was reported three or four days before anyone in Hyderabad could have known about the Vellore Mutiny, suggesting some sort of wider anti-British conspiracy. The events at Hyderabad's Hussain Sagar Cantonment were also important because they indicated widespread and severe discontent in the Madras Army. However, the incidents in the Nizam's capital are a puzzle, for the available records obscure the events with oblique language and a fog of political rhetoric. Captain Hastings Fraser, in his well-known work, *Our Faithful Ally, the Nizam*, gives a detailed account of intrigues at the Nizam's court, but carefully avoids mentioning the anti-British stance of Sikandar Jah, the Nizam, or the odd convulsions of the Subsidiary Force, which the British Resident attributed to the work of agents of the Hyderabadi nobility.[1] Nevertheless, what happened in Hyderabad was more than a sideshow of the Vellore Mutiny. Indeed, viewed in the context of the Company's long-term diplomatic effort at the Nizam's court, the discontent of the Subsidiary Force acquires both coherence and even greater significance.[2]

The Hyderabad Subsidiary Force was the Madras Army's largest concentration of troops, consisting of HM 33rd Foot, two regular Madras cavalry regiments, six sepoy battalions, a train of field artillery, gun lascars, and pioneers—altogether over 9,000 men. In 1806, the strength of the garrison reflected the centrality of the Company's subsidiary alliance with Nizam Sikandar Jah. The subsidiary alliances with Mysore and Poona had been made possible, in part, by the previous Nizam's willingness to support British interests in south India. In turn, the treaties with Purnaiya (the *Diwan* of Mysore) and the Peshwa had been strengthened by older alliances between the Company and the Rajas of Cochin and Travancore. With the fall of Mysore, the attention of the British had been drawn to the northern Deccan. Strategically, the subsidiary forces stationed at Poona and Hyderabad established a forward line of defence against attacks by Holkar or Sindiah, and thus spared the Company's directly-administered territories from the dangers and ravages of war. Major John Malcolm, furthermore, noted that the maintenance of a subsidiary force at Hyderabad had a positive effect on the military labour market.

> The subsidiary corps which has been fixed some years at Hyderabad has many of the inhabitants of the Deckan in it, and they are a finer class of men than either those of the Carnatic or Mysore. By these corps being occasionally relieved, a Superior body of men will be gradually introduced into the Madras native army, and a provision will be made for the employment of great numbers of the most idle and . . . dangerous class of the inhabitants of the Country of the Subah of the Deckan.[3]

Nizam Ali Khan—toothless, bald, and paralytic—had signed the subsidiary alliance treaty with the Company in 1798, to the dismay of the Hyderabadi *paigah* nobility, who viewed the alliance with the British as yet another in a long line of European interventions in the affairs of the Deccan.[4] Prince Sikandar Jah, the heir apparent at the Asafiya court, had been the chief opponent of Nizam Ali Khan's alliance with the Company, and his cause had been seconded by his chief creditor, Raja Mahipat Ram, an important courtier and former *sheristidar* to the commander of the Corps Français de Raymond.[5] Aristu Jah, the Diwan who had negotiated the alliance with the British, had been feared and hated by many Hyderabadis, and his funeral procession in 1802 had been disrupted by a mob, which had pelted his corpse with rocks and shouted words of abuse.[6]

Many *sipahis* of the Corps Français de Raymond also had been dismayed by the subsidiary alliance treaty, as most of them had been disbanded as a result of it. In May 1800, two of these *sipahis* had tried to assassinate Major James Achilles Kirkpatrick, the British Resident. Kirkpatrick, a controversial figure, had not been able to imagine which of his enemies had sought his death. His marriage to Mir Alam's grand-niece, Khair-un-Nissa, has come down to the present as a romantic story of cross-cultural exchange in old Hyderabad, but at that time it was a great scandal. According to a special enquiry undertaken by the Madras Government, members of the Residency staff had known that a sexual relationship between Kirkpatrick and Khair-un-Nissa had begun before their marriage, while Mir Alam was leading the Nizam's contingent against Seringapatam in 1799.[7] The Nizam's courtiers also had known of the affair, of which the more traditional nobles disapproved. Rumours of the affair had even been bandied in the streets, and had been the stuff of ribald handbills put up around the Char Minar. In any event, the assassins had been captured by the Resident's escort, and had turned out to be discharged *sipahis* of the Corps de Raymond, but no other clues as to their intentions had been uncovered.

Sikandar Jah had taken his father's place on the *masnad* of Hyderabad on 11 August 1803, a few months after the opening of the Second Anglo-Maratha War, to which his father had committed 6,000 infantry and 9,000 cavalry under the terms of the alliance with the Company. Sikandar Jah had failed to raise the full number of troops promised, and those forces he had sent to join Wellesley's army had turned out to be a rag-tag mob who would have served the allied cause best by remaining in Hyderabad. In fact, while the Company's troops had been desperately engaged with the Marathas at Assaye on 23 September 1803, the Nizam's army, under the 'command' of Raja Mahipat Ram, had looted the British camp. After the battle, when Wellesley had sought permission to leave nearly one thousand of his wounded soldiers in hospital at Daulatabad, the *qiladar* of the place had refused to receive them. Elsewhere in the Nizam's dominions, *qiladars* had fired on passing British columns, or had refused to allow Company supply convoys to shelter from enemy raiders within the walls of their forts. Sir Arthur Wellesley had penned strongly-worded complaints to his elder brother, the Governor-General, and to Kirkpatrick, at Hyderabad, accusing Sikandar Jah of being either treacherous or dangerously incompetent.[8]

Kirkpatrick had conveyed in open *darbar*, the government's displeasure to the Nizam and on 9 January 1804, had compelled him to amend the subsidiary alliance treaty of 1798, adding a new clause that gave British troops access to all strongholds in time of war. When Aristu Jah died, only four months later, Kirkpatrick urged the Governor-General to secure the appointment of a pro-Company *diwan*, preferably Mir Alam, who long had been sympathetic to the Company's interests, and who furthermore was his wife's former guardian.[9] Sikandar Jah had agreed to appoint Mir Alam to be his new *diwan*, but he had made no secret of the fact that he personally favoured Raja Mahipat Ram. When the latter had returned from the Maratha War in October 1805, he had informed the Acting Resident, Captain Henry Russell, that he alone could reconcile the Nizam to the subsidiary alliance that so chaffed his pride. Not long afterward, Sikandar Jah had summoned the Resident to his palace and had insinuated that Mir Alam should be a mere figurehead *diwan*, while all real power should be held by Raja Mahipat Ram.[10]

Angered by these intrigues, Mir Alam had asked Captain Russell to intercede on his behalf and persuade the Nizam to order Raja Mahipat Ram to return to his newly-granted *jagir* of Berar. Sikandar Jah, however, had no desire to banish his favourite from court, and soon had begun to lobby the Resident to secure the government's approval of Raja Mahipat Ram's appointment as *peshkar*, or treasurer, a post that Mir Alam had hoped to give to his own son, Munir-ul-Mulk.[11] Russell himself did not consider Raja Mahipat Ram to be a potential threat to the Company Raj, but he had served at Hyderabad long enough, as Kirkpatrick's assistant, to be wary of securing too much power for a courtier who was so indifferent to British interests and so close to the Nizam.[12] The more Sikandar Jah had pressed the Resident to support his proposals, therefore, the more the Resident had thrown his weight—and that of the Government of India—behind Mir Alam. Meanwhile, Mir Alam himself had been busy mobilizing support by winning over Nizam Ali Khan's influential widows, Bakshi Begum and Tiniyat-un-Nissa Begum, as well as several important nobles who all had their own reasons not to trust Raja Mahipat Ram.[13]

Shortly after Captain Thomas Sydenham had become Resident on 3 January 1806, a political tempest had arisen at the Hyderabad *darbar*.[14] Mir Alam, through Bakshi Begum and *umara* friendly to his cause, had submitted a *wajid-ul-arz* to Sikandar Jah, demanding the Nizam's confidence and additional powers to appoint both the *peshkar* and a special minister for 'English Affairs'. Raja Mahipat Ram and his confederate, Ismail Yar Jang, had advised Sikandar Jah to alter the terms of the *wajid-ul-arz* in such a manner that its claims would be negated. They had argued that the British were the real authors of Mir Alam's demands, and that placating the *Diwan*, in this instance, would amount to an abrogation of sovereignty. Raja Mahipat Ram had urged Sikandar Jah to stand forth as the unquestionable political authority in Hyderabad, whose policies were not to be dictated by the Company's Resident. At the end of the day, however, the Nizam had been swayed by the advice of Umzat-ul-Mulk, a friend of Mir Alam, and he had signed the original *arz* presented by the *Diwan*. Encouraged by this turn of fortune, Mir Alam then had secured from the Nizam an order sending Raja Mahipat Ram off to Berar. Fearful now of losing all influence at court, Raja Mahipat Ram had turned to the Resident, asking how he might win the Company's approval. Sydenham had suggested that staying out of court intrigues and returning to Berar would be a good start, and that if he really sought to impress the British, he would reform the *silladari* horse and revenue-collection arrangements in that unhappy province.[15] Deflated, Raja Mahipat Ram had retired from Hyderabad to his *jagir*, and Raja Chandu Lal—the Resident's choice—had been appointed *peshkar*.[16]

Sydenham had sent the following report—a rather misleading one—to Bentinck in April:

> At Hyderabad everything remains quiet, and the Nizam evinces the greatest satisfaction at the changes which have lately taken place at that Court. The Pindaries have been entirely expelled from Berar without the interference of the British force stationed in that province.[17]

The officers and men of the 11th Native Infantry would have been astonished by the Resident's confident report. Both battalions of the regiment had been serving with the Hyderabad Subsidiary Force since 1798, and during that time they had been on active service almost continually. After taking part in the last war with Tipu Sultan, the 2/11th Native Infantry had marched to the Raichur Doab to join the operations against Dundiya Waugh.[18] After a brief rest in Hyderabad, the corps had marched again, in the summer of 1803, to join Wellesley's army just prior to the Battle of Assaye.[19] Finally, in

January 1804, both battalions had proceeded to Berar, under Lieutenant-Colonel Ross Lang, to drive out parties of Maratha cavalry who had been ravaging the countryside. When this mission had been accomplished—more or less, for Pindari horse had a way of vanishing, only to return again—the 1/11th Native Infantry had joined the field force in Khandesh, participating in several perilous assaults.[20] The 2/11th, meanwhile, had detached two companies to escort Acting Resident Robert Jenkins to the court of Sindiah. This escort, after joining the Maharajah's camp, had been mobbed by riotous Maratha cavalry on 27 December 1804, and had lost several men before forming square around the Acting Resident's tent, and driving off their assailants with disciplined volley fire.[21] Both battalions were together again, in April 1805, for an attack on Fattehpur, and had returned to Hussain Sagar Cantonment, at Hyderabad, at the end of the spring of 1806, much in need of rest and replacements.[22] At that time, Lieutenant-Colonel Ross Lang had departed to take charge of Wallajahbad, and Colonel Thomas G. Montresor, a King's officer, had arrived from Malabar to assume command of the Subsidiary Force.

'AN UNCOMMON DISTURBANCE AND UPROAR . . . '

On the night of 11 July 1806, several British officers of the 2/11th Native Infantry reported to Colonel Montresor that their sepoys were acting strangely, having been stirred into a passion by irrational fears. Montresor himself consequently sent the following explanation to Sydenham:

> . . . That there was an idea among the troops that it was the intention of Government to force them to relinquish everything that distinguishes one caste from another, and by degrees to convert them to Christianity; that they also suspected the Europeans intended to massacre the native troops. There were several other alarms and ridiculous reports of Europeans being about to make an human sacrifice, but however ridiculous these reports were, they evidently worked in a great degree upon the minds of the natives. At first I could scarcely credit what appeared to me so absurd, but I soon learnt that a very general alarm did prevail, and officers were warned by people attached to them not to venture out.[23]

In their original reports to Montresor, the officers of the 2/11th Native Infantry also complained that their men had served under difficult conditions for many years, and furthermore had suffered a significant loss of pay due to the need to exchange Star Pagodas for Hyderabadi rupees. The sepoys themselves expressed their feelings more openly the next day, thronging the cantonment bazaar, the men of the 11th Native Infantry, in particular, 'shew[ing] . . . a mutinous disposition'. Some of the sepoys who participated in the protest had been under arms, which meant either that sentries had walked from their posts to join their comrades, or that the troops had taken muskets from their battalion bell-of-arms without permission.[24]

Another riotous assembly, described as 'an uncommon disturbance and uproar', occurred that evening, at about eight o'clock, behind the sepoy lines. Montresor ordered his aide-de-camp to turn out the picquet at the Main Guard and block the Cantonment Road, and later sent more troops into the lines to quell the disturbance that had been reported. How this happened is not known; nor is it clear, from Montresor's report, exactly what sort of assembly had been broken up. In his report, however, the commander of the Subsidiary Force stated that the disturbance had been some sort of military protest against the new turban.

The next day the natives seemed all convinced that they had been alarmed without cause, and at present I believe there is little or no jealousy entertained relative to the Europeans, which change of sentiment, in a few days, may be imputed to the native troops having had meetings of their own, and being now confident in their numbers. . . . In the 2nd Battalion 15th N.I. the men publicly declare their fixed resolution never to submit to wear [the new turbans], and every other corps is without doubt decidedly of the same opinion. I have endeavored to learn what dependence I could have upon any corps, in case of a sudden rising. I am sorry to add no confidence is to be placed in any. The reports from Lieutenant-Colonel Doveton of the 3rd Native Cavalry, whose information is to be depended on, are clear as to what may be expected from the cavalry. They saw they will never draw their sword[s] in suppressing a riot occasioned by persevering in causing the new turband [*sic*], or hats as they call them, to be worn. It therefore is evident that a very serious disturbance must ensue if that is attempted. . . .[25]

What seemed even more ominous than the manifest discontent of the troops, however, was a report that an *amir* at the Nizam's court, Raja Rao Rambha, sent his son to Hussain Sagar on 11 July, mounted on an elephant and accompanied by armed followers. He was said to have spent the afternoon at a merchant's *dukan* in the Cantonment Bazar. Some of Nur-ul-Umara's household troops also entered the Cantonment, and when challenged by sentries, declared that they were out hunting and were lost.[26] The *prima facie* evidence, to British observers suspicious of the Hyderabadi nobility, suggested some sort of collusion between mutinous sepoys and elements at the Nizam's court who were opposed to the subsidiary alliance.

Montresor's options were limited. He could employ his European corps to overawe the sepoys, of course, but British soldiers were not sent to India, in the early nineteenth century, to guard against the mutiny of Indian troops. On the contrary, the Government of India's established policy was to discourage the use of European forces against sepoys unless the latter already were in open mutiny. It was thought, with some justification, that any clash between British troops and sepoys would erode the latter's confidence in the government. Indeed, Montresor himself was fully aware that drastic action might precipitate an open confrontation—which, at Hyderabad, was to be avoided at all costs, as it might prove fatal to British prestige at the Nizam's court. Montresor thus sought to remove every possible source of misunderstanding, and when detailed reports of the Vellore mutiny finally reached him, he tried to win over the two cavalry regiments of the Subsidiary Force with parade ground speeches about the loyalty shown by the sowars of the 7th Native Cavalry.[27] The sepoys, however, did not relish standing in the heat, listening to Montresor laud those who had cut down the Vellore mutineers. Indeed, after the parade, the native officers told their British commanders that the anger of their men was 'hourly increasing'.[28]

Captain Sydenham sent express riders to Nagpur and Poona to warn the Residents in those cities about the Vellore mutiny and the unrest among the troops at Hyderabad. He himself went to see Mir Alam in an effort to quell the many rumours that had begun to circulate in the city's bazars.[29] The *Diwan* 'appeared surprised and shocked' by Sydenham's 'official' version of the events at Vellore, but he congratulated the Resident on the Company's swift recovery of the fort, and that evening took the matter before the Nizam. Sydenham and Montresor, meanwhile, decided they had to act quickly, on their own initiative, to avert a crisis, there being no time to await instructions from either Calcutta or Madras.[30] Montresor sent a note to the Resident, suggesting that 'in this critical state of affairs', it would be best to 'do away [with] everything that may be deemed a just, or at least a general cause of complaint'.[31] Sydenham agreed, and in his reply underscored the important military and diplomatic role of the Subsidiary Force. Were the military strength of the contingent seen to be weak, as a result of discontent and the mutinous behaviour of the Indian troops, the strategic position of the British in the Deccan would be undermined, and the authority of the Resident with it.[32] Accordingly, Montresor assembled the entire Subsidiary Force for a grand parade, at which he formally rescinded the order to adopt the new pattern of turban, as well as the 'objectionable' new regulations regarding *vibhuti* and ornaments.[33] He concluded his speech to the troops by stressing that the Company harboured no designs against anyone's religion or caste, and when he was finished, sullen grumbling gave way to spontaneous and genuine cheers—a rather unusual occurrence in the Madras Army. The sepoys, apparently, were overcome with relief. For them, the crisis had passed, and they had won the day.[34]

SYDENHAM CHALLENGES THE UMARA

Captain Sydenham was convinced that the new turban and regulations were the main causes of the disturbances that had occurred in the Subsidiary Force, but he was not prepared to rule out the possibility that powerful *umara* at the Nizam's court may have been toying with the sepoys' morale. Spreading rumors in the bazars was an old and rather potent political tactic in Hyderabad, with its large and rather riot-prone population, large numbers of whom were connected with the Nizam's government in one way or another. Also, as had happened at Vellore, local people had told the sepoys of the Subsidiary Force that they would not 'associate or intermarry' with them if they should 'conform to the habits and dress of Europeans'. Sydenham's dilemma, however, was that there were so many enemies of the Company around Sikandar Jah that it was impossible to fix on a single culprit—and extremely dangerous to lay a blanket charge.

There are doubtless thousands of turbulent persons in or about Hyderabad who would gladly cooperate in such an insurrection, and would join the standard of any Nobleman sufficiently aspiring and audacious to become their leader. Men of this description would not be wanting at this Court, of sufficient rank and consequence to shake the power of the reigning Prince to its very foundation, and perhaps such a leader might be found in the family itself of His Highness. It is probable that [Fariddun Jah] would require no better opportunity of aspiring to the [masnad], and there can scarcely exist a doubt that he would be joined by the most respectable part of the nobility and nearly the whole of the Nizam's army.[35]

When the disturbances in the Subsidiary Force first had been reported to Sydenham, he already had begun a discreet investigation, through his escort commander, Major Hemmings, into the desertion of several sepoys. He had become convinced that Raja Rao Rambha and Nur-ul-Umara were enticing the Company's troops to leave their posts and enlist in their own household guard—possibly with the connivance of Bakshi Begam. Sydenham suddenly decided that these two *umara* also must be behind the disturbances in the Subsidiary Force, and after only a few days' investigation, presented Mir Alam with 'proof' of the nobles' treachery.[36] At first, Mir Alam pretended to be unaware of the discontent of the Subsidiary Force, but when Sydenham insisted that calm had been restored, he subtly let the Resident know that he was well-informed of the anxiety of the Company's troops, who he described as being 'in despair'—using the Urdu phrase *be-dil aur lechar*—regarding the new turban. Mir Alam expressed amazement that the British, with all their years of Indian experience, could have introduced such a 'perilous' innovation. Sydenham assured the Diwan that the Company had meant no harm, and Mir Alam accepted his assurances, but pointed out that sepoys were not men of reason, but simple sons of the soil and inclined to be swayed by deep-rooted feelings, especially regarding any matter touching dress or *mamul* (custom). Mir Alam remarked that although the British thought their sepoys might fight better if they looked like European soldiers, 'courage resides in the breast, and not in dress'. The Diwan thought that the rescinding of the turban and the new regulations had been a clever ploy, one that would win over the sepoys, but warned Sydenham that the pursuit of any accusations against members of the nobility might be seen as an affront to the Asafiya dynasty. Nevertheless, Mir Alam promised Sydenham to help him make a very quiet and secret investigation of both the disturbance in the sepoy lines and those *umara* who might have been connected with it.[37]

Both Mir Alam and Captain Sydenham conferred with the *peshkar*, Chandu Lal, whose spies kept the Diwan well-informed regarding the secret affairs of the court, the city, and the neighbouring cantonment. In Mir Alam's estimation, Raja Rao Rambha was a 'weak and rash' individual, known for his anti-British stance, and according to the spies' reports, he had opened a suspicious correspondence with the Maratha leaders Holkar and Sindiah. However, the substance of Raja Rao Rambha's dealings with the Marathas was not known. In any event, Mir Alam considered Nur-ul-Umara to be the most dangerous of the Nizam's courtiers. The feisty Nur-ul-Umara did not hide his hatred of the British behind a mask of acquiescence. Indeed, he had been frequently heard to remark that he could—with proper support—drive the British from the Deccan. It was well known at court that Nur-ul-Umara was a desperate character, who twice had offered to murder his former patron, Azim-ul-Umara. Mir Alam and Chandu Lal both agreed that of all the Nizam's courtiers, Nur-ul-Umara was also the most useless, holding a *jagir* worth twenty-five lakh rupees a year, yet maintaining only fifty *sowars* for the Nizam's houschold cavalry.[38]

Sydenham's evidence against Nur-ul-Umara, however, was merely a story gleaned from a deserter who had been returned to the Subsidiary Force. According to the deserter, Nur-ul-Umara's *jamadar* had recruited some twenty sepoys of the Company's battalions with offers of higher pay and promotion. A *naigue*, for instance, claimed that the *jamadar* approached him one day, offering to make him a *subadar*, on 100 rupees a month, if he could convince one hundred sepoys to desert with their arms and equipment. Sydenham himself had traced only four deserters who were known to have enlisted in Nur-ul-Umara's household forces, but he assured Mir Alam that the *amir* had given the other men new names when he had entered them in the *arz-o-chehra* of his *paltan*.[39] Mir Alam and Chandu Lal probably realized that Sydenham's 'evidence' was mainly conjecture, but they had their own reasons to diminish the anti-British faction at court, and consequently asked Sikandar Jah to arrest Raja Rao Rambha and banish Nur-ul-Umara from the capital. The Nizam was visibly shaken by these requests, as well as by reports he had heard of the unrest in the Company's army; he feared what might happen if he compounded people's fears by seeming to purge his nobles under pressure from the British Resident. Any noble who thought he was likely to be arrested would fly to his *jagir* and raise an army, no doubt seeking aid from the Marathas to even the odds. Mir Alam and Chandu Lal, however, suggested that Raja Rao Rambha be captured by subtle means. They proposed that the Nizam invite him on a hunting expedition, out toward the old, sprawling hill fort of Golkonda, where he could be seized suddenly and conveyed directly to the royal dungeons.[40] The Nizam agreed to this plan, but was unhappy with such trickery. As soon as the *Diwan* and the *peshkar* departed, Sikandar Jah ordered Amzud-ul-Mulk to assemble all of the *paigah* and their troops, some two thousand men. The nobles moved from their suburban villas into the palace, while their household troops patrolled the surrounding streets and the environs of the Char Minar. Sydenham was shocked to see such a demonstration, but Mir Alam cautioned him against lodging formal complaints, for the Nizam was alarmed, and felt that a strong guard was necessary for his own safety.[41]

In fact, Sikandar Jah was just as concerned about rebellious nobles as he was about the machinations of the British Resident. The Nizam decided that Raja Rao Rambha and his family possessed 'claims' on the Asafiya dynasty that could not be overlooked. Mir Alam and Chandu Lal were informed that Raja Rao Rambha was not to be insulted by being summarily arrested, but ought to be ordered, discreetly, to retire to his *jagir*. Nur-ul-Umara, however, was an adventurer who could be turned out of the kingdom without a second thought. Nevertheless, Sikandar Jah called Sydenham to his *darbar* to ask him to explain his case against the two noblemen. The Nizam's question put the Resident in a difficult situation, since none of his information—spurious to begin with—was corroborated or verified by any other source. However, Mir Alam, quoting the Maratha statesman, Nana Farnavis, said: 'Matters of state (*raj karan*) [are] not [to] be settled by a *panchayat*'.[42] The *Diwan* insisted that they must act swiftly, and thus take the conspirators by surprise, before they could raise a revolt. Sikandar Jah, for the moment, gave in to this united effort on the part of Mir Alam and the Resident. The very next day, he announced his decrees to the assembled courtiers: Raja Rao Rambha was to leave Hyderabad and return to his *samasthanam.* Nur-ul-Umara's *jagir* was to be sequestered, and he himself was warned to quit the Nizam's dominions without delay. Finally, the *paigah* were instructed to send their household troops out of the city, the 'crisis' having passed.[43]

SYDENHAM AND MONTRESOR INVESTIGATE THE DISTURBANCES IN THE SEPOY LINES

Sydenham made no mention of his diplomatic activities in his first report to Bentinck, merely remarking that order had been restored at Hussain Sagar Cantonment, while rumours had subsided in the bazars of Hyderabad.[44] Only in mid-August did the Resident inform the Madras Government that he believed native officers of the Subsidiary Force to be involved in a conspiracy with some of the Nizam's courtiers.[45] By this time, however, the Governor-in-Council had instructed Colonel Montresor to investigate whether or not Tipu Sultan's sons had fomented the mysterious disturbances in the sepoy battalions at Hyderabad.[46] Meanwhile, the Supreme Government had given provisional approval of the steps that Sydenham and Montresor had taken to reassure the Indian troops of the Subsidiary Force, thus indicating, in a subtle manner, their as yet undeclared view that Cradock's new turban and regulations were the main causes of the Vellore crisis.[47]

Between 24 July and 9 August 1806, Sydenham investigated the possibility that there had been treasonable contact between the Nizam's subjects and inhabitants of the Cantonment.[48] Montresor, meanwhile, gathered information about the extent of disaffection among his troops, relying on his own spies as well as the confidential men of each battalion. The Resident's enquiry began with the interrogation of five men arrested in connection with an alleged plot to rescue Prince Fariddun Jah from his 'restraint' at the fortress of Golkonda. Two of the men, Narasingha Rao and Degambara Rao, were *mutassadies*, or petty officials of the local revenue establishment. A third, Mansurah, was a cantonment *bania*, and the remaining two prisoners, Venkatirayulu and Kottanayaka, were British officers' servants. According to the practice already well-established for such cases, the two *mutassadies* were handed over to the *Diwan*, who imprisoned them in Golkonda. The others were detained at the Residency, tried under Company law, and deported to Madras.[49] Sydenham questioned the prisoners four times, and on the basis of their testimony arrested two more individuals. One of these, Hub-bub-ullah, was a former sepoy of the 2/9th Native Infantry, who had become a servant of Raja Rao Rambha.[50] The other man arrested was Shaikh Tipu, formerly a servant of Captain Johnson, but now a cantonment *bania*. Sydenham obtained no useful information from either of these men, but the very act of interrogating prisoners seemed to increase the Resident's conviction that a terrible plot would be revealed. In his official report of his 'findings', Sydenham pointed out that Hyderabad was an extensive city, with straggling suburbs that intermingled with the Hussain Sagar Cantonment. People were constantly passing back and forth between the city and the cantonment, and therefore the possibilities for seditious activity were legion.[51]

Montresor, meanwhile, seized four native officers of the Subsidiary Force who he considered to be 'ringleaders'. Three of these men were subadars of the 1/15th Native Infantry—Sidi Hussain, Qadi Beg, and Umar Ali. The fourth suspect was Subadar Shaikh Sultan of the 2/11th Native Infantry.[52] Montresor considered Sidi Hussain and Qadi Beg to be those most deeply implicated in the recent disturbances, but he noted that the sepoys of the 11th Native Infantry had been particularly reticent and uncooperative during his investigation.[53] Sydenham thought the Subsidiary Force commander should arrest every sepoy suspected of treason, sending them all to Fort St. George for a general court martial. The Resident insisted that those found guilty deserved life imprisonment at the very least. However, at no point in his tirade did Sydenham specifically state what it was the sepoys had done to warrant such harsh punishment.[54] In any case Montresor did not concur with Sydenham. He explained that the Resident's scheme exceeded his authority, and was perhaps too severe. Montresor added that it was not even practical to arrest all of the disaffected native officers and sepoys, implying that to do so would decimate his command. At the most, the 'ringleaders' could be sent to Masulipatam to await the Council's decision regarding their fate.[55]

Both Sydenham and Montresor, in their reports to Calcutta and Madras, remarked that no material evidence or testimony had been revealed, yet, corroborating their opinions regarding the guilt of the above individuals. Indeed, the charges against their prisoners amounted only to a perceived pattern of suspicious behaviour. Nothing whatsoever had been turned up to suggest a connection between the Vellore mutiny and the disturbances at Hyderabad.[56] Nevertheless, when the Governor-in-Council received the above reports, Montresor's plan to send the 'ringleaders' to Masulipatam was approved.[57] By mid-August, Montresor's investigation had progressed further, but his evidence merely confirmed earlier opinions that the sepoys of the Subsidiary Force had legitimate grievances. In his report of 17 August, he explained that the 'conspiracy' in the sepoy battalions had been confined to a small group of native officers, mostly Muslims, who had employed a 'system of terror' to induce others either to support their scheme, or to remain silent about it.[58] Sydenham did not forward a detailed report to the government until 22 August, but for the first time he provided his superiors with a substantial analysis of the situation in Hyderabad. The Resident divided the causes of the sepoys' unrest into three broad categories: (1) the new turbans and regulations, (2) service conditions unique to the Subsidiary Force, and (3) local orders issued by Lieutenant-Colonels Elliott and Ross Lang while they had been in command of the garrison between March and June 1806.[59]

Sydenham felt that the new turban, both in shape and appearance, must have looked very much like a *topi* to 'ignorant and credulous natives'. Indeed, following Montresor's order rescinding the new turban and regulations, several Hindu sepoys had performed ceremonies giving thanks 'for having escaped the choice between 'the sacrifice of their faith and insurrection against the Company's Government'.[60] The peculiar service conditions of the Subsidiary Force, meanwhile, had long been a subject of correspondence between the officers of the garrison and the Madras authorities. Since 1798, the Governor-in-Council had repeatedly read reports regarding the substantial financial loss suffered by sepoys, in both Hyderabad and the Circars, due to the unfavourable exchange rates between Star Pagodas and local currencies. Sydenham's final category of the causes of sepoy discontent focused on two unpopular local orders and Cradock's general demand that native infantry regiments display better discipline, emphasizing strict adherence to military regulations and uniformity of appearance. On 20 June, a General Order had been sent out from Choultry Plain, enjoining all commanders of sepoy battalions to drill their troops intensively, and to increase the number of inspections.[61]

Shortly after the 11th Native Infantry returned to Hyderabad from their recent operations in Berar, new standing garrison orders had been issued by Lieutenant-Colonel Elliott. Sepoys were ordered to remain at their posts throughout their watches, and to turn out for roll call every hour.[62] More specifically, the soldiers were not allowed to leave their posts even to urinate or defecate; for high caste Hindu sepoys, this meant running the risk of pollution, for guard posts usually were very public places, without either water or clean earth. Another of Elliott's orders banned the use of tom-toms in the Cantonment—a provision that made it impossible for sepoys to celebrate weddings, religious festivals, and funerals according to established custom. As a result of the new emphasis on the turn-out of the battalions, sepoys also were forced to spend many tedious hours cleaning their equipment, or sending their uniforms to be laundered, at no small expense. After years of active service in the field, most sepoys at Hyderabad probably had become lax about matters of 'interior economy', and resented suddenly being ordered into a spit-and-polish mode by officers who, only a few weeks before, had been content to overlook irregularities. In fact, many sepoys could not keep up with the new pace of drills and inspections, and several men were summarily dismissed—a severe blow to the cohesion of their platoons and companies.[63]

Sydenham felt that most sepoys would have shrugged away the above orders as a temporary nuisance if their impact had not been felt in a wider context of strange and provocative rumors.

> It was generally reported, and believed, both in the Cantonment and the City, that an oracle from one of the neighbouring pagodas, had revealed to some favoured person the existence of considerable treasure in the bottom of the well in the European Barrack, which treasure, however, would not be discovered until a certain number of human heads had been sacrificed to the titular Deity of the well. The Europeans were, of course, to be employed in waylaying persons by night to cut off the number of heads necessary to the discovery of the treasure. A man who was about that time found dead

near the Residency, without his head, and an unfortunate accident, by which a drunken European artilleryman wounded a native sentry, so completely confirmed the absurd rumor that scarcely any native could be prevailed upon to leave his house at night. The workmen at the Residency, and at [Mir Alam's] buildings, would not work after four o'clock in the evening, and it was seriously reported, both to [Mir Alam] and to His Highness the Nizam, that a hundred bodies without heads were laying along the banks of the [Musi] River. At one time it was reported that the Europeans had built a church, which . . . required a sacrifice of human heads to sanctify. At another time it was given out that the Europeans would be ordered to massacre all the natives, excepting those who should erect the sign of the cross on the doors of their dwellings. These, and several other reports, equally monstrous, were industriously circulated, and produced the most distressing alarm amongst all ranks of natives.[64]

Sydenham was convinced that these stories served sinister purposes, angering and also scaring sepoys. Hiding in their lines from occult murderers, the troops did not witness the exchange of 'secret agents' between the city and the cantonment. It seems odd that so many men, hardened by war, who had risked their lives only recently against shot and shell, dreaded the supernatural and demonic more than a visible, material, and entirely human threat. In any event, the sepoys of the Subsidiary Force perceived a 'systematick design to force them to receive the Christian faith'. Sydenham remarked that the troops had been loyal before the receipt of Cradock's new directives, and that the Company's enemies had been able to build their rumours of forced conversion to Christianity on those 'obnoxious orders'.[65]

THE COMPANY'S SEPOYS AND THE HYDERABADI UMARA

At the end of August, Sydenham wrote to the Supreme Government in Bengal, offering additional 'information' regarding the disturbances at Hyderabad. He claimed, in his report, that 'every improper kind of intercourse' existed between the sepoys of the Nizam's guard of honour and 'persons about the court'. Although the guard of honour was commanded by a European officer, the small details of sepoys assigned to accompany Sikandar Jah and his sons all were led by native officers. Both the officers and the men of these details were on friendly terms with a variety of people in the city, and many of them had taken an interest in local politics. According to Sydenham, the Nizam's courtiers encouraged the sepoys to become political actors in their own right.

They were treated with considerable and unusual familiarity by Moors in a much higher condition in life than themselves in the bazars, in drinking houses, and in brothels; they became very intimate with some of the most licentious and turbulent characters in the city. The native officers and men were occasionally fed and entertained, either by the Princes over whom they were placed on duty, or by persons of rank in the neighbourhood of the Princes' dwellings. As their tour of duty lasted a week, and as that tour frequently recurred, the men had time to improve the acquaintances which they at first casually established. They had leisure to compare the severity of their discipline with the liberty and licentiousness of the Nizam's troops, and they became naturally liable to the impressions produced by such vicious examples. As the characters, pretensions, and views of every principle person at the capital are freely discussed in the city, the sepoys became gradually acquainted with all those topics, and acquired a very dangerous species of knowledge, while there is reason to fear that some of them, and especially the Musselmans [*sic*], found their attachment to the British Government and their obedience to the regular discipline of the service to be shaken by the example and insinuations of their vicious associates.[66]

Wary of this high degree of fraternization between the people of Hyderabad and their Indian troops, British commanders had withdrawn the honour guards protecting the Nizam and his sons. However, Sydenham assumed that many native officers and sepoys who had served on such details carried on their friendships with the *umara*, entering the city while off duty, 'without their regimentals'. This supposition, however, was conjured from a simple report that, some time around 5 or 6 July 1806, Raja Rao Rambha had made a recruitment offer to the Company's sepoys.[67]

Sydenham's information about Raja Rao Rambha had been provided by a deserter, unnamed in his report, who was apprehended by Major Hemmings—the same individual whose testimony had led to the arrest of Sidi Hussain, Qadir Beg, and other native officers of the 15th Native Infantry, who allegedly were the Raja's contacts in the Cantonment. A *naigue* corroborated the deserter's tale, but added that no one had seen Raja Rao Rambha's agents, as they moved in secrecy. Later, however, the *naigue* added that a woman who 'frequented' the lines of the 15th Native Infantry had told him that she knew all about the communications between the *umara* and the sepoys of the Subsidiary Force. Sydenham's efforts to locate this woman, however, were in vain; tipped off, perhaps, she stopped visiting the sepoy lines. In pursuing these leads, however, the Resident learned that Raja Rao Rambha's 'adopted and favourite son', Imam Muhyi-ud-Din Khan, had been slipping into the Cantonment at night, unattended. Indeed, Sydenham's *harkaras* claimed to have seen the young man, but as he was on horseback, and they on foot, he was able to gallop away. The Resident tried to lay a trap for Imam Muhyi-ud-Din Khan, but he, too, seemed to have heard that a 'secret' investigation was being made. Perhaps he also had heard a rumour that the Nizam had decided to banish his father from the city.[68]

Sydenham's reports to his superiors invariably follow the same pattern. They begin with a kernel of dubious information—usually some obscure court gossip, or a bazar rumour. Sydenham extrapolates this kernel of information into a dangerous conspiracy aimed at the destruction of British influence in the Deccan. Finally, at the end of his reports, the Resident admits that his analysis rests on no substantive evidence. This construction of the reports is so repetitive that one almost suspects the pattern to be a deliberate attempt to ride the fence regarding the alleged disaffection of the sepoy battalions, for Sydenham knew full well that although the British representative at the Nizam's court was to be watchful, he could not afford to read alarm into every cryptic utterance. Sydenham's reports, in fact, are primarily political rhetoric rather than an impartial analysis of intelligence, and therefore must be used with caution. The Sydenham brothers owed their rapid advance to the patronage of the Wellesleys, and were known to be proponents of the aggressive 'forward' policy that Lord Mornington had adopted *vis-à-vis* the Indian states, junior members of the same clique of pro-empire Company diplomats to which John Malcolm and Barry Close also belonged.[69]

Apart from a few native officers, Raja Rao Rambha's other contacts in the Cantonment were *dubashes*, most of whom Sydenham believed to be former native officers and sepoys, who had taken their discharge at Hussain Sagar, staying on to take service with British officers of the Subsidiary Force, but remaining in the Cantonment as shop-keepers after their employers were transferred elsewhere.[70] Other such men had managed to secure positions under the *umaras*. Initially, these men had been in Sydenham's eye because he thought they might be involved in a plot, hatched by Raja Rao Rambha and Nur-ul-Umara, to free Fariddun Jah and raise a revolt against the Nizam. The Resident was informed that, four months earlier, during Muharram, Narasingha Rao had told Degamba Rao, a relative, that the British might depose Sikandar Jah, with whom they had become dissatisfied.[71] Consequently, Narasingha and Degamba Rao had decided to suggest Fariddun Jah as a possible successor, but their scheme did not go far, for the prince himself, languishing at Golkonda, dismissed the plan as 'impracticable'. Fariddun Jah, in fact, was eager to curry favour with the British, and had contacted the Assistant Resident's *dubash*, Kistnappah, through his foster brother. Kistnappah informed Assistant Resident Henry Russell that Fariddun Jah preferred to speak with him face-to-face, ostensibly regarding the repair of his foster brother's house, a proposal that Russell could not endorse.[72] Such a meeting would have required formal permission from Sydenham and Mir Alam, neither of whom wanted to encourage Fariddun Jah.[73] Sydenham concluded his report by dismissing this investigation of the Cantonment *dubashes* and merchants as a matter of no importance—at any rate, one unconnected with the disaffection of the sepoy battalions. Fariddun Jah, the Resident noted, had tried to contact him several times since the beginning of the year, once asking to be made Mir Alam's *naib*, or deputy. The request, perhaps, indicated a degree of desperation. Sydenham, in any event, considered him harmless; he lived under close guard, and spent most of his monthly stipend of three thousand Hyderabadi rupees 'collecting well-wishers' at court.[74]

Colonel Montresor, meanwhile, concentrated on determining whether or not Raja Rao Rambha's offers had led to disaffection among his troops. One sepoy of the 2/11th Native Infantry admitted that when he was in Hyderabad city, at the time of the disturbances, people had asked him if he intended to desert to the Raja. Questioned further, the soldier explained that the *amir* had set up a tent pavilion in a *deohra* near Raymond's old gunfoundry, less than a mile from the Cantonment.[75] Native officers from the nearby sepoy lines visited the pavilion, in disguise, conferring with the Raja's *jamadars*. Naigue Subha Singh of the 1/15th Native Infantry added that rumours continued to circulate in the lines after 24 July, spread by Subadars Sidi Hussain and Qadir Beg. On one occasion, the sepoys heard that they were to march to Chicacole, where they would be forced to don the new turban. On another occasion, it was said that the Madras European regiment was marching from Masulipatam, with two regiments of *Allemaun* cavalry, to force the sepoys at Hyderabad to accept the new turban.[76]

The Supreme Government usually received Sydenham's reports within five to seven days, for they were sped northward by mounted *harkaras.* Thus far they had approved of Sydenham's efforts, but the last spate of dispatches finally convinced the Governor-General in Council that the Resident had become bogged down in conspiracy theories. In their letter of 1 September, the Bengal Council urged Sydenham not to be overzealous in his effort to build a connection between the intrigues of the Nizam's court and the feelings of the sepoys. The authorities in Calcutta had read the Resident's reports closely, and could see that his long diatribes were founded on nothing but hearsay; Sydenham was told to view the 'obnoxious orders' about the dress of the sepoys as 'unquestionably . . . the foundation' of the Army's discontents. It was only natural, the Bengal Council remarked, for those who disliked the Company Raj to seek some advantage in the sepoys' anxiety about the new turban, and in a rather sarcastic turn, they reminded Sydenham that they were well aware that the British Government had its detractors in Hyderabad. That there were enemies of the Company at the Nizam's court had always been known, and the Resident had to expect that the *umara* always would act counter to British interests. Sydenham was instructed to adopt the same policy that had been laid down for the guidance of the Government of Madras: to preserve the security of the Raj by making it clear to the sepoys that they had nothing to fear. Montresor was given leave to subject his three ringleaders to a summary court martial, but with that symbolic sacrifice, the investigations at Hyderabad were to end. Indeed, they had become nothing more than a witch hunt. Sydenham, in fact, was instructed to go to the Nizam and ask that the orders banishing Raja Rao Rambha and Nur-ul-Umara be rescinded, for the latter had departed for Delhi, and the Bengal Council preferred to keep him in the Deccan, where he was relatively harmless. Nur-ul-Umara, at the head of his own private army, with a personal treasure estimated to be in excess of twenty-five lakh rupees, had the potential to be a source of trouble for the British, especially in the still-turbulent area around the old Mughal imperial capital; the Nizam, the Supreme Government suggested, would do the Company a great favour by simply settling the *amir* down in his *jagir*.[77]

CONFRONTATION BETWEEN THE RESIDENT AND THE NIZAM

The Supreme Government could not have expressed their desire to terminate the investigations at Hyderabad more clearly if they had enclosed a letter of dismissal with their response of 1 September. However, Sydenham does not seem to have taken their admonishing letter seriously. On 11 September, the Adjutant of the 2/9th Native Infantry, Lieutenant A. MacLeod, was approached by a confidential sepoy of his battalion, who handed him a letter that he claimed was written by Subadar Shaikh Hussain, of the 15th Native Infantry, some time in mid-July. When MacLeod asked about the origins of the letter, the sepoy explained that he had obtained it from a 'friend' in the Nizam's service—a Palace sweeper. The sweeper had 'found' this particular letter, and claimed that others, of a similar nature, could be found if required. The letter turned out to be an *arz*, or petition, and was turned over to the Resident for translation. Sydenham, who translated the document himself, reported that Subadar Sidi Hussain was the author—not Subadar Shaikh Hussain, as both MacLeod and the confidential sepoy had stated. In any event, the *arz* was highly incendiary, treasonous material from the perspective of any British officer:

> We, Ghulam Siddee Hoosain, the Chief of the English Force, and all the Subahdars, Jemidars, and Commandants of the sepoys of infantry and cavalry humbly state that the English propose to us to receive their faith and to wear the dress of hat-wearers, that we will not consent to depart from the faith of the Islaam, or to embrace that of the hat-wearers; that we consider your Highness to be our Sovereign (Malik), and therefore we represent that if your Highness will honour us with your orders, or communicate your auspicious intention by going on a hunting excursion, or to the fort of Mahomed Nuggar, that five days after that concerted signal, we will extirpate the English every one and all, by murdering them. We further represent

that we have always enjoyed the bounty of your Highness, and in the same manner we hope henceforth to enjoy your support and protection; that excepting your Highness, the Shadow of God, there is now no one to whom we look up. That after the perusal of this arzee, if our designs should meet with your Highness' approbation, we request the order may be issued, otherwise that the transaction should be kept secret. We swear by the Prophet that it shall not be revealed.[78]

That the Nizam could have received such an *arz* without reporting it to the British or Mir Alam made Sydenham exceedingly suspicious. However, because Sikandar Jah was inclined to be wary of everyone, Sydenham decided to overlook the matter for the time being—perhaps confident that his report to Madras would *not* be ignored.[79] Indeed, as if to maximize the impact of this new 'evidence', Sydenham—through Montresor—had sent a copy of his translation to Lieutenant-Colonel Thomas Reynell in Mysore.[80]

Bentinck and the other members of the Madras Council received Sydenham's translation of the *arz* on 23 September, whereupon the Governor immediately moved that the native officers sent to Masulipatam by Montresor be summarily discharged and transported, for life, to Penang.[81] The resolution was adopted at once, and Cradock announced that it would be published before the Army without delay.[82] In his own minute on the matter, the Commander-in-Chief remarked that the situation in Hyderabad merely offered additional proof of the existence of a widespread, anti-British conspiracy in which native officers of the Madras Army were linked with rebellious elites. Cradock stated that he had always considered the Nizam's regime to be untrustworthy, and suggested that the sepoys of the Subsidiary Force had been so 'tampered with' that their units should be replaced, at once, with 'fresh' battalions. Nothing came of this bluster, however, for the Company simply could not afford to move that many troops, all at once, for any reason other than the outbreak of a major war.[83]

As the Supreme Government had feared, Sydenham had gone too far, and now the Nizam was seriously annoyed. Raja Mahipat Ram and his friends at court had regained Sikandar Jah's confidence, and had opened a secret correspondence with the Maratha *sardars*, apparently with the Nizam's approval. When Sydenham presented the Governor-General's views regarding Nur-ul-Umara's banishment, via Chandu Lal, Sikandar Jah interrupted the *peshkar* several times as he read the Resident's letter.

At the end of that sentence in which I observed that I had already received from the Mir an official communication of His Highness' determination relative to Noor-ool-Omrah and the rest of the persons mentioned, and that I had immediately conveyed it to the Governor-General, His Highness observed, 'What is it to me that he (the Resident) received such a communication? Of course he did, and he wrote it to the Governor-General, for every Resident is an akhbar-nawees [*sic*].' Where I mentioned that Noor-ool-Omrah received the formality of his dismissal, His Highness exclaimed, 'What is that to the Resident. I may give an hundred paundauns [*sic*] of leave in a day, and taken them back again, if such be my pleasure.' At my observation that His Highness's new resolution might be hurtful to the dignity and interests of his State, he said, 'Who is to judge of my interests and dignity but myself? How do they concern the Resident? If I choose to hurt and degrade myself, I alone can suffer it. It is of no consequence to any other person.'[84]

Sydenham himself believed that Sikandar Jah had been raised to the *masnad* of Hyderabad with every intention of throwing off the connection that Nizam Ali Khan had formed between the Asafiya dynasty and the Company. First, the British victory over the Marathas in 1803 had placed him in an awkward position, but then the 'defeats' inflicted by Holkar's forces in northern India in 1804–5 had been hailed across the Deccan as severe blows to the Company's military might and prestige. Sikandar Jah was even told that Holkar and Scindia had designs on Berar, and might attack him in order to regain the province. The disaffection of the Subsidiary Force, in this wider context, must have left the Nizam feeling uneasy, for the British, once before, had 'betrayed' the Asafiya cause rather than stand with their ally against a Maratha attack.[85]

Mir Alam worried that Sikandar Jah had no faith in the protection offered by the Company, and therefore had been misled by Mahipat Ram into seeking a secret, separate alliance with Holkar and Scindia.[86] In an effort to head off a potential collision between the Nizam and the British, Mir Alam threatened to resign unless the Resident demanded that Sikandar Jah cut-off all ties with Raja Mahipat Ram and his associate, Ismail Yar Jang. Sydenham, impressed by the *Diwan's* insistence, asked the Supreme Government to address a threatening letter to the Nizam, but before the Bengal Council could respond, Mir Alam precipitated a major crisis. On 21 September the Diwan fled across the Musi River to the Residency, declaring his life to be in danger. Sydenham at once requested an audience with the Nizam, but was told that he could not come to the *darbar* until he agreed to allow Nur-ul-Umara to retire to Ellichpur.[87] Sydenham shot back a terse note reminding Sikandar Jah that he had no right, under the treaty of subsidiary alliance, to set conditions on the Resident's right to an audience. The Nizam relented, but when Sydenham arrived at the *darbar*, he was confronted by a hall filled with angry *umara* and their armed retainers; no doubt was left in his mind regarding the court's new political stance.[88] The Resident's meeting with the Nizam went about as well as one might expect, under the circumstances, but the Bengal Council instructed him to stand his ground, declaring that the Government was 'prepared to adopt such measures as . . . may . . . be indispensably requisite for our security'.[89]

The alarm occasioned in Hyderabad by this open rupture between the court and the Residency was acute; the troops of the Subsidiary Force stood on full alert, ready to fight the Nizam's army, throughout the tense confrontation. Finally, when the Governor-General's letter arrived on 28 November, Sydenham personally delivered it to Sikandar Jah along with a speech intended to persuade him that the subsidiary alliance was beneficial both to his government and that of the Company. The *umara* were unimpressed, the Nizam unconvinced.[90] Intrigues continued, and on 5 December Sydenham reported that Mahipat Ram and his allies were gathering armed followers in the countryside, the Judge and Magistrate of Cuddapah having warned the Resident that 'hundreds' of Pathan horsemen were making their way up to Hyderabad to take service under the *umara*. Rather than await an attack, unprepared, Sydenham asked Montresor to organize a field force for immediate action: the cavalry *risala*, two sepoy battalions, and two batteries of artillery. Suddenly feeling confidence in the loyalty and military strength of the Subsidiary Force, Sydenham told the Nizam to order Mahipat Ram to retire from Berar to Sagar fort, in *zilla* Gulbarga. To some extent, it was a bluff, but the Nizam folded, for he could not counter the Resident's demand, under the circumstances, without running the risk of a war with the

Company. As Sydenham had anticipated, Mahipat Ram himself refused to comply with the Nizam's order to fall back, and Montresor at once marched against him, accompanied by Chandu Lal's brother, Raja Govind Bakshi, the newly-appointed governor of Berar. The very news that the Subsidiary Force was on the march terrified Mahipat Ram, and he fled, leaving his men to scatter. The crisis, however, did not end with his flight.[91]

From Sagar, Mahipat Ram continued a 'seditious' correspondence with the Nizam, the Hyderabadi *umara*, and the Maratha *sardars*. His patience worn thin, Sydenham demanded that Mahipat Ram retire from political life and make a pilgrimage to Benares—for the rest of his life.[92] The rebellious exile, however, seemed determined not to be cowed again. He withheld the tribute due from his *jagirs*, using the money to raise an army instead. When Mir Alam's persistent leprosy finally killed him in early February 1808, Mahipat Ram lashed out. At the time, the Nizam and the Resident were arguing about the appointment of a new *Diwan*, and the Nizam's troops, undisciplined, and only recently placed under the command of British officers, were cut to pieces near Shahpur by Mahipat Ram's army. Now Sikandar Jah realized the value of the Subsidiary Force, for it saved his weak regime from collapse. Once more, Mahipat Ram fled at the approach of the Company's troops, becoming a restless exile at Holkar's court. It later was said that a mutinous Maratha trooper murdered him in a brawl in Indore, and thus he met the end common to many such adventurers at a time when military adventuring, for both Europeans and Indians, had come to an end in the Deccan and south India.[93]

NOTES

1. Captain Hastings Fraser, *Our Faithful Ally, the Nizam* (Delhi, 1985 [reprint]), pp. 226-9.
2. Peter Wood, *Vassal State in the Shadow of Empire: Palmer's Hyderabad, 1799-1867*, University of Wisconsin–Madison Ph.D. Thesis (unpublished), 1981; William Hollingberry, *A History of his Late Highness Nizam Alee Khan, Soobah of the Deccan* (Calcutta, 1805); Zubaida Yazdani, *Hyderabad during the Residency of Henry Russell, 1811-1820* (Oxford, 1976).

3. UN, Major John Malcolm to Bentinck (confidential), 6 April 1804, Portland MS, PwJb/32, ff. 10-11.
4. Wood, p. 38.
5. When the subsidiary alliance first had been signed, Sikandar Jah and Mahipat Ram had favoured it, for the British had supported the former's right to the Asafiya throne over the designs of his younger brother, Fariddun Jah. Nizam Ali Khan had made Sikandar Jah his regent, thereby indicating his right of inheritance, but as has been remarked already, Muslim dynasties in south India did not have an established pattern of succession. Sons born of concubines were ranked equally with those born of wives, and thus Sikandar Jah and Fariddun Jah struggled for power as Nizam Ali Khan's health failed in 1796. Before the British intervened, in fact, Fariddun Jah had been gaining the upper hand, for he was supported not only by the *paigah* nobles, but also by the Corps Français de Raymond. For a more detailed account of this succession struggle, see Nani Gopal Chaudhuri, *British Relations with Hyderabad, 1798-1843* (Calcutta, 1964), pp. 98-106.
6. BL/OIOC, Henry Russell to Hastings, 24 November 1819, *Hyderabad Residency Records, Sarojini Regani,* Nizam-British Relation, 1724-1857 (Hyderabad, 1963), op. cit., V. 57, p. 253.
7. William Dalrymple, *White Mughals: Love and Betrayal in Eighteenth-Century India* (New York, 2002), op. cit., BL/OIOC, Report of an Examination Instituted by the Direction of . . . the Governor-General, Fort Saint George, 7th Nov. 1801, *HMS,* V. 464.
8. Sir Arthur Wellesley to Major James Kirkpatrick, 2 December 1803, *The Maratha War Papers of Arthur Wellesley, January to December 1803,* Anthony S. Bennell, ed. (Gloucestershire, 1998), p. 401; Sir Arthur Wellesley to Major James Kirkpatrick, 16 January 1804, *A Selection from the Despatches, Memoranda, and Other Papers Relating to India of Field-Marshall the Duke of Wellington,* Sidney J. Owen, ed. (Oxford, 1880), pp. 185-7.
9. NAI, Wellesley to Sikandar Jah, 22 May 1804, *Hyderabad Residency Records,* V. 27, pp. 231-47.
10. NAI, Captain Henry Russell to GGC/FW (Governor-General-in-Council, Fort William), 23 October 1805, *Hyderabad Residency Records,* V. 29, letter no. 8.
11. Ibid.
12. NAI, Captain Henry Russell to GGC/FW, 20 December 1805, *Hyderabad Residency Records,* V. 29, letter no. 16, paras. 12-13.
13. Nizam Ali Khan was functionally illiterate, and therefore the highly-educated women of his *zenana* played an important role in state affairs. Bakshi Begum was one of the most important of his wives, and well

into her old age controlled the privy purse. Tiniyat-un-Nissa, meanwhile, long had been in charge of the crown jewels, which were worth a considerable fortune. See Chaudhuri, p. 107, op. cit., BL Add. MSS, no. 13,582, Copy No. 51, para. 9.

14. Captain Thomas Sydenham, an officer of the Madras Engineers, had been transferred from Poona, where he had been Acting Resident during the absence of Colonel Barry Close. Earlier, Sydenham had served in Mysore, where he took part in the storming of Seringapatam. In fact, he may have been one of the British officers who entered the Palace, with Major Alexander Allan, to accept the surrender of Tipu Sultan's sons.
15. NAI, Sydenham to GGC/FW, 30 May 1806, *Hyderabad Residency Records*, V. 29, Letter no. 13.
16. NAI, Sydenham to GGC/FW, 15 May 1806, ibid., Letter no. 12, para. 15.
17. UN, Sydenham to Bentinck, 2 April 1806, Portland MS, PwJb/32, f. 225.
18. Wilson, V. 3, p. 15.
19. Ibid., p. 61.
20. Ibid., pp. 125-6, 130-4.
21. Ibid., pp. 134-6. The detachment was commended in General Orders for 21 May 1806, the families of those who had been killed in this affair being granted the same extra allowances accorded to those who had died in the Second Anglo-Maratha War.
22. Ibid., pp. 137-40.
23. BL/OIOC, Montresor to Sydenham, 21 July 1806, *HMS*, V. 507, pp. 539-40.
24. Neither sepoys nor British soldiers were allowed to have access to their firelocks when off duty. Muskets not in use were locked to wooden racks in each battalion's 'bell-of-arms', a small armoury situated at the end of each line of barracks or sepoy huts. The armoury was so called because a small bell was rung whenever the guard was changed, or if there was some emergency requiring the men to turn out under arms.
25. BL/OIOC, Montresor to Sydenham, 21 July 1806, *HMS*, V. 507, pp. 540-3. Montresor's information was obtained from the battalion commanders, who in turn had received reports from their 'confidential men'.
26. BL/OIOC, Sydenham to Edmonstone, 26 August 1806, *HMS*, V. 509, pp. 281-96.
27. Immediately after the Vellore Mutiny, Gillespie, on his own initiative, sent an unofficial report to both Montresor and Sydenham. Other private correspondence brought much detailed information about

the Vellore affair to Hyderabad that week. BL/OIOC, Sydenham to Mountstuart Elphinstone, 19 July 1806, *HMS*, V. 507, pp. 520-2.

28. UN, Montresor to GC/FSG, 18 July 1806, Portland MS, PwJb/25, pp. 390-3.
29. The first rumors of a 'disturbance' at Vellore were reported as early as 12 July 1806—before word of the mutiny there could have reached Hyderabad.
30. Although the Residency's mail was carried to both Calcutta and Madras by express riders, the journey nevertheless took about a week.
31. BL/OIOC, Montresor to Sydenham, 21 July 1806, *HMS*, V. 507, pp. 538-45.
32. BL/OIOC, Sydenham to Montresor, 21 July 1806, *HMS*, V. 507, pp. 537-8.
33. This was a local order, applying only to the Subsidiary Force.
34. BL/OIOC, Sydenham to GC/FSG, 24 July 1806, *HMS*, V. 507, pp. 525-6.
35. BL/OIOC, Sydenham to N.B. Elphinstone, 23 July 1806, *HMS*, V. 507, pp. 529-31.
36. Sydenham's reports do not offer the reader many dates, and consequently it is not possible to reconstruct an exact chronology of his meetings with Mir Alam and Sikandar Jah during the Vellore crisis. The order of the meetings, however, can be worked out roughly from oblique references to various events for which dates are known.
37. TNSA, Sydenham to Barlow, 31 August 1806, *MSP*, V. 5-A, pp. 1731-55.
38. TNSA, Sydenham to Buchan, 15 September 1806, *MSP*, V. 5, pp. 1731-55, paras. 9, 21.
39. Ibid., para. 9. The *arz-o-chehra* of an Indian prince's army was the equivalent of a British roll book, recording the name and detailing the physical description, equipment, and country of origin of all recruits.
40. The royal dungeons were located in the half-ruined fort, which had fallen into disrepair since the Mughal conquest.
41. Ibid., paras. 11-14.
42. The Hindustani words in parentheses appear in Sydenham's account of his interview with the Nizam, giving some insight into the tenor of his translations.
43. TNSA, Sydenham to Buchan, 15 September 1806, *MSP*, V. 5, pp. 1731-55, paras. 15-19.
44. BL/OIOC, Sydenham to Bentinck, 24 July 1806, *HMS*, V. 507, pp. 525-6.
45. BL/OIOC, Sydenham to Bentinck, 14 August 1806, *HMS*, V. 509, pp. 48-58.

46. BL/OIOC, Buchan to Montresor, 31 July 1806, *HMS*, V. 507, pp. 550-1.
47. BL/OIOC, Brown to Buchan, 7 August 1806, *HMS*, V. 508, p. 108.
48. Like all other Madras Army cantonments in south India, the Hussain Sagar station was under British military law. This had been the case since at least the 1770s, when the number of altercations between the Company's subjects and those of the Nawab of Arcot necessitated placing cantonments under martial law.
49. The punishment of the men, essentially, was banishment from the cantonment.
50. The 2/9th Native Infantry had been formed from the 27th Circar Battalion, a unit raised primarily to act as sibbandies in Vizagapatam District. A mutiny had occurred in this battalion in 1797, after which the troops were sent to Hyderebad under Colonel Roberts. In 1799, they fought at Seringapatam, and were one of the sepoy battalions that participated in the assault, staying in the city afterward as part of its garrison. It was determined, however, that Hubbub-ullah was a subject of the Nizam, and therefore he, too, was sent to the dungeons of Golkonda.
51. BL/OIOC, Sydenham to Bentinck, 14 August 1806, *HMS*, V. 509, pp. 48-58.
52. BL/OIOC, Montresor's Memorandum, 9 August 1806, *HMS*, V. 509, pp. 58-61.
53. BL/OIOC, Montresor to Sydenham, 11 August 1806, *HMS*, V. 509, pp. 62-8.
54. BL/OIOC, Sydenham to Bentinck, 14 August 1806, *HMS*, V. 509, pp. 48-58.
55. BL/OIOC, Montresor's Memorandum, 9 August 1806, *HMS*, V. 509, pp. 58-61.
56. Ibid.
57. BL/OIOC, GC/FSG to Sydenham, 29 August 1806, *HMS*, V. 509, pp. 69-70.
58. BL/OIOC, Montresor to Buchan, 17 August 1806, *HMS*, V. 509, pp. 110-12.
59. BL/OIOC, Sydenham to Edmonstone, 22 August 1806, *HMS*, V. 509, pp. 259-80.
60. Sydenham, of course, reads into these ceremonies his own interpretation of the sepoys' intentions.
61. BL/OIOC, Sydenham to Edmonstone, 22 August 1806, *HMS*, V. 509, pp. 259-80.
62. These regulations would seem to have been framed with a view to curbing desertions.

63. BL/OIOC, Sydenham to Edmonstone, 22 August 1806, *HMS*, V. 509, pp. 259-80.
64. Ibid. At the time of these events, the Palladian-style Residency, begun by Kirkpatrick, was being completed. Mir Alam, meanwhile, had commenced a number of construction projects nearby in 1804, including the building of a large tank and several irrigation channels. These projects were finished early in 1807. The 'church' mentioned in the rumours may reflect indigenous suspicions about the activities of the British officers' Masonic lodge. There was no Protestant garrison chapel at Hyderabad in 1806, although there was a Roman Catholic mission church in the Gunfoundry area, just outside Hussain Sagar Cantonment.
65. Ibid.
66. Ibid.
67. Ibid. Raja Rao Rambha offered any Company sepoy who joined his standard the same pay that he currently received from the British, plus an *inam* of twenty to twenty-four rupees.
68. Ibid.
69. BL/OIOC, Sydenham to Edmonstone, 26 August 1806, *HMS*, V. 509, pp. 281-96.
70. This sort of opportunistic career pattern was not at all uncommon for native officers of the Madras Army in the late eighteenth century.
71. Narasingha Rao was a former *darogah* of Azim-ul-Umara.
72. Henry Russell, an officer of the Madras Engineers, had become Assistant Resident only recently, and would become Resident after Sydenham. He already had been in Hyderabad for several years, supervising the construction of the Residency and Mir Alam's tank.
73. BL/OIOC, Examination of Degamba Rao, Narasingha, Kulinayaka, and Venkatrayalu, by Sydenham, no date, *HMS*, V. 509, pp. 299-311.
74. BL/OIOC, Sydenham to Edmonstone, 26 August 1806, *HMS*, V. 509, pp. 281-96. It was not entirely unknown, in Hyderabadi politics, to be in disgrace one day, and in power the next; Mir Alam, for instance, had been sent to prison by Aristu Jah in 1800, over a serious disagreement at court, but within six months he had been released, and was reinstated.
75. This was the site of Raymond's *lashkar*.
76. BL/OIOC, Sydenham to Buchan, 14 September 1806, *HMS*, V. 509, pp. 343-54. 'Allemaun' is clearly a corruption of the French word for 'German', and its use may indicate that the native officers were former Pondicherry sepoys. Both the French and the British had used small troops of German dragoons in Hyderabad, the Circars, and the Carnatic during the wars of the 1750s, and it is possible that the term entered

the local languages as a synonym for heavy cavalry at about that time. It may have been applied, indiscriminately, to all European cavalry, or, perhaps, many sepoys thought the King's cavalry regiments raised for special service in India were composed of Germans, since the only British troops sent to India before the 1780s had been infantry or artillery.

77. Edmonstone to Sydenham, 1 September 1806, quoted in Hyderabad State Committee for the History of the Freedom Movement in India, *The Freedom Struggle in Hyderabad: A Connected Account, 1800-1857*, V. 1 (Hyderabad, 1956), pp. 28-31.
78. BL/OIOC, Translation of *arz* found in the Nizam's Palace, HMS, V. 509, pp. 355-6. The *arz* was found, undated, without a seal. On the outside of the letter, however, the following warning appeared: 'Let this be delivered to His Highness, the Nizam. If it should fall in other hands, and be opened, may the curses of their father and mother fall on their heads.' Clearly, neither the Palace sweeper nor the confidential sepoy were that concerned about their parents' good opinion!
79. BL/OIOC, Sydenham to Buchan, 14 September 1806, *HMS*, V. 509, pp. 343-54.
80. BL/OIOC, Montresor to Lieutenant-Colonel Thomas Reynell, 12 September 1806, *HMS*, V. 509, p. 367. It is rather odd that a translation of the *arz* should have been sent to Mysore before one was sent to Madras.
81. BL/OIOC, Bentinck's Minute, 23 September 1806, *HMS*, V. 509, pp. 356-61. The Company, at that time, operated a penal colony near Penang, to which many political prisoners were sent from south India, including both sepoy mutineers and *palegaru* rebels.
82. BL/OIOC, General Order of Government, 23 September 1806, *HMS*, V. 509, pp. 361-4.
83. BL/OIOC, Cradock's Minute, 21 September 1806, *HMS*, V. 509, pp. 365-6.
84. Sydenham to Edmonstone, 25 September 1806, quoted in *Freedom Struggle in Hyderabad*, V. 1, p. 37.
85. This was the war of 1795, in which Governor-General John Shore decided not to support Aristu Jah's scheme to reconquer the Deccan; the result was the humiliating defeat of Nizam Ali Khan's army at Khardla, from which the Asafiya dynasty never really recovered. Since the war had been viewed, in Hyderabad, as a defensive campaign against the expansive Marathas, the *umara* did not understand the Company's indifference. After all, the Company had been willing to go to war, in 1790, to support the Raja of Travancore after his territory had been invaded by Tipu Sultan.

86. Sydenham to Edmonstone, 25 September 1806, quoted in *Freedom Struggle in Hyderabad*, V. 1, pp. 38-41.
87. NAI, Sikandar Jah to Sydenham, *Hyderabad Residency Records*, V. 29, note no. 1 and letter no. 17. This demand does not make much sense, given that the British Government wanted Nur-ul-Umara to stay in the Deccan anyway.
88. NAI, Sydenham to GGC/FW, 11 October 1806, ibid., V. 29, letter no. 22.
89. NAI, Edmonstone to Sydenham, 25 October 1806, ibid., V. 33.
90. NAI, GGC/FW to Sydenham, 24 November 1806, ibid., V. 33, letter no. 24.
91. Sarojini Regani, *Nizam-British Relations, 1724-1857* (Hyderabad, 1963), pp. 206-7.
92. Aristu Jah had demanded the same of Nana Farnavis in 1794, and Sydenham's request was no doubt meant as an echo of that famous threat.
93. *Freedom Struggle in Hyderabad*, pp. 52-5.

6

'The Conspiracy Has Extended Beyond All Belief'

The Vellore Mutiny and associated disturbances in Hyderabad and Wallajahbad plunged the Madras Government into a crisis of confidence: the Company Raj depended on a military system composed mainly of Indian troops, but could those Indian troops be trusted? To experienced civilians such as William Petrie, the second member of the Council of Fort St. George, such a question could have only one answer: the sepoys had to be trusted, or the Raj would not exist. Detachments of sepoys gave the Company's new civil administration a powerful response to those who tried to resist British efforts to replace the pre-colonial political system with bureaucratic institutions and a Western model of the rule of law. Without these detachments of sepoys the civil authorities were powerless, the new courts and the Company's revenue collection schemes meaningless. Although European soldiers almost always led the way in battle, being seen as shock troops, the dirty work and drudgery of colonial 'peace-keeping' fell to sepoys and their officers. Such operations entailed difficult, onerous duties, and required knowledge of local customs and languages.[1] For many years, the Madras authorities, both military and civil, had recognized that British soldiers and sepoys, although not the same, were two complementary halves of a whole. However, from this realization flowed the Madras Government's doctrine that European troops alone could not hold the country. Sepoy loyalty, therefore, was a crucial component of British power; as Petrie observed, 'With India on our side, we may set our European foes at defiance, but if we lose the affection of our native subjects, our sovereignty in the East will vanish like a dream.'[2]

SPREADING DISCONTENT

Through August and September of 1806, British officials in Madras issued confidently-worded General Orders and proclamations, but the tenor of debate behind the closed doors of the Council chamber was quite different. Separating fact from fancy in reports from the *mofussil* was not always easily done, for the detailed information-collecting that was the essence of the Company Raj was a slow and laborious process.[3] For instance, on 3 August Cradock laid before the Council the depositions of two Indian soldiers, taken at different times and places. The first of these was a statement by Subadar Sikandar Khan, a cavalry trooper who had been interviewed during the investigations at Wallajahbad; the second was the confession of Jamadar Sheikh Qasim of the 1/1st Native Infantry.[4] Subadar Sikandar Khan insisted, in his statement, that the entire Madras Army was seething with anger, especially the 4th, 5th, and 7th regiments of cavalry, which all were stationed in the Carnatic. This unrest, he added, was aroused by agents from Vellore, representing Tipu Sultan's sons, who were abetted by large numbers of sepoys who once had been *sipahis* in the Sultan's army. The *sipahis,* Sikandar Khan assured his British officers, were 'active instruments . . . spreading disaffection'. It was said that Cuddalore was a major centre of unrest.[5] Jamadar Sheikh Qasim's narrative of the Vellore Mutiny supported the above report, both implicating Tipu Sultan's sons and claiming that the cavalry detachments at Arcot and Konnatur had been sympathetic to the mutineers' cause.[6]

Cradock insisted that the unrest reported in the cavalry regiments indicated a conspiracy to overthrow the Company Raj and restore the fallen Muslim dynasties of Mysore and the Carnatic. The regular cavalry regiments of the Madras Army had been annexed directly from the Nawab's army; most of the *sowars* were Muslims, and the cavalry recruiting regulations were framed to assure that most of the troopers would remain Muslim.[7] Many troopers had close ties to the Wallajahi dynasty, and there had been serious protests and riots by the *sowars* in the 1780s and 1790s, leading British officers to look upon them with suspicion despite their otherwise brilliant combat record.[8] Colonel Alexander Campbell's reports from Trichinopoly confirmed Cradock's suspicions. Several deserters—many of them from Vellore—had been captured, probably at the Cauvery crossings, and had been taken to Trichinopoly for questioning, telling British officers all manner of fantastic stories. Considering these reports alongside those from Wallajahbad and Hyderabad, the Madras Government assumed the worst, and placed an inordinate emphasis on the remarks of Subadar Sikandar Khan.[9] Indeed, at the very sight of Sikandar Khan's deposition, Bentinck had written to Sir Thomas Maitland, the Governor of Ceylon, requesting that a detachment of British troops be sent to the mainland at once.[10] To Major Mark Wilks, the Acting Resident at Mysore, Bentinck wrote that a 'dangerous indifference' had taken root among the men of the sepoy battalions.[11] Lieutenant-Colonel Thomas Munro, meanwhile, was warned, at about the same time, 'not to place too much dependence on any of the Native troops', for 'the conspiracy has extended beyond all belief, and has reached the most remote parts of our army'.[12]

More than a month passed, after the first spate of alarming reports, before officials at Madras realized that many of the urgent communications they had received were, in fact, merely symptoms of panic. Nowhere could terrified British officials produce convincing proof that the cause of their fears was real. In many sepoy battalions, the daily round of *daftar* duties, drill, and guard-mounting went on as before, with both European officers and Indian troops bewildered by what they heard about the Vellore affair.[13] Civil administrators, furthermore, found no trace of popular or even secret support for the Vellore mutineers in their districts.[14]

Government policy drifted with the tide of information. At first, reports that all was well were disregarded, and the Council, following Cradock's lead, had pursued the theory that the Vellore Mutiny must have resulted from a far-flung and elaborate anti-British conspiracy. The first shock to the Council's chosen course came on 9 August, when the Mixed Commission, which had been sifting through the Vellore enquiry documents since 21 July, drafted its report, concluding that the 'late innovations as to the dress and appearance of the sepoys were the leading cause of the mutiny, and the other was the residence of the family of the late Tippoo Sultaun at Vellore'.[15] Lieutenant-Colonel Thomas Munro, however, thought the mutiny an isolated, strictly military affair. He discounted the idea that Tipu Sultan's sons could have fomented such a rebellion, pointing out that the restoration of a detested Muslim dynasty could not have appealed to so many Hindu sepoys. Nor did Munro think the sepoys had yielded to bribery, for Haidar Ali and Tipu Sultan had made better offers, during the Anglo-Mysore Wars, but relatively few of the Company's sepoys had defected at that time, even though the Madras Army was beaten, exhausted, and often unpaid. No, Munro argued, Cradock's orders were to blame for the mutiny: they had been 'converted into an attack upon religious ceremonies' in a manner 'well calculated to enable artful leaders to inflame the minds of the ignorant. . .'. The government itself had spread the disaffection throughout the Army with its succession of General Orders, transmitted by express *tappal*—an extraordinary and unprecedented response to a sepoy mutiny. Once British officers calmed themselves, Munro thought, they could expect their men to be calm, too. By mid-September, there was a sudden shift to a policy of reconciliation as the government became aware that sepoys were reacting negatively to British surveillance.

The Supreme Government, meanwhile, intervened in the Vellore crisis, urging Bentinck and his colleagues to avoid unnecessary investigations, to remember that their primary duty to the Company was to restore and maintain the peace. The Court of Directors would want to know what had caused the mutiny, of course, but they would not have patience for an investigation that clearly had been tainted by local political considerations. For its part, the Supreme Government rejected the idea of an anti-British plot, asserting instead that the 'orders in themselves were notorious enough to create the late disaffection and agitations'.[16] Governor-General Barlow also urged Bentinck to be as lenient as possible, punishing only those 'chiefly responsible' for the uprising at Vellore; as if to underscore the point, Barlow flatly refused to send Bentinck the British troops he had requested.[17]

Lord Bentinck, now aware that he now stood on very thin ice, politically—ice that was melting very quickly in south India's summer heat, at once moderated his views. On 26 August, he proposed a General Order granting sepoys 'full liberty' to wear as many 'joys and ornaments' as they liked.[18] Cradock, supported by Petrie and Oakes, argued that such an order would undermine the discipline of the Army, for the sepoys would see that their officers had been scolded by the Company, while protestors were exonerated—even rewarded.[19] At first Bentinck was ready to override the Council and publish his proposed General Order under his own authority, but he eventually relented and sought a compromise. A similar, but more tactfully-worded version of the General Order was circulated to the Army on 24 September.[20]

Bentinck's reversal of opinion did little to restore the government's authority. Indeed, his proposed General Order set the civil authorities against the military. Instead of taking Cradock into his confidence, and sharing responsibility for the many mistakes that the government had made thus far, Bentinck chose to paint himself as the reasonable civilian official struggling against a blustering soldier fixated on the principle of blind obedience to orders. The Governor even went so far as to whitewash his own panicked decisions, and those moments when he had agreed with Cradock. 'It is unfortunate that the Commander-in-Chief and the Government should have taken a different view of these transactions', Bentinck wrote to Jacob Bosquet. 'Differing as to the causes of the distemper, our opinions necessarily differed upon the remedy.'[21]

The remedy to which Bentinck referred was the punishment of the Vellore mutineers. Over 1,000 Indian officers and soldiers had been implicated in the uprising, and more than 600 of them faced court martial proceedings.[22] Among the latter, nineteen already had been sentenced to death, but by early September, the disagreement between Bentinck and Cradock had reached such a pitch that the two men could not even agree on the manner in which these condemned prisoners were to die. Cradock desired a spectacle—three mass executions, at Vellore, Trichinopoly, and Mysore—calculated to terrorize as many people as possible, to get the word out that the British were not to be trifled with. The Commander-in-Chief wanted the remaining prisoners sent into exile for life, preferably to Penang; their battalions, meanwhile, would be dissolved and struck from the Army List.[23] Bentinck looked upon these ideas with horror, although it was precisely such bluster that made it easy for him to cast Cradock as the very caricature of a martinet. Bentinck suggested that making a spectacle of the mutineers' deaths would overthrow the Supreme Government's hopes for reconciliation. The condemned men, Bentinck argued, should all be executed at Vellore, without delay, while the survivors received clemency. Petrie and Oakes supported this view.[24]

Nineteen of the Vellore mutineers were executed on the western glacis of the fort on 23 September 1806. Six mutineers were strapped across the muzzles of cannon and blown in half; eight were hanged; five were shot. Never before, in the history of the Madras Army, had so many sepoys been executed as the result of a formal court martial, and for many of those who watched them die, the grim, ritualized military executions seemed more unjust than anything for which the mutineers had been condemned. Their deaths opened a new phase of the crisis.[25]

The executions shocked thousands of sepoys, especially in battalions whose men were associated with those of the two mutinous units through ties of kinship, marriage, or friendship. One such battalion, the 2/18th Native Infantry, was headquartered at Bangalore, with a detachment at Nandidurgam, in Mysore. When a native officer of the 2/18th reported seditious talk among his comrades at Nandidurgam, his British officers at once assumed the existence of a conspiracy. Hundreds of sepoys, going quietly about their duties, suddenly found themselves cast by their own officers into the role of villain. A court of enquiry later uncovered many stories of odd and suspicious activities, but no incontrovertible evidence that there had been a plot to take over the fort of Nandidurgam. What was started at Nandidurgam, however, soon spread to Seringapatam and Bangalore; every unusual occurrence or rumour was read as a cryptic sign that Maratha or even French agents were at work, undermining British influence in Mysore. Even Purnaiya, Raja Krishnaraya Udaiyar's *Diwan*, was implicated in one of the more elaborate conspiracy theories—an absurd conclusion that embarrassed the government and compelled the Council to take steps to arrest the panic that was undermining both the loyalty of the army and the credibility of the Raj.

PANIC AT NANDIDURGAM

Sepoys were overheard frequently, during the summer of 1806, muttering about their officers—but usually about particular British officers. At many military stations, the very officers who read the

General Order intended to soothe their sepoys were themselves convinced that every Indian soldier was a potential mutineer and murderer. Major James Welsh, the officer commanding at Palaiyamkottai, continued to fear his men even after disarming a large number of them simply because they were Kallars—a people frequently associated, in local folklore and colonial rhetoric, with criminal activity. Welsh's own commanding officer, Lieutenant-Colonel Dyce, was no better, referring to the Wallajahbad incident as an 'insurrection' in a letter sent to Welsh from his retreat at Papanasam.[26] Many British officers found it difficult to contain their fear, for they often were isolated, receiving little or no accurate information, and seeking to solicit loyalty from hundreds of men belonging to different ethnicities, religions, and castes, and speaking different languages. At most cantonments, British officers were the only foreigners present, with no European troops to support or protect them; it was easy, under the circumstances, to expect the worst—that the Madras Army was about to collapse under the weight of too many internal contradictions. In assessing the attitudes and actions taken by officers such as Welsh and Dyce, it is important to recall that the decisions regarding the Vellore crisis thus far had been made in secret meetings, on the basis of confidential reports. Even relatively high-ranking officers in the *mofussil* could follow the crisis only through sporadic, often contradictory circulars and rumours—the former statements often couched in alarmist rhetoric, the latter often too mysterious to be deciphered. Many officers' reports to the government that summer drew attention to this lack of knowledge—not only regarding the intentions of their sepoys, but also regarding the reasoning behind the Council's decisions. From the point of view of *mofussil* officers and officials, it seemed that the Madras authorities were being too optimistic, and that the situation, in fact, was deteriorating rapidly. At this point in the Vellore crisis, several British officers succumbed to hysteria, precipitating a series of unfortunate events.

The hill fort of Nandidurgam, where Cradock had intended to spend a relaxing summer with his wife, in a relatively cool, picturesque, and pastoral environment, was garrisoned by four companies of the 2/18th Native Infantry.[27] The Nandidurgam outpost was located 31 miles north of Bangalore, in the village of Nandi, on the road to Anantapur.[28] From the summit of the adjoining granite mountain of Nandidurgam, over 4,800 feet above sea level, an elaborate network of fortifications commanded every possible approach. The fort itself covered, although it did not command, branching roads connecting Bangalore with Bellary, the Raichur Doab, and the eastern Ceded Districts. The heights had been captured by the Madras Army, after a daring assault, on 18 October 1791, and the Company's troops had indulged in a night of pillage, rape, and murder, one of the few incidents in which the discipline of the sepoy battalions had broken down after a victory.[29] The harsh treatment meted out to Tipu's garrison had been inspired by the popular idea that Nandidurgam was the place where Haidar Ali and Tipu Sultan had flung captured European and Indian soldiers from the top of perpendicular cliffs nearly 1,000 feet high.[30] A sepoy battalion was stationed at Nandidurgam in 1799, but although the fort was not pulled down or rendered indefensible, it was not considered a practical location for a permanent garrison. The Company's Tamil and Telugu sepoys found the exposed, rocky heights too cold, especially at night, when damp mist enveloped the mountain top. Furthermore, supplies were nearly impossible, as everything had to be carried up a narrow footpath by coolies.[31]

As in the days of Haidar Ali and Tipu Sultan, the garrison lived at the foot of Nandidurgam, to the north-west, between the half-ruined town of Sultanpettah and the village of Nandi. Visiting the cantonment in 1809, shortly after the troops were withdrawn, Major James Welsh noted that the town was 'extensive, and was formerly connected with the foot of the hill by a line of works and deep ditch, now out of repair and useless'. Nevertheless, the bazars were well-stocked with potatoes, soft sugar, and exotic European fruits.[32] Few British officers posted to Nandidurgam had been able to resist the urge to plant English gardens and the fruit trees common to temperate climates, and many had built villas on the nearby hills in order to enjoy the spectacular views and the cool breeze. The surrounding jangal was full of big game, and officers spent much of their time away from the outpost, tracking tigers.[33]

Nandi itself was merely a village, but its squat, Chola-period Bhoga Nandiswara *mandir* was wellknown throughout south India. Thousands of pilgrims attended the Sivaratri festival, at which

Mysore's famous white pack bullocks were marketed. Captain Thomas Baynes, who organized the pack bullock corps of the Army during the Second Anglo-Maratha War, was one of the officers stationed at Nandidurgam in 1806. 'Conversant with all the country languages', Baynes had become the *de facto* European adjutant of the garrison.[34] The sepoy barracks and Baynes' quarters were located in an ornately-carved stone *choultry* attached to an abandoned temple in the middle of Nandi village. When off duty, the sepoys usually retired to a line of huts along the path to Sultanpettah, where their wives and children resided.[35] The villages around Nandi were full of sepoys' families, and during the autumn furlough, hundreds of men from various battalions—but especially the 2/4th Native Infantry—could be found in the area.[36] The local *rayats*, descendants of Telugu migrants, had a long tradition of military service; they had served a succession of rulers since the days of the Vijayanagar kings, and after 1799, they had taken up the Company's arms.

In 1806, the Nandidurgam garrison consisted of companies detached from Bangalore, the battalion headquarters of the 2/18th Native Infantry, which was under the command of Major Alexander Muir-head. The 1/18th Native Infantry, meanwhile, had been moved to Vellore, to take over garrison duties in the aftermath of the mutiny. According to Harcourt, they had been so cowed that they acted more like servants than sepoys.[37] They were assigned to guard the imprisoned mutineers, and no doubt were disturbed by the executions they were assembled to watch on September 23. As frequently happened, news passed back and forth from one battalion to another, for each was linked with several others through the frequent drafting of men—especially native officers—from one corps to another. Thus the men of the 2/18th Native Infantry at Nandidurgam were well-informed about events in Vellore.[38]

Subadar Abdul Qadir of the 1/5th Native Infantry arrived at Nandidurgam, on leave from Bellary, on 7 October. At that time, he was told by several people that the men of the 2/18th Native Infantry had been depressed since the slaughter that ended the Vellore Mutiny. Indeed, at that time, many sepoys had sent their families away, asking their wives and children to forgive them—a gesture usually made only when there was the possibility of imminent death. Since then, however, the turban order had been rescinded, and the sepoys' families had returned to Nandidurgam. Nevertheless, continuing reports of disaffection prompted Colonel Cuppage to ask Subadar Abdul Qadir to employ four men to discreetly spy on the garrison.[39]

According to Subadar Kasturi of the 2/18th Native Infantry, the collapse of the garrison's morale had begun long before the Vellore Mutiny, in March, with the arrival of rumours from the Maratha country. At that time, apparently, the sepoys discussed the possible return of Tipu Sultan's nephew, the son of Karim Sahib, with a detachment of Holkar's army, which would advance via Hyderabad. Kasturi claimed that some sepoys said they would join Karim Sahib's son, if he was successful, and that after the Vellore Mutiny, they had vowed that the revolt there would be repeated at Nandidurgam. The emergence of such talk coincided with the arrival of four *faqirs* from Hindustan, an observation that Jamadar Sheikh Dawood, the Acting Adjutant, confessed to be true.[40]

There was an old man, two young men, and one boy. They started at the [*asura khana*] near the Barracks. They applied to the native officers for leave to exhibit some puppets, etc., before them, particularly as their show represented the Padshah of Delhi on his masnad. . . . Subidar Mahomed Raza said he would see it afterwards. The other native officers said they would see it at a time [when] there was neither parade nor drill.[41]

In order to keep the puppeteers in Nandi until the next off duty day, the non-commissioned officers had taken up a collection, to which all had contributed according to their rank. Subadar Kasturi stated that the whole matter was kept secret, the *subadars* and *jamadars* swearing an oath on their swords. At the same time, seditious comments also had been made about an alliance between Karim Sahib and the princes at Vellore. 'When an order came from the latter', Kasturi explained, 'a rising was to take place, and if a revolution was affected, the native officers [would] hold in the new service the rank[s] from General downwards, with their pay.'[42]

Jamadar Sheikh Dawood, however, recalled that it was not easy for the non-commissioned officers to reach a consensus. Jamadar Shaikh Ahmad, for one, did not agreed, at first, to contribute to the *faqir's* fund because 'he had no rupees'. Sheikh Dawood offered to pay the half-rupee requested from Shaikh Ahmad, whereupon Subadar Muhammad Reza said, 'We are all of one mind, and we can jump together into this tank', making reference to the stone tank in the middle of the Barrack Square. Jamadar Shaikh Ahmad, however, said that if they jumped into the tank, he would throw stones on their heads. Muhammad Reza was alarmed by this outburst, but Sheikh Dawood had soothed Shaikh Ahmad, eventually reconciling him to the plan. Thus they all swore the oath, on their swords, to keep the puppet show a secret.[43]

The *faqirs* displayed their puppets that evening, and gave additional performances during the next several days. They set up their puppet theatre twice in the Barrack occupied by the 3rd line company, once at the *kotwal's choultry*, and a few more times at the houses of *subadars* and *jamadars*.[44] At the latter locations, the *faqirs* had received five rupees from each family. According to Kasturi, the puppet shows 'corrupted' most of the non-commissioned officers—Subadar Muhammad Reza in particular. During one performance, he was said to have remarked to Subadar Venkatchellam that the scene depicted the *masnad* of the Padshah in Delhi, but that it was 'now occupied by Europeans'.[45]

Jamadar Sheikh Dawood recalled that at one point during the show, Muhammad Reza, Venkatchellam, Havildar Sheikh Nattar, and two sepoys quietly sent someone to bring arrack into the Barracks. Later, quite drunk, these men led Sheikh Dawood out of the village to a small Hanuman temple, stopping along the way to procure another bottle of arrack. The men 'drank the arrack, and . . . then took an oath to be true to each other on every occasion, and that their secrets were to be kept in their own minds, without opening them to any other person'. By this time, however, Sheikh Dawood was so drunk he could scarcely stand, and Venkatchellam and Muhammad Reza carried him home. At the door of his hut 'they told him they would assist him on all occasions, and he must do the same to them'.[46]

When the companies at Nandidurgam were informed about the order altering the shape of their turbans, some of the native officers were shocked. The cohesion which had formed easily under the influence of arrack, suddenly dissolved. Jamadar Muhammad Reza vowed not to wear the new turban, but Sheikh Dawood counselled following the lead of 'the eldest battalions', stating that he himself would be the first to remake his turban according to the new pattern.

Subadar Venkatchellam and Jamadar Tika Ram, however, were less annoyed by the announcement regarding the new turban than by the apparent relish with which Subadar Kasturi read the order. 'You were made a [subadar] for killing a [*qiladar*]', they said, 'and now you want a [*palankin*] and a medal on account of these turbans'.[47]

Subadar Kasturi heard a lively discussion in front of the Main Guard of the barracks square on the evening of 28 September, only five days after the executions at Vellore. According to his report, Subadar Venkatchellam pointed out that political power in south India had passed from the 'Malabars' to the Muslims, then to the French, and finally to the British.[48] Havildar Qadir Beg, however, pointed out that Muslim astrologers had predicted the fall of the Europeans before a resurgent Islam, notwithstanding their present power and government. At this point, Subadar Kasturi interjected his own views: the British, he said, were faithful paymasters. He was shouted down by Venkatchellam, Subadar Muhammad Reza, and Jamadar Dekka Ram. These three officers maintained that the Company Raj was built on treachery, draining away the wealth of the country and giving its sepoys 'only [a] trifling allowance'. They asked Kasturi how the British could prevail if the 'Malabars', Muslims, and Marathas all united against them. Kasturi replied with a cautionary tale:

> There was a fish in the sea of a prodigious size (literally, Lord of the Fishes), which the rest were combined to destroy; while they held their consultation, the large fish was providentially informed of their conspiracy, and advised to prepare against the impending danger. The Deity then gave it a [*chakram*], or celestial wheel, and advised it to affix it to its tail, and dash it against the water at the approach of the other fish, that it would cause a whirlpool, and advised it to open its mouth at that instant, when all those in conspiracy would be drawn into its belly, thereby, and to shut its mouth.

The message of the story was clear enough: the Company Raj would prevail not by treachery, or even by force, but by its mastery of information, and through divinely ordained good fortune. The other soldiers were unimpressed; they jokingly retorted that 'Hindoos, Mussulmen and Mahrattas are one; the French have a country of their own, but the English [have] only their . . . merchandise.'[49]

Subadar Kasturi relayed this story to Major Muirhead on 9 October, placing Subadar Muhammad Reza at the centre of an extensive web of intrigue. Muhammad Reza was alleged to possess a sacred text, brought from Mecca, foretelling the 'downfall of the Europeans by the sword of the Mahomedans'.[50] According to Kasturi's deposition, meetings were held at Muhammad Reza's house, from which he was excluded, the other sepoys apparently realizing he was the company's 'confidential' man. According to another soldier, Naigue Abdul Qadir, a Muslim sepoy was overheard telling his comrades about a mysterious order to rise and kill the commanders and all other Europeans and their offspring.[51] On the strength of these reports, Muirhead arrested both Muhammad Reza and Venkatchellam—an action that stunned the little garrison.[52] The sepoys already saw Kasturi as something of an officious martinet; now they shunned him altogether.

On the afternoon of 17 October, Sepoy Ranga of the 2/18th Native Infantry walked to nearby Ballapur with several comrades.[53] Along the way, Sepoy Venkatchellam spoke of the arrests made by Kasturi, and added, 'Wait . . . three months, and see what will happen.'[54] Sepoy Virash recalled how Venkatchellam spoke 'as if there was some evil in his mind'.[55] Muirhead, by this time, had begun to fear trouble, and applied for a troop of dragoons—a rather extreme response to a Subadar's failure to control his men. The two companies that had been under Muhammad Reza and Venkatchellam were marched off to Bangalore to join Lieutenant-Colonel Alexander Cuppage's command, and the next day, Cuppage requested permission from the officer commanding the Mysore Division to withdraw a third company from Nandidurgam.[56]

At about three o'clock in the afternoon on 18 October, Acting Adjutant Sheikh Dawood returned from a visit to Seringapatam and was informed of the recent arrests and of the departure of the two 'disaffected' companies. Two sepoys told him that 'something' would happen that night, and the Acting Adjutant assumed that by 'something' the soldiers meant a mutiny. Instead of warning his European officers, however, Sheikh Dawood joined a party that had been sent out to buy *kumblis* from the local shepherds. As they traversed the countryside around Nandi, they met a man named Abdullah Khan, who described himself as the *moniyagar*, or renter, of 'a small place' near Gauribidanur in the Ceded Districts.[57] Calling the troops aside, he explained that he had heard about the Vellore

Mutiny, 'and that in a little time the same scene was to be acted at [Nandidurgam]'. He offered to support the sepoys with five hundred men, 'properly and stout, [who] . . . could assemble in the hills . . . with baked bread, and could fall upon the Europeans suddenly'. Abdullah Khan added that the Vellore mutineers had failed because they had risen before their friends outside the fort had been ready to assist them.[58]

Even before the sepoys' meeting with Abdullah Khan, there had been talk among the native officers that day about the possibility of various communities and classes joining together to support a military rising.[59] When word of Abdullah Khan's promises was brought back to Nandi, the sepoys' excitement quickly reached a point of crisis. At around five o'clock, Subadar Kasturi noticed men milling around in front of the barracks in small groups, and at seven o'clock, a sepoy and one of the villagers informed him that the soldiers' families were leaving Nandi.[60]

By the early evening hours of 18 October, Subadar Kasturi and the remaining British officers at Nandidurgam were obsessed with the idea that the two companies left to guard the station intended to mutiny that night, before they could be sent off to Bangalore. Naigue Arnasum, according to Kasturi, reported that several sepoys were meeting with a *faqir* in the old abandoned temple near the barracks. According to the Naigue, the sepoys had said, 'This Pariar Subidar has made all our Secret Public, but wait and see what will happen in two [*garis*]. . . .' Furious, Kasturi stormed over to the Main Guard, where he ran into Sepoy Sheikh Muhyi-ud-Din, who was walking with Havildar Viragu and several others, muttering, 'This subadar always makes new regulations, but see what will happen in two or three *garis*. . . .' Kasturi immediately ordered the men to arrest and confine Sheikh Muhyi-ud-Din. There is a problem, however, with Kasturi's testimony; Naigue Arnasum later told a court of enquiry investigating the Nandidurgam incident that he did not understand Hindustani, and therefore had no idea what the sepoys and lascars had been discussing with the *faqir* in the old pagoda.[61] Either Kasturi put words into Arnasum's mouth, or one of his own sepoys had called him a Paraiyar—in any event, the Subadar leaped to the conclusion that the two companies remaining at Nandidurgam intended to mutiny.[62]

Muirhead now was convinced that he and his officers would be murdered in their beds if they did not act quickly; he sent an urgent request for British troops to Bangalore, collected his fellow European officers and a few 'loyal' sepoys, and retreated to a more or less secure room inside the barracks square.[63] There was no mutiny in Nandidurgam, but *something* happened. Sepoy Ramdu left the barracks to go to the lines at half past seven in the morning, and found the huts empty 'except for a few old women'. Shortly afterward, however, the sepoys' families began to return, and the lines were reoccupied by ten o'clock, when Subadars Kasturi and Abdul Qadir appeared. The two native officers at once went to the house of an old pensioner of the 1/5th Native Infantry, Shaikh Madar, and demanded to know what had happened. The pensioner explained that during the night an old woman had awakened him, asking how he could sleep so calmly while all were fleeing. The battle-hardened veteran had replied that he was an old, infirm man, and did not care whether he was killed or not.[64]

Lieutenant-Colonel Henry Davis of HM 22nd Light Dragoons, meanwhile, had set out from Bangalore with two troops of cavalry and a galloper gun, expecting to find, at the end of his march, a repeat of the scenes of Vellore, only on a smaller scale. Instead, as he noted later, 'I . . . arrived . . . before two o'clock and found all quiet'. The sepoys of the two companies sat 'dismally quiet in their barracks', no doubt wondering why their officers had gone into hiding.[65] Over the next few days, the sepoys began to vent their anger and frustration. On the evening of 19 October, Jamadar Jerober Singh saw several horses tethered in front of Captain Baynes' quarters, and remarked to Sepoy Sheikh Mirah that the animals ought to be fed and put in the stables for the night. The sepoy, however, retorted, 'they (meaning Europeans) have now plenty of riches, but when their power is gone they must be starved to death'. The next day, a stranger named Shaikh Muhyi-ud-Din approached the Main Guard and asked for Lance Naigue Sheikh Bari. He told the sentries he had come from Gudibanda, and added that there was a rumour, at the time of the Vellore Mutiny, that the Nandidurgam garrison also was to have risen.[66] The stranger explained to the sentries that a wave of mutinies was to have plunged the region into chaos, preparing the way for an invasion by the united armies of Holkar and Sindiah at New Year. A French force (*rumi-ki-fauj*) would support the Marathas, and the whole population would rise and fight with the sepoys. The Raja of Cochin, the man continued, had already begun hostilities against Purnaiya's troops in Wynaad, and there would be 'fighting by sea' before the rebellion was over.[67] Havildar Venkatram corroborated both Jerober Singh's story and the visit by Sheikh Muhyi-ud-Din.[68] Other native officers had been pulled aside for short, cryptic conversations. Subadar Abdul Qadir, for instance, met Jemadar Sheikh Dawood near the barracks and remarked that both the Hindus and Paraiyars had withdrawn from the 'general combination', and that it now was difficult to hold any private conference.[69]

Lieutenant-Colonel Davis ordered a court of enquiry to investigate the events at Nandidurgam—a decision that anticipated Cradock's own orders. The Commander-in-Chief, however, ordered Major-General Hay MacDowall, the officer commanding the Mysore Division, to expand the enquiry to include the companies of the 2/18th Native Infantry stationed at Bangalore. A wing of HM 22nd Light Dragoons, stationed at Arcot, was sent to reinforce Davis and assist MacDowall in arresting the 'progress of disaffection'.[70]

The Nandidurgam enquiry dragged on for weeks. After examining and cross-examining a variety of witnesses and informants, including both sepoys and villagers, British officers found no evidence of a conspiracy to mutiny. However, a number of those questioned by the court agreed that there had been a lot of suspicious behaviour among the troops of the garrison. The most alarming testimony presented to the court, however, was that of Jamadar Sheikh Dawood, who said that he had returned to Nandidurgam from Seringapatam on 18 October to find 'three-fourths' of the corps prepared to 'kill the Europeans, plunder all they could, and . . . run off'.[71] Sheikh Dawood asserted that both wings of the battalion were joined in a conspiracy, communicating frequently by means of letters and messengers. When the court pressed him for proof, however, the Jamadar merely said that 'in his heart [he believed] that such was the case'.[72]

Major-General MacDowall arrived at Nandidurgam on 29 October to review the court of enquiry proceedings. In his official report, based almost entirely on Sheikh Dawood's opinions, the commander of the Mysore Division informed Lieutenant-Colonel Patrick Agnew, the Adjutant-General, that the 'most daring and atrocious acts' had been averted at Nandidurgam by prompt, vigorous action. South India was being saturated with anti-British propaganda, he wrote, the chief architects of this movement being a seditious conspiracy of disgruntled Indian officers, unseated *amildars,* and *palegaru* longing for the lost days of violence and plunder.[73] Lieutenant-Colonel Davis also accepted Sheikh Dawood's words at face value and added his own worst fears, reporting—without any evidence whatever—that Holkar and Tipu Sultan's nephew, Fatteh Ali, had 'sent hundreds, perhaps thousands of emissaries into Mysore and our own provinces' to raise the standard of revolt.[74] MacDowall harangued the men of the two companies at Nandidurgam in a furious address on the evening of 30 October. This made eleven sepoys so angry they asked to be discharged from the Army; the others 'promised an entire reformation and avowed their willingness to die for the Company'.[75] By this time, however, the crisis had spread to Bangalore, events there being influenced by MacDowall's assessment of the Nandidurgam incident.

THE SWAGGERINGS OF BHANG SMOKERS

Lieutenant-Colonel Samuel William Ogg, the officer commanding at Bangalore, was one of the officers who had been assigned the difficult task of clearing out Tipu Sultan's palace at Seringapatam in 1799. He had been assigned the job of cataloguing and packing up the Sultan's extensive library, which Lord Mornington had ordered to be shipped to the headquarters of the Asiatic Society in Calcutta. Ogg must have been aware of the many discoveries that were made, at that time, in the Seringapatam *daftar khanas,* as William Kirkpatrick and others combed through the intelligence reports that had been sent to the Sultan. Among other important documents, they had discovered carefully copied public and private papers from the Hyderabad Residency, forwarded to Tipu Sultan by Nizam Ali Khan's nephew, Imtiaz ul-Umara, who at that time had been the leader of the anti-British faction at the Nizam's court. British officers who had rifled through Tipu Sultan's papers had been left with the impression that the rulers of Mysore had scattered spies and agents throughout the Deccan. In 1806, it was perhaps only natural for officers like Ogg to wonder what Tipu's partisans had been doing during the last seven years, and to suppose that they had been plotting, secretly, to avenge their master's defeat.[76]

Upon hearing of the incident at Nandidurgam, Lieutenant-Colonel Ogg began to see cryptic importance in the most trivial occurrences. Too many people, he complained, were entering Bangalore from Kolar Sarai 'without any ostensible object in view'. The relative of a *naigue*, who seemed to 'avoid observation', was arrested merely because his behaviour was deemed suspicious.[77] Ogg was convinced that some secret conspiracy threatened the security of the garrison. *Pirs* and *faqirs*, he informed Cradock, were 'blowing the coals in the quarter'.[78] The sepoys of the 2/18th Native Infantry continued to carry out their duties without any hint of insubordination, leaving Ogg convinced that this good behaviour must somehow mask their true intentions.[79] A court of enquiry was assembled in the *diwan-i-aam* of the old summer palace inside Bangalore fort, the adjoining temple providing a convenient place in which oaths could be administered to high-caste Hindu witnesses.

By 22 October, Ogg was determined to unmask the conspirators, and to this end, he ordered a *munshi's* house to be searched for seditious materials. A bundle of papers was produced, among which Ogg claimed to find a letter that 'proved' the existence of a scheme to free the Mysore prisoners at Vellore, one that had been 'in contemplation for six years'.[80] Ogg also searched the residence of an itinerant *faqir*, Sayyid Muhammad, and again claimed to find evidence of sedition.[81] A few days later, another letter turned up, in the fort of all places, alluding to a plot to destroy the 'principal European officers'. Several men were arrested on the basis of this rather spurious document.[82] MacDowall was impressed, however, and ordered Ogg to expand the scope of his investigation.[83]

Parties of sepoys, under British officers, began to conduct a house-to-house search in the walled city of Bangalore, arresting all who resisted their intrusion. Strictly speaking, this search was illegal, as the premises in question belonged to Krishnaraya Wodeyar's subjects, and no permission for a search had been granted by the Raja's officials. Ogg, however, suspected that the *qiladar* of Bangalore and Purnaiya were both involved in some grand conspiracy against the Company's interests—an attitude that deeply offended the *Diwan*.[84] Purnaiya at once dispatched a formal complaint to Lord Bentinck, on behalf of the young Raja, via the Acting Resident, Mark Wilks. Hearing of this move by the *Diwan*, the military authorities at Bangalore scrambled to justify their recent acts, offering a substantial sum to anyone who could provide evidence of the existence of an anti-British plot.[85] A stream of witnesses appeared—sepoys, bazar women, *faqirs*, and others—all eager to provide Ogg's court of enquiry with stories about odd events, suspicious strangers, and seditious chatter. One soldier's tale even included a report that 'God had taken the form of a man, and is at this present time in Bangalore, and that he is the author of all these things'.[86]

Sepoy Ramaswamy, sworn 'in the most solemn manner in front of the idol', told the court that he had visited Jamadar Lullab-ullah Sayyid Hussain twenty days prior to the Nandidurgam 'mutiny'. At that time, the Jamadar told Ramaswamy that he would see, in ten days, a 'scene of confusion in this place, and . . . all the Europeans . . . put to death'. He explained to the Hindu sepoy that a soldier's brother had brought this warning from Nandidurgam, but that no one must know about it. Ramaswamy dismissed the Jamadar's words as nonsense, but came forward when he heard that his officers were seeking information about treasonous activities.[87] Jamadar Lullab-ullah Sayyid Hussain acknowledged Ramaswamy's visit, but denied the sepoy's version of their conversation. He said that when Havildar Qasim Khan had been about to go away on four months' leave, he had warned Sepoys Muhammad Gowse and Abdul Qadir that 'disturbances would occur in the battalion, and they should be careful'. According to the Jamadar, Ramaswamy came to him asking if there had been a disturbance at Nandidurgam, where his brother was stationed. The Jamadar had sent him away as a 'fool' who 'knew nothing'. Under a sharp cross-examination, however, Jamadar Lullab-ullah Sayyid Hussain admitted that an old woman, the mother-in-law of Sepoy Grenadier Abbas Khan, came to his house from Nandidurgam with stories about the garrison's low morale.[88]

Jamadar Muttiah, the battalion's 'confidential' native officer, discreetly plied Lullab-ullah Sayyid Hussain with money, offering five pagodas and a substantial reward from Lieutenant-Colonel Ogg if he could produce useful evidence for the court of enquiry. Nothing came of this request, but Muttiah was determined to root out the seditious members of the corps. He decided that if anyone in the battalion had engaged in treason, it probably was Havildar Qasim

Khan; if the fellow was not the author of the trouble, he undoubtedly would know about it. The court of enquiry, therefore, turned its attention to a conversation alleged to have taken place on 3 November when Sepoys Muhammad Gowse and Abdul Qadir met Havildar Qasim Khan outside the Delhi Gate, near an old tomb just north of the fort. According to Muhammad Gowse, the Havildar merely had told him to be alert at his post during the next several days, as there was 'sedition in the corps', and he himself was going away on leave. When the sepoy asked Havildar Qasim Khan to explain what he meant, however, the response was rather surly: 'You are a good-for-nothing fellow, and I can't trust you!' Sepoy Abdul Qadir testified that Muhammad Gowse's account of the exchange was more or less accurate, but that the Havildar's response to his question had been: 'I could tell you more, but you are a great son-of-a-bitch, and I don't like to trust you.' Before he could add more, however, Subadar Abdul Nabi appeared and the Havildar abruptly walked away.[89]

Havildar Qasim Khan, who had yet to go on leave, was brought before the court of enquiry to confront Muttiah's insinuations about his character. He defended himself by remarking that Sepoys Muhammad Gowse and Abdul Qadir, Havildar Venkatswami, and Jamadar Muttiah were well known to be his enemies. Muttiah, in fact, never missed an opportunity to harass him. Havildar Qasim Khan was asked why he had sent his sister away from Bangalore in early October, to which he angrily replied that she had gone to a wedding. Finally, he insisted that he had never spoken with the two sepoys outside the Delhi Gate. Seeing that their efforts were fruitless, the court of enquiry released the Havildar and turned to other evidence.[90]

Jamadar Muttiah continued to search for signs of unrest in the battalion, while sepoys, meanwhile, were encouraged to report any 'seditious' language they heard. On 11 November, Sepoy Sayyid Ibrahim told the court of enquiry that Naigue Muhammad Usman remarked that his brother, Muhammad Reza, had been arrested at Nandidurgam. According to Sayyid Ibrahim, the *naigue* said that if his brother was executed, he would kill 'some person of consequence' in revenge. This information was passed on to Sepoy Muhammad Gowse, who informed Jamadar Muttiah. The Native Adjutant, Jamadar Shaikh Hussain, reported the matter to the battalion commander, but added that Naigue Muhammad Usman had an otherwise 'unblemished' character. The court of enquiry accepted that the *naigue* was upset by the arrest of his brother, and wisely did not pursue the matter further.[91] However, Sepoy Sheikh Buddin brought evidence to his native officers that seemed to point to a widespread and very dangerous plot against the government. He said that a 'celebrated doctor' named Kallianu had come to the lines to treat a relative of his who had fallen ill. After his visit, the doctor told Sheikh Buddin that he would replace the hut in which he now lived with a much better house, explaining that he had heard, at the *amildar's* house, that the Company Raj would fall within a few weeks.[92] The doctor was arrested but when he appeared before the court of enquiry, he denied ever having said anything treasonous.[93] The fact that the *amildar* had been mentioned, however, added a new dimension to Ogg's investigation, for the native 'confidential' officers were convinced that Purnaiya's officials might be involved in some anti-British conspiracy—a point of view that British officers eagerly adopted. Subadar Abdul Qadir ordered Sepoys Muhammad Shalli and Shaikh Muhammad to mingle with the people of the *pettah* and report anything unusual they might overhear; similar orders were given to Sepoy Muhammad Gowse.[94] What they discovered, and the uproar that followed, is discussed in detail in the following chapter.

The court of enquiry endured such testimony for three weeks before throwing up its hands and concluding that there was no evidence, whatsoever, to suggest that the sepoys of the 2/18th Native Infantry were mutinous. Even Ogg had to accept the inevitable, and finally reported to MacDowall that 'this part of the battalion had been and still is steady in its fidelity and allegiance to Government'.[95]

Bentinck was deeply embarrassed by the affairs at Nandidurgam and Bangalore, especially the aspersions that had been cast upon Purnaiya's administration by MacDowall and Ogg. Cradock, meanwhile, clutched at what seemed to be his last opportunity to prove the existence of a far-flung, anti-British conspiracy. Having accepted the initial reports of MacDowall and Davis as accurate, Cradock expressed his firm belief that the 2/18th Native Infantry had been 'ready to renew the scenes of Vellore', but had been prevented from doing so by prompt action on the part of the military authorities.[96] Bentinck, however, made no comment on the reports from Mysore; too many false alarms and the censure of the Supreme Government finally had made him cautious. He accepted the view of Mark Wilks, who concurred with Purnaiya's colourful quip that Ogg's proceedings at Bangalore were the 'swaggerings of [*bhang*] smokers'.[97] What is astonishing, however, is that the Bengal authorities, despite their earlier censure of Cradock, now accepted, on the basis of circum-stantial evidence, that the men of the 2/18th Native Infantry at Nandidurgam had indeed been plotting to murder their officers.[98]

Rumours from Nandidurgam and Bangalore made even more British officers lose their composure, confirming the fears of those who already had given way to panic. Lieutenant-Colonel Dyce sent a lurid account of the Nandidurgam enquiry to the excitable Major Welsh, implying that the native officers of almost every sepoy battalion were deeply implicated in a general conspiracy weaving together the animosities and aspirations of every displaced and disgruntled political interest in southern India. 'The plan', he wrote, 'is supposed to have been traced in Holkar's camp, and to include the Nizam's brothers, Tippoo's sons, and some others.'[99]

Not every British officer lost his head. There were a few who clearly saw through the layers of misinformation and subterfuge, even without perusing all of the official documents. Lieutenant-Colonel John Malcolm, who replaced Mark Wilks as Resident at the Mysore court in March 1807, had been able to confer with both Wilks and Colonel Close regarding the matter.[100] Close himself tended to believe that there was some sort of plot against the Company's interests by disaffected and displaced Muslim élites, but Malcolm pointed out, in a letter to his friend, Sir Arthur Wellesley, that the 'weakness, distractions, and incompetence' of the government were to blame for the Vellore crisis. While the British had trounced their external foes, Malcolm lamented, the internal governance of 'this unfortunate empire' was in a state of near collapse.[101] In the wake of the storm over the Nandidurgam and Bangalore incidents, Wilks became dispirited; Malcolm found him feeling ill, and thinking about a furlough to Britain.[102] In October 1807, in a letter addressed to Lord Minto, the new Governor-General, Malcolm wrote that Barlow's decision to transfer authority over the Mysore Resident from Calcutta to Madras had not been wise. Military authorities were far less likely to challenge the Resident's authority if he represented the Governor-General, for they could not influence the Supreme Government in the same way that they could lobby the members of a local Presidency administration.

It is impossible (within the compass of this letter) to go into a detail of what has since occurred at Mysoor, but I can assure your lordship that such was the presumption of individuals upon expected support at Madras, that in the case of Lieutenant Colonel Ogg at Bangalore, which is upon record, and some others of still great magnitude, which are not so, nothing but the firm, honorable and decided personal support of Lord William Bentinck (who fully understood and highly admired the principles of our connection with Mysoor) could have enabled that able and virtuous public officer, Mark Wilks, to have carried on the duties of his station; and even with expectation of that support, he was at one period almost forced to resign rather than continue exposed to the vexation, intrigues and opposition of military officers in Mysoor, who were encouraged, if not stimulated, by the countenance of men high in power at Madras.[103]

Malcolm went on to point out that if Bentinck had failed to support Wilks, the Acting Resident's resignation would have led Purnaiya to resign as Diwan, or give way to the 'tide of the moment', to become a cipher of the Madras Government. Because Wilks and Purnaiya had held their ground, however, Mysore had been free of real disaffection during the Vellore crisis. 'Though the name of the family of Tippoo Sultaun was the watchword of revolt', Malcolm noted, 'not a man of the army of Mysore (upwards of 10,000 in number), not one inhabitant of that country, was convicted of either mutiny or treason, a proof (beyond all opinion) of the vigilance, vigour and excellence of the existing government.' Malcolm also remarked that the 'degradation' of Krishnaraya's government in the eyes of his subjects

. . . will generally have its origin in the abuses and excesses of the military, who (from their habits) do not much respect civil authority, and are too apt at times to treat the officers of the local government with contempt, and its subjects with oppression. This disposition can only be kept in check by the spirit and decision of the British resident, who must (however invidious the task) either evade his duty or come to issue on every question of this nature that arises, and this he cannot do unless he is fully supported by the government under which he acts. . . .[104]

NOTES

1. UN, Petrie's Minute, 30 January 1806, Portland MS., PwJb/140, not paginated. This minute, written prior to the Vellore Mutiny, was part of an exchange of ideas about the role of the Madras Army, and how the force should be structured in future, in order to reduce expenses and meet security needs.
2. BL/OIOC, Petrie's Minute, 17 July 1806, *HMS*, V. 508, pp. 249-57.
3. For Bentinck's circular, asking district officers to collect information about local disaffection, see BL/OIOC, Circular, 3 August 1806, *HMS*, V. 508, pp. 40-2.
4. BL/OIOC, Cradock's Minute, 2 August 1806, *HMS*, V. 508, pp. 3-5.
5. BL/OIOC, Subadar Şikandar Khan's Statement, *HMS*, V. 508, pp. 5-6.
6. TNSA, Sheikh Qasim's Deposition, *MSP*, V. 20, pp. 1225-45.
7. Wilson, V. 3, p. 151. In mid-1805, new regulations for cavalry recruitment stipulated that those enlisted as *sowars* should be between the ages of seventeen and twenty-five, at least four feet, five inches tall, and Muslims 'of good sects', or else Rajputs, Marathas, or Rachawars. A Muslim 'of good sect' meant those with some claim to Ashraf heritage, as opposed to local castes who had converted to Islam, or people whose ancestry was known to be mixed, such as the Tamil Labbai.
8. Ibid., V. 2, pp. 106-9, 150-5; Henry H. Dodwell, Sepoy Recruitment in the Old Madras Army (London, 1922), p. 29. Most of the Nawab's horsemen had been taken into the Company's service in 1780-4, during the Second Anglo-Mysore War. At that time, four of these recently-drafted *risalas* mutinied simultaneously at Arni and Arcot, under the direction of some of Muhammad Ali Wallajah's courtiers. To the horror of the Madras authorities, the *sowars* were supported by parties of sepoys and artillery lascars. Several British officers were taken hostage by the mutineers, but were overpowered by loyal forces within a few days.
9. BL/OIOC, *Secret Letters from Madras*, Series 1, V. 3, GC/FSG to SC/EIC, 30 September 1806, paras. 203-20.
10. BL/OIOC, Bentinck to Maitland, 3 August 1806, HMS, V. 508, pp. 27-31; Bentinck also wrote to Bengal, asking the Supreme Government to reinforce the Madras Army with at least one European regiment. See LB/OIOC, Bentinck to Barlow, 3 August 1806, *HMS*, V. 508, pp. 21-6.
11. BL/OIOC, Buchan to Wilks, 3 August 1806, *HMS*, V. 508, pp. 31-3.
12. Quoted in G.R. Gleig, *Life of Major-General Sir Thomas Munro* (London, 1830), p. 362.

13. For instance, Major-General Dugald Campbell reported 'perfect tranquillity and good order' in all of the garrisons of the Ceded Districts, TNSA, Campbell to Cradock, 17 July 1806, *MSP*, V. 19, pp. 1014-15. Similar reports were received from Colonel Harcourt regarding the 1/18th Native Infantry, occupying Vellore; from William Blackburne, the British Resident at Thanjavur, regarding the Tanjore Provincial Battalion; and from Mark Wilks and Major-General Hay MacDowall regarding the troops under their command in Mysore. See BL/OIOC, Harcourt to Cradock, 4 August 1806, *HMS*, V. 508, p. 65; BL/OIOC, Blackburne to Buchan, 4 August 1806, *HMS*, V. 508, pp. 101-2; and BL/OIOC, Wilks to Bentinck, 8 August 1806, *HMS*, V. 508, pp. 486-7. Blackburne, however, also remarked that he was pleased to 'counteract . . . the false and injurious impressions which were made at the court of his Excellency, the Raja, by the first vague and exaggerated reports of the affair in question'.
14. There were food riots in Madras in November and December, but these were occasioned by drought and rising food prices rather than the discontent of the Army. Indeed, sepoys were called in to put down the riots and guard the bazars. See BL/OIOC, Memorial of the Court of Directors to the Privy Council, 1807, *HMS*, V. 431, pp. 337-73.
15. BL/OIOC, Report of the Mixed Commission, *HMS*, V. 508, pp. 103-21.
16. TNSA, Barlow to Bentinck, 11 August 1806, *MSP*, V. 21, pp. 1847-50.
17. TNSA, Barlow's Minutes, 11 August 1806, *MSP*, V. 21, pp. 1850-60.
18. BL/OIOC, Bentinck's Minute, 26 August 1806, *HMS*, V. 509, pp. 33-4.
19. BL/OIOC, Minutes of Cradock, Petrie, and Oakes, *HMS*, V. 509, pp. 35, 47-8, 143-8.
20. BL/OIOC, Bentinck's Minute, 8 September 1806, *HMS*, V. 509, pp. 149-54. The order was released, as it turned out, the day after the execution of the condemned Vellore mutineers.
21. UN, Bentinck to Bosquet, 2 October 1806, Portland MS, PwJb/727, pp. 247-51.
22. BL/OIOC, Bentinck's Minute, 23 September 1806, *HMS*, V. 509, pp. 333-9. I have been unable to find the exact number of the prisoners, or a list of those who were to be tried by court martial.
23. BL/OIOC, Cradock's Minute, 2 September 1806, *HMS*, V. 509, pp. 104-8.
24. BL/OIOC, Bentinck's Minute, 3 September 1806, *HMS*, V. 509, pp. 113-19; BL/OIOC, Minutes of Oakes and Petrie, ibid., pp. 143-8, 185-92.

25. BL/OIOC, Harcourt to Agnew, 23 September 1806, *HMS*, V. 509, pp. 385-6. To add to the drama of the scene, the firing squad was composed of loyal sepoys of the 1/1st and 2/23rd Native Infantry battalions.
26. TNSA, Dyce to Welsh, 6 August 1806, *MSP*, V. 28, pp. 897-9. British officers stationed at Palaiyamkottai, and the civilian officials at Tirunelveli, had picked out the waterfalls of Papanasam as a sort of 'proto-hill-station' around the time of the Vellore Mutiny. The area was located near Ambasamudram, about thirty miles from Tirunelveli.
27. Although Nandidurgam might seem an oddly isolated place for the Commander-in-Chief's holiday, it was in fact located within 150 miles of most of the south Indian cantonments then occupied by European troops.
28. This road led, eventually, to Hyderabad.
29. Mohibbul Hasan, *History of Tipu Sultan* (Calcutta, 1971), pp. 222-3, op cit., Dirom, pp. 43-9; Hamid Khan, *Tarikh-i-Hamid Khan*, Bankipur MS, no. 619, ff. 88b-9a.
30. Some British officers were imprisoned in a cave at the foot of the durgam, but no evidence has been found to substantiate the rumours of British prisoners being hurled off the cliffs.
31. After the Fourth Anglo-Mysore War, Company troops occupied all of the major hill forts of Mysore and the Ceded Districts. These were systematically rendered indefensible by the demolition of the bastions defending their gates, and by the destruction of tanks and water channels.
32. The introduction of European fruit trees may have occurred under Tipu Sultan's rule; the Sultan was, as Buchanan notes, quite interested in horticulture, and maintained impressive gardens near Seringapatam.
33. Welsh, V. 1, pp. 310-18.
34. Ibid., p. 318.
35. Ibid., p. 310.
36. TNSA, Jamadar Shaikh Dawood's Testimony, *MSP*, V. 4, pp. 2423-4. '. . . He has heard that about 300 sepoys were on leave in the neighborhood, with arms, ammunition, etc., etc., from Vellore and other places, but he thinks they are gone. He also heard that many deserters from Vellore are hereabouts. . . .'
37. BL/OIOC, Harcourt to Cradock, 4 August 1806, *HMS*, V. 508, p. 65.
38. Wilson, V. 3, pp. 87-8. Both battalions of the 18th Native Infantry were raised at Bangalore and Nandidurgam in July 1800. The nucleus of the corps consisted of drafts from veteran battalions then serving in Mysore: the two battalions of the 1st Native Infantry, the 2/4th, 1/13th, and 1/14th Native Infantry battalions, and the crack 1/8th

and 1/12th Native Infantry corps. The rank and file of the 18th Native Infantry consisted mainly of demobilized *sipahis* who had been serving Tipu Sultan as late as May 1799. The 2/18th, known as the 'Nandi' battalion, was warned for active service during the Second Anglo-Maratha War, but missed the Battle of Assaye, being deployed to guard Wellesley's line of march.

39. TNSA, Subadar Abdul Qadir's Testimony, *MSP*, V. 4, pp. 2397-8.
40. TNSA, Subadar Kasturi's Testimony, *MSP*, V. 4, p. 2402.
41. TNSA, Jamadar Shaikh Dawood's Testimony, 26 October 1806, *MSP*, V. 4, p. 2416.
42. TNSA, Subadar Kasturi's Testimony, *MSP*, V. 4, p. 2402. This, Kasturi claimed, occurred before the Vellore Mutiny.
43. TNSA, Jamadar Sheikh Dawood's Testimony, 26 October 1806, *MSP*, V. 4, pp. 2417-18.
44. For more information about traditional Indian puppetry, see R.V.S. Sundaram, 'Puppetry', *Encyclopedia of the Folk Culture of Karnataka* (Madras, 1991), V. 1, pp. 383-99.
45. TNSA, Subadar Kasturi's Testimony, *MSP*, V. 4, p. 2402.
46. TNSA, Jamadar Sheikh Dawood's Testimony, 26 October 1806, *MSP*, V. 4, pp. 2418-19.
47. TNSA, Jamadar Sheikh Dawood's Testimony, 26 October 1806, *MSP*, V. 4, pp. 2420-1.
48. TNSA, Muirhead to Ogg, 12 October 1806, enclosing a translation of the Tamil deposition of Subadar Kasturi, Appendix No. 5 of Nandidurgam Enquiry Proceedings, *MSS*, V. 4, pp. 2428-36. It seems, given that he spoke Tamil, that Subadar Kasturi was a Labbai.
49. Ibid., pp. 2432-3.
50. Ibid., pp. 2437-8.
51. TNSA, Naigue Abdul Qadir's Desposition, *MSS*, V. 4, p. 2395.
52. This occurred on October 12. See TNSA, Major Alexander Muirhead to Lieutenant-Colonel Ogg, 12 October 1806, *MSP*, V. 4, p. 2429.
53. Present-day Chikballapur, about five miles north-east of Nandi.
54. TNSA, Sepoy Ranga's Testimony, *MSP*, V. 4, pp. 2408-9.
55. TNSA, Sepoy Virasah's Testimony, ibid., p. 2409.
56. Ibid., pp. 2485-6; 2661-3.
57. Located about thirty-four miles from Nandi.
58. TNSA, Jamadar Sheikh Dawood's Testimony, *MSP*, V. 4, pp. 2422-3.
59. Ibid., p. 2424.
60. TNSA, Testimonies of Subadar Kasturi, Naigue Arnasum, Sepoy Muttu, and Mussalmani, ibid., pp. 2402-7. The sepoy who brought this news later explained to the court of enquiry that he had gone out into a field near the village 'on a call of nature' and had seen the sepoys' wives and

children going away 'in parties . . . of ten or twelve'. He ran at once to the Barracks of his own company, but finding them deserted had gone to report to Kasturi. The villager who reported the evacuation of the sepoys' families was a local figure of some note, who had been a servant of (then) Captain Baird during his imprisonment at Nandidurgam—a scrap of information added to the proceedings as a cue to British officers that his testimony was 'reliable'.

61. Ibid.
62. There are several references, in the Vellore Records, to Muslim sepoys calling each other Paraiyars. For Muslims the term meant someone of low origin, such as a convert from one of the 'untouchable' communities. In this case, it may have been a slur against Kasturi for being a Labbai.
63. TNSA, Cuppage to Davis, 18 October, *MSP*, V. 22, pp. 2491-2.
64. Ibid.
65. TNSA, Davis to Reynell, 19 October 1806, *MSP*, V. 22, pp. 2492-4.
66. Guddibanda was a small town located in the hill country approximately thirty miles north of Nandi.
67. The man's reference to the Raja of Cochin seems to have been a rather confused account of a minor revolt that occurred at Cochin earlier that year.
68. TNSA, Testimony of Jerober Singh and Havildar Venkatram, *MSP*, V. 4, pp. 2410-12.
69. TNSA, Jamadar Sheikh Dawood's Testimony, ibid., p. 2427.
70. TNSA, Cradock to MacDowall, October 1806, *MSP*, V. 22, pp. 2496-8.
71. If this had been the case, the men would have been very disappointed with the plunder available at Nandidurgam, which was a pathetic shell in 1806, compared to what it had been in Tipu Sultan's day, when the fort was destroyed and ransacked by the Marquess of Cornwallis' troops.
72. TNSA, Jamadar Sheikh Dawood's Testimony, *MSP*, V. 22, pp. 2416-25; 2427-8.
73. TNSA, MacDowall to Agnew, 31 October 1806, *MSP*, V. 22, pp. 2766-73.
74. TNSA, Davis to Cradock, 4 November 1806, *MSP*, V. 23, pp. 2930-6.
75. TNSA, MacDowall to Agnew, 1 November 1806, *MSP*, V. 23, pp. 2892-5.
76. James Kirkpatrick, 'A View of the State of the Deccan, 4th June 1798', *Wellesley Papers*, BL Add. Mss 13582, f. 38, pt. 11.
77. TNSA, Ogg to Cradock, 15 October 1806, *MSP*, V. 22, pp. 2482-5.
78. Ibid.
79. TNSA, Ogg to Reynell, 20 October 1806, *MSP*, V. 22, p. 2663.
80. Ibid., 25 October 1806, *MSP*, V. 22, p. 2665.

81. TNSA, Ogg to Reynell, 25 October 1806, *MSP*, V. 22, pp. 2689-91.
82. Ibid., pp. 2688-9.
83. TNSA, MacDowall to Ogg, 28 October 1806, *MSP*, V. 23, pp. 2937-9.
84. UN, Portland MS, PwJb/49, pp. 365-90, Letters, November 1806. Ogg may have thought he was within his rights if he considered the city of Bangalore to be part of the 'cantonment'. At that time, there was no proper military station at Bangalore, and the Company's troops were housed in the old fortress and the adjoining streets—the practical result being that the area under British jurisdiction overlapped with that under the *qiladar*. Seringapatam was the only town in Mysore that had been placed entirely under Company jurisdiction.
85. TNSA, *MSP*, V. 23, pp. 2895-2919.
86. TNSA, *MSP*, V. 23, pp. 3157-68.
87. TNSA, Sepoy Ramaswamy's Testimony, 5 November 1806, *MSS*, V. 4, pp. 2446-8.
88. TNSA, Jamadar Lullab-ullah Sayyid Hussain's Testimony, *MSS*, V. 4, pp. 2448-51.
89. TNSA, Testimonies of Jamadar Muttiah, Havildar Venkatswami, and Sepoys Muhammad Gowse and Abdul Qadir, *MSS*, V. 4, pp. 2451-5.
90. TNSA, Havildar Qasim Khan's Testimony, ibid., *MSS*, V. 4, pp. 2453-6.
91. TNSA, Sepoy Sayyid Ibrahim's Testimony, 11 November 1806, *MSS*, V. 5, pp. 2599-2600.
92. TNSA, Sepoy Sheikh Buddin's Testimony, 12 November 1806, *MSS*, V. 5, pp. 2607-8.
93. TNSA, Kallianu's Testimony, 14 November 1806, *MSS*, V. 5, pp. 2609-10.
94. UN, Bangalore Court of Enquiry Proceedings, 18 November 1806, Portland MS, PwJb/57, pp. 4016-32.
95. TNSA, Ogg to MacDowall, 23 November 1806, *MSP*, V. 25, pp. 4174-7.
96. TNSA, Cradock's Minute, 9 November 1806, *MSP*, V. 23, pp. 3006-14.
97. UN, Wilks to Bentinck, 23 October 1806, Portland MS, PwJb/49, pp. 377-8.
98. TNSA, Barlow to Bentinck, 4 December 1806, *MSP*, V. 24, pp. 3764-71. The basis of this conclusion was that the 2/18th Native Infantry contained a large number of sepoys who formerly had served Tipu Sultan. According to this logic, however, over half of the battalions of the Madras Army should have been disbanded, for thousands of Tipu's *sipahis* had been recruited into every unit that had served in Mysore since 1799.

99. TNSA, Dyce to Welsh, *MSP*, V. 28, pp. 903-7.
100. Close had been the first British Resident at the Mysore court, in 1799, before being transferred to Poona; it was at that time that Mark Wilks took over as Acting Resident.
101. USL, WP1/166/4, Lieutenant-Colonel J. Malcolm to Major-General Sir Arthur Wellesley, 3 March 1807.
102. USL, WP1/170/72, Lieutenant-Colonel J. Malcolm to Major-General Sir Arthur Wellesley, 20 June 1807.
103. USL, WP1/175/25/3, Copy of a letter from Lieutenant-Colonel Sir J. Malcolm to Lord Minto, 8 October 1807. Malcolm was thinking, very specifically, of Major-General Cradock.
104. Ibid. Malcolm refers, of course, to the British military forces stationed in Mysore.

7

The *Faqir* Investigations

British officers in south India in 1806 were hamstrung by their own ignorance. If sepoy battalions had been managed efficiently, there should have been a better understanding of the indigenous people, their languages, and their customs. As mentioned in the previous chapter, the General Orders emanating from Fort St. George, although meant to calm the Army, occasioned dread wherever British officers and sepoys were essentially strangers to each other. Those officers most inclined to panic, however, were not the totally ignorant—most of whom were simply baffled by the Vellore crisis—but rather those who, like James Welsh, possessed enough superficial knowledge of south Indian society to attempt to comprehend what was happening. In the end, very often, such officers drew connections that were wholly unwarranted, especially between 'disaffection' in sepoy battalions and the teachings and movements of itinerant Muslim mystics, or *faqirs*. This is one of the most revealing aspects of the Vellore crisis.

The attention of the Council of Fort St. George was drawn to the issue of itinerant *faqirs* early in its review of the Vellore proceedings. Wandering holy men frequently attached themselves to sepoy battalions, and the Council could not overlook the fact that the Vellore conspirators had met at a Sufi *dargah*, the tomb of Amin Pir.[1] It also struck the Council that most of the conspirators were—or were thought to be—devout Muslims.[2] Indeed, one of the serving women of Haidar Ali's *mahal* testified that at least one *faqir* had been inside the palace during the Mutiny.[3] As the Vellore crisis expanded to other parts of south India, the authorities at Madras noticed that *faqirs* also were mentioned in association with the incidents at Nandidurgam and Bangalore, and elsewhere. The fact that *faqirs* were not mentioned in connection with the incidents at Wallajahbad or Hyderabad was never discussed in any of the Council's correspondence or minutes.

A number of Army officers, it seems, became convinced that *faqirs*, in fact, were the common denominator of the Vellore crisis—mysterious catalysts for anti-British sentiments. The *faqirs* were known to travel from one cantonment to another; therefore, they must have been the communication network linking groups of conspirators in different parts of the country.

In early November 1806, the Madras Government decided to determine whether or not the *faqirs* of south India were involved in an anti-British conspiracy. Like other investigations launched during the Vellore crisis, this, too, led down a dozen blind alleys. Like the other investigations, the quest for the 'rebel *faqirs*' is more important for what it reveals about the information-gathering techniques of the early Raj, and about Indian opinion, than for what it accomplished. In fact, this was one of the first times that the British directed their gaze at street-level, popular Islam. In 1806, the daily devotional life of south Indian Muslims was not well understood, and this lack of understanding was to lead to gross misinterpretations, false accusations of sedition, and—in a few cases—to incidents so ridiculous as to be funny.

HARCOURT'S INVESTIGATION OF THE SUFIS OF VELLORE

One way to begin to understand the role that *khanaqahs*, *dargahs*, and *faqirs* played in the Vellore crisis is to examine the Islamic institutions in the town of Vellore at the time of the mutiny. Three of these have been mentioned already: the mosque inside the fort, the 'white mosque' of Chanda Sahib (the Sundar Sahib-ki-masjid), and Amin Pir's tomb, or *dargah*.[4] Vellore had been a Muslim military and administrative centre since its conquest by the Qutb Shahis in the seventeenth century; a large number of north Indian Muslims, especially Pathans, were attracted to the town over the years, and they, in turn, drew Sufis seeking both patrons and disciples. Richard Eaton, in his *Sufis of Bijapur*, has examined the nexus of rising political power and ghazi culture in a typical Deccani garrison town.[5] The processes identified by Eaton in Bijapur also were manifested in Bellary, Cuddapah, Kurnool, and other outposts of the Islamic frontier in southern India; nor were these processes confined to the medieval period. In the seventeenth and eighteenth centuries, one could observe similar developments in Islamicized towns of the Carnatic and Mysore.

Whether most medieval ghazis had been spiritual warriors, or soldiers in a more literal sense, may be debated. What is important, for our purposes, is that in eighteenth-century Mysore and the Carnatic, these early standard-bearers of Islam were seen as sword-wielding heroes and martyrs. Muslim soldiers of the period, whether elite cavalry serving the Nawab of Arcot, or sepoys of the Company, were drawn to the shrines of these medieval Sufis as to a kindered spirit. The socio-political context of war had changed by 1800, but Muslim troops still spoke of conflict in terms of *jihad* (holy war of spiritual conquest) and *shehadat* (martyrdom). Indeed, this was the rhetoric often employed by Haidar Ali and Tipu Sultan. However, one could be a martyr even as a rebel against a Muslim overlord, or in a battle between two Muslim kings. Warfare was an integral part of the lifestyle of Muslim soldiers, an important factor in their identity. Several *dargahs* built in Tamil Nadu during the eighteenth century, in fact, celebrated men killed during the Carnatic and Mysore Wars, some of whom were native officers in the service of the East India Company.

In 1823, a Wallajahi court chronicler, Ghulam Abdul Qadir Nazir, described Vellore in his *Bahar-i-Azam Jahi*, an account of Nawab Azim Jah's colourful procession from Chepauk to Nagore.[6] Most locations mentioned in the Vellore Mutiny records are recognizable in this account. Most of the Islamic institutions and structures in Vellore in 1806, apart from those mentioned above, were the tombs of notable Muslim residents. The eldest of these, the tomb of Hazrat Nur Muhammad Qadiri, was located inside the fort, near the Jalakanteshwara mandir, and was said to date from the fourteenth century.[7] Most of the tombs, however, were built in the eighteenth century, and were clustered in the tree-shaded *muqabara* surrounding the *dargah*, *khanaqah*, and *naggar-khana* of Shah Ali Husayni Chishti.[8] Some Vellore *dargahs* were places associated with the high culture of the Wallajahi court, such as the tombs of Hazrat Shah Abu'l-Hasan Qadiri Qurbi, a noted jurist, and his son, Sayyid 'Abdu'l-Latif Dhawqi, a Persian poet who died only a few days before Haidar Ali's forces laid siege to the town in 1780.[9] Other *dargahs*, however, were associated with people on the fringes of Muslim society. One of these, the tomb of Hazrat Ali Sultan, a Chishtiyya *majdhub*, commemorated a mystic who had emerged as a local hero and symbol of anti-Mysore resistance during the siege of 1780–2. Despite the close blockade imposed by Haidar Ali's troops, Hazrat Ali Sultan managed to slip back and forth through the Mysore lines, apparently by making himself invisible. One day, however, he was captured, and Haidar Ali ordered him to be put to death. Three times soldiers executed him, and yet the day after each execution, he returned, still very much alive. Haidar Ali finally realized that he was up against a power beyond his control; he sent Hazrat Ali away, laden with money and gifts. The man gave this bounty to the astonished Mysore soldiers before returning to Vellore, where he soon died of natural causes.[10]

Amin Pir's tomb, like that of Hazrat Ali, was associated with an unusual manifestation of divine power. However, unlike the other *dargahs*, that of Amin Pir celebrated not a ghazi, a scholar, or even a mystic anchorite like Hazrat Ali, but a common labourer. In many ways, both material and spiritual, Amin Pir was a true *faqir*.

> Amin Pir was a porter. No one ever knew that he had attained moral perfection. The eyes of ordinary men could not judge his real worth. One day an oil-presser was filled with wonder at the fact that while other porters demanded more wages for lesser weight, this porter agreed for a low wage to carry a heavier load. He decided to ascertain from him the reason for his accepting a lower wage. Just then, the oil-presser directed his eye at him and discovered, to his great surprise, that the heavy bag placed by him on the head of the porter was one cubit above his head, and was rolling along like a piece of cloud. When he saw that, the oil-presser could not control himself. Immediately, he fell at the feet of Amin Pir, the porter, and became his faithful disciple.[11]

The discovery of 'the secret of his personality' was depressing for Amin Pir, however, for it brought his happy life of quiet anonymity to an end. The burden of living with his new fame soon caused him to fall ill and die, and his unwanted followers subsequently buried him near the Esplanade that separated the fort from the *pettah*. The oil-presser indirectly responsible for Amin Pir's demise was still alive in the 1820s, celebrating the urs of the Pir every year with great devotion.[12]

On 12 November 1806, the Madras Council ordered Colonel Harcourt, then the officer in command at Vellore, to submit a detailed report on the town's resident and itinerant *faqirs*. Harcourt could not carry out these orders to the letter without arousing undue suspicion. Yet his *harkaras* managed to produce, in only a few days, a list of local *faqirs*, their places of residence, and a tally of their disciples. The *harkara* reports startled the commander, who commented that 'the number of these persons now at Vellore appears so unaccountably great that, coupled with a knowledge of their general character, I cannot but entertain a considerable degree of suspicion of their intentions, though I have not the least apprehension of their exciting any serious disturbances'.[13] Within the town walls, the *harkaras* counted 150 *faqirs* and 32 *murids*. Outside the walls, they found 60 *faqirs* and 13 *murids*. Most of the *faqirs* were married men, which was usually the case, the disciples being, for the most part, young single men. Within the town, *faqirs* lived in several locations. Some had their own houses in the bazars, but others stayed at *dargahs*, in mosques, or as paupers in the streets around the *langar khana*. Harcourt's study, in fact, provides a vivid glimpse of the Sufi presence at Vellore. The report mentions four different *masjids*, four *dargahs*, one *tykha* inside the town, and a *masjid* and a *dargah* outside the gates. During their search, the *harkaras* found *faqirs* living in isolated locations on the hillsides above the town, under the trees near the drawbridge of the fort, near a small Indian Christian chapel, and at a sepoy guard post in the *pettah*. Outside the town, *faqirs* also lived at a prominent place known simply as 'Qadir Ali's Flag', and at the brassmen's *choultry*, immediately outside the north gate.[14]

Harcourt's alarm about the number of *faqirs* in Vellore is rather misleading. Given the size of Vellore, its location, and history, the number of *faqirs* found by the *harkaras* was rather small. Indeed, many of the itinerant *faqirs* may have left the town in July, shortly after the mutiny, when British officials first began to probe the identities of local people. Nor had the *faqirs* of Vellore given British officers any reason to suspect them of treachery. Indeed, two *faqirs* had tried to warn the British of the impending mutiny. Sepoy Mustafa Beg had gone to Lieutenant-Colonel Forbes primarily at the prompting of his brother, who shared his house, and who happened to be a *faqir*.[15] As noted earlier, the most dramatic and specific warning about the impending mutiny was given by Rustam Ali Shah, an itinerant *faqir* from Cuddapah, whose words were dismissed until his 'prophecy' came true.[16] Most of the Vellore *faqirs*, however, simply ignored the tumultuous events that unfolded in their town, as they ignored most other political activities. In this disregard for their surroundings, the *faqirs* were emulating the Sufi masters of the past. The goal of the *faqir*, after all, was to attain 'poverty', or detachment from the material world, thus making himself open to the presence of Allah. Ignoring the coming and going of sepoys, and turning a blind eye to the mutiny, was therefore a spiritual exercise. The conspirators had met in *dargahs* and mosques but none of the post-mutiny depositions or testimonies mentioned the participation or even name of a single *mullah* or *faqir*.

Curiously, the *faqir* who presided over Amin Pir's tomb was never accused of sedition by the British. The tomb was probably chosen as a meeting place by the conspirators because of its convenient location on the Esplanade. It already had been, for some time, a popular gathering place for both sepoys and Palace servants. Behind the *dargah* walls, men found a refuge from the prying eyes and ever-alert ears of 'confidential' sepoys and the Paymaster's ubiquitous *harkaras*. In Vellore town, the *dargah* of Amin Pir and the *madrasa* near the *jamma masjid* were places where people could discuss politics freely, assuming—correctly—that the *faqirs* around them were uninterested in their opinions and schemes.

The conspirators, however, did not meet in *dargahs* and mosques simply because these were safe places in which to plan a revolt. Most of the conspirators at Vellore were literate men with an interest, either political or personal, in Islamic theology. One of them, Sidi Muhyi-ud-Din of the 1/1st Native Infantry, was the son of a Vellore *faqir* and a 'perfect master of Persian'. However, being a *faqir's* son did not influence the young soldier's decision to join the conspiracy; by his own admission, he hoped to obtain the very worldly office of town *kotwal* if the mutiny had been successful.[17] Whatever the aspirations of individual conspirators, it was the inherently collective nature of Islamic institutions and the communal cohesiveness of Muslim society that brought them together. Shared interests and a common faith strengthened their relationships. Many of the conspirators were bound together, furthermore, by the knowledge that they shared similar past experiences. Those who had served Tipu Sultan had survived the catastrophic fall of Seringapatam, which had plunged them into a maelstrom of personal chaos, political displacement, economic hardship, and social degradation. Many of these men had wandered across the Deccan and the Carnatic, taking up the *faqir's* patched habit and begging bowl, seeking shelter in the *dargahs* of garrison towns. Most men who followed this path discreetly sought a fresh chance for military service.

A large number of Tipu Sultan's former soldiers attached themselves to insurgent bands, and were killed by the British during the two years immediately following the capture of Seringapatam. The story of Shaikh Mian was typical of ex-Mysore *sipahis* who became anti-British rebels during the period 1799-1802. After the British occupation of Mysore, and the dissolution of Tipu Sultan's army, Shaikh Mian was unable to support himself, but he had heard that rebel forces were gathering north of the Kaveri. For a time, he 'waited as a [*faqir*] in the [*masjid*]' at Palachi, subsisting on charity until he had put aside enough money to travel to Dundiya Waugh's camp. Accepted in the rebel army, he attached himself to a war band led by a *jamadar* named Muhammed Hashem. The band passed through British lines, travelling incognito, and breaking up into small groups; they reassembled at Virupakshi for a surprise attack on the lines of the 5th Native Cavalry at Coimbatore, but the British knew of their approach, and the entire war band was captured by the watchful garrison. Shaikh Mian's story is known from the testimony given before the court martial that sentenced him to be hanged for treason, along with several of his comrades.[18] Such stories were all too common in Mysore at that time. However, thousands of other *sipahis* chose a different life, taking the first opportunity to exchange a *faqir's* patched robe for the uniform of a Company sepoy.

MUHARRAM CELEBRATION AT BANGALORE

Immediately after the Vellore Mutiny, British officers commanding garrisons in Mysore expected some sort of trouble. Mark Wilks, the Acting Resident at the court of Krishnaraya Udaiyar, assured Major-General MacDowall and the Madras Government that the Diwan, Purnaiya, was a loyal ally, and that disorder, if it arose, would be suppressed by the local authorities. However, most British officers and officials had assumed that Tipu Sultan's sons had instigated the Vellore mutiny and concluded that a bloody uprising might occur in Mysore, where thousands of people still pined for the old regime, and daily cursed the new system of government introduced by Purnaiya and the Company. It was imagined that Seringapatam itself would be the most likely place to find the disaffected, but MacDowall's local investigation only resulted in an embarrassing incident in which several local people were dragged before a court of enquiry to explain that the French *tricoleur* that had been spotted was, in fact, an ordinary temple flag. Captain MacPherson, to whom the 'flag' was brought described it as a 'symbol of wretchedness and rags', consisting of a black *kumbli*, a piece of white cotton, and the red chintz end of a sari, sewn together. One can see why a British officer, from a distance, might mistake the flag for a French *tricoleur*, but one has to admit that if such a device had been hoisted over a Hindu temple, it was a rather shabby one.[19]

This incident, however, demonstrates how oblivious MacDowall was to the socio-economic condition of the city under his command. In 1799, when the British stormed its walls, Seringapatam and its suburbs were home to perhaps two hundred thousand people; thousands had fled during and after the siege, when every house in the city was sacked. Thousands more went to Vellore with Tipu Sultan's family, or dispersed across Mysore. A large number of Hindu inhabitants, meanwhile, had moved to Mysore city, to live near the new court. Other people, forcibly moved to the capital during Tipu Sultan's reign, drifted back to their old homes. Seringapatam was a gutted city in 1806, its population perhaps a tenth of what it had been in 1799, and this remnant was dependent on the employment and market offered by a relatively small, rear echelon garrison. The Muslim part of the population, for the most part, had been dispersed, as had any partisans who still hoped for the return of Tipu Sultan's regime.

In fact, many of the Muslims of Seringapatam had moved to join the already large and vibrant Muslim community of Bangalore. At the time of the Nandidurgam incident, in which *faqirs* seemed to play a prominent role, British officers wondered where the sympathies of Bangalore's Muslims lay. Haidar Ali and Tipu Sultan had patronized a number of Sufis there, some from as far away as Arabia. Even after Tipu Sultan's death, Bangalore continued to be a centre of Islamic learning, with several active, living *pirs* and at least one *madrasa.* As early as August 1806, before any signs of disaffection had been seen in the sepoy battalions stationed in Mysore, Lieutenant-Colonel Ogg prohibited native officers and sepoys from attending a religious ceremony presided over by a prominent local *faqir* who had been one of Tipu Sultan's *pirs.*[20] When he heard about the discontent of the detachment of the 2/18th Native Infantry at Nandidurgam, Ogg became convinced that wandering *faqirs* had encouraged the sepoys at Bangalore to disobey their officers, and that Madhu Ram, the district *amildar*, had also done his best to sow the seeds of discontent. He warned Davis, who had been sent up to Nandidurgam with a detachment of dragoons, that the two wings of the 2/18th Native Infantry seemed to have been 'conspiring'. Consequently, Davis moved his troop from Ascottah to a position north of Bangalore, while Ogg organized another dragoon picquet at the old Palace inside the walled city, which was reinforced with a field gun.[21]

A few days later, Ogg sent Cradock a copy of a 'lamentation', said to commemorate the death of Tipu Sultan, which had been sung during Muharram 'under the nose of the [*amildar*] and [*kotwal*]'. He added that he sought other 'seditious' writings, said to have been penned by a teacher at the Bangalore *madrasa.* Ogg, who probably could not read the 'lamentation', told Cradock that it contained the most virulently anti-British sentiments imaginable, and that those connected with it deserved severe punishment, lest they be 'encouraged to more daring attempts'. In his righteous indignation, however, Ogg ignored that the individuals in question were not the Company's subjects, but those of Raja Krishnaraya Wodeyar. Ogg's attempt to locate the source of anti-British propaganda in Bangalore was to lead British officers and sepoy investigators deep into the lives of the town's underworld of displaced persons, *faqirs*, and suspicious strangers.[22]

One of these sepoy investigators was Muhammad Gowse. He had been ordered to obtain information about the mysterious letter that had been thrown into the lines of HM 22nd Dragoons, and he reasoned that the *dargah* of Ibrahim Shah was a place where one was likely to encounter literate people. At the *dargah*, Gowse was hailed by a man named Mir Hussain, who also was known around town as Ghulam Hussain—the latter, perhaps, a 'religious' name.[23] When asked who he was, Gowse lied and said he was a cavalry trooper from Ranipet. The sepoy then asked Ghulam Hussain if he had been an *amildar* or *asaf* in the days of Tipu Sultan, but the man explained that he had been a *sowar*. Four hundred of his comrades, he added, were now soldiers of the 18th Native Infantry.[24] Muhammad Gowse knew something about Ghulam Hussain already, and had been told that the man possessed a book about Tipu Sultan. He asked if he could purchase the book for five rupees, but Ghulam Hussain replied—in a rather suspicious manner, the sepoy thought—that he had thrown all his books and papers into a well. Ghulam Hussain then turned the conversation to the events at Vellore, remarking that the men who had fought the British there had 'acted bravely, and died well'. He added that 'we should all have lost our honour, and been obliged to wear hats', were it not for their sacrifice. Repeatedly, as he said these things, the man exclaimed, 'O Sultan, why are you gone?'[25]

When the court of enquiry confronted Ghulam Hussain with Gowse's testimony, the man offered them a different version of what had transpired at the *dargah*. He said that Gowse sent for him at his home, offering a rupee if he would give him a copy of a *munaqbat* written in honour of Tipu Sultan.[26] Ghulam Hussain told the court how he replied that his papers all had been destroyed, but that he would ask if anyone else possessed such a book.[27] In seeking out a copy of the book for Sepoy Muhammad Gowse, Ghulam Hussain began with his son-in-law, Mir Ghulam Ali, son of the Bangalore *kotwal* and a student at Sheikh Ansur's *madrasa*. Mir Ghulam Ali, however, said he did not have a copy of that particular book.[28] What Ghulam Hussain did not know was that he was being tailed by a second sepoy, Sayyid Ismail. This second sepoy testified that Ghulam Hussain lived with the son-in-law of the *qazi* of Kolar. Sepoy Sayyid Ismail had met the *qazi's* son-in-law on the street on 8 November, and had been asked whether or not there had been a disturbance in the battalion. When Sayyid Ismail said that nothing had happened, the *qazi's* son-in-law declared, 'The English government will be destroyed shortly.'[29] Seeking more information about the mysterious dirge that Gowse had mentioned, the court of enquiry called the *kotwal's* son, Mir Ghulam Ali, and asked him if he had the *munaqbat* 'composed by Sheikh Ansur in praise of Tipu Sultan?' The witness said he did not possess that particular poem, but that it often was repeated by a certain *kaligar*, or tinman, during Muharram. The court then asked Mir Ghulam Ali if he himself remembered the words, to which the *kotwal's* son retorted: 'No—how could I recollect what was repeated by fifteen thousand people?' He added that his master, Sheikh Ansur, did not teach Muharram songs in his *madrasa*.[30]

A few days passed before the court of enquiry resumed their quest for the 'seditious' Muharram song, for it took the authorities some time to locate the *kaligar*, Shaikh Buddin. The man admitted that he had once possessed the *munaqbat* composed by Shaikh Ansur, but that he had given it to Sepoy Hussain Khan some time in May 1806.[31] Sepoy Hussain Khan confessed that he had looked at the book, but that he had returned it after having a *munshi* copy out several lines for him. When confronted together, however, the tinman and the sepoy quarrelled about every detail of their respective stories. The *dubash*, Akbar Ali Beg, interrupted the proceedings to inform the panel of British officers that during Muharram, Sepoy Hussain Khan had brought him the book in question. Perusing it, he had noticed that he contained all manner of abuse directed at the 'ministers' who 'betrayed' Tipu Sultan during the Fourth Mysore War, especially Purnaiya.[32] He himself had written in the margin of the book that such language was 'improper'. Akbar Ali Beg added that he was certain the soldier had returned the book; others had seen it, and had accosted him, calling him a *rafzi* for what he had written in the margin.[33]

Meanwhile, two other soldiers, Sepoy Grenadier Abbas Khan and Sepoy Muhammad Shalli, stumbled upon a second possible link to a 'seditious' plot involving the *amildar*. Sitting down at a Sufi's *makan* near the fort, Abbas Khan told Muhammad Shalli that 'God almighty himself had subjected them to this unfortunate service'. The remark—indeed, their whole conversation—was staged, for they hoped that they could lure possible traitors by making such inflammatory comments. As they had hoped, a stranger took an interest in what they were saying. He later was identified as Abdul Shakur, a *munshi* formerly in the service of the Mysorean princes who had been taken to Vellore. He was alleged to have said to the two sepoys: 'Alexander the Great . . . possessed the greatest power and dominion, and . . .

even he was destroyed'. According to Abbas Khan, the man concluded his diatribe on the transitory nature of political power by exclaiming, 'Can the European government possibly remain? This is only for a few days.' Later, Abdul Shakur asked the sepoys if they had met Abdullah Khan of Chaulur, but Abbas Khan replied that they knew no such person.[34] Abdul Shakur replied that it was dangerous to speak one's mind. A *faqir*, overhearing this exchange between the two sepoys and the *munshi*, admonished them all for speaking thus in the *dargah*, adding, 'I possess one corner under their government, and may God preserve their government'.[35]

The *faqir's* name was Adam Shah, and he told the court of enquiry a different version of the same story. He claimed that Abbas Khan had asked him to remain in the *makan* as a witness to what was said. Abdul Shakur, according to the *faqir*, said, 'Many sovereigns vanish from the face of the earth; they are birds of passage, like the swallow, and . . . the noon day remains with no man. So many emperors have vanished, this is going likewise.' Adam Shah, upon hearing this, remarked that 'he was contented with a small portion of *ragi*, and that whoever was lord of the country, he thought it his duty to pray for his welfare'.[36]

Subadar Abdul Qadir was in charge of the sepoy investigators, and as soon as he heard about Abdul Shakur he set out to arrest the man and bring him before Lieutenant-Colonel Ogg. At the Sufi's *makan*, however, he was told that the individual whom he sought had gone to the *amildar's* house. From the gate of the *amildar's* house, the Subadar was conducted into the presence of Madhu Ram by a peon, and explained that he was seeking a man named Abdul Shakur. According to Subadar Abdul Qadir, the *amildar* immediately cried out: 'Has the Colonel ordered you to force your way into everybody's house to catch people?' The Subadar protested with the age-old soldier's excuse that he was merely following orders. The *amildar* was not to be appeased, and retorted: 'The whole town is in a state of uproar and confusion—well it is enough!' Ordered to leave the house, Subadar Abdul Qadir had not walked one hundred paces down the street before the peon stopped him and beckoned him down a side lane. There, 'squatting on the ground', was Abdul Shakur, who was arrested on the spot. Arguing with 'the extremest [*sic*] violence of passion', the *munshi* was marched away by Naigue Sayyid Buddin, eventually to be handed over to Sepoy Grenadier Abbas Khan.[37] Oddly enough, Abbas Khan was instructed to present the prisoner to the *amildar* and ask that he be confined in the *choultry*.[38] The *amildar* refused the request, pointing out that the arrest had been made not only without his consent, but very much against his wishes. He told the sepoy that he no longer could trust 'any of you', and suggested, 'in a paroxysm of passion', that, if Lieutenant-Colonel Ogg was so insistent on imprisoning the man, he should confine Abdul Shakur to the Company's guard post at the fort.[39]

When brought before the court of enquiry, Abdul Shakur was both composed and well-spoken. He explained that he had heard one sepoy remark to another that the Company's service was hard, and that life had been easier when they had served Tipu Sultan. Abdul Shakur told the court he interjected, 'What is one dominion? The dominion of Alexander vanished. That of Abraham and his army [was] destroyed by stones dropped on their heads by swallows, by the order of the Almighty. . . . This is the thirteenth century, and an iron age it is. No rain has fallen; it is a crust season.'[40] Abdul Shakur admitted that he then had asked about Abdullah Khan of Chaulur, but that the *faqir* had asked him to be quiet, pointing out that Sepoy Grenadier Abbas Khan was a Company servant, and might be punished if someone heard him talking about such things. When questioned about his identity, Abdul Shakur declared that he himself was from Chaulur, where he had been a tutor ten years previously. For a time, he had taught the sons of Abdul Karim, a former *qiladar* of Bangalore. He had been away from the city, but had returned some time in 1805, and had taken up residence in the *pettah*.[41]

THE MYSTERIOUS TIPU SULTAN—*FAQIR* AND FORMER SEPOY

Subadar Abdul Qadir's squad of 'confidential' sepoys, meanwhile, had been busy pursuing yet another set of leads. Sepoys Muhammad Shalli and Shaikh Muhammad had been roaming the bazars for days, hoping to run into some sign of treason, but everywhere they turned, they found that people avoided them, or had no desire to speak with them. Tired, the two sepoys sat down to rest at the sepoy guard post near the *choultry*.[42] Not long after, a prisoner wearing leg-irons staggered up to the sepoys, attended by one of the *kotwal's* peons. His nose had been cut-off—a common form of punishment in Mysore, even for relatively petty offences. The man introduced himself as Timmanayaka, one of three hereditary *talaiyars* of Bangalore *pettah*. The sepoys explained that they were trying to learn who had thrown the strange letter into the dragoons' lines, and Timmanayaka informed them that the other *talaiyars* could answer that question. He himself entered into a lengthy account of how he had come to be disfigured and imprisoned. He explained that, the *amildar* and the other two *talaiyars* had been planning, had the Vellore Mutiny been successful, to seize Bangalore fort from the British. He himself had set out for Madras to foil their plot, but had been ambushed and arrested at the gates of the city. Timmanayaka added that the *amildar* and others were secretly supporting a mysterious individual known as the 'nawab', who lived in a village not far from the city, and who was believed to be receiving information from 'some distant country'. An itinerant Lingayat guru, said to hail from Kanara, also had been in Bangalore, telling people that the Company Raj would fall at the end of the 'Gentoo year', and that a 'new king' then would rise to power in the city.[43]

Sepoy Shaikh Muhammad corroborated the above story, adding that on the morning of 14 November he and Muhammad Shalli went to the village of Palaiyanu, along with Sepoy Muhammad Ismail, to seek out the so-called 'nawab'.[44] On the edge of the village, they met a Paraiyar woman and asked her if any Muslims lived in the area. She answered that there was a Muslim family in another village, not far away. When the sepoys asked her if she knew of any nawab there the woman immediately replied that the man lived nearby, and was said to be supported by a 'Brahmin of Bangalore'. She knew the woman who cooked for him, and from her she had learned that the man's name was Tipu Sultan. Their curiosity piqued, the three sepoys set off at once to meet this mysterious pensioner.[45]

The three soldiers soon came upon a man 'sitting on a piece of leather, on a stone, with two bags in front of him'. This was a typical *faqir* setting. Sepoy Shaikh Muhammad recalled how the man gestured to them to approach and sit down, asking from where they had come. The sepoys lied, saying they had come south from Chitradurga,[46] and were seeking service.[47] They were told not to be concerned about finding service, for soon there would be no end of work for soldiers. According to Shaikh Muhammad, the old *faqir* remarked that the Europeans were 'embroiled among themselves', and would 'soon fight and kill one another', upon which 'we shall all be happy, and have plenty to eat'. This was a shrewd political assessment, coming from a man living on a rock in the Deccan, but then his words ranged from the Napoleonic conflict to the supernatural. He added that God had taken the form of a man, and 'is at this present time in Bangalore, and . . . he is the author of all these things'. A revolt would sweep through Mysore, the *faqir* predicted, beginning at Nandidurgam and spreading to Bangalore and Seringapatam. In the latter city, a buried treasure, hidden away in the days of Tipu Sultan, would be discovered.[48] Until these things happened, however, the *faqir* advised the three sepoys to return to Chitradurga and wait there quietly. He also warned them not to go to Bangalore, as strangers appearing there were being questioned and arrested.[49]

The court of enquiry immediately called Timmanayaka and the other *talaiyars* as witnesses, hoping to find substantive proof of a conspiracy. They were disappointed. Timmanayaka, eager to lay his personal grievances before British officers, gave an elaborate but mostly irrelevant account of his career, stating that the other two *talaiyars* and the *amildar* had been plotting his downfall for years. When his nose had been cut-off by Tipu Sultan, they had threatened to punish any doctor who helped him; after Timmanayaka had gone to Kotagiri to have his wounds attended, his fellow *talaiyars* had seized his possessions and had imprisoned his family. Upon his return, Timmanayaka had encountered further trouble when he had defended a dancing girl who had sought his protection from the other two *talaiyars*. After this last struggle, he had been cast into the *choultry*, of the *kotwal*, where he had seen and heard many suspicious things. Timmanayaka informed the court about the guru 'Lingappah,' who passed the prison from time to time in his *palankin*, with a crowd of attendants. Timmanayaka also mentioned a gardener at the *choultry*, who told him there would be disturbances at Bellary, Sankaridurgam, and elsewhere. The *talaiyars*' peons began to patrol the streets at night after Ogg had published his proclamation calling on people to come forward with information, and they had taken the opportunity to abuse everyone they met. One man, who had gone out to the street to urinate late at night, was arrested and marched to the *choultry*, where the peons demanded five Kanterai *fanams*. In the morning, the man returned to the office of the *kotwal* to complain to the *havildar* of the guard. Perhaps sensing that the officers of the court were growing restless with this meandering tale, Timmanayaka hastily added that he had not told the sepoys about the 'nawab' or about the seditious activities of anyone who worked for the *amildar*.[50] The other two *talaiyars* had nothing to say regarding Timmanayaka's testimony; they simply explained that they had grown up with him, and that he always had been a liar and a thief, whose reputation was known to everyone in Bangalore.[51]

The court of enquiry dismissed Timmanayaka and called for the 'nawab'. This person explained that he changed his original name, Fath Muhammad, to Faqir Muhammad, following his 'distress'. The British officers of the court listened, incredulous, as he related the story of his life. He told them he was the son of Budhullah, a *sipahi* under Bahadur Hyder [*sic*] Ali Khan, who had married the daughter of Ibrahim Sahib, the Sufi whose tomb lay just outside the Delhi Gate of Bangalore fort. Since she was the sister of Tipu Sultan's mother, he thus claimed indirect relationship to the former ruling family. Faqir Muhammad then explained that he and his mother had followed Haidar Ali's standard to Dindigul and Madurai in the early 1750s, at the time of the Carnatic Wars. Budhullah's wife had died during the campaign, and since he himself could not care for a little boy while on the march, he left his son with a poor family and returned to Mysore with Haidar Ali. Faqir Muhammad thus had grown up in the southern Carnatic, and as a teenager, he had enlisted as a sipahi in Nawab Muhammad Ali Wallajah's army. Following the second siege of Thanjavur, he quit the Nawab's service and joined one of the Company's sepoy battalions. Faqir Muhammad explained the internal politics of the two sepoy battalions with which he served in Tirunelveli, and mentioned that his particular unit was transferred to Madras.[52] On the march to Madras, however, Faqir Muhammad fell ill, straggled behind, and encountered one of Haidar Ali's recruiting parties near Thiagur. Enticed by their promises he returned to Mysore to take service under Haidar Hussain, the *qiladar* of Bangalore.[53]

When Haidar Ali invaded the Carnatic in 1780, Faqir Muhammad was left behind in garrison for two years. He then went to the front and fought in the desperate, large-scale battles outside Cuddalore. During the last Anglo-Mysore War, he fought at Seringapatam as a 'jamadar of six men', and managed to escape during the storming of the city. For a year, he survived as a beggar at Mudur and Agapatanam before making his way to Bangalore. *Sowars* of the Company's cavalry supported Faqir Muhammad for a time, but he refused to follow them when they marched off to chase Dundiya Waugh. It was then that he had changed his name to Faqir Muhammad, once more roaming the countryside as a beggar. One day, however, Purnaiya had passed, on a tour with Lieutenant-Colonel Barry Close, then the Resident at Krishnaraya Udaiyar's court. Faqir Muhammad refused to salaam the *Diwan* and was arrested for his impertinence. Sent to Bangalore, he spent five days in the stocks, but the *banias* of the bazar supplied him with fruit and sweets. The *kotwal*, sensing that the people were on Faqir Muhammad's side, then decided to take him outside the city, to Krishnapuram, and quietly turn him loose. Not long after this, while begging in the villages north of Bangalore, he suffered a stroke and became a 'cripple'. Quite literally passed around from one village to another, he eventually was accepted by the people of Palaiyanu. Their meager charity, and occasional gifts from people in Bangalore, allowed him to subsist. The *amildar*, he insisted, was not among his patrons, however.[54]

When confronted with the testimony of the three sepoys, Faqir Muhammad said they were trying to put words into his mouth. It was they who spoke about a rebellion at Nandidurgam, he told the court; it was they who claimed that the sepoys there had taken over the hill fort, and were fighting the British. He told the court he did not care to hear such things, and had advised the sepoys to be quiet. He also claimed that he admonished the soldiers, reminding them that the only power left in south India that was willing to give service to Muslims was the Company Raj. If the sepoys proved unfaithful to the British, they would 'lose their caste and victuals'. He told them that it was precisely such self-seeking behaviour as theirs that had been the ruination of Tipu Sultan. Despite the clarity and historical accuracy of Faqir Muhammad's testimony, however, it was thrown out by the British officers who heard it. In the report of their proceedings, they glibly remarked, 'The man frequently runs into a kind of rhapsody, and then looks like an idiot. It is deemed unnecessary to ask him any more questions.'[55]

The court of enquiry finally considered the mysterious Lingayat guru mentioned by Timmanayaka. One of the *talaiyars* said that Lingappah was known to cure the sick, and had come to his house, once, to read prayers over his sister, who was ill. The *talaiyar* added, however, that he knew nothing of the man's origins. The other *talaiyar* confirmed this story, but called the guru Jotu Lingappah. He himself, he said, was a devotee of Venkatchellah, the Lord of Tirupati—a polite way of saying that he did not much care for Lingayats.[56] Once more the officers of the court were disappointed. When called before the court, the guru explained that everyone called him Jotu, but that his real name was Kuru Lingappah. He had come to Bangalore from a village near Savanur as a priest of the 'cow-keeper caste', and did not consider himself allied with the Lingayats.[57] He admitted that, during his travels, he had been to the Carnatic, but only as far as Venkatagiri; most of the time he stayed in Bangalore. He said he knew nothing of local politics, nor did he wish to discuss such worldly matters.[58]

At this point in their proceedings, the members of the Bangalore court of enquiry had become aware of the government's displeasure regarding their efforts. Desperate to find something that might justify their investigation, they pursued every lead, no matter how obscure. Sepoy Sayyid Muhyi-ud-Din mentioned that he met Sepoys Sayyid Ismail and Muhammad Gowse in the cloth bazar, and that a *qalandar* named Faqir-ud-Din told them about a *sipahi* of Holkar's army, who passed through Bangalore a month earlier.[59] The man had claimed to be on a mission to Mysore on behalf of Karim Sahib's son, and to be making his way to Annakul, to see his family, from whom he had been absent for twelve years.[60] While staying at Sita Sahib's *dargah*, the *sipahi* had offered to take Faqir-ud-Din north to join the Maratha army, but the *faqir* had refused the invitation. After buying flowers to strew over the Sufi's tomb, the *sipahi* had ridden away in the morning.[61] Faced with such evidence as this, Major-General Hay MacDowall wrote to the Governor-in-Council that the investigation of the conduct of Madhu Ram, his officers, and the people of Bangalore seemed pointless. Not a scrap of reliable evidence had been revealed—only ridiculous rumours spread by a 'depraved and infamous vagabond'.[62]

Lieutenant-Colonel Ogg managed to accomplish at least one thing with his investigations—he outraged the *amildar* of Bangalore. Madhu Rao penned formal complaints to several British officers, as well as to Purnaiya, who at once relayed the Raja's displeasure to the Acting Resident, Mark Wilks, as mentioned in the previous chapter. Major Wilks informed the Madras Council that Purnaiya, meeting with him in personally, displayed 'stronger marks of disgust and indignation' than he had ever seen before. Bitterly, the *Diwan* reminded Wilks that spies were employed to watch enemies, not to pry into the domestic affairs of allies.[63] Wilks himself, meanwhile, made his own investigations, cross-checking reports which had been sent to him from Nandidurgam and Bangalore. He pointed out in his own report to the Madras Government that Abdullah Khan, the *moniyagar* of Chaulur, who allegedly offered to assist the sepoys at Nandidurgam if they mutinied, was an inhabitant of the Ceded Districts, and therefore ought to be prosecuted by the Company's civil courts. All of the Udaiyar Raja's subjects mentioned in the reports were, in Wilk's view, harmless, and he recommended that the authorities forget about them.[64] Finally, as for Fatteh Muhammad, alias Faqir Muhammad, the 'nawab', Wilks informed the Madras authorities that he indeed had met Purnaiya and Close during their tour of Mysore in 1801. Immediately after the fall of Seringapatam, he had claimed to be Tipu Sultan himself; Purnaiya wanted to hang him, but Close suggested that the man be released after being whipped through the town. Now, apparently, Faqir Muhammad claimed to be one of Tipu Sultan's relatives, although he had bungled the details of the requisite genealogy.[65]

HERESY TRIAL IN BELLARY

Even as the Bangalore investigation dissolved, Cradock subjected his fellow members of Council to yet another enquiry into the activities of religious mendicants. At Bellary, the main cantonment of the Ceded Districts, a court of enquiry discovered information of an 'extraordinary and unaccountable nature', regarding a group of *faqirs* whose 'strange doctrine tends to the destruction of all order, [and] would loosen those bonds of union that maintain the relations of society alike in every country.'[66] The documents examined by the Council were translations of a very unusual enquiry that took place in early November, under the orders of Lieutenant-Colonel George Martin, the officer commanding at Bellary. Martin had explained, in a letter to Major-General Dugald Campbell, that certain native officers and sepoys of the 2/5th and 2/7th Native Infantry battalions had been charged with attempting to 'introduce doctrines threatening to disturb the public tranquillity of Bellary'. Because the matter was more of a civil than a military nature, the court of enquiry had been composed of 'men whose characters are well known'—prominent local *faqirs*, assistant *kotwals*, *munshis*, and Muslim native officers of the garrison. The *qazi* of Bellary, Shaikh Muhammad, had presided over the enquiry, with orders to 'expound the precepts of the Mussulman faith'.[67]

Sepoy Abdul Nabi of the 2/5th Native Infantry was charged with blasphemy—a rather unusual offence for which to try a soldier. He was accused of having said

> . . . that the [Qur'an] should be thrown away into the water, that prayers were useless, and that it was no crime to commit sodomy on the person who was at prayers; that there was no crime in commiting debauchery, nor [any] difference between good and evil; that a married woman and a strumpet were on the same footing; and that the whole of the doctrines in the books of religious morality were false and undeserving of belief, and that there was no harm in doing, in all respects, that which was forbidden; that by making use of this description of language, several men had been seduced from the faith of Mussalmen [*sic*], and had turned them from fear of the Day of Judgement.[68]

These charges were brought after Sepoy Abdul Nabi allegedly accosted a *munshi* at prayer in the cantonment *masjid*. According to the *munshi*, Abdul Nabi approached him and said there would be no harm in 'sodomizing him' in his present act. Outraged, the *munshi* threatened to drag the sepoy before the *qazi*, and several men who were present, including other sepoys, offered to help the *munshi*.[69] Jamadar Muhammad Tipu of the 2/7th Native Infantry was foremost among the soldiers who came to the *munshi's* aid, telling Abdul Nabi that 'if he [were] not a servant of the Honourable Company, [he] would slipper him'.[70] Subadar Mir Bakr, however, pointed out to the Jamadar that Abdul Nabi was a soldier of the 2/5th Native Infantry, and that it was 'improper' for an officer of one corps to beat a sepoy of another corps.[71]

According to the native commissioned and non-commissioned officers of the light company of the 2/5th Native Infantry in which Abdul Nabi served, the sepoy had been on a collision course with disaster for several months. For four or five months, Havildar Shaikh Buddai had noticed Abdul Nabi talking with Naigue Takub Khan of the light company, Subadar Mir Bakr and Naigue Abdul Giri of the 2/7th Native Infantry, and five or six others. Havildar Shaikh Buddai's descriptions of the group's conversations mirrored the charges brought against Abdul Nabi by the *qazi.* Those who actually conversed with Abdul Nabi gave a slightly different account of what happened.[72] Havildar Shaikh Hussain recalled that one day he asked Naigue Yakub Khan why he was not a practising Muslim. The *naigue* and Abdul Nabi who was present, both replied that the observance of custom was folly, that prayer, and even burial of the dead, were useless exercises. Abdul Nabi, however, took this line of thinking further, telling Shaikh Hussain that he himself was the 'Evil Spirit of Darkness, and the faker [*sic*] was his high priest'. Infuriated by such talk, the Havildar complained to Subadar Sayyid Ali, the native officer of the 7th line company and the recognized battalion authority on matters of Islamic law. The Subadar, however, merely observed that Abdul Nabi was a habitual trouble-maker. He added, rather cryptically, that sooner or later someone would kill him.[73]

It was not long before several non-commissioned officers and sepoys of the light company of the 2/5th Native Infantry complained to Jamadar Muhammad Bakr about Abdul Nabi's attitude toward orthodox Islam. According to the Jamadar, the men had accused Abdul Nabi and his friends from the 2/7th of becoming 'heretics'. Abdul Nabi himself was accused of claiming to be the 'author of a new Koran', and of saying that people were 'unacquainted with the precepts of a true religion, or with a God—that a stone with two [*lakhs*] and a nose was as good as a God. . . .'[74] Apart from his remarks about sodomizing those who dared to pray, Abdul Nabi was accused of declaring that all food and drink were lawful. These new doctrines had been taught at Subadar Mir Bakr's house by Abdul Nabi and his *pir*, an itinerant *faqir* named Alam Ali Shah.[75]

Meanwhile, the men of the 2nd line company of the 2/7th Native

Infantry were only slightly less displeased with Subadar Mir Bakr's behaviour. Sepoy Sheikh Medina described to the court of enquiry how the Muslim officers and a Telugu Hindu officer dragged the Subadar before the European Sergeant-Major of the corps.[76] When the Sergeant-Major heard the complaints against Subadar Mir Bakr, he told the latter that he was astonished that a man of his rank and status could be duped by someone as ingenuous as Abdul Nabi. To this, however, Mir Bakr was said to have replied, 'You do not know Abdul Nabi, for he is a lion heart, though in sheep's clothing.' The Sergeant-Major retorted that Abdul Nabi was an imposter, a cheat, and a dangerous man.[77] When Mir Bakr later explained what happened to his friend, Naigue Yakub Khan, the latter told him that Abdul Nabi had nothing to fear, for he was 'at times invisible, and no one [was] sufficiently skilful to find him out. . .'.[78]

Jamadar Muhammad Bakr explained to the court of enquiry that he tried to stop Abdul Nabi's activities before they led to serious disturbances in the sepoy lines. Jamadar Muhammad Tipu added that matters came to a head when Abdul Nabi began to heckle Muhammad Shah, one of the most prominent *faqirs* in Bellary, who led a Koran study group among the men of the 2/5th Native Infantry. As Muhammad Shah was Jamadar Muhammad Bakr's *pir*, the latter could not idly stand by and allow Abdul Nabi to abuse him; he told the sepoy's friends from the 2/7th Native Infantry to return to their barracks and never associate with Abdul Nabi again.[79] Jamadar Muhammad Bakr then brought the matter before Subadar Sayyid Ali of the 7th line company of the 2/5th Native Infantry, who was recognized as 'head of the Mussulmen [*sic*] of the corps. . .'. Subadar Sayyid Ali questioned Abdul Nabi about his alleged heresy, but the sepoy flatly denied everything, refusing even to discuss the matter. For about a month after that, according to Jamadar Muhammad Bakr, Abdul Nabi and his friends avoided the lines of the 2/5th Native Infantry, but all the while they met secretly in the barracks of the 2/7th Native Infantry. When this became apparent to the native officers, some time in July or August, Abdul Nabi was ordered to avoid his friends altogether, a command to which he assented with reluctance.[80]

Jamadar Muhammad Bakr, however, was still suspicious of Abdul Nabi; donning a disguise, he followed the sepoy when he was off duty. Indeed, as Subadar Sayyid Ali had predicted, Abdul Nabi still met his associates.[81] One of the confidential sepoys of the 2/5th Native Infantry told Jamadar Muhammad Tipu that the 'heretics' met at night in a room off the Main Guard. Part of an old stone structure that dated from the heyday of the Vijayanagar Empire, the room in question had only a few small windows. It could not be approached silently by armed sentries, as they had to ascend an irregular flight of stone slab steps, and the jingling of their equipment would give them away. As Muhammad Tipu was on guard duty, however, he had no reason to sneak around in disguise—or to be silent. Lighting a lantern, as was normally done before checking sentry posts, the Jamadar proceeded directly to the room off the Main Guard, with a havildar and a *naigue*, and surprised Abdul Nabi and Mir Bakr in conversation. The latter was confronted about his nocturnal meetings with Abdul Nabi the next day, but retorted: 'You are a child, and are uninformed.' A few days later, however, after Abdul Nabi was accused once more of accosting a *faqir*, Muhammad Tipu told Mir Bakr that he had better be careful, or he might be hanged for what he was doing.[82]

Confronted by the court of enquiry, Subadar Mir Bakr tried to explain that Abdul Nabi was not the leader of some sort of movement, nor himself a follower. He stressed that his own lineage was 'descended from priests', and that he abhorred heresy.[83] Mir Bakr furthermore insisted that there was nothing improper about his connection with Abdul Nabi, or with the *faqir*, Alam Ali Shah; the root of the problem was that Jamadar Muhammad Bakr sought to build up a following for his own *pir* in the two battalions at Bellary! Mir Bakr explained that the Jamadar warned his brother, Mir Abdullah Jamadar—in his own presence, no less—that he was going astray, and ought to become a follower of Muhammad Shah. When Mir Bakr scoffed at this suggestion, Muhammad Bakr began to harass him, in concert with several other native officers and sepoys who recognized Muhammad Shah as their *pir*.[84] This testimony introduced an intriguing new element into the Bellary proceedings—that of *faqirs* competing for the patronage of sepoys—but unfortunately Mir Bakr's story was not corroborated by any other witnesses. Abdul Nabi himself realized that the best thing he could do, before such a court of enquiry, was deny everything. He stated, rather bluntly, that although he had been accused of heresy by several people over the last five or six months, no 'disinterested evidence' could be produced to substantiate the charge. Defiantly, he offered to plead 'guilty' if the court could produce any proof of his alleged wrong-doing.[85]

Lieutenant-Colonel George Martin was unable to comprehend the meaning of these events. In his report to Major-General Dugald Campbell, he pointed out that two *faqirs*, Alam Ali Shah and Nur Khalil Shah, came to Bellary from Hindustan shortly before the Vellore Mutiny, and that both men taught 'evil doctrines'. They were quiet at first, but on receiving the patronage of Sepoy Abdul Nabi and Subadar Mir Bakr, they began to openly espouse their real sentiments. However, in sharp contrast to the tone of Cradock's minute of 27 November, Martin made it clear that the teachings of the two *faqirs* at Bellary had nothing to do with the disturbances in the rest of the Army. In fact, almost every sepoy of the 2/5th and 2/7th Native Infantry battalions had regarded the two mendicants and their followers with disgust and horror. They had been so unpopular, in fact, that as soon as their protectors were arrested, they fled across the Tungabhadra into the Raichur Doab. The *qazi* assured Martin that if they had not run, someone in Bellary would have killed them; indeed, if the matter had not been made public, there might have been a mass murder of all the alleged heretics. There remained, however, the problem of disposing of Subadar Mir Bakr and Sepoy Abdul Nabi, the latter held in irons in the *choultry* inside the fort. Captain Wright, commander of the light company of the 2/5th Native Infantry, reported that the Subadar refused to believe he had done anything wrong, and was 'sullen and discontented'. To Martin, these facts were sufficient to warrant the removal of both men from the service. As his 'confidential' sepoys had assured him the two corps were loyal, he decided he would not compel the troops to accept a non-commissioned officer and a sepoy who they thought to be 'obnoxious'.[86]

Far from according the Bellary incident the same importance Cradock attached to it, the Council of Fort St. George merely recorded having read the relevant correspondence, and turned their attention to other matters. If what happened at Bellary demonstrated anything, it was that the average Muslim, orthodox in his beliefs, quiet and law-abiding, harboured no secret hatred of the Company Raj. Indeed, in Bellary, a new *masjid* had been built in 1806, and had been endowed with *inam* lands by the principal British administrators of the district.

NOTES

1. BL/OIOC, for example, see Jamadar Shaikh Qasim's Confession, 31 July 1806, *HMS*, V. 508, pp. 7-17.
2. UN, Second Report of Forbes and Coombs, 30 December 1806, Portland MS., Pwjb/59, pp. 4403-62.
3. BL/OIOC, Chumeen Khorah's Testimony, *HMS*, V. 507, pp. 282-3. The unnamed *faqir* seemed to be one of the guests at the wedding.
4. A Persian inscription in the 'Chanda Shah' mosque bears the date AH 1148 (1735-6), and therefore the *masjid* probably came to be associated with Chanda Sahib's name later, perhaps as a corruption of its original name. See Ziyaud-din A. Desai, *A Topographical List of Arabic, Persian, and Urdu Inscriptions of South India* (New Delhi, 1989), p. 156, no. 1586.
5. Richard M. Eaton, *Sufis of Bijapur, 1300-1700: Social Roles of Sufis in Medieval India* (Princeton, 1978).
6. Ghulam 'Abdu'l-Qadir Nazir, *Bahar-i-A'zam Jahi*, tr. S. Muhammad Husayn Nainar (Madras, 1950), pp. 125-34. The Nawab did not take the most direct route, but his intention was to visit several Sufi shrines along a route that also would take him to the scattered remains of his royal estate. Nagore, his destination, was one of the most important centres of Islamic culture on the Coromandel Coast.
7. Ibid., p. 128.
8. Ibid., p. 129.
9. Ibid., pp. 128-9. The *maqabara* was located in the courtyard of the *jamma masjid*, which had been built in 1737-8. See Desai, p. 156, no. 1587. Also see Bayly, pp. 178-9.
10. Ibid., pp. 129-30.
11. Ghulam 'Abdul 'I-Qadir Nazir, *Bahar-i-A'zam Jahi*, tr. S. Muhammad Husayn Nainar (Madras, 1950), pp. 125-34. Also see Susan Bayly, *Saints Goddesses and Kings: Muslims and Christians in South Indian Society, 1700-1900* (Cambridge, 1989).
12. This particular oil-presser was one of Vellore's chief merchants, and he appears frequently in the Company's revenue records as one of those charged with the upkeep of certain Hindu shrines in the area. It seems, therefore, that Amin Pir's tomb attracted both Hindu and Muslim devotees, which was not unusual.
13. TNSA, Harcourt to Buchan, 19 November 1806, *MSP*, V. 5, pp. 2689-91; 'List of Fackeers [*sic*] within the Pettah Walls, Vellore', 19 November 1806, ibid., pp. 2692-6; 'List of Fackeers [*sic*] residing in places adjacent to the Pettah of Vellore', 19 November 1806, ibid., pp. 2697-8.
14. Ibid.

15. BL/OIOC, Mustafa Beg's Testimony, *HMS*, V. 508, pp. 182-6.
16. UN, Second Report of Forbes and Coombs, Appendix no. 28, Portland MS, PwJb/59, pp. 4557-64. After the mutiny, 'the old killedar of Arcot' said to Rustam Ali Shah: 'Rustam faqir, you are a true prophet; what you have foretold has come to pass.'
17. Ibid., pp. 4491-2.
18. TNSA, Shaikh Mian's Testimony, 8 June 1800, *Madras Board of Revenue Proceedings*, V. 255-B, pp. 5759-61.
19. UN, Portland MS, PwJb/49, pp. 337-48, Captain MacPherson's Report.
20. TNSA, Ogg to MacDowall, 21 August 1806, *MSP*, V. 22, pp. 2463-6. Ogg felt that 'improper conversation . . . would take place at meeting[s] of . . . this kind.'
21. TNSA, Ogg to Davis, 7 November 1806, *MSS*, V. 5, pp. 2589-90.
22. TNSA, Ogg to Cradock, 11 November 1806, *MSS*, V. 5, pp. 2591-2.
23. 'Mir' is an honorific for those claiming a relation to the Prophet. It was a common Ashraf title in south India.
24. This may have been true; the 18th Native Infantry, like other Madras units stationed in Mysore, had recruited back up to strength, following the last war with Tipu Sultan, by taking in hundreds of former Mysorean soldiers, and Bangalore had been a major requirement centre.
25. TNSA, Muhammad Gowse's Testimony, 10 November 1806, *MSS*, V. 5, pp. 2584-6.
26. The word is translated, incorrectly, as *munkabbat* in the *Madras Secret Sundries.*
27. When asked why his books and papers had been destroyed, Ghulam Hussain said they had been of 'no consequence', merely being 'lamentations' sung during Muharram. He added that the boys studying in the *madrasa* were more interested in these songs than in their theological studies, and therefore he had destroyed them.
28. TNSA, Ghulam Hussain's Testimony, 10 November 1806, *MSS*, V. 5, pp. 2586-7.
29. TNSA, Sepoy Sayyid Ismail's Testimony, 10 November 1806, *MSS*, V. 5, p. 2587.
30. TNSA, Mir Ghulam Ali's Testimony, 10 November 1806, *MSS*, V. 5, pp. 2587-8.
31. TNSA, Shaikh Buddin's Testimony, 14 November 1806, *MSS*, V. 5, p. 2613.
32. It was widely believed, in the aftermath of Tipu Sultan's death, that he had been betrayed by a number of commanders and ministers, including Purnaiya, some of whom may have been bribed by Mir Alam on behalf of the Nizam of Hyderabad.

33. TNSA, Testimony of Sepoy Hussain Khan and Comments by Akbar Ali Beg, 14 November 1806, *MSS*, V. 5, pp. 2613-14.
34. Chaulur, written 'Chowloor' in the old records, was a small hamlet in the Hindupur Taluq of Anantapur District, not far from Nandidurgam.
35. TNSA, Sepoy Abbas Khan's Testimony, 10 November 1806, *MSS*, V. 5, pp. 2595-6.
36. TNSA, Adam Shah's Testimony, 10 November 1806, *MSS*, V. 5, pp. 2596-7.
37. TNSA, Subadar Abdul Qadir's Testimony, 10 November 1806, *MSS*, V. 5, pp. 2592-5.
38. For Subadar Abdul Qadir to send a subordinate to speak with Madhu Ram, after what had happened, was a subtle insult to the *amildar*. However, as Abdul Shakur was a subject of the Raja of Mysore, turning him over to the *amildar*—and eventually to the town *kotwal*—was merely proper legal procedure.
39. TNSA, Sepoy Grenadier Abbas Khan's Testimony, 10 November 1806, *MSS*, V. 5, pp. 2598-9. The *amildar* seems to have been trying to trick Ogg into violating Abdul Shakur's rights as a subject of Mysore, perhaps to build a case against the British commander.
40. During the last few months of 1806, south India had begun to feel the effects of a region-wide drought that would, by the following year, become acute, if not as severe as the great droughts and famines of the late nineteenth century.
41. TNSA, Abdul Shakur's Testimony, 10 November 1806, *MSS*, V. 5, pp. 2597-8.
42. UN, Sepoy Shaikh Muhammad's Testimony, 19 November 1806, Portland MS, PwJb/57, pp. 4043-52.
43. TNSA, Sepoy Muhammad Shalli's Testimony, 12 November 1806, *MSS*, V. 5, pp. 2603-5.
44. Palaiyanu was said to be near Devanahalli, the birthplace of Tipu Sultan, north of Bangalore, on the route that troops had been taking to and from Nandidurgam.
45. TNSA, Sepoy Muhammad Ismail's Testimony, 14 November 1806, *MSS*, V. 5, pp. 2612-13.
46. Old British records usually refer to this town as Chittledroog.
47. This statement would seem to suggest that the sepoys were wearing ordinary peasants' clothes rather than regimentals.
48. In 1799, right after the fall of Seringapatam, the British camp was full of stories about a treasure buried somewhere by the late Sultan. According to legend, the treasure was cursed, and had fallen into the hands of Mir Alam—thus becoming the source of the leprosy from which the Nizam's minister suffered. In fact, Aristu Jah was so certain

that Mir Alam had 'stolen' this treasure that he confronted the general about the matter in open *darbar*. Mir Alam even spent a few months in prison over the matter, before his name was cleared.

49. TNSA, Sepoy Shaikh Muhammad's Testimony, 14 November 1806, *MSS*, V. 5, pp. 2610-12. Sepoy Muhammad Shalli gave a slightly different account of the meeting. According to him, the *faqir* said that because there would soon be 'a tempest' in Bangalore, all men who wanted service soon would have it. Instead of 'God' being incarnate at Bangalore, the *faqir* had specifically said that the Imam Mahdi had been born there, and that this was 'the last age'. At the end of the year, he himself would begin the great revolt against the Raj, supporting by an 'invisible army'. See Sepoy Muhammad Shalli's Testimony, 19 November 1806, Portland MS, PwJb/57, pp. 4032-43.
50. UN, Timmanayaka's Testimony, 19 November 1806, Portland MS, PwJb/57, pp. 4052-90.
51. UN, Testimonies of Handi Anantapur Timmanayaka and Nagar Bawa Timmanayaka, 19 November 1806, Portland MS, PwJb/57, pp. 4122-5.
52. Faqir Muhammad's stories concerned the schemes of various native officers to become Native Commandant of the battalion, which had involved visits to the Nawab's court at Chepauk and secret meetings with the Governor's personal *dubashes*.
53. UN, Testimony of Fath Muhammad, alias Faqir Muhammad, 19 November 1806, Portland MS, PwJb/57, pp. 4125-35.
54. Ibid. It is reasonably certain that Faqir Muhammad told the court the truth, for his story contained information that was not widely known at the time, but which was historically accurate. He seems to have had a very clear understanding of the political history of his day, and was far less confused about such matters than most men who served as sepoys.
55. Ibid., pp. 4135-6.
56. UN, Testimonies of Handi Anantapur Timmanayaka and Nagar Bawa Timmanayaka, 19 November 1806, Portland MS, PwJb/57, pp. 4122-5.
57. He perhaps meant the Goaluru, a major cattle-herding caste of the Mysore Plateau.
58. UN, Kuru Lingappah's Testimony, 19 November 1806, Portland MS, PwJb/57, pp. 4136-8.
59. The use of the term *qalandar* to describe Faqir-ud-Din indicates that he was, like most *faqirs* associated with the Vellore Crisis, a so-called *be-shar*, or non-*tariqa* Sufi. In Iran and India, the term *qalandar* often was used to refer to beggars whose outward religiosity was merely a

performance calculated to win sympathy and alms. See Cyril Glassé, *The New Encyclopedia of Islam* (New York, 2001), pp. 367-8.

60. Karim Sahib was the mentally disabled elder brother of Tipu Sultan, tentatively backed by many people in Holkar's entourage as a pretender to the throne of Mysore.
61. TNSA, Testimonies of Faqir-ud-Din, Sepoy Sayyid Muhyi-ud-Din, and Sepoy Sayyid Ismail, 14 November 1806, *MSS*, V. 5, pp. 2614-16.
62. UN, MacDowall to GC/FSG, 27 November 1806, Portland MS, PwJb/57, pp. 3997-9. The 'depraved and infamous vagabond' seems to have been Faqir Muhammad, although the same phrase might be applied to several of the court's witnesses.
63. UN, Wilks to GC/FSG, 28 November 1806, Portland MS, PwJb/57, pp. 3989-97.
64. Ibid., pp. 3977-89.
65. Ibid., pp. 3989-97.
66. TNSA, Cradock's Minute, 27 November 1806, *MSS*, V. 4, p. 2753.
67. TNSA, Lieutenant-Colonel George Martin to Major-General Dugald Campbell, 12 November 1806, *MSS*, V. 4, pp. 2754-9.
68. TNSA, Proceedings of the Bellary Court of Enquiry, 5 November 1806, *MSS*, V. 4, pp. 2759-61.
69. TNSA, Evidence of Muhammad Surmust, 5 November 1806, *MSS*, V. 4, p. 2761.
70. TNSA, Evidence of Jamadar Muhammad Tipu, 5 November 1806, *MSS*, V. 4, pp. 2768-71. By 'slipper', the Jamadar meant to beat the sepoy with his sandals—a common punishment for those presumed to be guilty of defiling acts.
71. TNSA, Defense of Subadar Mir Bakr, 7 November 1806, *MSS*, V. 4, pp. 2775-6.
72. TNSA, Havildar Shaikh Buddai's Testimony, 5 November 1806, *MSS*, V. 4, pp. 2761-3.
73. TNSA, Evidence of Havildar Shaikh Hussain, 5 November 1806, *MSS*, V. 4, pp. 2767-8.
74. A reference to the anthropomorphic Hindu deities installed in temples, and to the large endowments often set aside for their worship and maintenance.
75. TNSA, Jamadar Muhammad Bakr's Testimony, 5 November 1806, *MSS*, V. 4, pp. 2763-7.
76. Most sepoy battalions, by 1806, had at least one European non-commissioned officer attached to them to supervise drill instruction. These men were transferred to the sepoy battalions from the Madras European Regiment, and after spending several years in south India were able to speak local languages. Many of the men also were married

to Indian women. Some sepoys, however, viewed the presence of European non-commissioned officers with chagrin, for they often did not salute Indian officers, and in all cases out-ranked even commissioned Indian officers.

77. In Tamil and Telugu, many of the words for 'disturbance' also carry connotations of mutiny, riot, and even revolt—but without 'violence'. The nearest English equivalent, perhaps, would be 'uproar'.
78. TNSA, Sepoy Sheikh Medina's Testimony, 7 November 1806, *MSS*, V. 4, pp. 2772-4.
79. TNSA, Evidence of Jamadar Muhammad Tipu, 5 November 1806, *MSS*, V. 4, pp. 2768-71.
80. TNSA, Jamadar Muhammad Bakr's Testimony, 5 November 1806, *MSS*, V. 4, pp. 2763-7.
81. Ibid.
82. TNSA, Evidence of Jamadar Muhammad Tipu, 5 November 1806, *MSS*, V. 4, pp. 2768-71.
83. Obviously, the English translation of the proceedings is somewhat faulty; instead of 'priests', Mir Bakr undoubtedly told the court that he was a Sayyid.
84. TNSA, Defense of Subadar Mir Bakr, 7 November 1806, *MSS*, V. 4, pp. 2775-6.
85. TNSA, Defence of Sepoy Abdul Nabi, 7 November 1806, *MSS*, V. 4, p. 2774.
86. TNSA, Lieutenant-Colonel George Martin to Major-General Dugald Campbell, 12 November 1806, *MSS*, V. 4, pp. 2754-9.

8

'The System of Confidence'

Rumours circulating among British officers in Mysore led to unfortunate events in the Southern and Central Divisions of the Madras Army. At Palaiyamkottai, major James Welsh decided, without cause, that his troops were about to mutiny; he disarmed the Muslim sepoys of the garrison and warned the commanding officer at Quilon, Lieutenant-Colonel Robert Grant, that he should do the same. This was a drastic step, for disarming troops in this manner obliterated the cohesion and tactical effectiveness of entire battalions, inflicting more damage on the Army than might be occasioned by a major war. On the strength of an unfounded rumour, therefore, almost all of the Company's regular Indian troops in Tirunelveli and Travancore were disarmed, leaving a vast and very strategic area entirely undefended. Such rash behaviour finally moved Major-General Cradock to issue a strongly-worded order to all battalion commanders, demanding that they display confidence in the fidelity of their sepoys. This order broke the spell that had been cast over the Madras Army by the Vellore disaster. Before Cradock's order could be circulated throughout the Presidency, however, two more incidents occurred, one at Wallajahbad, and another at Sankaridurgam. By now the government was immune to alarms from the *mofussil*, and the reports of these 'threats' were thrown out as false. At last, six months after the Vellore Mutiny, the Council was able to frame and implement a policy that quickly ended the crisis—at least in India.

When word of the Vellore Mutiny reached England in late December 1806, the Directors of the East India Company were shocked. The 'Indian Interest' in Parliament and the Board of Control clamoured for the immediate recall of Bentinck and Cradock, but the Court of Directors delayed making a decision until the arrival of the Madras dispatches. Once these documents were laid before the Court, however, the process of ordering the recall of the Governor and the Commander-in-Chief became a mere formality. We cannot investigate here the politics behind the Court's decisions. Bentinck and Cradock received orders to step down and return to England in September 1807, and both men reached London early the following year. Even before their arrival, factions within the Court of Directors had begun another major battle in a series of such conflicts over Company policy. The Vellore Mutiny became a symbol, for all parties, of the many problems associated with British rule in India.

The 'Indian Interest' in the Court of Directors argued that the Vellore Mutiny was caused by the activities of evangelical Christians, whose 'violent attacks' on Indian society and religion aroused animosity against European influence. The so-called 'Saints', pro-missionary Directors headed by the redoubtable Charles Grant and Edward Parry, countered this allegation with a simple appeal to facts. There were but a handful of European missionaries in south India in 1806, none of whom were British.[1] Indeed, the condition of the existing Christian missions in south India was at a rather low ebb, compared to what it had been even in the middle of the eighteenth century.[2] At no point were missionaries mentioned in the various court of enquiry or court martial proceedings. Furthermore, most missionaries in the Madras Presidency were respected by the Indian population. Even Haidar Ali and Tipu Sultan had respected Friedrich Schwartz, who had spoken out in favour of peace during the destructive Anglo-Mysore Wars. Except in the area around Tirunelveli and Palaiyamkottai, Indian Protestant congregations were very small and, generally, very quiet.[3] Nevertheless, a long, public, and heated debate ensued regarding the future of the Company's policy regarding Christian missions in India.[4] The debate eventually was won by the 'Saints', but only in alliance with the powerful 'Free Trade' lobby in Parliament, many of whose members shared their evangelical leanings. As part of the package of compromises attached to the renewal of the Company's Charter in 1813, an Act of Parliament opened British India to missionary organizations that met with the Government's approval.[5]

PANIC IN THE SOUTHERN AND CENTRAL DIVISIONS

On 16 November 1806, Major James Welsh was told that 'blood' had been splashed across the entrance of a church in Palaiyamkottai fort.[6] A trail of the stain led from the threshold of the chapel to the cemetery, circled one of the graves, and led to another, where it stopped. The discovery of this strange 'sign' was followed, the next day, by a report that the fort was haunted. A ghost (*bhut*) was said to have accosted several people, demanding 'bread and water'.[7] Welsh interpreted this information as a 'friendly warning of danger'.[8] Several days later, a sepoy leaving for Srivilliputtur warned Welsh that 1/3rd Native Infantry was mutinous, and that 'if the Gentlemen introduce this turban again . . . or any way do any oppressive act, [the sepoys] will kill all the Gentlemen'.[9] Placing great faith in this particular soldier's testimony, Welsh went at once to the District Magistrate, George Stratton. After listening to Major Welsh's account of the strange occurrences at the fort, Stratton showed him the circular ordering the investigation of all religious mendicants. That evening, after the troops performed poorly on parade, Welsh and his officers decided that the sepoys were distracted by 'some malicious design'.[10] The next morning, gossiping over breakfast with their friend, Captain George Pepper, Welsh and his wife became convinced that the troops—and even many of their own servants—were conspiring to slaughter the entire European community at Palaiyamkottai, and that the attack would occur some time within the next ten days.[11]

The senior military and civil officers at the station met at once to discuss their situation. Worried that their movements had been noticed by would-be insurgents, Welsh suggested that the entire European population leave Palaiyamkottai at once. He offered to stay behind, alone, with the sepoys, and 'let things take their course'. Stratton and the Collector, James Hepburn, argued that it would be better to 'surprise' the battalion and disarm the troops.[12] The officers agreed that they must adopt this second course of action, but realized that the disarming would have to occur immediately, before anyone could anticipate their scheme. Returning to the fort, Welsh ordered the two most influential native officers on a routine errand to Tirunelveli town, a few miles away. One of the men objected, at first, and neither hurried to execute the order, thus confirming Welsh's worst suspicions; he immediately informed Lieutenant-Colonel Dyce that the time had come to disarm the corps.[13]

Welsh and his fellow officers armed themselves and paraded the battalion. They ordered the sepoys to pile their muskets, which was done with the alacrity one might expect of professional soldiers. The sepoys returned to their ranks to be informed that there were traitors at work among them, who had to be rooted out at all costs. While the troops were still absorbing this alarming news, they were marched, by companies, to the central *maidan*, some distance from their piled muskets, and halted. There, all of the non-Muslim soldiers were ordered to fall out and form up in a separate division. Having separated the 150 Hindu sepoys from their 450 Muslim comrades, Welsh issued muskets to the former and informed the latter that they were being deprived of their arms as a 'temporary measure', pending an investigation of the alleged plot to murder the European officers. The Hindu sepoys, meanwhile, were sent to the various gates and guard posts, while the Muslim sepoys were marched out of the fort, where they dispersed quietly. The Muslim officers, however, were confined.[14]

Thus far Welsh had carried out his 'pacification' of Palaiyamkottai without incident. He sought to secure the garrison further by sending to Madurai and Trichinopoly for reinforcements. His letters, however, written in a sensational style, gave the impression that he was anticipating an immediate attack by some overwhelming rebel force, rather than presiding over a disarmed and cowed garrison. He informed his division commander, for instance, that 'I have now, with a handful of men, quiet possession of the garrison. . . . We look for immediate succour, and shall defend our present position with our lives.'[15] Indeed, the confined Muslim officers, confused and scared by what had happened, pleaded with their officers 'that they were ready to embrace our religion . . . [and to] wear topies and crosses to convince us of their fidelity!'[16]

Welsh harboured an extreme hatred for Islam that pre-dated the Vellore crisis. He frequently referred to Muhammad, in his correspondence, as the 'False Prophet'. Fierce Christian that he was, he took a sadistic pleasure in his degradation of the Muslim prisoners. Their pleading, far from soothing him, merely intensified his conviction that there was a widespread Muslim conspiracy, the immediate aim of which was the overthrow of the Company Raj. Welsh's active and bigoted imagination required little prompting.[17] He wrote to Sir Thomas Maitland, Governor of Ceylon, asking for three companies of European infantry, and described the situation in Tirunelveli District as tantamount to a full-scale revolt.[18] Unfortunately for both Welsh and the Madras Government, Maitland immediately forwarded this letter and his own more level-headed opinions to London aboard a special packet brig, the Ariel.[19] Nor did Welsh's folly end there. Hearing that a local *faqir* had set out for Quilon, he wrote to Lieutenant-Colonel Grant, commanding the Travancore Subsidiary Force, urging him to disarm his own corps before it was too late. 'The followers of the False Prophet', he wrote, 'are unanimously corrupted.'[20]

Lieutenant-Colonel Alexander Dyce hurried to Palaiyamkottai from his retreat at Papanasam. After hearing Welsh's report, and hoping to confirm the loyalty of the Hindu portion of the battalion, he ordered all of the sepoys to swear an oath of allegiance under the regimental colours. Five of the Hindu sepoys were promoted to subadar, another five to jamadar, twenty-five to havildar, and twenty-five to *naigue* on the spot.[21] Needless to say, this generosity pleased men who could not have expected such promotions—and the pay raise attending them—for many years.[22] The Muslim officers in confinement, however, were deeply distressed. It seemed to them that the Hindus had 'renounced the faith and . . . worship of their forefathers'.[23] Dyce was even prepared to put the Muslim officers in irons, but Welsh restrained him, arguing—in a sudden outburst of compassion for men he himself had humiliated—that soldiers who had distinguished themselves in so many battles for the Company ought not to be disgraced.[24]

Welsh's desperately worded warning to Lieutenant-Colonel Grant reached Quilon on 21 November, shocking the British officers of the Travancore Subsidiary Force. The garrison under Grant's command consisted of two sepoy battalions and a company of European artillery, and the officers immediately decided to use the latter to overawe the former. Hand-picked sepoys were placed over the magazine, guards, and other important posts, while the guns were trained on the sepoy lines.[25] However, as S. MacDowall remarked, in his reply to Welsh, these precautions 'seemed to create no alarm, nor did the motive seem to be understood'.[26] Cautioned by Welsh not to trust any appearance of loyalty on the part of his men, Grant ordered the sepoy battalions to be disarmed the next morning, meanwhile depriving them of their cartridge boxes and side-arms. The native officers, called away from the lines, were informed of Welsh's letter and assured that no aspersion was cast upon them. However, they also were told that they would be separated from their troops for the time being. The following day, Grant offered a reward of five hundred Star pagodas for the discovery of 'emissaries or any disaffected persons'. With such an incentive, it should not have been too difficult for some enter-prising person to find suspicious characters in and around Quilon, but no one stepped forward to claim the reward. Nothing happened. On 25 November, Grant received word from Palaiyamkottai that he should rearm his troops.[27]

Upon receiving Welsh's plea for help, the commander of the Southern Division, Major-General Alexander Campbell, organized a 'relief force' of 250 *sowars* of the 6th Native Cavalry.[28] The next day, realizing that most of the troopers were Muslims, and might not act if called upon in an emergency, Campbell dispatched a column of European troops and sepoys to carry the flag through the Tirunelveli palaiyams, ready to move off, in an instant, either to Palaiyamkottai, or to chastise any of the petty rajas who chose to fight.[29] However, Campbell knew Welsh to be an excitable rumour-monger, and in a letter to the Chief Secretary to Government, he wrote, 'I fear [Welsh] . . . has been precipitate. But I cannot judge correctly.'[30] In another letter, Campbell urged Dyce to be discreet, even to disavow Welsh's actions, however 'repugnant to . . . private feelings'.[31] By the time Campbell reported the Palaiyamkottai incident to the Government, the panic that had taken root after the earlier 'insurrections' had been replaced by scepticism. Welsh was informed by the Chief Secretary to Government that if he could not demonstrate a sound reason for separating the Hindu sepoys from their Muslim comrades, he would 'incur his Lordship's dissatisfaction'.[32]

Cradock was furious. When he heard that Grant had disarmed the Travancore Subsidiary Force on the basis of a rumour circulated by Welsh, couched in fearful, unmilitary language, it became clear to the Commander-in-Chief that a substantial portion of the European officer corps was so caught up in post-Vellore hysteria that they could not be trusted to exercise proper judgement or retain authority over their troops. Welsh and Grant were battle-hardened veteran officers with years of experience in India. How Grant could disarm two thousand sepoys, at the same time writing to the Adjutant-

General that no symptoms of disaffection had appeared was beyond Cradock's comprehension. Cradock requested that Grant immediate resign his post and proceed to Madras to explain his conduct.[33] The Commander-in-Chief also issued a circular to all battalion commanders, urging them to 'recall the military mind'. He informed them that he would tolerate no more reports of non-existent rebellion—if an officer used the words 'mutiny' or 'revolt' in a report, there had better be actual fighting involved—and to rub salt into this stinging order, Cradock told the officers of the Army to demonstrate some 'manliness' for a change.[34] The authorities, meanwhile, ordered Welsh to travel to Choultry Plain and justify his actions before a court of enquiry.[35] The Muslim troops at Palaiyamkottai were allowed to re-enter the fort and take up their arms again. At Quilon, a formal apology was read to the sepoys; the entire Subsidiary Force was informed that their European officers would pay dearly for doubting, even for a moment, the Indian soldier's loyalty to the Company.[36]

As Cradock was preparing to dispatch his admonishing circular, however, another strange 'incident' occurred—precisely the sort of thing the Commander-in-Chief did not want to hear about. This time the agitation began when a woman informed Captain William Oliver that the sepoys at Wallajahbad were speaking of 'something' happening after they drew their pay on 1 December. At the time, the two battalions in garrison were the 2/1st and the 1/6th Native Infantry, the latter having arrived recently from Masulipatam.[37] Captain Robert Hughes, employing one of his *naigues* as a confidential agent, promised to promote him if he uncovered a secret plot within the battalion. Two days later, the hopeful *naigue* presented Sepoy Shaikh Nattar, whom he claimed to have 'won over' from a band of desperate, would-be mutineers of the 1/6th Native Infantry.[38]

Major Joseph Hazlewood, commanding the 2/1st Native Infantry, proceeded to Madras and briefed Cradock on this turn of events, explaining that the 1/6th contained a large number of Paraiyar sepoys, including 130 Christians—an unusually large concentration of converts in a sepoy battalion.[39] The men of the battalion were convinced, apparently, that they had been marched from Masulipatam to Wallajahbad to be the first unit of the Army forcibly converted to Christianity, as most of them were low-caste men. 'Mussulman principles and interests' were behind the men's disaffection, Hazlewood reported. The Hindus, he believed, would wait, and then join the 'strongest party'. The officers at Wallajahbad urged Cradock to post four troops of dragoons at Kaveripak, midway between Arcot and their cantonment, in the hope of forcing the chief conspirators among the sepoys to reveal themselves.[40]

When Cradock presented the above information to the Council, he viewed it with scepticism, but Bentinck—rather oddly—gave the matter serious attention.[41] Cradock argued, however, that he would not overthrow the 'system of confidence' by rushing dragoons around the Carnatic on the strength of rumors.[42] Petrie agreed with Cradock, suggesting that the deployment of European cavalry would provide 'complete confirmation of our intentions to trample their religion, to erect our churches on the ruins of their temples, and to make them converts by force to the Christian faith'.[43] Oakes favoured a proclamation reminding everyone that the Company Raj was a tolerant regime, committed to the protection of all religions and customs.[44] Ultimately, Oakes' recommendation was adopted, and the proclamation was issued on 3 December.[45] Nevertheless, Lieutenant-Colonel Thomas Munro was sent to Wallajahbad to investigate the latest incident of alleged 'disaffection'.[46]

Munro's knowledge of Hindustani and Telugu enabled him to thoroughly and accurately interrogate the witnesses and informants in Wallajahbad. Within a few days, he established that nothing very serious had happened. Shaikh Nattar admitted that there were only some sixty or seventy disgruntled sepoys in the 1/6th Native Infantry, and that they were the 'worst characters in the corps', inclined to loiter in a *nallah,* behind the cantonment, drinking arrack and smoking *bhang.* There had been loose talk about the Vellore Mutiny and its aftermath, but nothing more than the idle gossip of drunken friends. As for the serving woman who originally warned Captain Oliver of the 'conspiracy', Munro determined that she had merely passed on a rumour relayed by her brothers, who claimed to receive their information from a Muslim subadar. She and her brothers were from Burhanpur, in the Deccan; they were strangers in the Carnatic, and did not know the Muslim subadar in question very well.[47]

Major Hazlewood, for one, was not relieved by Munro's confident report. As he marched the 2/1st Native Infantry north toward Masulipatam, he became obsessed with the idea that his men were plotting to mutiny. This time, however, the letters that he addressed to Agnew and Cradock were not dignified with responses. Nor did the Military Board even acknowledge the receipt of his reports.[48] When the 2/1st finally arrived at Masulipatam, Hazlewood wrote to the Governor-in-Council, announcing that he possessed evidence of a well-organized movement, sponsored by French agents, which aimed to destroy British power in south India.[49] By now the government was weary of these outrageous conspiracy theories, and Bentinck even wondered if Hazlewood had lost his mind. Agnew suggested that his evidence had been 'purchased' in an effort to gain promotion for himself.[50] The magistrate at Masulipatam sent his own report to the Council, remarking that Hazlewood seemed to be 'very credulous'.[51] Nevertheless, the government decided to let Hazlewood try to prove his case; in any event, it could not hurt to remove him, temporarily, from a corps he did not trust.[52]

After examining Hazlewood's remarkably creative report, the Governor-in-Council appointed A. Scott, John Malcolm, and John Munro to make a thorough enquiry. These officers endured fifteen days of fanciful testimony, a collage that brought together every conspiracy theory that had by now been foisted upon the Madras Government. In their report, the committee declared that Hazlewood had proved nothing. The Major himself, they recorded, had been overcome by Francophobia and anti-Muslim prejudice, and also probably had been misled by 'discontented' native officers.[53]

The final act of the Vellore crisis concerned, appropriately enough, the officer whose notorious new turban galvanized the grievances of the Madras Army in the first place. Major Paul Bose and the 2/14th Native Infantry was transferred from Wallajahbad to the hill fort of Sankaridurgam during the summer. Like many other British officers suspicious of their men, Bose employed spies to bring him reports of unusual activities or talk among the sepoys. On 4 December, Bose was informed that the native adjutant of the battalion, Jamadar Perumal Nayaka, had received a letter from Seringapatam telling him that the sepoys at that station were united in some mysterious cause. When the adjutant invited the other native officers to his house, Bose concluded that they were planning to murder him, and were timing their mutiny to coincide with an outbreak at Seringapatam. Bose reported his worries to Major-General Campbell on 7 December, and the next day wrote to Major-General Fuller. His men, he insisted, were sending their families away from the *pettah* below the fort, which could only mean that they anticipated some violent action. Bose requested that a party of British troops be sent to Sankaridurgam to help him disarm his corps.[54]

Unfortunately for Bose, his alarming notes arrived at Trichinopoly just as the authorities there received Cradock's circular urging officers to cease making scandalous, unfounded accusations regarding the loyalty of their troops. Campbell informed Bose that no European troops could be spared to disarm his battalion, and that government 'sentiments' regarding the morale of the Army had changed.[55] The Madras Council also disavowed Bose's report. Thus it was that the Vellore crisis finally came to an end. Stray incidents of civil unrest occurred in various parts of the Carnatic during late 1806 and early 1807, but none of these events were believed to be related to the discontents of the Army.

'VINDICATING THE LAW AND JUSTICE'

Meanwhile, hundreds of sepoys, taken prisoner after the Vellore Mutiny, had languished at Vellore and Poonamalee, awaiting their fate. It was the government's hope that these men could be disposed of as quietly as possible, although Cradock, in September 1806, had asked the Council to support a resolution to transport them all to Penang. Bentinck, however, had pointed out that the guilt of the prisoners varied considerably, and that some of them probably were victims of circumstance, caught in the wrong place at the wrong time. Furthermore, they had been moved to mutiny by orders that were, from their point of view, greatly insulting. 'We are punishing murder rather than . . . resistance to orders', Bentinck had stated, adding: 'We are vindicating the law and justice, rather than gratifying revenge.' Banishment was viewed by most Indians—especially Hindus—as a drastic punishment, equivalent to execution. Six hundred sepoys simply could not be shipped overseas for the rest of their lives without benefit of trial; the rest of the Army would be outraged. At the same time, however, so many mutineers could not be turned loose, angry, and without any means of support.[56] The Governor favoured temporary confinement, a measure to which Cradock had strongly objected.[57] Petrie and Oakes had supported Bentinck with respect to the disposal of the prisoners, but preferred Cradock's argument that the 'honour of the Army' demanded the removal of the Vellore battalions from the Army List.[58] Bentinck opposed expunging the battalions, for fear of making the men seem 'martyrs to religion'. His veto, however, was overturned, eventually, by the Supreme Government.[59]

During the rest of 1806, while debates over protocol caused occasional skirmishes between members of the Madras Council, Lieutenant Colonel Forbes and Coombs, who was now a captain, continued to investigate the causes of the Vellore Mutiny and the relative guilt of the remaining prisoners. Their first report, submitted to the government on 6 September 1806, had concerned only the activities of the mutineers during the fight for the fort. Their second report, which was distributed to the Council on New Year's Eve, provided much-needed insight into the conspiracy to mutiny. Forbes and Coombs argued that the disaster at Vellore had but 'one evident and undoubted source'. They dismissed the increasingly popular verdict that the new turban and the 'obnoxious orders' in the new regulations had motivated the mutineers. 'Reason', they wrote, 'would forbid us to believe that . . . [the mutineers'] minds, however weak, could be brought to that scale of malignity and depravity to resolve, deliberately and inhumanely, [to] perpetrate the massacre of their officers and the European troops, with the sole object of resisting a change of dress.' Instead, Forbes and Coombs asserted that the rising was the work of 'interested and designing persons', both sepoys and servants of the princes of Mysore. The second report of Forbes and Coombs also noted the fact that all of the chief conspirators, with only one exception, were Muslims, and that Hindus, whether native officers or sepoys, had not played a conspicuous role in the mutiny. Most of the conspirators also had been soldiers in Tipu Sultan's army before enlisting in the Company's forces, and some of them had served in Tipu's bodyguard—probably in the so-called *Sher-ki-paltan*, or Tiger Corps, so named for their red-and-green *bubri*-pattern *kurtas.* Under these circumstances, frequently guarded by their father's old soldiers, the motivation of the Princes seemed obvious to Forbes and Coombs.[60]

The love of freedom is a principle inherent in our nature, a powerful desire which the human mind never ceases to feel, under any circumstances of misfortune or misery. To attempt the recovery of our liberty, when deprived of it, is but natural, and if to such sufficiently powerful incentive is added a prospect of sovereign authority and independence, it will excite less surprise that the captive princes of Mysore should anxiously seek and eagerly embrace an opportunity of attempting their emancipation, and that in the prosecution of those views, they should not hesitate in endeavouring to corrupt the fidelity of the native troops by whom they were surrounded, troops of the same caste, faith, and religion as themselves, and amongst whom they found individuals who had been, to use a common phrase, nourished by their father's salt, and who might, from that circumstance, be the more readily disposed to enter into their views.[61]

Bentinck claimed not to be convinced by the above arguments, although in the marginal notes of his personal copy of the report, he indicated that he could find few flaws in their presentation.[62] However, the Supreme Government had directed the Madras authorities to resolve the Vellore affair without further ado. Bentinck was eager to dispense with further pointless discussions about the mutiny and its causes. In any event, the second report of Forbes and Coombs arrived too late to alter the Council's determination to pursue the policy upon which it finally had settled after so many weeks of rancor and debate. The 1st and 23rd Regiments of Native Infantry ceased to exist on 1 January 1807, and were replaced by the newly-raised 24th and 25th Regiments. The 2/1st Native Infantry was incorporated into the 24th, while the 1/23rd Native Infantry became the 1/25th.[63] Finally, in the late spring and early summer of 1807, after nearly a year of imprisonment, the survivors of the mutiny being held at Vellore and St. Thomas Mount were released. The native officers among them were given small stipends in an effort to encourage them not to turn to banditry, or become mercenaries. This policy of clemency proved, in time, to be a complete success. The Vellore mutineers never again troubled the Company Raj. Indeed, before long, many of them were back in uniform, having quietly enlisted in other battalions.

'WHAT IS COME OVER THE ARMY OF FORT SAINT GEORGE?'

Shortly before Christmas of 1806, nearly six months after the Vellore Mutiny, an American ship brought the first news of the uprising to England. The story, however, was garbled, and the *Times of London* reported it as a rumour, almost too ludicrous to be believed.

It appears that a very disagreeable affair occurred at Vellore. . . . A battalion of Sepoys, in consequence, it is supposed, of a quarrel about some women, fell upon the 16th Regiment of Native Infantry, and put every man to death, including two officers, Major Charles Armstrong and another. Immediately after this bloody outrage, a Regiment of Cavalry was sent for to Arcot, which hastened to attack the Sepoys, to whom no quarter was given, nor did the Dragoons think their vengeance complete until every one of the guilty battalion were sacrificed. We have the satisfaction to state that this unpleasant affair did not originate in any spirit of disaffection to the Government.[64]

Shortly after New Year, more accurate accounts of the uprising appeared in British newspapers and journals. Many young officers had hurriedly written home, in July 1806, to reassure their families and friends that they were safe; excerpts from these letters were printed in January and February 1807, providing the public with an increasing amount of detail, as well as different perspectives on what had happened.[65] The first wave of reports emphasized the limited extent of the mutiny and how promptly it had been put down, clarifying the number of casualties, and providing the names of European officers who had been killed or wounded.[66] It took two months for the press to begin sorting fact from fiction, however. Charles Armstrong, for instance, had been killed, as first reported, but only because he happened to be passing Vellore Fort in his palanquin during the Mutiny. Furthermore, neither battalion of the 16th Native Infantry had been involved in any of the disturbances associated with the Vellore crisis.[67] Major-General Sir Arthur Wellesley, awaiting his next assignment, read these reports and could not believe that the very sepoy battalions he had led to victory in 1803 could be guilty of killing their officers just three years later.

Alas! . . . What is come over the army of Fort St. George? What are we to believe? Is it possible that the princes at Vellore can have corrupted the detachment at Hyderabad at the distance of five hundred miles? Surely these princes, in confinement, and possessing but limited pecuniary means, could never have had the power of creating a general interest in their favor throughout the whole of the native army of Fort St. George, dispersed as it is over thousands of miles! I am all anxiety upon this subject, and yet I have not received a line from a soul. Nobody believed the accounts which have been received from India upon this subject, notwithstanding the character and credit of those who have transmitted them, and the mind of every man is filled with suspicion and alarm. Surely the brave fellows who went through the difficulties and dangers of the Mahratta [*sic*] campaign cannot have broken their allegiance! I can never believe it till I shall see it proved in the clearest manner.[68]

Needless to say, the news from Madras astounded the Court of Directors when it finally reached Leadenhall, and there was a furious clamour in the Court of Proprietors. *The Times* even went so far as to report a 'partial insurrection . . . amongst the poligars' on 12 January 1807—doubtless responding to the rash and wildly inaccurate reports that had been dispatched by Welsh and forwarded to England by the Governor of Ceylon.[69] One of the Directors confessed, in a letter to former Governor-General, Warren Hastings, that he could not bring himself to believe the story in the absence of official reports.[70]

The first official account of the Mutiny did not reach London until 17 February, and to the consternation of all concerned, it was not a very informative report.[71] The Acting Governor-General, George Barlow, sent one of the Company's 'extra' ships, the brig *Sara Christiana*, to convey the Madras Government's reports and records concerning the Vellore crisis to London.[72] However, the vessel did not leave Fort St. George until 15 October, by which time she had to labour against the incoming monsoon all the way down the Coromandel Coast. The *Sara Christiana*, therefore, was still at sea when the Court of Directors sat on 24 February to officially discuss the crisis for the first time. Some members of the Court demanded the immediate recall of both Bentinck and Cradock, but cooler heads prevailed, and their motion was tabled until the next regular session.[73] Meanwhile, George Tierney, the President of the Board of Control, announced that he was prepared to support any recommendation made by the Court of Directors.[74]

The Court of Directors continued to discuss the Vellore crisis in early March, but although most of the members had reached their decisions about the matter, they tactfully refused to make a judgement until they saw the dispatches being sent aboard the *Sara Christiana*.[75] Finally, on 23 March, the Madras dispatches were laid before the Court by its President, William Elphinstone. Major James Leith, the Judge Advocate General, who accompanied the dispatches on behalf of the Madras Council, to answer any questions the Court might have, confessed to Bentinck that 'I was too late in getting here. I found the public mind preoccupied and fortified with prejudice against any further impression.'[76] Leith's mission had been made virtually impossible by the arrival of the *Ariel*, from Colombo, bearing Welsh's alarming letters about an 'insurrection' around Palaiyamkottai. The *Ariel* also had brought documents suggesting that sepoys had mutinied at Wallajahbad and Nandidurgam. Although all of the *Ariel's* dispatches, except Sir Thomas Maitland's cover letter, consisted of nonsense, they already had given the Directors and the Proprietors an impression that there had been a catastrophic collapse of authority in the Madras Army.[77]

The Court of Directors decided to recall Bentinck and Cradock, but this was not as unusual as it seems on the surface. Governors and Commanders-in-Chief—even Governors-General—had been removed by the Directors in the past. Generally, the Directors preferred men who had risen through the Company's hierarchy rather than outsiders such as Bentinck and Cradock. It was not easy to earn the unreserved support of the twenty-four Directors; they each were powerful individuals in their own right, and collectively they controlled financial resources and political influence sufficient to persuade Parliament and the Ministry to attend to their interests. The Duke of Portland, as the leader of the attack on the Company's privileges in the 1770s and 1780s, had won the undying enmity of many of the Directors, animosity that was poured out on Bentinck when he became Governor of Madras. Many of Bentinck's decisions had annoyed the Directors, and some of his ideas had outraged them. Bentinck had been forced to deal with the Vellore crisis knowing that the Directors were unlikely to support him; he also had been aware that many Civil and Military officers were alienated by his particular style of governance. Bentinck's lack of popularity in Madras worked against him in London during the spring of 1807. Cradock, meanwhile, was a man without influence or strong patrons.[78] Few people hesitated to demand Cradock's removal from the Madras Army, for he was an unexceptional, expendable general. In fairness to the Directors, however, it must be noted that they were under considerable pressure to act as they did.[79] As Major Leith informed Bentinck, 'the reason generally assigned [for your recall] in common conversation is that it was necessary to shew the Natives that the Legislature at home would not suffer the Government of the Country to remain longer in the hands of those in whose justice the Natives had not confidence'.[80]

The Court of Directors officially voted to recall Bentinck and Cradock on 7 April. The Governor was removed by a majority vote, the order described as 'expedient for the restoration of confidence in the Company's Government'. Cradock's recall, however, was unanimous and brusque. The Court made no mention of his 'zeal and integrity', as they had in Bentinck's case.[81] After these orders were sent out to Madras, a second set of letters was prepared, clarifying the reasons for the Court's displeasure and defending their decisions. The Directors argued that Bentinck's responsibility for the Mutiny was indirect, but that he lacked 'that prudence and discernment so requisite in administering the government of a numerous and peculiar people'. Maintaining discipline, they warned, should not have taken precedence over the 'prejudices of the Native troops'.[82] Meanwhile, the Directors dispatch made a devastating attack on Cradock, who was described as an incompetent and ignorant martinet.[83]

Lord Bentinck's father, the Duke of Portland, had become Prime Minister on 24 March, and Robert Dundas had replaced George Tierney at the Board of Control on 6 April, yet these changes in His Majesty's Government had no effect on the proceedings of the East India Company. Bentinck's friends had asked the Duke of Portland to intervene on his son's behalf, but he declined.[84] Dundas, meanwhile, informed the Prime Minister that the Board was scarcely in a position to commit the Home Government to a contest with the Company.[85] However, Dundas had been able to soften the original language of the order recalling Bentinck—a scrambling effort, on his part, that may well have saved the young Governor's career. The altered order read:

> Though the zeal and integrity of our present governor of Madras, Lord William Bentinck, are deserving our approbation, being of opinion that circumstances which have recently come under our considerations, render it expedient for the interest of our service that a new arrangement of our government of Fort St. George should take place without delay, we have felt ourselves under the necessity of determining that his Lordship should be removed. . . .[86]

The wording of the order that recalled Cradock, however, remained unaltered. The Court's dispatch ended by appointing William Petrie to be Acting Governor of Madras. Finally, additional orders were sent out removing Lieutenant-Colonel Patrick Agnew and Major Pierce from the General Staff, and demanding their return to England to explain why they had pressed Cradock to approve the 'obnoxious orders' in the new code of regulations.

The orders reached Madras late at night on 9 September 1807, stunning both the Governor and the Commander-in-Chief.[87] Bentinck obediently resigned on 11 September. Cradock, although willing to relinquish command of the Company's troops, nevertheless refused to give up command of the King's troops, petulantly maintaining that the Court of Directors had no right to remove him from a Crown-appointed position. Petrie was forced to threaten Cradock with severe disciplinary action in order to persuade him to relent and return to England.[88] Lord and Lady Bentinck set sail on 29 September, Admiral Sir Edward Pellew offering them free passage aboard the frigate HMS *Pitt.* Bentinck departed amid great fanfare, carrying numerous letters from well-wishers who found his summary removal unjust.[89] Cradock, meanwhile, was forced to wait two months 'without rank or salary' until the departure of the next Europe convoy—and then was forced to pay £3,500 to secure passage for his family and their servants. This was nothing, however, compared with the chagrin he felt on losing the immense prestige attached to his position. Once he had fallen from grace—and power—there were many who took the opportunity to subject him to 'vexatious treatment and petty attacks'. The former Commander-in-Chief restrained himself, saving his anger for a furious battle with the Company.[90]

Bentinck also went back to England determined to confront the Court of Directors. He hoped to obtain a pardon 'as public as . . . [the censure] which imposed . . . the stigma from which my character suffers.'[91] Obtaining a hearing before the Directors, however, was a difficult and drawn-out process. Upon returning to London in early 1808, Bentinck sought an interview with William Elphinstone, the new President of the Court of Directors. Following the meeting, however, Bentinck confided to his diary that 'the conversation was very unsatisfactory, and Mr. E. appeared to me to be nothing better than a canting rascal'.[92] The Company's apparent lack of interest in his case moved Bentinck to draft a lengthy memorial clarifying and defending his actions. This memorial was presented to the Directors on 7 February 1809, by which time they also had received a copy of Cradock's *Detailed Letter Relative to the Insurrection at Vellore.* In this diatribe, and in his *Sketch of the Situation of Sir John Cradock*, submitted to the Court in September 1808, Cradock offered an interpretation of the Vellore crisis that clashed with the one provided by Bentinck. However, Cradock also questioned the Company regarding his pay and allowances, the Directors having informed him that he had drawn almost ninety thousand rupees more than the amount approved for the expenses of his position.[93]

The Court of Directors, by the late spring of 1809, finally possessed copies of all official correspondence, proceedings, and records concerning the Vellore crisis. These materials were reviewed carefully, and on 25 July, a final judgement was passed upon Bentinck, Cradock, Agnew, and Pierce. The Directors determined that Bentinck was not responsible for the orders that caused the Vellore Mutiny, but that he should have displayed 'greater care and caution . . . in examining . . . the real sentiments and dispositions of the sepoys before measures of severity were adopted'. However, in his handling of the aftermath of the Vellore rising, Bentinck was said to have demonstrated 'moderation, clemency, and consideration' worthy of 'unqualified praise'. In other words, Bentinck was guilty merely of a lapse in good judgment.[94] Cradock, meanwhile, was held to be innocent of that 'wanton and imprudent violation of caste which was generally imputed to him'. However, the Directors thought his style of command unsuited to the nature of the people with whom he had to deal.[95] Ironically, Agnew and Pierce were exonerated, the latter receiving a mere censure for including unofficial orders in the new regulations in such a way that they appeared to have been approved already by the Governor-in-Council. Both officers were permitted to return to India, and became eligible for reappointment to their former posts.[96]

Neither Bentinck nor Cradock were satisfied. The former published a memorial defending his administration, while the latter pressed the Directors for redress and complained of how Bentinck's publication vilified him. For all practical purposes, however, the Vellore crisis had begun to melt into history. By the summer of 1809, the ranting of Bentinck and Cradock was just another monotonous Regency libel case, arousing little public sympathy and incapable of resolution. Both Bentinck and Cradock went on to serve in the Peninsular War during the grim period of the Coruña disaster.[97] The patronage of the Marquess of Wellesley and Lord Castlereagh eventually secured Bentinck an important mission to the exiled Neapolitan court in Sicily. Sir Arthur Wellesley, meanwhile, used his steadily mounting influence to obtain an Irish title—Baron Howden—for Cradock, and eventually an appointment as Governor of Cape Colony, South Africa.

Agnew and Pierce returned to Madras, as did Major James Welsh. The former Adjutant General was relieved, no doubt, to have been absent during the infamous 'White Mutiny' of 1809. Welsh, who had returned earlier, was contacted by mutinous officers, many of whom were his friends, but wisely remained neutral as the officers' ill-conceived contest with the Madras Government took its inevitable course.[98] What Agnew, Pierce, and Welsh had done during the fateful year 1806 was forgotten after the scandals and bloodshed of the officers' mutiny of 1809, in which many British officers who had been in Mysore and at Hyderabad during the Vellore crisis, such as MacDowall and Ogg, were implicated. Welsh, for one, tried to avoid further discussion of his own role in the Vellore crisis. In his memoirs, in coming to the latter part of 1806, he merely noted: 'Toward the end of the year, an event took place, which although injurious to my own prospects and fortune, under the signal blessing of Providence terminated most fortunately. Time has now spread his oblivious wings over the whole occurrence, and I will not attempt to remove the veil.'[99]

NOTES

1. Francis Buchanan, then touring Mysore and Kanara, was technically a missionary, but had suspended his evangelical activities to carry out research for the government.
2. All of the Protestant missionaries in south India in 1806 were Lutherans, mostly educated at the German seminary of Halle, who worked for the

Royal Danish Halle Mission, first established at Tranquebar in 1706. This mission was closely linked with the S.P.C.K. (Society for the Propagation of Christian Knowledge), and had branched out from the Danish settlement of Tranquebar to Tanjore, Trichinopoly, Tirunelveli, and Vepery. In 1806, Tranquebar had been occupied by the British for five years. Most of the other missionaries in south India were Roman Catholics, mainly French and Italian priests who had fled to India—or been abandoned there—after the French Revolution. Because these priests tended to be pro-monarchist and pro-Bourbon, the Company tolerated their activities throughout the period of the Napoleonic Wars.

3. Even in Tirunelveli and Palaiyamkottai, the Christians were a 'microscopic minority'.
4. This debate stemmed from William Carey's 'challenge' to the 'English-speaking peoples'. Carey, a Baptist missionary working at the Danish settlement of Serampore, in Bengal, mad made an effort, in 1793, to compel Parliament to insert a so-called 'pious clause' in the Charter Renewal Act.
5. Fisch, pp. 22-70.
6. For a brief (partisan) account of this church, which was built by Indian Christians, see Reverend George Pettitt, *The Tinnevelly Mission* (London, 1851), pp. 1-12. This chapel had been built by Clarinda, 'a Brahminee woman' who was baptized by the German missionary Christian Friedrich Schwartz. The congregation, consisting of some 100 local converts, was under the direction of an ordained Lutheran minister named Sattiyanathan. The community was thriving in the 1790s, but a series of violent incidents during the period 1799–1802, allegedly encouraged by the Tirunelveli palaiyakkars, temporarily stemmed the rise of this evangelical Protestant community.
7. A rather unusual request for a Tamil or Telugu ghost!
8. TNSA, Welsh to Dyce, 25 November 1806, *MSP*, V. 24, pp. 3537-8.
9. TNSA, Sepoy Aitwar Singh's Deposition, *MSP*, V. 27, pp. 60-1.
10. TNSA, Welsh to Dyce, 25 November 1806, *MSP*, V. 24, pp. 3540-1.
11. Ibid.
12. TNSA, Hepburn's Deposition, *MSP*, V. 28, pp. 859-61.
13. TNSA, Welsh to Dyce, 25 November 1806, *MSP*, V. 24, pp. 3544-5; TNSA, Dyce's Deposition, *MSP*, V. 28, p. 733.
14. TNSA, Dyce to Buchan, 25 November 1806, *MSP*, V. 24, p. 3527.
15. TNSA, Welsh to Campbell, 19 November 1806, *MSP*, V. 23, pp. 3261-2.
16. TNSA, Welsh to Dyce, 25 November 1806, *MSP*, V. 24, pp. 3553-4.
17. For instance, see James Welsh, *Military Reminiscences*, V. 1 (London, 1830), pp. 259-60. Returning from the Second Anglo-Maratha War in

January 1806, Welsh's battalion marched through Mysore. In the hills near Chitradurga, the Muslim sepoys asked for permission to visit a well-known *faqir* who lived some distance from the line of march. When these troops returned from their pilgrimage, a few days later, they reported to Welsh that the *faqir* had predicted the fall of British rule shortly after the celebration of Muharram in the spring of 1806. Welsh wrote, 'This imposter certainly gulled them completely, and was likely to have done us a serious injury, had not Providence watched over our safety, and proved him, like his Arabian master, a false prophet.'

18. TNSA, Dyce to Buchan, 25 November 1806, *MSP*, V. 24, pp. 3633-44.
19. PRO, CO/54/22, ff. 211-12, Maitland to Windham, 24 November 1806. The Madras Government was not informed that this information had been sent to England. See Bentinck, p. 39.
20. TNSA, Welsh to Grant, November 1806, *MSP*, V. 24, pp. 3510-11.
21. Such on-the-spot promotions were technically a violation of Madras Army regulations.
22. TNSA, Dyce to Campbell, 21 November 1806, *MSP*, V. 23, pp. 3411-14.
23. Ibid., pp. 3416-18.
24. Ibid.; TNSA, Dyce's Deposition, *MSP*, V. 28, pp. 793-7.
25. TNSA, Grant's Deposition, *MSP*, V. 28, pp. 930-69.
26. TNSA, MacDowall to Welsh, 22 November 1806, *MSP*, V. 24, pp. 3569-70.
27. TNSA, Grant to Macaulay, 23 November 1806, *MSP*, V. 24, pp. 3520-1; TNSA, Grant's Deposition, *MSP*, V. 28, pp. 930-6.
28. TNSA, Campbell to Buchan, 21 November 1806, *MSP*, V. 23, pp. 3258-9.
29. TNSA, Campbell to Buchan, 22 November, 1806, *MSP*, V. 23, pp. 3400-3. The detachment consisted of the 1/4th Native Infantry, the light company of HM 69th Foot, and a detail of artillery. See TNSA, Campbell to Dyce, 22 November 1806, ibid., pp. 3403-7.
30. TNSA, Campbell to Buchan, 21 November 1806, *MSP*, V. 23, pp. 3260-1.
31. TNSA, Campbell to Dyce, 22 November 1806, *MSP*, V. 23, pp. 3403-7.
32. TNSA, Buchan to Dyce, 25 November 1806, *MSP*, V. 23, pp. 3263-5. Since Welsh already had sent out several different accounts of the affair at Palaiyamkottai, several of which were now part of the official record, there was very little he could do to couch his actions in neutral words.
33. TNSA, Cradock's Minute, 1 December 1806, *MSP*, V. 24, pp. 3555-9.
34. TNSA, Circular to Battalion Commanders, *MSP*, V. 24, pp. 3560-2.

35. TNSA, Agnew to Welsh, December 1806, *MSP*, V. 24, pp. 3563-4.
36. TNSA, *MSP*, V. 24, pp. 3564-7.
37. TNSA, *MSP*, V. 24, p. 3785.
38. Ibid., pp. 3463-9.
39. TNSA, *MSP*, V. 24, p. 3785. Although the Government frowned upon the recruitment of Indian Christians, and discouraged sepoys from converting, a few converts always managed to slip into the Army. Usually, however, there were never more than five to ten Christians in a battalion.
40. TNSA, *MSP*, V. 24, pp. 3469-71.
41. TNSA, Bentinck's Minute, 2 December 1806, *MSP*, V. 24, pp. 3472-3.
42. TNSA, Cradock's Minute, 2 December 1806, *MSP*, V. 24, pp. 3473-5.
43. TNSA, Petrie's Minute, 2 December 1806, *MSP*, V. 24, pp. 3475-82.
44. TNSA, Oakes' Minute, 2 December 1806, *MSP*, V. 24, pp. 3483-8.
45. BL/OIOC, GC/FSG to SC/EIC, 11 January 1807, *Secret Letters from Madras*, Series 1, v. 3.
46. TNSA, *MSP*, V. 24, pp. 3488-92.
47. TNSA, Munro's Report, *MSP*, V. 24, pp. 3781-3805.
48. TNSA, Hazlewood to Agnew, 3 January 1807, *MSP*, V. 27, pp. 332-45.
49. TNSA, Hazlewood to Buchan, *MSP*, V. 28, pp. 445-8; Hazlewood to Reynell, ibid., pp. 524-5.
50. UN, Tod to Bentinck, 12 February 1807, Portland MS, PwJb/44; TNSA, Hazlewood to Reynell, 7 February 1807, *MSP*, V. 28, pp. 524-5.
51. UN, Tod to Bentinck, 12 February 1807, Portland MS, PwJb/44.
52. TNSA, *MSP*, V. 28, pp. 522-3.
53. TNSA, Report of the Committee, *MSP*, V. 29, pp. 1217-27.
54. TNSA, Bose to Campbell, 7 December 1806, *MSP*, V. 24, pp. 3737-43; TNSA, Bose to Fuller, 8 December 1806, ibid., pp. 3733-6.
55. TNSA, Campbell to Bose, 9 December 1806, *MSP*, V. 24, pp. 3731-2.
56. BL/OIOC, Bentinck's Minute, 13 September 1806, *HMS*, V. 509, pp. 227-337.
57. BL/OIOC, Cradock's Minute, 14 September 1806, *HMS*, V. 509, pp. 237-40.
58. BL/OIOC, Oakes' Minute, 6 September 1806, *HMS*, V. 509, pp. 148-9; BL/OIOC, Petrie's Minute, 10 September 1806, ibid., pp. 185-92.
59. Lord William Bentinck, *Memorial Addressed to the Honourable Court of Directors . . . Containing an Account of the Mutiny at Vellore, with the Causes and Consequences of that Event* (London, 1810), pp. 31-5.
60. UN, Second Report of Forbes and Coombs, Portland MS, PwJb/59, pp. 4403-62.

61. Ibid., p. 4429.
62. For example, see ibid., p. 4419.
63. TNSA, *MMP*, Range 256, V. 2, pp. 454-60.
64. *Times of London*, 23 December 1806.
65. For those accounts printed in the *Times of London*, see 5 January 1807, 9 January 1807 (an unusually complete, well-balanced, and insightful account written by an 'officer at Madras to his Friend at Edinburgh'), 12 January 1807, and 18 February 1807.
66. The names of British private soldiers were not provided. Indeed, the Army did not publish lists of casualties among 'Other Ranks' until the 1880s.
67. Wilson, V. 3, p. 187. Also see Dodwell and Miles, *Officers of the Madras Army* (London, 1838), pp. 2-3. Captain (not Major) Armstrong had halted his *palankin* near the glacis of the fort, opposite the north-east cavalier, and had stepped out to hail a party of sepoys holding that position. Apparently, he did not realize the garrison had mutinied, and was shot by one of the sepoys in the cavalier. At the time of his death, Armstrong was serving as Hindustani instructor to the cadet company stationed at Cuddalore.
68. Major-General Sir Arthur Wellesley to Lieutenant-Colonel John Malcolm, 23 February 1807, quoted in John William Kaye, *The Life and Correspondence of Major-General Sir John Malcolm* (London, 1841), p. 376.
69. *Times of London*, 12 January 1807.
70. BL, Sweny Toone to Warren Hastings, Add. MSS 29182, f. 50.
71. BL/OIOC, *HMS*, V. 510, p. 411; BL/OIOC, GGC/FW to SC/EIC, 30 July 1806, *Secret Letters from Bengal and India*, V. 8, pp. 409-14. These reports were sent overland, via Egypt and the Mediterranean. They stressed that the rising was extremely localized, and had been thoroughly crushed.
72. BL/OIOC, N.B. Edmonstone to Buchan, 25 August 1806, *HMS*, V. 509, pp. 252-4. The ship was to have sailed 'at once' from Bengal, and was not to be detained at Madras for more than forty-eight hours.
73. BL/OIOC, CD/EIC Minutes, 24 February 1807, *Court Book*, V. 115, pp. 1274-5.
74. UN, Portland MS, PwJb/216a.
75. BL/OIOC, CD/EIC Minutes, 4 March 1807, *Court Book*, V. 115, pp. 1304-5.
76. UN, Portland MS, PwJb/25, Leith to Bentinck, pp. 502-3.
77. UN, Portland MS, PwJb/750.
78. Cradock's most important 'friend' in London, Sir Arthur Wellesley, was reluctant to assist him in the aftermath of the Vellore Mutiny,

primarily because Cradock sought to blame the affair on Bentinck. Wellesley was much closer, socially, to Lord and Lady Bentinck, than he ever was to Cradock. In any event, Wellesley was fiercely opposed to what he called 'party spirit', and generally tried to remain aloof during crises.

79. UN, Charles Grant to Bentinck, Portland MS, PwJb/218a.
80. UN, Leith to Bentinck, Portland MS, PwJb/25, pp. 502-23. One wonders what comfort Bentinck was to have derived from this information, but Major Leith had never been known for his tact.
81. BL/OIOC, CD/EIC Minutes, 7 April 1807, *Court Book*, V. 115, pp. 1466-7.
82. BL/OIOC, CD/EIC to GC/FSG, 7 April 1807, *HMS*, V. 510, pp. 765-850, paras. 3, 10, and 22.
83. Ibid., paras. 10, 14, 16, and 23.
84. UN, Portland MS, Pwjb/25, pp. 502-23.
85. UN, Robert Dundas to the Duke of Portland, 16 April 1807, Portland MS, PwJb/216a.
86. BL/OIOC, Draft Order of Recall, *Board of Control*, V. 13-F, pp. 529-31.
87. UN, Bentinck's Journal, Portland MS, PwJb/677/1.
88. BL/OIOC, *HMS*, V. 510, pp. 897-914; Cradock, pp. 1-15.
89. UN, Portland MS, PwJb/750; PwJb/667/1.
90. Cradock, pp. 1-15.
91. UN, Portland MS, PwJb/317a.
92. UN, Portland MS, PwJb/750.
93. BL/OIOC, CD/EIC, July 1810, *Correspondence Reports*, V. 34, pp. 640-4.
94. BL/OIOC, CD/EIC Minutes, 25 July 1809, *Court Book*, V. 118, pp. 572-5.
95. Ibid., pp. 575-6.
96. Ibid., pp. 576-7, 586-7, 593-5.
97. Bentinck commanded a wing of the British army trapped at Coruña, while Cradock covered Lisbon with a small force of 5,000 men, and nearly abandoned the city in a sudden panic. When word of Sir John Moore's death at Coruña reached London, Sir Arthur Wellesley was ordered to return to the Peninsula and replace Cradock.
98. See Alexander Cardew, *The White Mutiny: A Forgotten Episode in the History of the Indian Army* (London, 1929).
99. James Welsh, *Military Reminiscences*, V. 1 (London, 1830), p. 275.

9

'It Was a Hat and Not a Turband'

On the surface, it may seem absurd that a change in dress could occasion a violent mutiny, shake the discipline of an army, and call into question the foundations of an empire. However, this sense of the absurdity of the 'new' turban and its connection with the Vellore Mutiny arises from the modern observer's alienation, in a global economy founded on mass-production and mass-marketing, with respect to the identity-shaping power of culture. Scholars have long been aware that 'clothing matters'—as a symbol of status, either claimed or ascribed, as a conscious expression of individual or group identity, and as a mark of defiance. At the time of the Vellore Mutiny, Europeans, no less than Indians, communicated complex statements about themselves through clothing, ornament, and hairstyles. As European fashion was undergoing a sea change in those years, it is difficult to imagine that British officials in India, in 1806, were insensible to the cultural significance of dress. British officials—especially military officers—sought the causes of the Vellore Mutiny everywhere but in the new turban. Almost every sepoy deposed before the various courts of enquiry, however, underscored the centrality of the new turban in an extensive and complex matrix of grievances. Too much had been read into the sepoys' words, and not enough attention has been paid to what disaffected Indian soldiers actually said about the sources of their discontent.

As the preceding narrative of the Post-mutiny enquiries has revealed, no conspiracies lurked behind the Vellore crisis, although here and there we can discern the activities of very small, relatively powerless groups of men, each with its own narrow agenda. Nor does the preceding narrative suggest that the sepoys of the Madras Army were moved to act as they did by strong anti-British sentiments. The colonial authorities had hoped to find signs of general disaffection, but to their chagrin had to admit that the people of south India, despite worsening economic conditions, were not on the brink of revolt against the Raj. This admission was embarrassing, for it meant that the frustration of the average Madras sepoy was generated within the Army, not by external provocateurs. It seemed that the British would not be able to blame the Vellore crisis on either angry princes, or the French, or the weather, or even the mismanagement of previous regimes, as was so often done when disaster struck the foundations of the Raj. There were political and material causes behind the Vellore Mutiny, but these were not directly linked with the event, and this is what has puzzled so many historians. Only an analysis of the Vellore records, taking each selection of evidence in its specific context, permits us to discern and appreciate exactly what it was about the new turban that sepoys dreaded.

THE CLOTHING OF THE MADRAS ARMY

Throughout the Vellore crisis, sepoys pointed to the new turban as a major source of anxiety and discontent. Their negative response to the new turban was embedded in socio-cultural values and practices shared—but viewed rather differently—by both Hindus and Muslims. Sepoy Shaikh Ahmad of the 1/1st Native Infantry, for instance, recalled how, in January 1806, the palace servants of Vellore remarked to the sepoy sentries in the *mahals* that their uniforms were beginning to resemble those of British soldiers. Indeed, since the exiles had arrived at Vellore, the Madras sepoy's dress had been transformed. Between 1800 and 1803, white waistcoats and high, standing collars, or stocks, were added to the sepoy's uniform, and *kamarbands* were discontinued. Major Bose's new turban—or *topi*, as everyone called it—was a significant step toward conforming the Madras Army to the pattern of the British Army. Aesthetics and military discipline, in those days, were much more closely related than they are today. Only a few months after Sepoy Shaikh Ahmad had been chided about his uniform, however, another incident drew attention to the significance of differences in European and indigenous dress. A *maulvi* who taught in the sepoy lines accused the Muslim troops of apostasy for serving *kafiron aur topiwalle*—infidels and hat-wearers. The *maulvi* shunned the sepoys, refusing to read prayers at the burial of a Muslim woman whose son was serving in the 2/5th Native Infantry.[1]

In May, a sepoy of the 2/4th Native Infantry spelled out the objection to the new turban, patterns for which had arrived at Vellore, in the clearest possible manner: '. . . it was a hat and not a turband; that if [we] wore it [our] caste would not supply [us] with water, neither would [we] marry [our] daughters'.[2] For many sepoys, the prospect of ostracism compelled them to consider leaving the Army—a step which no sepoy ever took lightly.[3] Sepoy depositions concur that the threat of ostracism originated outside the Army, which suggests that knowledge about the nature of the new turban—including its hat-like shape—was widespread even before the Vellore Mutiny. We must accept the possibility that the negative associations attached to the new turban drew much of their force from a general anxiety regarding the Company's recent, dramatic conquests, which had turned key elements of south Indian society upside down.[4] Sepoys, however, had known they were to receive a new turban since the circulation of a General Order on 15 November 1805; they made no objection to it until late April and May of 1806, when the patterns began to reach the battalion stores.[5] As soon as the *darzi* sepoy of the grenadier company of the 2/4th Native Infantry opened the sealed pattern of the new turban, sent from the Adjutant-General's office, he remarked that it looked like a drummer's *topi* or hat. Kot Havildar Shaikh Imam warned the *darzi* not to use the word *topi* in earshot of the sepoys, and to keep his opinions to himself. Why was the hat-like shape of the turban so important that it was considered provocative even to mention it?[6]

Viewed as a drummer's hat, the new turban was a symbol articulating the fears of many sepoys, especially caste Hindus and Muslims. Unfortunately, there is confusion, among historians, about the appearance of the new turban, and whether or not it could be considered a *topi*.[7] To a great extent this uncertainty arises from the alleged similarity of Major Bose's turban and that which had been adopted by the Army in March 1797. The distinction between these two turbans is important, because the men who had to wear them—and many others—viewed the two patterns very differently. When the sepoy battaiions first had been formed through the linking of independent mercenary companies in the late 1750s, a turban, or *pagri*, had been part of their uniform, and turban cloth of a standard colour may have been distributed by European and native officers to improve the appearance of their men. The most reliable paintings and drawings of sepoys, dating from the early period of the Madras Army's development, suggest that sepoy turbans were similar to the *urumal* worn by most Telugu and Tamil men at that time.[8] European observers often described this early turban as 'flat' or 'loose'. In any event, every sepoy would have wrapped his turban differently, depending on the custom of his sect or caste, and therefore it was possible to distinguish a Kallan sepoy, for instance, from a Reddi or a Paraiyar, a Pathan from a Labbai. Jafar Sharif of Elluru, in his *Qanoon-i-Islam*, identifies seventeen styles of turban that were worn in the Carnatic and the Deccan in the 1820s—in fact, the number of different turban styles was much greater than this.[9]

In 1797 a General Order of the Commander-in-Chief, George Harris, instructed the Army to make up a new type of turban, larger and more uniform than the old *urumal*. This turban, like that ordered to be adopted in 1806, was wrapped around a frame. However, its shape was distinct, and could not be mistaken for a European hat.[10] Tapering down to the head, the turban of 1797 rose to a wide, flat top, which sloped down from right to left.[11] Most sepoys wore this turban at a sharp angle—an impractical concession to fashion, but also a subtle and significant indicator that this turban was popular, seen as rakish and rather dashing. It was not adopted throughout the Army, however, and the old *urumal* style of turban was being depicted by soldier-artsists, in sketches of sepoys, as late as 1804. The turban of 1797 clearly had not been considered a *topi*, however, and all who wore it, or saw it, recognized it as a turban. Some battalions, in fact, had worn such a turban since the early 1790s.[12] In its colour and manner of construction, the turban of 1797 was even similar to one worn by Tipu Sultan's soldiers.[13] Since *topi-wallah* was one of Tipu's favourite terms of abuse for the British, it is extremely unlikely that he would have ordered anything resembling a European hat to be worn by his troops.

Major Paul Bose, the creator of the new turban of 1806, objected to the manner in which sepoys were wearing the turban that had been ordered for the Army in 1797. The jaunty tilt of the old turban—precisely what made it a turban in the eyes of indigenous observers—seemed unmilitary to Bose. Worn at such a sharp angle, the old turban fell off easily, preventing sepoys from moving quickly.

Consequently, Bose designed his new turban to rest firmly on the head. Indeed, it was made so that it simply could not be worn at an angle, unless a sepoy happened to have a particularly large head! In the General Order of 15 November 1805, both officers and sepoys were given some idea of the new turban's appearance.

Each turban to be made sufficiently large to reach low down upon the head, and to fit so firmly as to prevent the turban becoming unsteady when the soldier moves at an accelerated pace. The turban shall be worn even upon the head and touching the eyebrows.[14]

When the sealed patterns of the new turban arrived at battalion storage godowns in May 1806, other features of the new turban were revealed, such as its shape and ornamentation. The *darzi* sepoy of the grenadiers of the 2/4th Native Infantry, for one, was struck immediately by the fact that the new turban sloped from front to back, rather than from one side to another, and had a 'feather' fixed at the crown.[15] This shape was significant, for it reflected, although it did not exactly mirror, the shape of the shako adopted around 1800 by the King's and Company's British troops in India, a version of which was also worn by the musicians of sepoy battalions. Like the British soldier's shako, the new turban was crowned with a ball tuft fixed in a leather cockade.[16] The only similarity between the old and new turban, in fact, was the iron frame on which they were both wrapped, and the decorative white tape stretched diagonally across them. Neither British officers nor sepoys seemed to recognize the new turban as a proper *pagri.* Indeed, many of the former accidentally referred to it as a *topi* in conversations with sepoys. In the 1830s, a Madras Army officer alluded to these cross-cultural blunders in a letter to a friend.

Sepoys are a *genus irritabile* with which poets may not be compared, and of which as adequate idea can only be formed by contact. Would you believe that I have known a company absolutely stirred to mutiny by an officer who, from ignorance of the language, called their head-dresses caps, when they chose them to be considered turbans?—the head-dress bearing, the while, as strong similitude to a turban as to a whale.[17]

The new turban, as has been noted before, was part of a process of modernization in both the King's and Company's armies, one in which the latter copied patterns established in the former. The scarlet broadcloth coats issued to sepoys in the mid-1750s approximated those worn by the Madras European Regiment at that time, with their full skirts and wide lapels and cuffs. Military fashion, in turn, reflected European civilian fashion, which changed very rapidly during the latter half of the eighteenth century. Every few years, in fact, the Military Board altered the cut of the coats made for the Company's troops, and gradually these were transformed into the close-fitting jacket, with short skirts and narrow facings, which had been adopted around the year 1799. Apart from cross-belts and pouches, however, the rest of the sepoy's uniform was Indian rather than European. Under his red coat, the sepoy wore a loose, white blouse, with no collar and an open neck, opening on either the right or left side, depending on the man's religion. Instead of the white breeches and stockings worn by European soldiers, sepoys wore knee-length *janghirs*, or *challanas*—'short drawers' in the British records—which were slightly longer than those worn by some south Indian *rayats.*[18] As a concession to modesty, an additional blue or black cloth, passing between the legs, had been worn on the outside of these drawers by most sepoys. Thus, apart from their red coats and distinctive turbans, the Company's sepoys resembled the soldiers of most other South Asian rulers of the time. European-style neck cloths were added to the uniform in 1796, but as an indigenous equivalent of this article existed already, the cravat was not seen as a foreign innovation.[19] By the mid-1790s, however, the sepoy's uniform had begun to change radically, primarily because the matter of military clothing was being centralized and standardized, like everything else in the Army.

One of the most important steps toward centralizing the management of the Army was the formation of the Adjutant General's office under the Military Board. Very quickly, the Adjutant General replaced the colonel as the prime decision-maker regarding matters of military dress. Formerly, sepoys were attired in inexpensive, readily-available materials suitable to the Indian climate and amenable to the soldiers' cultural biases, but by 1800 this expedient approach gave way to a policy of altering the dress of the Madras forces, that they might conform to the prevailing standards of European military fashion. However, European military fashion, at the time, was dictated more by romantic fads than by considerations of martial utility. The romance of the latest light cavalry fashions, for instance, was not lost on Rebecca Chase, a young Englishwoman who admired the men of the 5th Madras Native Cavalry, who she observed training at Arcot, with rather a close eye.

Their dress alone would be sufficient to captivate many a fair [lady] . . . a white capanore cloth jacket with a belt round the waist, buckled in front, on the side of which hangs a large sword and [sabretache], handsomely ornamented with a silver fringe. I should tell you that the jacket cuffs and collars are green, trimmed with silver, and silver buttons. This is their undress; their dress is short scarlet jackets, very handsome, trimmed with silver. They have three kinds of hats with their dresses, one with a plaited crown, with a plume of black feathers. Besides these, when they go on exercise, they wear helmets ornamented in a very handsome manner with silk and silver, and crimson sashes round their waists, over their belts.[20]

Officers of the King's Army, who dominated the new General Staff under the Commander-in-Chief, began to define, with great precision, how a sepoy was to appear. A General Order of Government for 7 July 1801, for instance, transformed the sepoy's old, open coat into a short-skirted jacket, buttoned and cross-laced to the waist, with narrow facings. Stocks were added in December of the following year, while the epaulettes and shoulder-knots that once had distinguished native officers were replaced with white chevrons—markings that, in the British Army, designated non-commissioned officers and musicians.[21] Native officers, wearing breeches, stockings, and boots, acquired a very European appearance; indeed, they looked just like British officers, the only difference being that they wore turbans.[22] These changes, however, did not occur quite as regularly as the authors of works on uniforms and militaria suggest. The dashing cavalrymen described by Rebecca Chase were an exception, an elite corps, stationed near the depots of Fort St. George. Matters were very different for the infantry, especially those at *mofussil* outposts, where tattered uniforms and broken or lost equipment could not be replaced easily. Few battalions were ever found to be 'complete' when inspected by the Commander-in-Chief or the generals commanding the divisions.

It is ironic that the East India Company, one of the foremost cloth dealers of the world, experienced great difficulty clothing its troops in India, troops which—in many cases—were deployed to guard cloth-weaving villages. The jackets of the Company's armies were made of sturdy, woollen cloth, imported from Europe. Even Indian princes purchased imported broadcloth for their armies, as it held up, on campaign, much better than the fine cotton fabrics produced by Indian weavers. As in the British Army, soldiers of the Company expected to receive a new set of clothes every year, in return for which part of their pay was 'stopped' every month by their officers.[23] It once had been the responsibility of regimental commanders to procure cloth and other materials, and have them 'made up' into uniforms by local artisans. Long periods of service in the field, with no fixed base, however, often made it impossible for officers to prepare clothing in a systematic, efficient manner. In 1801, in an effort to standardize Army uniforms, Lieutenant-General James Stuart decided to use local materials, which were to be procured and made up into clothing through a system of Indian contractors. The new uniforms would be kept in a central Army Clothing Depot, and sent out to battalions from Madras.

> The inferiority of the Army clothing in quality, fashion, and make, which has always been a subject of regret since I have known the service; it's yearly enhanced price, and the disappointment to which the troops were constantly subject from not receiving their clothing until it had been some years due, were the facts which induced me to recommend to the Board, in September 1802, that, as an experiment, a year's clothing should be made up, under certain regulations, by the Deputy Adjutant-General, and in doing so I had in view to ascertain as well the actual cost of the clothing of the different ranks of the Army, as the time necessary to provide such clothing.[24]

The Deputy Adjutant General, however, had been in the field, and the Army's clothing was delayed until October 1803. When he returned to Madras after the Second Anglo-Maratha War, the Deputy Adjutant General was shocked to find that the Indian contractors had not produced any uniforms. He was informed that violent monsoon rains had made it impossible for the contractors' people to make up the troops' clothes, and that buttons and trimming had been in short supply. Furthermore, the cotton tape provided by the Indian contractors had been inferior, in colour and durability, to the worsted tape formerly imported from England. Stuart concluded that it was more efficient, in the long run, to clothe the Army using European materials, although most of the buttons needed—

hundreds of thousands of them—could be made 'cheaply and well' in Madras.[25]

With the prospect of peace following the Second Anglo-Maratha War, and with most of the troops in proper garrisons, a concerted effort was made to standardize Army dress. Cradock's new regulations of 1806, however, carried the alteration of the sepoy's uniform to an extreme, providing specific descriptions of how every article of clothing was to be worn. This penchant for detailed, almost scientific, instruction was a practice current in the King's service, but utterly impractical given India's climate and the sensibilities of Hindu and Muslim sepoys. For instance, the troops were informed that

> . . . short drawers should be made to reach above the hip, so as not only to admit the under jacket being well tucked into them, but to ensure that the upper part of the short drawers, fastened with a running string, shall be perfectly covered by the lower edge of the regimental jacket, [and] reach the thigh 1 in. above the upper part of the knee pan. . . . The Commander-in-Chief . . . directs that no ligature whatever shall be passed from above, between the thighs, on the outside of the drawers.[26]

When sepoys considered that their uniforms now consisted of a white 'underjacket' and a red, jacket-like coat, it must have seemed that the above regulation sought to transform their short drawers into breeches. Such an unnecessary measure could only have been part of an effort to give sepoys a European appearance.[27] Furthermore, the manner in which they were ordered to wear their short drawers must have seemed quite outrageous, for without the 'ligature' the men's genitals would not only lack support, but also would be—if not exactly exposed—quite obviously present to the observer.[28] Under the circumstances, it would have been surprising if sepoys had not considered the new, shako-like turban to be anything other than the particular type of hat that was the quintessential mark of European culture throughout India.

THE CROSS-CULTURAL CONTEXT OF THE NEW TURBAN

The grenadiers of the 2/4th Native Infantry described the new turban as a threat to their caste.[29] They pointed out that acceptance of the new turban would result in their being cast out of their communities, and some of the men even went so far as to suggest that their own wives and children would forsake them. Subadar Shaikh Imam set forth his complaint, however, in a slightly different manner, explaining that the new turban would disgrace them, as it resembled a drummer's hat.[30] These were the views held by most of the men of the 2/4th Native Infantry. They had discussed the new turban, and those who agreed to refuse to wear it held that it was a *topi*, and therefore objectionable, no matter what others chose to call it; wearing it could have grave social and personal consequences. Identities might become confused, reputations would be compromised, and families torn apart. Nevertheless, the Indian commissioned officers questioned after the protests by the 2/4th Native Infantry assured British officers that neither a caste Hindu nor a Muslim of high status could object to the new turban on religious grounds.[31] All of the talk about caste had led British officers to focus on the leather cockades as a possible source of alarm, but the remarks of the native commissioned officers suggested that this was a mistake. Rather than investigate the sepoys' grievances further, the European officers decided that they were facing insubordination and defiance of orders rather than a legitimate complaint.

Sepoy attitudes about the new turban became increasingly negative after the protest of the 2/4th Native Infantry at Vellore. The troops began to view the new headgear not as an accidental source of ritual pollution, but as a deliberate scheme to defile sepoys as a class, for even Paraiyar sepoys were upset by the new turban. What remains constant throughout the Vellore crisis is the characterization of the turban as a hat. The Princes' servants continued to tease the sepoys at Vellore, telling them they would soon have to wear hats, and sometimes warning them not to wear the *topi* about to be issued to them, which would make all sepoys 'of one caste', and lead to their conversion to Christianity.[32] Invalid Subadar Sayyid Chandmand testified that what sepoys feared most about the new turban, however, was its shape, not its ornaments.[33] The sepoys at Vellore saw the new turban as a tool for erasing the distinctions between castes, and assumed that it would be followed by a change in diet—the final step that would result in the outcasting of the entire Army.[34] A few sepoys thought this outcasting would be followed by conversion to Christianity, but most of the men who joined the mutineers did not draw this conclusion.[35] For Sepoy Grenadier Murthi, the issue was not what the turban might lead to, but the turban itself; he took up arms at Vellore because 'the [*kafirun*] wanted . . . [us] to wear hats, leather stocks, and to cut . . . [our] whiskers'.[36] During the Vellore Mutiny, the contractor who made the new turban was attacked, along with his Paraiyar workmen, but very few sepoys were seen destroying the new turban, and many of them were wearing it when they were captured. Therefore it seems reasonable to conclude that the new turban was despised not because of what it was, but because of what it symbolized.[37]

The primary causes of the unrest that resulted in the Vellore Mutiny were clearly the new turban and, to a lesser extent, the new regulations forbidding the use of *vibhuti* while on duty.[38] Although the Palace servants had encouraged the sepoys to resist the new turban, neither their encouragement nor their schemes seem to have been central to the mutiny plot, which was dominated, in its planning and execution, by soldiers rather than representatives of the Princes. At other stations where disturbances occurred, the significance of the turban tended to be overshadowed by other considerations. Among the troops at Wallajahbad there was much less concern about the new turban than about hard drill and the additional expense of keeping white waistcoats clean.[39] Complaints about hard drill were made at Vellore, as well, especially be men of the newly-raised 2/23rd Native Infantry, who had been training rather hard, under Adjutant Coombs, when their battalion was ordered to march from Trichinopoly to join the Vellore garrison.

All of the above complaints were made by the sepoys at Hyderabad, whose feelings about the new turban were similar to those voiced by their comrades in Vellore. The sepoys of the Subsidiary Force feared ostracism and separation from their families if they showed themselves willing to conform to the habits and dress of Europeans.[40] The little circle of 'conspirators' at Hyderabad also had told their fellow soldiers that the new turban would be forced on them in order to bring about a negative cultural transformation, and the rather dubious *arz* that was found in the Nizam's palace argued that sepoys were to be compelled to wear the dress of 'hat-wearers' and to receive their faith.[41]

It is difficult to discern exactly how the sepoys at Nandidurgam felt about the new turban. The troops clearly opposed the new turban for they vied with each other to be the first to declare their refusal to accept it.[42] A local *faqir*, Madar Shah, explained that after the order to adopt the new turban had been circulated, Havildar Shaikh Imam and a growing number of sepoys began to meet at his *makan* for secret discussions. After the first meeting, one of the sepoys told the *faqir* that the Havildar, in fact, had smashed his wife's bangles, and had declared himself prepared to die—an example followed by others. These meetings continued, in fact, until 18 October, the last of them being the one witnessed by Sepoy Arnasum and reported to Captain Baynes.[43] The fears of the men of the 2/18th Native Infantry, however, were encouraged by soldiers of the 2/4th, who were on leave in the Nandidurgam area, or who had deserted, returning to their home district to hide. One such deserter, Muhabbat Khan, was arrested in October, and confessed that he had attended the puppet shows given by the sepoys of the garrison. In a desperate mood, the deserter remarked to Jamadar Jerobar Singh who was sent to interrogate him: 'We conquered the country for Europeans . . . [but] the Europeans never conquered for us. They are not such great people, and . . . the English power could not force us to wear the turband.'[44] The unrest at Nandidurgam is significant because it continued even after the order rescinding the new turban was received. What, then, were the sepoys there concerned about? It seems that the execution of the condemned men at Vellore struck a chord at Nandidurgam and Bangalore because of the close personal ties between the men of the 2/18th and the 1/1st Native Infantry battalions. However, it also is apparent that the morale of the Nandidurgam garrison was quite low, and that long-standing disagreements among the Indian officers contributed much to the collapse of discipline at the station. These disagreements themselves were almost all related, in one way or another, to the changing tenor of military service—especially to the increased emphasis on drill and 'regularity'. At Nandidurgam, the turban was clearly a symbol that came to absorb a variety of grievances.

The General Staff was too distracted, seeking evidence of a political conspiracy behind the Vellore Mutiny, to appreciate the significance of the new turban. Cradock insisted that the new turban was a mere device that the conspirators had used to sabotage the loyalty of otherwise faithful sepoys.[45] The Commander-in-Chief pointed out that protests against the new turban were confined to certain battalions, while others greeted the new headgear with ambivalence. The Military Board, in defence of the new regulations, presented reports from several battalion commanders, all of whom indicated that *vibhuti*, earrings, and beards had not been tolerated in their regiments. This evidence, however, was carefully vetted, and certainly did not represent the general practice of the Army. Nor did the Military Board's report take into account that beards were not fashionable in south India at that time—even among Muslims—or that many sepoys simply were unable to grow them.[46]

The Mixed Commission's report of 9 August 1806, however, suggests that how sepoys responded to the new turban may have had something to do with how much they knew about the new headgear, and about the events that had unfolded at Vellore after the protest of the 2/4th Native Infantry. For instance, 460 men of the 1/1st Native Infantry were detached to Chitoor and Chandragiri, where they heard little about the mutinous plotting by their comrades—perhaps only rumours. Indeed, the men of the detachments, being separated from the battalion adjutant, heard nothing about either the new regulations or the new turban, and remained calm after the Vellore Mutiny.[47] The Mixed Commission also singled out the shape of the new turban as the aspect of the innovation most offensive to sepoys. This was obvious, as well, to Thomas Oakes, next to Petrie the most experienced member of the government. Oakes believed that the sepoys' fears were quite real—that they truly believed the government sought to overthrow their culture by altering their dress. The Third of Council pointed out that officers conversant with Indian customs recognized that innovations such as the new turban were 'pregnant with danger', threatening the 'fondest prejudices' of the castes that supplied the Army with most of its manpower.[48]

WHO WAS THE MADRAS ARMY SEPOY?

Caste and the sacred status connected with it were prized by the Madras Army, and this was an important element underlying the military strength of the Company Raj. Ironically, however, many British officers referred to the need to 'conciliate' the 'fondest prejudices' of sepoys, indicating their lack of understanding of the role that caste played in the discipline of sepoy battalions. The

Company's tolerant attitude regarding caste restrictions enabled a sepoy, in theory, to pursue a promising military career in the service of a foreign power without sacrificing reputation or religious scruples.

As early as the late 1760s, the Company's commanders had held up the ideal image of an Army composed mainly of high-caste soldiers.[49] The Bengal Army was largely successful in its drive to bar low-caste men from military service, but in the Carnatic the situation was quite different as the Madras Army competed for manpower with several other rather large armies.[50] By 1765, the Madras forces were taking any men capable of shouldering a musket—and quite a number who could not even do that much.[51] Sir Archibald Campbell complained, in 1788, of the difficulty he encountered trying to locate good recruits in the Carnatic, an assertion repeated every recruiting season until the end of the Maratha Wars.[52] Cornwallis lamented, after the Third Anglo-Mysore War, that 'it [was] impracticable to procure in a short time a considerable number of men of proper caste and of sufficient size and strength for the duties of a soldier'.[53] Colonel Floyd, commanding the Southern Division of the Army, added: 'In my opinion . . . these countries do not now produce, whatever they may have done, any number of proper-built men.'[54]

Indian princes offered their soldiers better pay, but they also tended to keep their troops in arrears in order to prevent desertion. Nor was there any provision for wounded or elderly veterans in the armies of the princely states, apart from the occasional grant of a village.[55] The Company sepoy, on the other hand, earned less money than a prince's *sipahi*, but he almost always received his salary on time, and in full—minus the usual stoppages.[56] On retirement, or after being wounded, he could look forward to a pension, just as regularly paid. If he died in the Company's service, his family received a survivor's allowance sufficient to meet most of their wants. In the Madras Army, however, an Indian soldier traded opportunity for security. The prospect of a pension was a 'great draw' for sons of the soil—the sort of conservative, village folk the British wanted for regiments of native infantry. Such men took up service as a way of earning money with which to improve the lot of their families back in the village—they would stay with the Army, through good times and bad, and would remain faithful.[57]

Adventurers and men of ambition entered the Company's armies only to obtain military training before moving on to serve the Nizam, the Maratha sardars, Tipu Sultan, or the Raja of Travancore.[58] The Company's conquest and demilitarization of south India, however, had begun to close off these options for military adventurers by the 1790s, and thousands of such men were stranded, as it were, in the Madras Army, where their ambition was frustrated by racial barriers against promotion and the strict system of seniority that governed most advancement within sepoy battalions. By 1806, the sepoy battalions were filled with men who had served Tipu Sultan or some rebellious *palaiyakkar* only a few years before.[59] Furthermore, during the period 1780-1800, the Madras Army absorbed almost all of the Nawab of Arcot's troops, sometimes annexing entire companies and battalions of men at a time.[60]

The Company sepoy's monthly pay of two pagodas (or seven rupees)—minus stoppages—did not change much after the 1780s, despite the sharp increase that occurred in prices and the wages of non-military labourers. A slight pay increase was accorded all ranks in 1800, but during periods of scarcity sepoy families had to rely on paddy distributed by government depots. For thousands of men displaced from the service of Indian princes, enlisting in the Madras Army meant accepting significantly lower pay than that to which they had become accustomed—not to mention much more arduous conditions of service. Lieutenant-General John Brathwaite attempted to alert the Madras Government to the sepoy's rapidly deteriorating situation in a series of letters written in 1800, shortly after the Company's triumph over Mysore, when Lord Mornington felt inclined to reward the Army for its bravery during recent campaigns. Brathwaite noted that

> . . . it [is] well known that the [Army's] pay is seldom adequate to the subsistence of the sepoy, and never sufficient to render the service an object of attainment. . . . The miserable materials of which the mass of our native regiments are composed, and the difficulty of procuring even this inferior class of men for the service, must be well known to every military man. The cause is equally obvious—a sepoy, harassed with continual duty, subject to severe discipline, and often exposed to situations of considerable hardship and imminent danger, receives a smaller recompense for his service than the lowest [coolie] who accompanies the camp. . . . During the late campaign, officers of experience were more than usually struck with the want of strength and substance in the men of the Coast native corps. The mass of the sepoys

are hardly capable of sustaining the weight of their arms, [and] to use them with vigour and effect is not to be expected of them for any long continuance of service. . . . So many years as I have been in this service, I have never known the Native Battalions reduced to the necessity of taking such bad recruits as has been the case latterly, and although they now take almost anything that offers, your Lordship will see how very deficient [in numerical strength] they are.[61]

Specific information about the composition of the Army at the time of the Vellore Mutiny is not available. However, strong inferences can be made on the basis of prize money lists, rolls that have survived from the early 1820s, and from lists of sepoys detained during the Vellore crisis. Finally, general impressions about the composition of the Army are available in correspondence that appears in the Military Consultations. These materials indicate that the Madras Army, before the Vellore Mutiny, was composed mainly of men belonging to the Right Hand castes (including Paraiyars) and Muslims. Most recruits were drawn from the Northern Circars, the Carnatic, and Mysore. A handful of Nayars, Mappilas, Marathas, and Rajputs were also found in most regiments. Muslims of Deccani heritage formed the largest group within the Army, followed by Telugus and Tamils, in that order.[62]

Military historians who have studied the Company's sepoy battalions have often remarked that in the Madras Army, less emphasis was placed on caste than in the Bengal Army. Philip Mason, for instance, offers the statement of 'an old subadar' from the 1830s, who reputedly said, 'We put our religion into our knapsacks whenever our colours are unfurled.'[63] This, indeed, had been Cradock's view of the Madras Army before the Vellore crisis. He arrived in south India under the impression that the disciplinary system of the Madras Army was framed to 'abolish, to the greatest practicable extent, the observance of local usages'. He was under the impression that British officers, in most sepoy battalions, persuaded their men to 'disregard, on duty, all distinctions and observances of caste, and to assimilate the conduct and appearance . . . of European troops'.[64] As the Vellore Mutiny demonstrated, this perception was fundamentally incorrect. All sepoys—including Muslims and Paraiyars—were deeply concerned about 'caste' and 'prejudice'. The sepoys of the 2/4th Native Infantry, in particular, demonstrated just how strongly this sense of common interest united them. They stood together to oppose innovations that seemed to threaten their traditionally high sacred and secular status, a status that was being eroded, steadily, by the Europeanization of the Army, deteriorating service conditions, and the general condition to which the south Indian economy had sunk during the early stages of British rule.

THE SEPOY'S SENSE OF HONOUR, DUTY, AND LOYALTY

Every sepoy recruit, upon completion of his military training, was administered an oath of fidelity by a *pujari* of his own caste, or by a mullah, if he was Muslim. The words of the oath changed over time, but most of the sepoy mutineers of 1806 had recited the following version, or something very close to it:

> I, A. B., sepoy, do swear to serve the Honourable Company faithfully and truly against all their enemies while I continue to receive their pay and eat their salt. I do swear to obey all the orders I may receive from my Commanders and Officers, never to forsake my post, abandon my Colours, or turn my back to my enemies, and that I will, in all things, behave myself like a good and faithful sepoy, in perfect obedience, at all times, to the rules and customs of war. . . .[65]

Philip Mason, describing the concepts which held sepoy battalions together, writes of the oath:

> The regiment, the colours, were British; destiny and fidelity to salt Muslim; the essential message of the Bhagavad Gita, which some regard as the core of Hinduism, is that each man shall perform his proper function. All three understood the concept of honour. The oath at enlistment, the sacredness of the colours, the ceremonial of guard-mounting—these rubbed in the point.[66]

Mason's rhetoric must be treated with caution, especially his reference to the *Bhagavad Gita*, which was nowhere near as significant to Indian perceptions of Hinduism in 1800 as it became a century later. To many of the desperate characters who entered the Madras Army during the period 1800-5, the rather idealistic oath quoted above may well have been meaningless. They represented a very different military tradition, of which Orme had observed: 'The armies of the

Mahomedan princes of Indostan are composed of a number of distinct bodies of troops enlisted by different leaders; who, with their bands, enter into, and quit the service of different princes, according to the advantages which they expect to receive.'[67] Nevertheless, it is clear that many other sepoys interpreted the oath-taking ritual as the formation of a dynamic bond between themselves and the Company, a bond which they expected to endure for life, for sepoys, in describing conversations with each other, made frequent reference to different aspects of their oath.

While sepoys pledged to serve the Company, they expected their officers and the *sarkar* to provide payment and respect, and to take care of their families. Major James Welsh met many such soldiers in the Madras Army. One of them, Subadar Ali Khan, after being nearly cut in half by a cannon ball during the Battle of Argaum (1804), insisted on being carried forward as his battalion advanced. Realizing he did not have long to live, he remarked that 'he was not afraid of death; he had often braved it in the discharge of his duty, and only regretted that he should not be permitted to render further services to his honourable masters'.[68] Sepoys often mentioned having 'eaten' the 'Company's salt', which implied an obligation to serve, stated more specifically in the phrase *namak ada karna*, 'to repay one's salt'. *Halal* is an Islamic term, a reference to that which is proper, as opposed to *haram*, that which is forbidden.[69] The expression *namak-halal* conveyed a sense of loyalty, submission, faithfulness, and gratitude; it conveyed, at least in part, the dynamics of the client-patron relationship in India.

Another concept important to the Company sepoy was *izzat*, which may be defined loosely as 'reputation'. Sepoys also often used another, similar term, *ghairat*, which conveyed the idea of a petulant sense of honour centred on one's status as perceived by others.[70] Lieutenant-Colonel John Malcolm observed in 1811 that the 'native soldier of the Company, intelligent and quick in his conception, full of vanity and love of pre-eminence, if not of glory, is of all men the most sensible to the effect of attention, or neglect'.[71] Native Commandant Muhyi-ud-Din of the 14th Native Infantry, for instance, was offered a choice between a medal and a *palankin* allowance in recognition of his heroism at the siege of Ambur in 1767, and selected the latter, explaining to a British officer that a 'palanquin is looked upon by the Moors as a great thing, and therefore will be a more distinguishing mark . . . as it will be seen and known by everybody on what account it is given, whereas a medal would only be seen by a few friends'.[72] Such symbolic distinctions were—and are—of great significance in Indian society. Those who enjoyed the privilege of displaying them were accorded deference and respect which, in itself, signified superior status and honour. Many sepoys risked death to secure their share of *ghairat.* Major James Welsh recalled one such man, Hussain Khan, who attained the rank of subadar by recruiting two hundred men. During the assault on Ahmadnagar (1803), hoping to distinguish himself before Welsh and other British officers, he pushed his way to the top of a scaling ladder by pulling down the men ahead of him, only to be shot off the top of the city wall and mortally wounded.[73]

The Muslim sepoy's world-view, in particular, was shaped by the concept of *shariat*, 'what Muslims conceive of as "the good", whether moral or political'.[74] In the proceedings of the Bellary court of enquiry, we have seen how the concept of *shariat* guided Muslim sepoys as they themselves, with some input from Hindu comrades, but without the intervention of British officers, resolved a potentially serious disciplinary problem in their regiment. Notably absent from the formation of *shariat*, in south India, however, was a strong sense of the *umma*, or 'community of the faithful', except in a few towns and villages with large concentrations of Muslim residents. Among south Indian Muslims, the *umma* was less important than *biradari* (brotherhood, or kinship ties) and 'class'—the distinction between the *ashraf* Muslims of Arcot or Hyderabad, and the Pathans of Cuddapah and Kurnool, or the Lubbai communities of the Coromandel Coast. The Vellore Papers, however, indicate that in sepoy battalions something like an *umma* developed, on a small scale, around certain highly-respected individuals. Indeed, what is particularly striking is how vibrant the Muslim sepoy's religious life was, as indicated by the presence of so many *pirs* and *faqirs* in and around garrison towns, of informal Islamic study groups, and the intense religiosity of individual soldiers. Some sepoys, such as Havildar Shaikh Adam of the 2/18th Native Infantry, prepared themselves, through prayer and fasting, to be both sepoys and *faqirs*, and encouraged their fellow soldiers to pursue spiritual renewal.[75]

European officials and military officers found it difficult to explain why Indian soldiers were loyal. Mark Wilks, for instance, interpreted India's political condition as a state of 'oriental despotism', a 'fact so familiar to every reader that it seems to be received as we receive the knowledge of a law of nature, without any troublesome investigation of the causes'.[76] Bentinck himself, in February 1806, wrote that 'the inhabitants of India have . . . no political opinions, and are without any national predilections. Religion and custom prevent every type of revolt—social or political'.[77] Such views, of course, were reflected in the European interpretation of indigenous military systems. Francis Buchanan noted that:

[Hindu] military men are the only class that seem to have a strong attachment to their princes; and they serve faithfully, so long as they are regularly paid, or gratified by a permission to plunder; but provided these pay them better, they are equally willing to serve a Mussulman or Christian leader, as a Hindu prince. Terror is . . . the leading principle of every Indian government; and among the people, in place of loyalty and patriotism, the chief principles are an abject devotion to their spiritual masters, and an obstinate adherence to custom, chiefly in matters of ceremony and caste.

The Abbé Dubois, however, remarked that it was precisely this 'adherence to custom' and the warrior's concern about ceremony and caste, that was 'the chef-d'oeuvre, the happiest effort of Hindu legislation'. Caste, he argued, preserved India's indigenous civilization, despite foreign conquest, because it was, in itself, a system of government.[78] Lieutenant-Colonel Thomas Munro, considering social conditions in the Ceded Districts, reached a similar conclusion, which he shared with William Petrie in a letter of August 1805:

What is effected . . . by property in other parts of he world is accomplished here by the disctinction of casts [*sic*] and the manners of the people. The lower, the middle, and the higher classes of inhabitants preserve mutually as just degree of respect and subordination as the different orders in England.[79]

Indeed, Dubois believed that the British could secure their power over India best by linking the basis of loyalty to the Company with caste affiliation and other hierarchical aspects of Indian society. On the other hand, the quickest way for the British to lose India, he thought, was to ignore Hindu 'prejudice'. Shortly before the Vellore Mutiny, he made the following cautionary statement:

Let [the Europeans] take care, lest [they] bring about, by some hasty or imprudent action, catastrophes which would reduce the country to a state of anarchy, desolation, and ultimate ruin, for in my . . . opinion, the day when the Government attempts to interfere with any of the more important religious and civil usages of the Hindus will be the last of its existence as a political power.[80]

Dubois also predicted that the British might rue the day they had developed the sepoy military system, introducing European weapons and tactics to the Indian scene—a 'sad and fatal gift, which [the people of the country] may perhaps one day use against those who brought it to them.'[81] The Vellore Mutiny, meanwhile, made Bentinck see, if only briefly, that religion and caste could be catalysts for violent change rather than a check on social and political revolt. Cradock's military reforms, he noted, led sepoys 'to suppose the destruction of all [their] religious distinctions and prejudices'. This, in turn, undermined the sepoy's respect for his British officers.[82]

Ultimately, it is not at all surprising that the relationship between sepoys and British officers began to breakdown during the years preceding the Vellore Mutiny. The few documents left to us by sepoys strongly suggest that they viewed their military service as a reciprocal process; the British, for their part, were expected to honour caste and religion, thus preserving the high status of the profession of arms, and, consequently, of sepoys as a class. This was the compelling force behind the oath of fidelity—a public act, made in the context of caste affiliation, which concerned both personal and group honour. However, from the sepoys' perspective, the introduction of the new turban was the last straw in a series of violations of the unspoken agreement inherent in the oath of fidelity—the patron's obligation to protect his servants' interests. According to this point-of-view, it was not the sepoy who was guilty of plotting *ghadr*—an act of deceit, fraud, and treachery—but the Company itself. As William Petrie had observed, sensing the breach of faith that infuriated the Madras Army in 1806, 'These men have long fought our battles, they shared in our adversity, and their valor and attachment have eminently contributed to our prosperity, and I trust the justice and munificence of the British Government will never be insensible to their merits.'[83] The dialogue that once had allowed officers to learn about grievances and diffuse problems before they became crises had broken down, and consequently many soldiers saw violence as the only option left for seeking redress.[84] As many people at Nandidurgam and Bangalore remarked, the Vellore mutineers fought not only for their own rights, but for the very foundations of Indian society, making a sacrifice so terrible that it stayed the hand of the colonial power and prevented all castes from being transformed into one.

FROM DISCIPLINE TO DISCONTENT

The Vellore Mutiny was not a revolt against the Company as much as the dramatic resolution of a crisis that threatened the sepoy's *izzat* and the performance of his own particular dharma. The primary causes of the mutiny were military in nature, concerning only sepoys and those close to them, but the rising had results that were beneficial to traditional south Indian society as a whole. The mutiny was—at least from a Hindu perspective—a classic dharmic event, involving different but interconnected warrior communities. For Muslim soldiers there was a deep sense that some dramatic demonstration, perhaps even martyrdom, was necessary to preserve basic privileges. For Muslim sepoys of the Madras Army, mutiny and martyrdom tended to be seen as very similar concepts, since the former usually led to the latter. When all was said and done, the Vellore Mutiny was a sacrificial act intended to preserve the Indian soldier's social status and cultural identity.[85]

Hundreds of men were killed, but the Madras Army, as an institution, survived. More than that, sepoys drove home a point that India's colonial rulers, at least in the Madras Presidency, never forgot. Never again were the religious beliefs and caste interests of Madras sepoys threatened in such a cavalier manner. After Vellore, European officers were compelled to pay strict attention to the welfare and feelings of their Indian troops. Henry Bevan, writing of the Madras Army in the 1820s, remarked that:

> A great error, committed by young officers on first joining the Indian Army, is to affect contempt for the soldiers whom they are to command, calling them 'black fellows,' 'niggers,' etc. A residence of a few months at a Mofussil station soon clears the head of that nonsense. . . . There is nothing so efficacious in destroying the feelings of mutual prejudice as the sense of mutual dependence.[86]

Madras sepoys, in turn, accepted the ongoing Europeanization of the Army. By the 1840s, the Madras Army had become a fully westernized military system.[87] The legacy of Vellore paid off, for the British, when most Madras sepoys ignored the mass mutiny of the Bengal Army in 1857. Instead, mutinies in the Madras Army continued to be localized and highly dependent on the personalities of those involved in them, just as they had been before the disaster at Vellore.

The new turban and regulations symbolized broken promises and insensitivity, the unwillingness of British officers to honour the 'contract' inherent in the sepoy's oath of loyalty, as mentioned above. Yet other factors determined the subsequent course of the crisis: the presence of the Mysore princes in Vellore, for instance, or the political machinations of the Hyderabadi elite. Nevertheless, these were matters of local significance, peculiar to certain places, to particular battalions, or even to specific individuals, as in the case of the Bellary 'disturbances'. Some sepoys were motivated to acts of 'mutiny' by personal slights, such as having been passed over for promotion by a native officer, or having been insulted by a European. These cases, trivial in themselves, accumulated so that even petty discontents became dangers to military discipline—especially where tensions were not identified and diffused by dialogue. All serious disturbances during the Vellore crisis were preceded by a breakdown of the dialogic relationship between British officers and Indian officers, and between both sets of officers and the men under their command. When dialogue, the familiar process of *panchayati raj*, was replaced by an inflexible, impersonal disciplinary code, morale immediately entered a crisis.[88] Under the new disciplinary system, complaints from the ranks were viewed not as information, but as signs of unrest. Native officers quickly learned to silence their men, to give British officers false reports that their men were content. British officials, in turn, did not receive the information necessary to carry out their duties effectively. Even those European officers who could chat with their soldiers in Urdu found the men unwilling to speak freely for fear of punishment. A system meant to improve discipline made it impossible, in fact, for officers to command their troops.[89] A dramatic illustration of this breakdown in communication occurred at Palaiyamkottai on the anniversary of Qadir Aliyah, shortly after the Vellore Mutiny.

A soldier named Shaikh Haidar raised a flag over the masjid in the fort, upon which a fellow Muslim, Subadar Sikandar Khan, suggested that he ought to inform Major James Welsh of his intentions before flying Islamic flags inside a Company fort. Shaikh Haidar was reported to have said, 'I will mention it to the gentlemen', before laughing sarcastically at the very proposition that he should seek Welsh's permission for a private act of religious devotion.[90]

The Third Member of the Madras Council, Thomas Oakes, correctly observed that the manner of introduction of the new turban brought about a situation in which sepoys associated merit with resistance.[91] The grenadiers of the 2/4th Native Infantry, in their initial protest against the new turban, aired a minor grievance in the time-honoured tradition of the service. They had attempted to bring the matter to the attention of British officers earlier, but their warnings had been turned aside by native officers and *dubashes.* Lieutenant-Colonel Darley had sought the counsel of the battalion's Indian adjutant, and it was this native officer who had suggested the idea of challenging each sepoy individually, before his comrades—rather unwise advice, as it turned out.[92] The culture of the Madras Army could not abide a situation in which soldiers were asked to make a public choice between obedience to regulations, on the one hand, and loyalty to comrades and caste on the other.[93] An even greater mistake was Cradock's insistence upon absolute obedience to orders, which transformed the new turban into the very embodiment of the Commander-in-Chief's authority to govern and change the Army. Sepoys who rejected the new turban, therefore, came to be seen not as men who disliked an article of dress, but as men in defiance of the military hierarchy. As the Army was the core institution of the Raj, disobedient sepoys were threats to the security of the colonial state. Raising protest to the level of rebellion was both unnecessary and extremely reckless on the part of British authorities.

A few sepoys thought in terms of political revolt in 1806, but they were not numerous or successful enough to impart much political significance to the Vellore Mutiny. The political impact of the disturbances is to be seen primarily in the government's rather awkward handing of the crisis. Most of the Vellore mutineers would have been happy simply to have received permission to keep their old turbans. Nothing would have come of the petty conspiracies associated with the Vellore crisis if the Military Board had not introduced the new turban, or if the turban order had been rescinded earlier. Similarly, the turban order would not have raised such profound issues in the first place, nor been viewed as such a threat, if it had not occurred within the context of a widespread disintegration of the bonds which once had connected British officers and sepoys in the Madras Army.

NOTES

1. BL/OIOC, Lieutenant-Colonel Forbes' Deposition, 24 July 1806, *HMS*, V. 508, pp. 144-5.
2. Plural sense in the original.
3. UN, Vellore Court of Enquiry Proceedings, 17 May 1806, Portland MS, PwJb/57, pp. 23-7.
4. For instance, see BL/OIOC, Govind Rao's Testimony, 27 July 1806, *HMS*, V. 508, pp. 279-80. The pedda sherishtadar of the Collector of Arcot District reported that villagers around Taiyur, a small town near Vandavasi, began, in early June, to speak about a mass, forced conversion to Christianity. It was said that Europeans were going to force them to wear crosses. Such stories, in 1806, tended to be very localized, and remind one of the sporadic anti-missionary violence seen in India in the 1990s.
5. BL/OIOC, Sepoy Shaikh Abdul Qadir's Testimony, 5 August 1806, *HMS*, V. 508, pp. 532-4. The men of the 2/23rd Native Infantry heard about the new turban while in Trichinopoly, but did not become angry about it until they arrived at Vellore in June, and actually saw for themselves what it looked like.
6. UN, Kot Havildar Shaikh Imam's Defence, Portland MS, PwJb/57, pp. 103-4. Every company of a sepoy battalion had a tailor, whose job was to repair or alter uniforms. Most darzi sepoys were Muslims, often of low caste.
7. Curiously, during the three years that I have been giving presentations about the Vellore Mutiny in the United States, most of my listeners, when shown a picture of the new turban, have insisted that it does not appear, to them, to be a hat. My own feeling is that one's interpretation of Major Bose's turban depends on cultural influences.
8. Urumal is the Tamil form of the Hindu and Urdu *rumal*, or kerchief.
9. Jafar Sharif, *Qanoon-e-Islam; or, the Customs of the Mussulmans of India*, 2nd edn (Madras, 1863), Appendix no. 3, p. ix. The first English version of this work was translated and published by G.A. Herklots in 1832.

Many of the turbans described by Sharif were royal *pagris,* such as appear in the *darbar* paintings of Hyderabad. Others, however, were associated with particular martial communities, such as the Rachawars of Bobbli zamindari, in the Northern Circars.

10. The frame was originally made of wicker, but this proved to be too heavy, and was changed to a light frame of iron and wire. That this change occurred before 1806 is apparent because the sepoys of the 2/4th Native Infantry were ordered to send their old turbans to the stores to have the 'irons' reshaped according to Bose's model.
11. W.Y. Carman, *Indian Army Uniforms, under the British, from the 18th Century to 1947* (London, 1961-9), V. 2, pp. 131-2.
12. For example, see William Daniells, *Oriental Scenery,* V. 3, plate no. 14, *Ousoor, in Mysore, 4 May 1792.* In this watercolour, Daniells includes the four sepoys of his escort, seated in the shade of a small *choultry.* Their uniforms are clearly and accurately depicted, and include the 'flat-topped' turban described in the General Order of the Commander-in-Chief of March 1797.
13. See *Captives of Tipu: Survivors' Narratives,* ed. Arnold W. Lawrence (London, 1929), p. 231. James Scurry, a sailor captured by the French and handed over to the Mysore during the Cuddalore Campaign, 'coverted' to Islam, and was inducted into Tipu Sultan's army. As part of the process of indigenization to which he was subjected, Scurry was ordered to wear a turban not unlike that ordered for Madras sepoys in 1797. When he escaped from Mysore, he found he had to remove this turban before anyone would recognize him as a European.
14. General Order of the Commander-in-Chief, 15 November 1805, quotes in Carman, V. 2, p. 132.
15. UN, Kot Havildar Shaikh Imam's Defence, Portland MS, PwJb/57, pp. 103-4.
16. On the British soldier's shako, the ball tuft, or hackle, was fixed to the front of the crown, whereas on the sepoy's turban, it was in the middle of the crown.
17. Major Samuel C. Macpherson, *Memorials of Service in India,* ed. William Macpherson (London, 1865), p. 15. The passage quotes a letter written to an anonymous friend in 1829.
18. For a reference to short drawers worn by the peasantry, see Benjamin Lewis Rice, *Mysore and Coorg,* V. 1 (Bangalore, 1877), p. 358.
19. Carman, V. 2, p. 137.
20. Quoted in Carman, V. 1, p. 129. Note the reference to the headgear as a 'hat' or 'helmet'. The hat to which Rebecca Chase refers sounds like the Tarleton-style helmet then worn by British cavalry officers; the helmet, however, sounds like the turban worn by the sowars.

21. The fifers and drummers of British and sepoy regiments wore coats with chevrons extending all the way down the sleeves.
22. Carman, V. 1, pp. 133-4.
23. It was also a custom, in India, to present servants with a new set of clothes once each year, a gift that symbolized the patron-client relationship.
24. TNSA, Lieutenant-General James Stuart to GC/FSG, 6 March 1804, *MMC*, V. 319-A, pp. 865-6.
25. Ibid., pp. 866-70.
26. Carman, V. 1, pp. 135-6.
27. BL/OIOC, L/MIL/17/3/490, *A Code of Regulations for Various Departments of the Military Establishment of Fort St. George, Established by a General Order of Government, 11 March 1806*, p. 71. The sepoy's kit, apart from his red coat, consisted of one turban, three 'white underjackets', three short drawers, one pair of suspenders, two pairs of knee-bands, a knapsack, a *kambli* (woollen) watch coat, and a belt plate. Sandals were not standard issue until 1812.
28. In the spring of 2002, the British Library displayed pictures, paintings, and documents illustrating the East India Trade in an exhibit entitled *Trading Places*. The poster advertising the exhibit featured a period painting, in the Company style, of a European, in late eighteenth-century costume, standing beside an Indian prince. Their own sense of modesty compelled the Library's publicity staff to have the crotch of the European air-brushed to obscure embarrassing details!
29. By caste what the Records refer to really is *jati*, or birth-group. This is clearly the context in which the sepoys couched their concerns, as they spoke of commensality and marriage rather than occupation.
30. UN, Havildar Subharaya's Deposition, Portland MS, PwJb/57, pp. 36-7.
31. UN, Jamadar Chain Singh's Testimony, Proceedings of a General Court Martial, 9 June 1806, Portland MS., PwJb/57, pp. 145-6.
32. BL/OIOC, Sepoy Bawa Sahib's Testimony, 24 July 1806, *HMS*, V. 508, p. 146; TNSA, Havildar Yusuf Khan's Confession, 10 August 1806, *MSS*, V. 2-A, pp. 1183-9.
33. BL/OIOC, Invalid Subadar Sayyid Chandmand, 13 July 1806, *HMS*, V. 508, pp. 135-6.
34. BL/OIOC, Sepoy Mustafa Beg's Testimony, 27 July 1806, *HMS*, V. 508, pp. 182-6.
35. One of the Palace eunuchs, Muhammed Martaba, recalled that during the mutiny, one of the sepoys told him that the Army's new uniform made the men look like 'Christians'. See TNSA, Muhammad Martaba's Testimony, 4 August 1806, *MSS*, V. 2-A, pp. 978-86.

36. TNSA, Sepoy Grenadier Murthi's Testimony, *MSS*, V. 2-A, pp. 921-4.
37. BL/OIOC, Marriott's Testimony, 25 July 1806, *HMS*, V. 508, pp. 148-66.
38. The orders about the use of *vibhuti*, earrings, and hair styles, were mainly of concern to Hindu sepoys, and are rarely mentioned in the depositions of Muslim sepoys. As Sepoy Shaikh Abdul Qadir of the 2/23rd Native Infantry remarked, after a discussion of the order regarding 'caste marks', some sepoys were upset by the regulation, but it was clear that 'others did not care'. See BL/OIOC, Sepoy Shaikh Abdul Qadir's Testimony, 5 August 1806, *HMS*, V. 508, pp. 532-4.
39. BL/OIOC, Lang to Cradock, 26 July 1806, *HMS*, V. 507, pp. 433-4.
40. BL/OIOC, Sydenham to Edmonstone, 23 July 1806, *HMS*, V. 507, pp. 526-35.
41. BL/OIOC, Sydenham to Bentinck, enclosing *arz* to His Highness, the Nizam, 14 August 1806, *HMS*, V. 509, pp. 48-58.
42. TNSA, Jamadar Sheikh Dawood's Testimony, 26 October 1806, *MSP*, V. 4, p. 2421.
43. TNSA, Madar Shah's Testimony, 27 October 1806, *MSS*, V. 4, p. 2427.
44. TNSA, Confession of Sepoy Muhabbat [alias Faqir] Khan to Jamadar Jerobar Singh, 27 October 1806, *MSS*, V. 4, p. 2426.
45. BL/OIOC, Cradock's Minute, 23 July 1806, *HMS*, V. 507, pp. 275-6.
46. TNSA, Report of the Military Board, *MMP*, Range 256, V. 25.
47. BL/OIOC, Report of the Mixed Commission, 9 August 1806, *HMS*, V. 508, pp. 103-21.
48. BL/OIOC, Oakes' Minute, 6 September 1806, *HMS*, V. 509, pp. 143-8.
49. Exactly what is meant by high caste, with respect to sepoys, is a matter of some confusion. In the Madras Army, this meant Brahmins and Rajputs, as in the Bengal Army, but there were only a handful of the latter available in south India, mostly immigrants from northern India. The main Hindu warrior castes of southern India were the so-called *sat sudra* castes, such as the Kammas, Reddis, and Vellalars.
50. For instance, when two Circar battalions were raised at Elluru in 1778, Major Matthews could only find 300 recruits, and needed 619 more men to complete his two units. His efforts were hampered due to the presence of the Nizam's jamadars, who also were recruiting in the area. See TNSA, *Military Miscellany*, V. 1, 1778, pp. 347-9.
51. TNSA, GC/FSG to Major Charles Campbell, 9 April 1765, *MMC*, p. 272. From time to time, British officers mentioned seeing sepoys' wives carrying their muskets or backpacks on the march.
52. TNSA, Sir Archibald Campbell's Minute, 14 October 1788, *MMC*, pp. 3058-60.

53. *Cornwallis Correspondence*, V. 2, p. 569.
54. TNSA, Colonel Floyd to GC/FSG, 10 August 1795, *MMC*, pp. 2444-5.
55. For instance, see an *akhbar nawis*' report from Seringapatam to Nizam Ali Khan, dated 3 June 1776 (5 Muharram 1181 AH), in *Newsletters, 1767-1799* (*Nawab Mir Nizam Ali's Reign*), ed. Yusuf Husain (Hyderabad, 1955), p. 3. The news-writer reported that Haidar Ali's army was threatening to disband unless it received its arrears of pay.
56. From time to time, however, there were significant problems paying the Madras Army, due primarily to the need to exchange Star Pagodas for local currencies, which might reduce a sepoy's income by up to 20 per cent.
57. TNSA, Brathwaite to GC/FSG, 25 May 1800, *MSC*, V. 11, p. 614.
58. TNSA, Brathwaite to GC/FSG, 11 July 1800, *MSC*, V. 11, p. 613.
59. For instance, most of the peons in the service of the Raja of Ramnad (Ramanathapuram) joined the Madras Army in 1795, although they waited to enlist until after they had collected the arrears owed to them by their former master. See TNSA, *Military Miscellany*, V. 45, p. 510, and ibid., V. 46, p. 26.
60. For instance, see Wilson, V. 2, pp. 106-9.
61. TNSA, Brathwaite to Lord Edward Clive (confidential), 11 July 1800, *MSC*, V. 11, pp. 595-615. Brathwaite was not exaggerating, for after the Fourth Anglo-Mysore War, the sepoy battalions of the Madras Army, all told, were 12,000 men below their established strength.
62. See Dodwell, *Sepoy Recruitment*, pp. 40-1. Dodwell found that the ratio of Muslims to Hindus in the Madras Army varied from one unit to another. Much depended, in the early years, upon when and where a battalion was raised. Generally, between 40 and 60 per cent of a military unit's manpower were Muslim, as were about half of all Indian commissioned officers.
63. Mason, p. 23. By the 1830s, however, this comparison of the Madras and Bengal Armies was something of a trope of colonial literature. It also is unlikely that an Indian soldier would have spoken of religion in the sense presented by this quote. The quote may be a fabrication.
64. BL/OIOC, Cradock's Minute, 2 October 1806, *HMS*, V. 510, pp. 275-7.
65. Wilson, V. 1, p. 227. The rest of the oath consisted of a promise to return all equipment issued by the Company, in good condition, upon retirement from the Army. Significantly, Major Pierce shortened the oath in the Regulations of 1806 by removing the references to salt, or *namak*. The new oath read: 'I, A. B., private in the [regiment] swear to be true to the Company; to serve it honestly and faithfully against all its enemies, to obey the Government, and all Generals and officers set over me. I swear also that I will not abandon these colours, but always

defend them to the utmost of my power.' See *Code of Regulations* (1806), XVI, pp. 154-6.

66. Mason, p. 126.
67. Robert Orme, *Military Transactions,* V. 1, 4th edn. (London, 1861). Also see Buchanan, V. 2, p. 73.
68. Welsh, V. 1, pp. 193-4.
69. Majda Asad, *Indian Muslim Festivals and Customs* (New Delhi, 1988), p. 17.
70. Mason, p. 127.
71. Malcolm, p. 514.
72. Captain Calvert to GC/FSG, 21 December 1767, quoted in S.C. Hill, 'The Old Sepoy Officer', pp. 264-5.
73. Welsh, V. 1, pp. 161-2. Welsh himself carried the subadar to a dressing station, and thus missed the assault. Hussain Khan died of his wounds a few days later.
74. Farzana Shaikh, *Community and Consensus in Islam: Muslim Representation in Colonial India, 1860-1947* (Cambridge, 1989), p. 11.
75. TNSA, *Bangalore Court of Enquiry Proceedings,* Appendix no. 12, *MSS,* V. 4, p. 2442.
76. Wilks, p. 22.
77. UN, Bentinck's Minute, 12 February 1806, Portland MS, PwJb/729, p. 88, etc.
78. Dubois, p. 29. Note: This passage, like all passages quoted from Dubois here, is selected because it seems to represent the author's 'updating' of the otherwise plagiarized and much older French work on which *Hindu Manners and Customs* is based.
79. BL/OIOC, Munro Correspondence, 151/125 (1), Munro to Petrie and MBOR, 25 August 1805, para. 7.
80. Dubois, p. 97, see n. 78, above.
81. Ibid., pp. 679-80, see n. 78, above.
82. BL/OIOC, Bentinck's Minute, 24 August 1806, *HMS,* V. 509, pp. 5-9.
83. UN, Petrie's Minute, 14-17 July 1806, Portland MS, PwJb/57, p. 301.
84. BL/OIOC, Sir Thomas Maitland to Lord Minto, 20 October 1806, *HMS,* V. 510, pp. 399-409. The Governor of Ceylon, for instance, remarked to the Governor-General of India that the history of the Madras Army had been, essentially, the story of British officers persuading sepoys to 'abandon their prejudices', yet he did not believe 'sepoys themselves' to be responsible for the unrest that emerged in the Army in 1806.
85. This idea of the Vellore Mutiny as a dharmic event was expressed by

more than one witness at Nandidurgam, and is hinted at in the quote from William Petrie in n. 83.

86. Henry Bevan, *Thirty Years' Service in India*, p. 89.

87. For an excellent illustration of this transition, see Captain Albert Hervey, *A Soldier of the Company: The Life of an Indian Ensign, 1833-43*, ed. Charles Allen (London, 1988), pp. 73-4. In this particular passage, Hervey describes how a protest made by the men of his company in 1834 was handled at each level of the battalion. He increased the sepoys' stoppages in order to increase the allowance of the company *dhobi-wallahs*. Afterward, he left the subadar to pay the soldiers, while he himself visited a young Englishwoman in cantonments. The sepoys, meanwhile, refused their pay, and Hervey was compelled to hurry to the parade ground to persuade them to obey orders. By the time he reported the matter to his commanding officer, however, the colonel already had been informed of the situation, and Hervey was suspended from active command—a humiliating but effective punishment. This was exactly how the internal monitoring system of the Madras Army was supposed to operate. Also contrast the 1806 regulations with the *Standing Orders of 1848* (BL/OIOC/L/MIL/17/3/480, Adjutant General's Office, *Standing Orders for the Native Infantry of the Madras Army* (Fort St. George, 1848).

88. Each battalion's non-military affairs were regulated by a special sepoy *panchayat* in which ranks rather than castes were represented. These groups took care of all disciplinary problems not addressed by the Articles of War. See BL/OIOC, *Code of Regulations* (1806), XVI, pp. 158-9. Also see Buchanan, V. 1, p. 343. At Nandidurgam, in 1801, Buchanan observed that 'Hindus of all descriptions . . . are indeed very desirous of having every kind of business discussed in public assemblies.' Also see Louis Dumont, *A South Indian Subcaste: Social Organization and Religion of the Pramalai Kallar*, tr. M. Moffatt, L. and A. Morton (Delhi, 1986), pp. 320-1. Dumont found, in studying village *panchayats* among the Kallars of Thanjavur, that a high social value was placed on men adept at settling disputes. Village *panchayats*, furthermore, were inclined to seek out the most efficient, and very often equitable, solutions to their problems—but almost always their decisions were consistent with local custom.

89. BL/OIOC, Bentinck's Minute, 24 August 1806, *HMS*, V. 509, pp. 5-9. Also see TNSA, Bentinck's Minute, *MSP*, V. 28, pp. 1025-31, in which the Governor observed, in reference to the Quilon affair, that 'every Native will say what is pleasing without consideration of truth'.

90. TNSA, Examination of Subadar Sikandar Khan, n.d., *MSS*, V. 8, p. 17.

91. BL/OIOC, Oakes' Minute, 6 September 1806, *HMS*, V. 509, pp. 143-8.
92. UN, Captain James Moore's Testimony, 19 May 1806, Portland MS, PwJb/57, pp. 38-41; UN, Lieutenant-Colonel John Darley's Testimony, 17 May 1806, ibid., pp. 23-7.
93. UN, Lieutenant-Colonel John Darley's Testimony, 19 May 1806, Portland MS, PwJb/57, pp. 36-7. Havildar Subharaya, unable to speak directly with Darley (who did not know Telugu), was forced to report the grenadier company's concerns to the commander's *dubash*. Later, Darley rather awkwardly explained to the court of enquiry that 'this circumstance only came to my knowledge yesterday, *but the purport of it had been taken down in writing by my head servant, at his own house, some days ago*' (emphasis added).

Bibliography

PRIMARY ARCHIVAL SOURCES
REFERENCED OR CONSULTED

1. Tamil Nadu State Archives (TNSA)
   Madras Board of Revenue Proceedings, V. 255-B.
   Madras Judicial Proceedings, V. 13.
   Madras Military Consultations (*MMC*), V. 261-A, 310, 319-A.
   Madras Military Miscellany, V. 1, 45.
   Madras Military Proceedings (*MMP*),V. 2, 24-25, 48, 50, 69, 72-75, 78, 80.
   Madras Political Consultations (*MPC*), V. 6, 9-10.
   Madras Secret Constultations (*MSC*), V. 11.
   Madras Secret Proceedings (*MSP*), V. 4, 5-A, 19-25, 27-29.
   Madras Secret Sundries (*MSS*), V. 2-A, 4, 5-A, 8.
   North Arcot District Records, Revenue Letters Sent, V. 3-5, 8.
   Pre-Mutiny Political Pension Records, V. 39.

2. British Library/Oriental and India Office Library Collections (BL/OIOC)

   Bengal Secret and Political Consultations, V. 191.
   Board of Control, V. 13-F.
   Code of Regulations for Various Departments of the Military Establis-hment of Fort St. George, General Order of the Commander-in-Chief, 11 March 1806.
   Correspondence Reports, V. 34.
   Court Book, V. 115, 118.
   Despatches to Madras, E/4/902.
   Fort St. David Records, V. 10.
   Home Miscellaneous Series (*HMS*), V. 431, 459, 464, 486, 504, 507-510.

Military Despatches to England, V. 1.
Munro Correspondence, 151/125 (1).
President's Secret Correspondence, V. 1.
Secret Letters from Bengal and India, V. 8.
Secret Letters from Madras, Series 1, V. 3.
Standing Orders for the Native Infantry of the Madras Army, L/ MIL/17/3/ 480.

3. BRITISH MUSEUM/MANUSCRIPT READING ROOM (BM)

Original Correspondence of Warren Hastings, V. 51, January-October 1807, BM/Add.MSS. no. 29182.

Liverpool Papers, BL/Add. MSS. No. 23405.

4. NATIONAL ARCHIVES OF INDIA (NAI)

Hyderabad Residency Records, V. 27, 29, 57.

5. PUBLIC RECORDS OFFICE (PRO)

Colonial Office/54/22.

6. UNIVERSITY OF NOTTINGHAM (UN)

Portland Manuscripts, *Bentinck Papers,* PwJb/25, 28, 32, 44, 49, 57-60, 81, 96, 140, 155, 157, 216a, 218a, 317a, 667, 677, 727, 729, 750.

7. UNIVERSITY OF SOUTHAMPTON (USL)

'Grievances of Native Soldiers', *Wellington Papers,* WP1/184/8.

Lieutenant-Colonel J. Malcolm to Major-General Sir Arthur Wellesley, 3 March 1807, *Wellington Papers,* WP1/166/4.

Lieutenant-Colonel J. Malcolm to Major-General Sir Arthur Wellesley, 20 June 1807, *Wellington Papers,* WP1/170/72.

'Copy of a Letter from Lieutenant-Colonel Sir J. Malcolm to Lord Minto, 8 October 1807', *Wellington Ppaer,* WP/175/25/3.

CONTEMPORARY PUBLISHED SOURCES

Bentinck, Lord William Henry Cavendish, *Memorial Addressed to the Honourable Court of Directors. . . . Containing an Account of the Mutiny at Vellore, with the Causes and Consequences of that Event,* London, 1810.

Blackiston, John, *Twelve Years' Military Adventure in Three Quarters of the Globe . . . between the Years 1802 and 1814,* London, 1829.

Elers, George, *Memoirs of George Elers, Captain in the 12th Regiment of Foot, 1777-1842,* Lord Monson and George L. Gower, eds., New York, 1903.

Hamilton, Francis Buchanan, *A Journey from Madras, through the Countries of Mysore, Canara, and Malabar. . . .* 3 vols., London, 1807.

Hollingberry, William, *A History of His Late Highness Nizam Alee Khan, Soobah of the Deccan,* Calcutta, 1805.

Valentia, George Annesley, Viscount, *Voyages and Travels in India, Ceylon, the Red Sea, Abyssinia, and Egypt, in the Years 1802, 1803, 1804, 1805, and 1806,* London, 1809.

Welsh, James, *Military Reminiscences: Extracted from a Journal of Nearly Forty Years' Active Service in the East Indies,* 2 vols. London, 1830.

Wilks, Mark, *Historical Sketches of the South of India, in an Attempt to Trace the History of Mysoor: from the Origin of the Hindu Government of that State to the Extinction of the Mohammedan Dynasty of 1799* (1810), Mysore, 1932.

Williams, John, *An Historical Account of the Rise and Progress of the Bengal Native Infantry,* London, 1817.

SECONDARY SOURCES

Aitchison, C.V., *A Collection of Treaties, Engagements and Sanads Relating to India and Neighbouring Countries,* Calcutta, 1909.

Alavi, Seema, *The Sepoys and the Company: Tradition and Transition in Northern India, 1770-1830* , Delhi, 1995.

Ali, B. Sheikh, *British Relations with Haidar Ali, 1760-1782* , Mysore, 1963.

Asad, Majda, *Indian Muslim Festivals and Customs,* New Delhi, 1988.

Aspinall, A., *Cornwallis in Bengal,* Manchester, 1931.

Baden-Powell, B.H., *Land Systems of British India,* 3 vols. (1892), New York, 1972.

Barat, Amiya, *The Bengal Native Infantry: Its Organization and Discipline, 1796-1852* , Calcutta, 1962.

Bayley, W.H., ed., *A Gazetteer of Southern India,* Madras, 1855.

Bayly, C.A., *Empire and Information: Intelligence Gathering and Social Communication in India, 1780-1880,* Cambridge, 1996.

Bayly, Susan, *Saints, Goddesses and Kings: Muslims and Christians in South Indian Society, 1700-1900,* Cambridge, 1989.

Bennell, Anthony S., ed., *The Maratha War Papers of Arthur Wellesley, January to December 1803,* Gloucestershire, 1998.

Bevan, Henry, *Thirty Years in India: Or, a Soldier's Reminiscences of Native and European Life in the Presidencies, from 1808 to 1838,* 2 vols., London, 1839.

Beveridge, Henry, *A Comprehensive History of India,* London, 1862.

Boulger, Demitrius C., *Lord William Bentinck: Rulers of India Series,* Oxford, 1897.

Bowen, H.V., *Revenue and Reform: The Indian Problem in British Politics, 1757-1773,* Cambridge, 1991.

Brittlebank, Kate, *Tipu Sultan's Search for Legitimacy: Islam and Kinship in a Hindu Domain,* Delhi, 1997.

Cadell, Patrick, *History of the Bombay Army,* London, 1938.

Cardew, Alexander, *The White Mutiny: A Forgotten Episode in the History of the Indian Army,* London, 1929.

Carman, W.Y., *Indian Army Uniforms, under the British, from the 18th Century to 1947,* 2 vols., London, 1961-9.

Chaudhuri, Nani Gopal, *British Relations with Hyderabad, 1798-1843,* Calcutta, 1964.

Chinnian, Perumal, *The First Struggle for Freedom in South India in 1806: Sporadic Events after the Vellore Mutin,* Erode, 1983.

———, *The Vellore Mutiny: The First Uprising against the British,* Madras, 1982.

Collingham, E.M., *Imperial Bodies: The Physical Experience of the Raj, c. 1800-1947,* London, 2001.

Colville, John, *Strange Inheritance,* Salisbury, 1983.

Cox, Arthur F., *A Manual of the North Arcot District in the Presidency of Madras,* Madras, 1981.

Dalrymple, William, *White Mughals: Love and Betrayal in Eighteenth-Century India,* New York, 2003.

Desai, Ziyauddin A., *A Topographical List of Arabic, Persian, and Urdu Inscriptions of South India,* New Delhi, 1989.

Dirks, Nicholas, *The Hollow Crown: The Ethnohistory of an Indian Kingdom,* Cambridge, 1987.

Dodwell, Henry H., *Dupleix and Clive: The Beginning of Empire* (1920), London, 1967.

———, *Report on the Madras Records,* Madras, 1929.

———, *Sepoy Recruitment in the Old Madras Army,* Calcutta, 1922.

Dubois, J.A., *Hindu Manners, Customs and Ceremonies,* tr. Henry K. Beauchamp (1906), Madras, 1992.

Dumont, Louis, *A South Indian Subcaste: Social Organization and Religion of the Pramalai Kallar,* tr. M. Moffatt, L. and A. Morton, Delhi, 1986.

Dunlop, Robert, *Life of Henry Grattan*, Philadelphia, 1889.

Eaton, Richard M., *Sufis of Bijapur, 1300-1700: Social Roles of Sufis in Medieval India*, Princeton, 1978.

Embree, Ainslie, *Charles Grant and British Rule in India*, New York, 1962.

Feiling, Keith, *Warren Hastings*, London, 1954.

Fisher, Michael H., *First Indian Author in English: Dean Mahomed (1759-1851) in India, Ireland, and England*, Oxford, 1996.

———, *Travels of Dean Mahomet: An Eighteenth-century Journey through India*, Berkeley, 1997.

Foreman, Amanda, *Georgiana, Duchess of Devonshire*, London, 1998.

Fortescue, John, W., *History of the British Army*, V. 4, Part I, London, 1906.

Frykenberg, Robert E., *Guntur District, 1788-1848: A History of Local Influence and Central Authority*, Oxford, 1965.

Fuller, John F.C., *Sir John Moore's System of Training*, London, 1925.

Fyzee, A. A. A., *Outlines of Muhammedan Law*, Oxford, 1964.

Gleig, G.R., *Life of Arthur, Duke of Wellington*, London, 1889.

Guha, Ranajit, *Elementary Aspects of Peasant Insurgency in Colonial India*, Delhi, 1983.

Gupta, Maya, *Lord William Bentinck in Madras and the Vellore Mutiny, 1803-1807*, New Delhi, 1986.

Hasan, Mohibbul, *History of Tipu Sultan*, Calcutta, 1971.

Hervey, Albert, *A Soldier of the Company: The Life of an Indian Ensign, 1833-43*, ed. Charles Allen, London, 1988.

Hill, S.C., *Yusuf Khan: The Rebel Commandant*, London, 1914.

Holt, Peter, *In Clive's Footsteps*, London, 1991.

Hyderabad State Committee for a History of the Freedom Movement in India, *The Freedom Struggle in Hyderabad: A Connected Account, 1800-1857*, V. 1, Hyderabad, 1956.

Irschick, Eugene F., *Dialogue and History: Constructing South India, 1795-1895*, Berkeley, 1994.

Jones, Mark Bence, *Clive of India*, London, 1974.

Kaye, John William, *A History of the Sepoy War in India, 1857-58*, London, 1896.

———, *Life and Correspondence of Major-General Sir John Malcolm*, London, 1841.

Kirby, Charles F., *The Adventures of an Arcot Rupee*, 3 vols., London, 1867.

Kolff, Dirk, *Naukar, Rajput and Sepoy: The Ethnohistory of the Military Labour Market in Hindustan, 1450-1850*, Cambridge, 1990.

Lawford, James P., *Britain's Army in India: From Its Origins to the Conquest of Bengal*, London, 1978.

———, *Clive, Proconsul of India: A Biography*, London, 1976.

Lawrence, Arnold W., ed., *Captives of Tipu: Survirors' Narratives*, London, 1929.

Longer, V., *Red Coats to Olive Green: A History of the Indian Army, 1600-1974*, Bombay, 1974.

Lawson, Charles, *Memories of Madras*, London, 1905.

Love, Henry Davison, *Vestiges of Old Madras, 1640-1800*, 3 vols., Indian Records Series, London, 1913.

Ludden, David, *Peasant History in South India*, Princeton, 1985.

Mackesy, Piers, *British Victory in Egypt, 1801: The End of Napoleon's Conquest*, London, 1995.

Macpherson, Samuel C., *Memorials of Service in India*, ed. William Macpherson, London, 1865.

Majumdar, Ramesh Chandra, *History of the Freedom Struggle in India*, Calcutta, 1962.

Marshall, P.J., *The Impeachment of Warren Hastings*, Oxford, 1965.

Marshman, John Clark, *The History of India, from the Earliest Period to the Close of Lord Dalhousie's Administration*, London, 1867.

Martin, Robert Montgomery, *The Despatches, Minutes, and Correspondence of the Marquess Wellesley during his Administration in India*, 5 vols., London, 1837.

Mason, Philip, *A Matter of Honour: An Account of the Indian Army, its Officers and Men*, London, 1974.

———, *A Shaft of Sunlight: Memories of a Varied Life*, London, 1978.

McHugh, Roger J., *Henry Grattan*, New York, 1937.

Mill, James, *History of British India*, London, 1844.

Mukherjee, Nilmani, *The Ryotwari System in Madras, 1792-1827*, Calcutta, 1962.

Munro, Innes, *The Munro Letters*, ed. Arthur H. Haley, Liverpool, 1992.

Musgrave, Sir Richard, *Memoirs of the Different Rebellions in Ireland*, 4th edn. (1802), Fort Wayne, 1995.

Nazir, Ghulam Abdul Qadir, *Bahar-i-Azam Jahi*, tr. S. Muhammad Husayn Nainar, Madras, 1950.

Oman, Carola, *Sir John Moore*, London, 1953.

Orme, Robert, *A History of the Military Transactions of the British Nation in Indostan* (1773), New Delhi, 1861.

Owen, Sidney J., *A Selection from the Despatches, Memoranda, and Other Papers Relating to India of Field Marshall the Duke of Wllington*, Oxford, 1880.

Pande, Sita Ram, *From Sepoy to Subedar: Being the Life and Adventures of*

Subedar Sita Ram, a Native Officer of the Bengal Army, Written and Related by Himself, tr. Lieutenant-Colonel Norgate, ed., James Lunt, London, 1970.

Parker, Geoffrey, *The Military Revolution: Military Innovation and the Rise of the West, 1500-1800*, Basingstoke, 1991.

Parkinson, Cyril N., *War in the Eastern Seas, 1793-1815*, London, 1954.

Parkinson, Roger, *Moore of Corunna*, London, 1976.

Pettitt, George, *The Tinnevelly Mission*, London, 1851.

Philips, Cyril H., *East India Company*, Manchester, 1940.

———, *The Correspondence of Lord William Henry Cavendish Bentinck, Governor-General of India, 1828-35*, 3 vols., New York, 1977.

Phythian-Adams, E.G., *Madras Infantry, 1748-1943*, Madras, 1943.

Price, Pamela G., *Kingship and Political Practice in Colonial India*, Cambridge, 1996.

Rajayyan, K., *Rise and Fall of the Poligars of Tamil Nadu*, Madras, 1974.

———, *South Indian Rebellion: The First Indian War of Independence, 1800-1801*, Mysore, 1971.

Rao, C. Hayadavana, ed., *Mysore Gazetteer: Compiled for Government*, V. 5, Bangalore 1930.

Rao (Bahadur), Rajakaryaprasakta, *Modern Mysore: From the Beginning to 1868*, Bangalore 1936.

Rao, Velcheru Narayana, et al., *Symbols of Substance: Court and State in Nayaka Period Tamilnadu*, Delhi, 1992.

Regani, Sarojini, *Nizam-British Relations, 1724-1857*, Hyderabad, 1963.

Renick, M.S., *Lord Wellesley and the Indian States*, Agra, 1987.

Rice, Benjamin Lewis, *Mysore and Coorg*, V. 1, Bangalore, 1877.

Roberts, Michael, *The Military Revolution, 1560-1660*, Belfast, 1956.

Roberts, P.E., *India under Wellesley, 1797-1805* (1929), Gorakhpur, 1961.

Rogers, Clifford J., ed., *The Military Revolution Debate: Readings on the Transformation of Early Modern Europe*, Boulder, 1995.

Rosselli, John, *Lord William Bentinck: The Making of a Liberal Imperialist, 1774-1839*, London, 1974.

Sen, Siba P., *The French in India, 1763-1816*, Calcutta, 1958.

Shaikh, Farzana, *Community and Consensus in Islam: Muslim Representation in Colonial India, 1860-1947*, Cambridge, 1989.

Sharif, Jagar, *Qanoon-i-Islam: Or, the Customs of the Mussulmans of India*, 2nd edn., revised, Madras, 1863.

Singh, Nihar Nandan, *British Historiography on British Rule in India: The Life and Writings of Sir John William Kaye, 1814-76*, Patna, 1986.

Singh, Paul Madan, *Indian Army under the East India Company*, New Delhi, 1976.

Sivakumar, S.S. and Chandra, *Peasants and Nabobs: Agrarian Radicalism in Late Eighteenth Century Tamil Country*, Delhi, 1993.

Srinivasta, B.B., *Sir John Shore's Policy Toward the Indian States*, Allahabad, 1981.

Stein, Burton, *Thomas Munro: The Origins of the Colonial State and his Vision of Empire*, Delhi, 1989.

Subramanian, K.R., *The Maratha Rajas of Tanjore (1928)*, Madras, 1988.

Sutherland, Lucy Stuart, *The East India Company in Eighteenth-century Politics*, Oxford, 1952.

Thornton, Edward, *A History of the British Empire in India*, London, 1843.

Trevelyan, Charles E., *The Mutiny of Vellore: Its Parallelisms and Its Lessons*, Calcutta, 1857.

Whelan, Kevin, *Fellowship of Freedom: The United Irishmen of 1798*, Cork, 1998.

Wickremesekera, Channa, '*Best Black Troops in the World,': British Perceptions and the Making of the Sepoy, 1746-1805*, New Delhi, 2002.

Wilson, J.W., *History of the Madras Army*, London, 1887.

Wink, André, *Land and Sovereignty in India: Agrarian Society and Politics under the Eighteenth-Century Maratha Swarajya*, Cambridge, 1986.

Yazdani, Zubaida, *Hyderabad During the Residency of Russell, 1811-1820*, Oxford, 1976.

ARTICLES

Bhadra, Gautam, 'The Mentality of Subalternity: Kantanama or Rajdharma', *Subaltern Studies* VI, ed. Ranajit Guha (1989), pp. 54-91.

Chaudhuri, Haripado, 'The Vellore Mutiny: A Reappraisal', *Modern Review*, 98, 1955, pp. 125-8.

Fisch, Jörg, 'A Pamphlet War on Christian Missions in India, 1807-1809', *Journal of Asian History*, 19, no. 1 (1985), pp. 22-70.

Frykenberg, Robert E., 'New Light on the Vellore Mutiny', *East India Company Studies*, Papers Presented to Sir Cyril Phillips, Hong Kong, 1986, pp. 207-31.

Grier, Sydney C., 'The Mutiny at Vellore in 1806', *Bengal, Past and Present* (October-December 1924), pp. 166-7.

Guha, Ranajit, 'On Some Aspects of the Historiography of Colonial India', *Subaltern Studies I: Writings on South Asian History and Society*, ed. Ranajit Guha, Delhi (1982), pp. 1-8.

Gupta, Maya, 'The Vellore Mutiny, July 1806', *Journal of Indian History*, 49, 1971, pp. 91-112.

Hill, Samuel C., 'The Old Sepoy Officer', *English Historical Review*, 28, 1913, pp. 260-91, 496-514.

Hoover, James, 'The Recruitment of the Bengal Army: Benyond the Myth of the Zamindar's Son', *Indo-British Review*, 21, no. 2, 1996, pp. 144-56.

Ingram, Edward, 'Timing and Explaining Aggression: Wellesley, Clive and the Carnatic, 1795-1801', *Indo-British Review*, 21, no. 2, 1986, pp. 104-15.

Mitra, S.K., 'The Vellore Mutiny of 1806 and the Question of Christian Mission to India', *Indian Church History Review*, 8, no. 1, 1974, pp. 75-82.

Peers, Douglas M., 'Contours of the Garrison State: The Army and the Historiography of Early Nineteenth Century India', *Orientalism, Evangelicalism, and the Military Cantonment in Early Nineteenth-Century India: A Historiographical Overview*, ed. Nancy G. Cassels, Queenston, Canada, 1991, pp. 89-124.

Rice, Elizabeth R. Talbot, 'Sudden Anger or Premeditated Pot: Vellore 1806 and the Aftermath', *National Army Musuem Report*, 1985, pp. 19-30.

Sastri, K.N. Venkatasubba, 'Petrie Papers', *Indian Historical Records Commission*, V. 18, pp. 288-96.

C.S. Srinivasachari, 'The Nawabas of the Carnatic', *Politics of the British Annexation of India*, 1757-1857, ed. Michael H. Fisher, Oxford, 1993.

Stephen, Sir Leslie and Lee, Sir Sidney, 'John Francis Caradoc', *Dictionary of National Biography*, V. 4, pp. 936-7.

Sundaram, R.V.S., 'Puppetry', *Encyclopedia of the Folk Culture of Karnataka*, Madras, 1991, V. 1, pp. 383-99.

Times of London, various articles, 1802-7.

UNPUBLISHED THESES

Samuelraj, Pakkianathan, 'The Mutiny at Vellore and Related Agitations', 1806-1807, University of Saskatchewan Ph.D. thesis, 1972.

Thangavelu, A., 'Military Administration of the East India Company in the Madras Presidency', 1800-1857, Madurai Kamaraj University Ph.D. thesis, 1988.

Wood, Peter, 'Vassal State in the Shadow of Empire: Palmer's Hyderabad', 1799-1867, University of Wisconsin-Madison, Ph.D. thesis, 1981.

Index

GS
12/11/07

(2)

A3